CHAPTER 1: AGITO CADETS

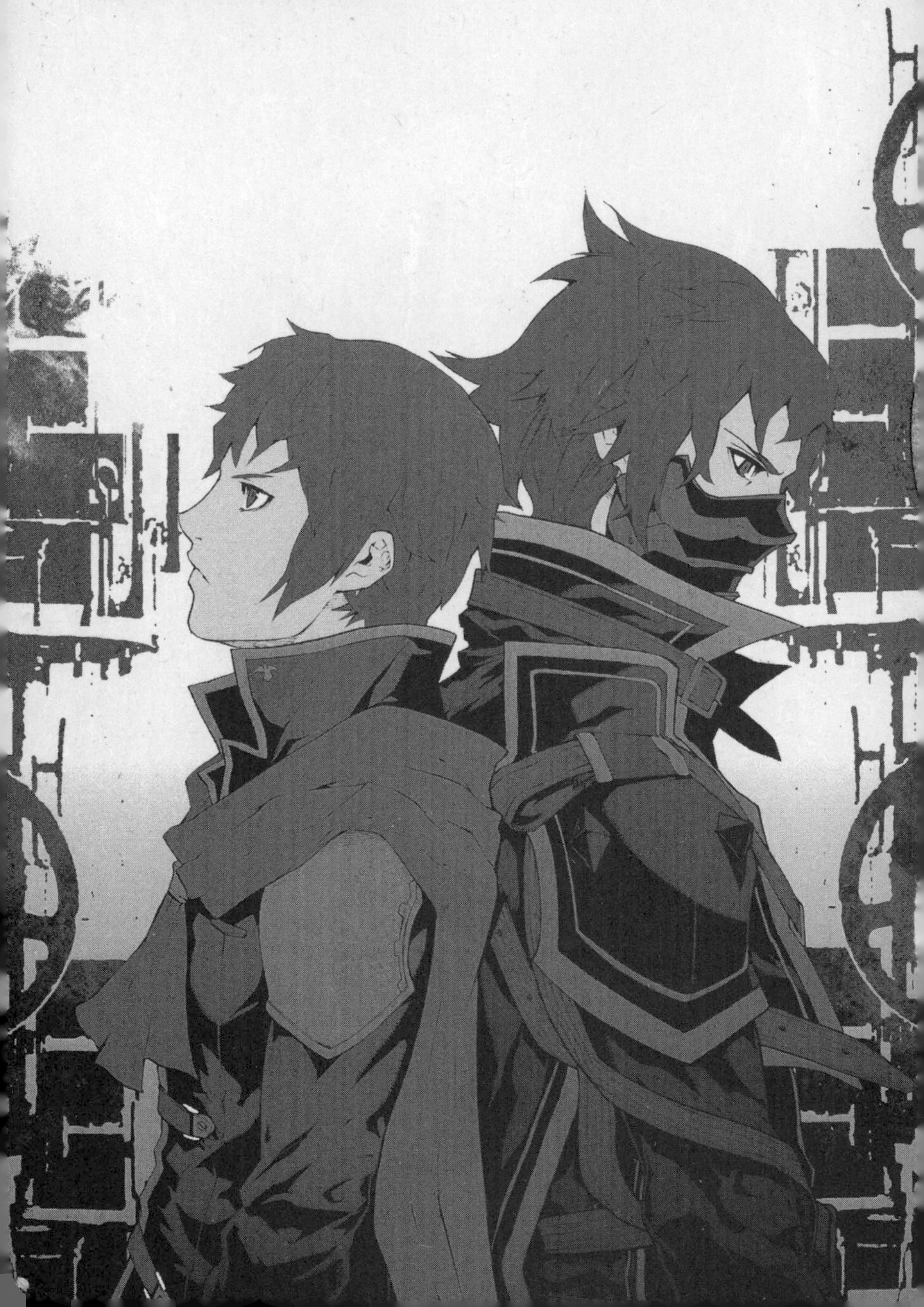

FINAL FANTASY. 零式 TYPE-0™
SIDE STORY
The Ice Reaper

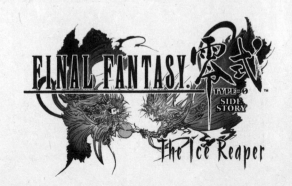

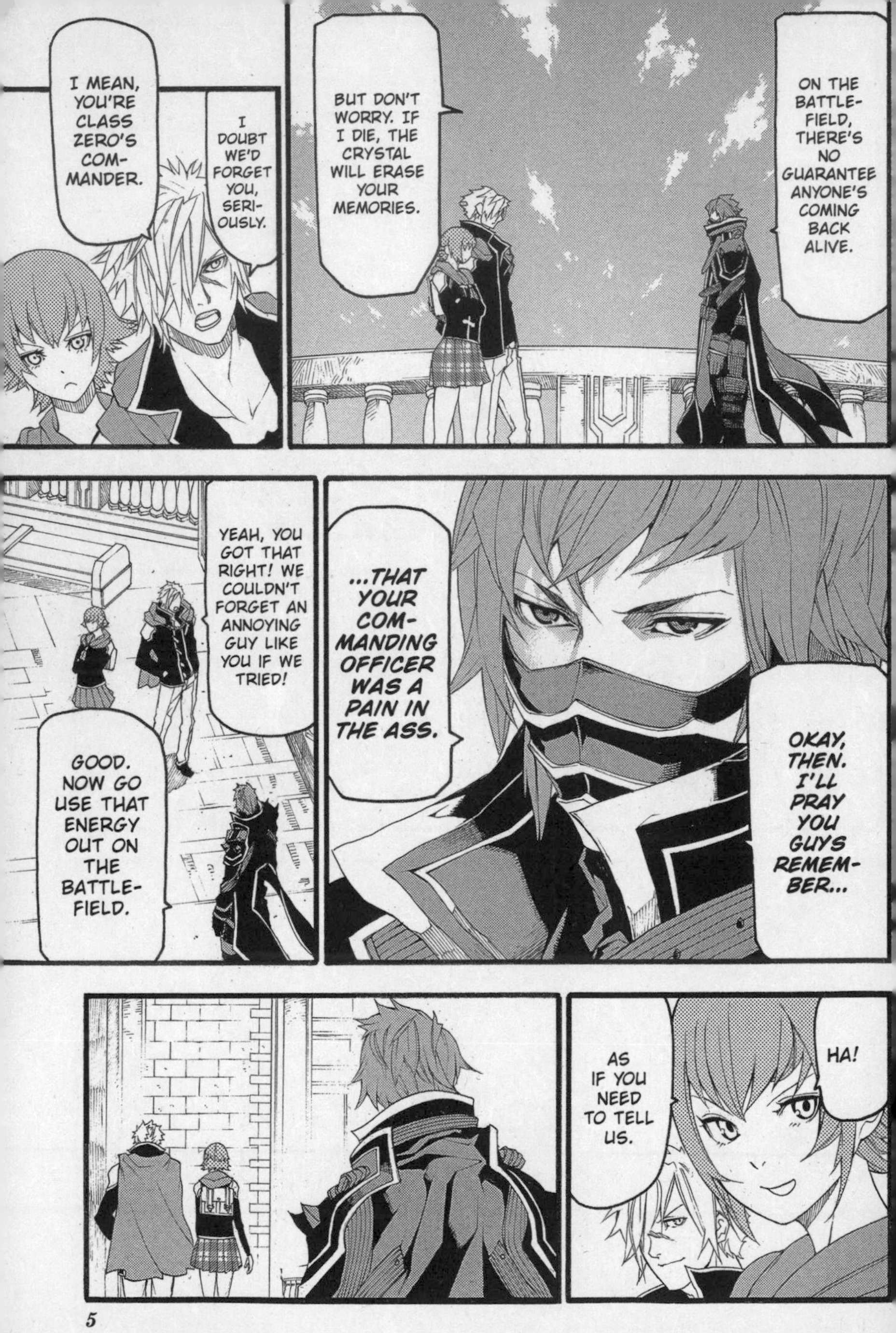
ON THE BATTLEFIELD, THERE'S NO GUARANTEE ANYONE'S COMING BACK ALIVE.
BUT DON'T WORRY. IF I DIE, THE CRYSTAL WILL ERASE YOUR MEMORIES.
I DOUBT WE'D FORGET YOU, SERIOUSLY.
I MEAN, YOU'RE CLASS ZERO'S COMMANDER.
OKAY, THEN. I'LL PRAY YOU GUYS REMEMBER...
...THAT YOUR COMMANDING OFFICER WAS A PAIN IN THE ASS.
YEAH, YOU GOT THAT RIGHT! WE COULDN'T FORGET AN ANNOYING GUY LIKE YOU IF WE TRIED!
GOOD. NOW GO USE THAT ENERGY OUT ON THE BATTLEFIELD.
HA!
AS IF YOU NEED TO TELL US.

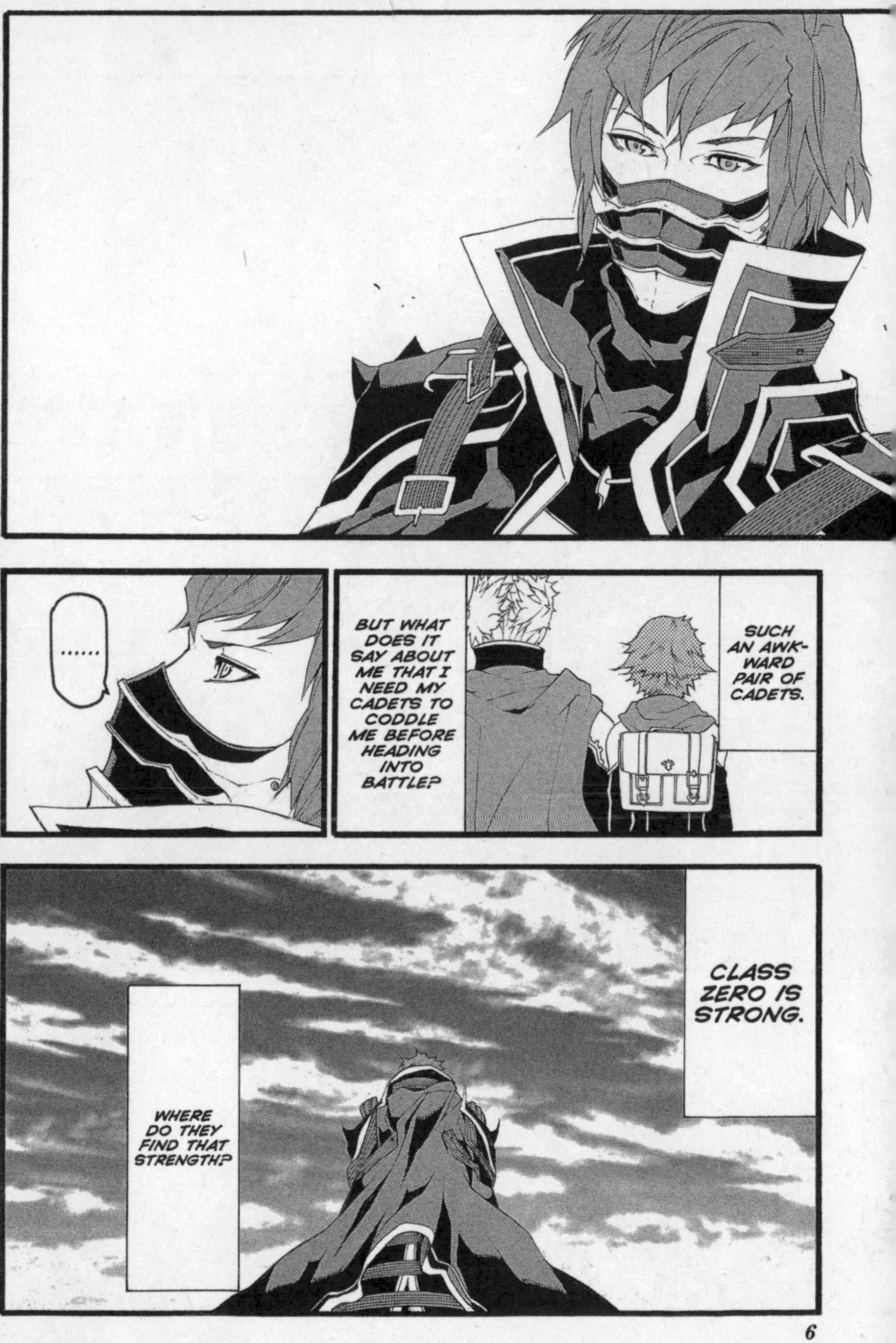
SUCH AN AWK-WARD PAIR OF CADETS.
BUT WHAT DOES IT SAY ABOUT ME THAT I NEED MY CADETS TO CODDLE ME BEFORE HEADING INTO BATTLE?
......
CLASS ZERO IS STRONG.
WHERE DO THEY FIND THAT STRENGTH?

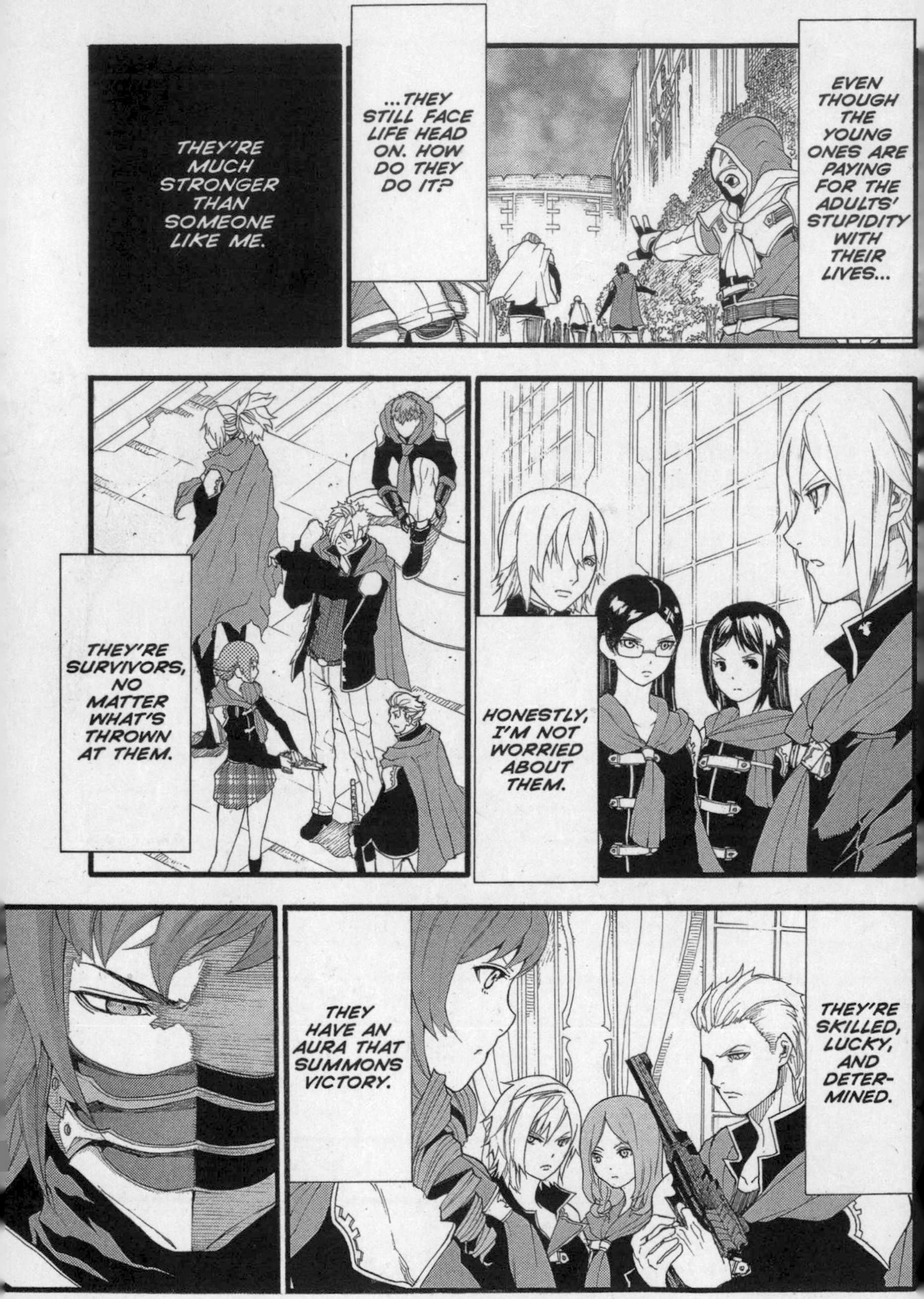
EVEN THOUGH THE YOUNG ONES ARE PAYING FOR THE ADULTS' STUPIDITY WITH THEIR LIVES...
...THEY STILL FACE LIFE HEAD ON. HOW DO THEY DO IT?
THEY'RE MUCH STRONGER THAN SOMEONE LIKE ME.
HONESTLY, I'M NOT WORRIED ABOUT THEM.
THEY'RE SURVIVORS, NO MATTER WHAT'S THROWN AT THEM.
THEY'RE SKILLED, LUCKY, AND DETER-MINED.
THEY HAVE AN AURA THAT SUMMONS VICTORY.

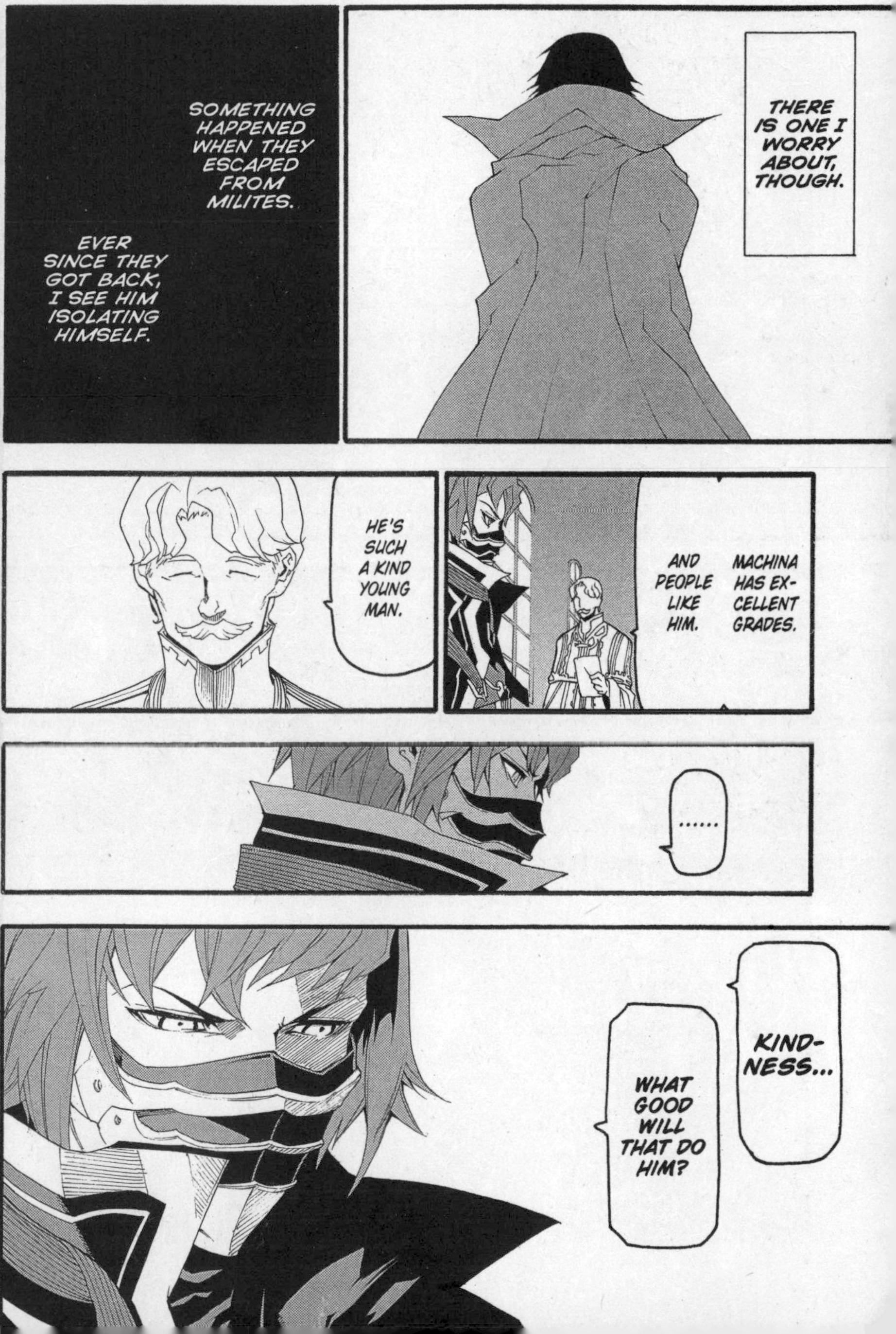
THERE IS ONE I WORRY ABOUT, THOUGH.
SOMETHING HAPPENED WHEN THEY ESCAPED FROM MILITES.
EVER SINCE THEY GOT BACK, I SEE HIM ISOLATING HIMSELF.
MACHINA HAS EX-CELLENT GRADES.
AND PEOPLE LIKE HIM.
HE'S SUCH A KIND YOUNG MAN.
......
KIND-NESS...
WHAT GOOD WILL THAT DO HIM?

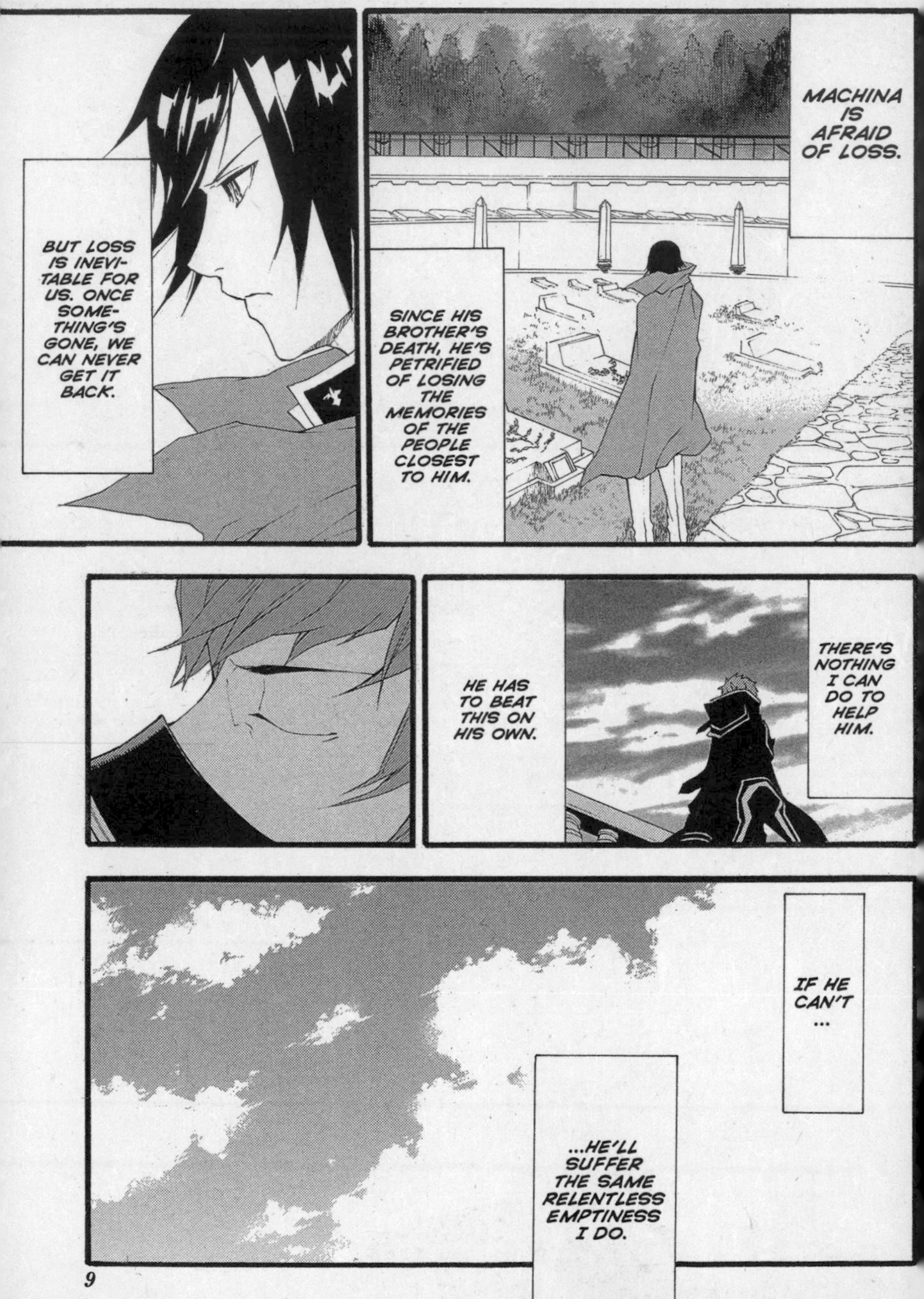
MACHINA IS AFRAID OF LOSS.
SINCE HIS BROTHER'S DEATH, HE'S PETRIFIED OF LOSING THE MEMORIES OF THE PEOPLE CLOSEST TO HIM.
BUT LOSS IS INEVITABLE FOR US. ONCE SOMETHING'S GONE, WE CAN NEVER GET IT BACK.
THERE'S NOTHING I CAN DO TO HELP HIM.
HE HAS TO BEAT THIS ON HIS OWN.
IF HE CAN'T...
...HE'LL SUFFER THE SAME RELENTLESS EMPTINESS I DO.

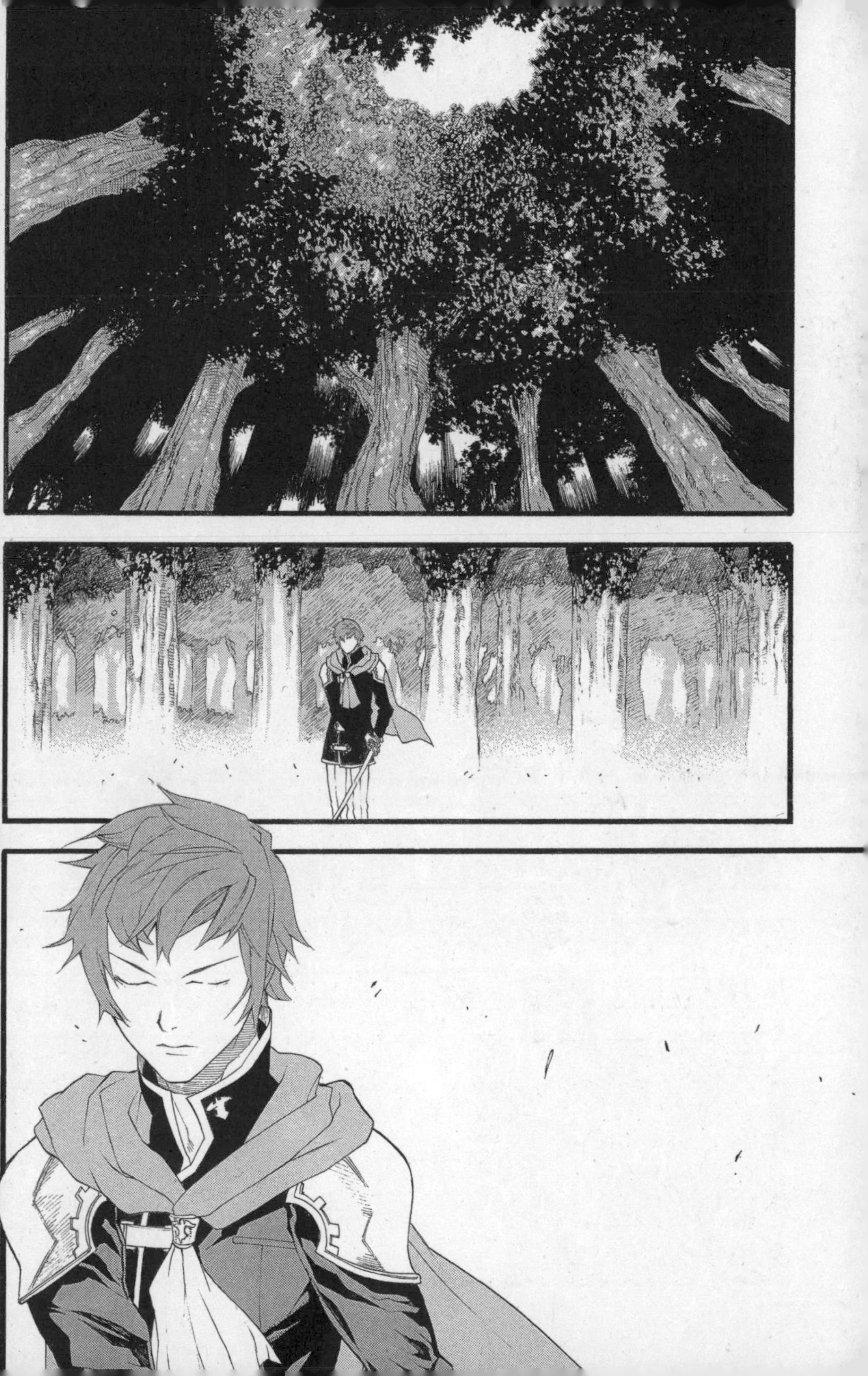

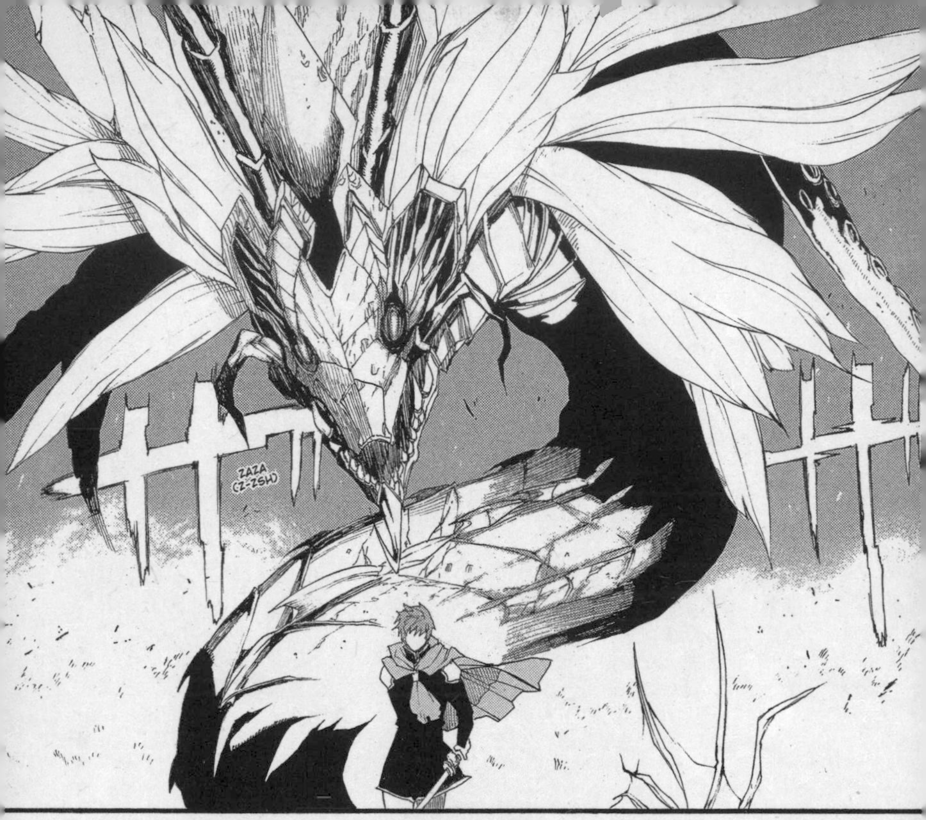
ZAZA
(Z-ZSH)
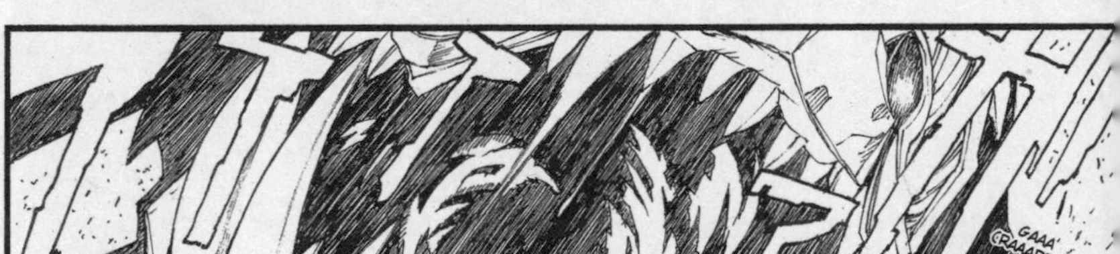
GAAA
(RAAARRR)
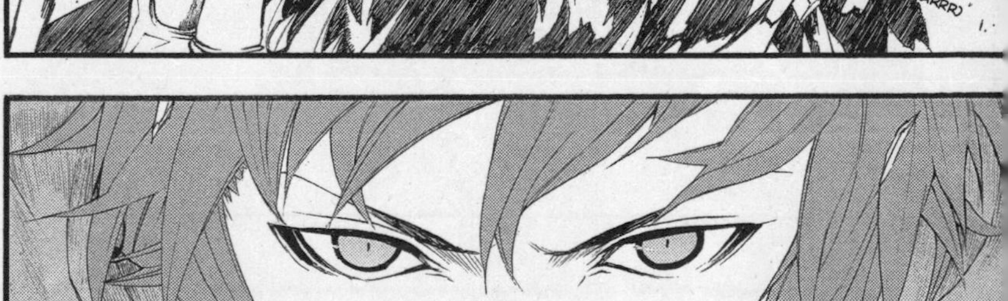

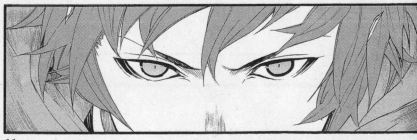

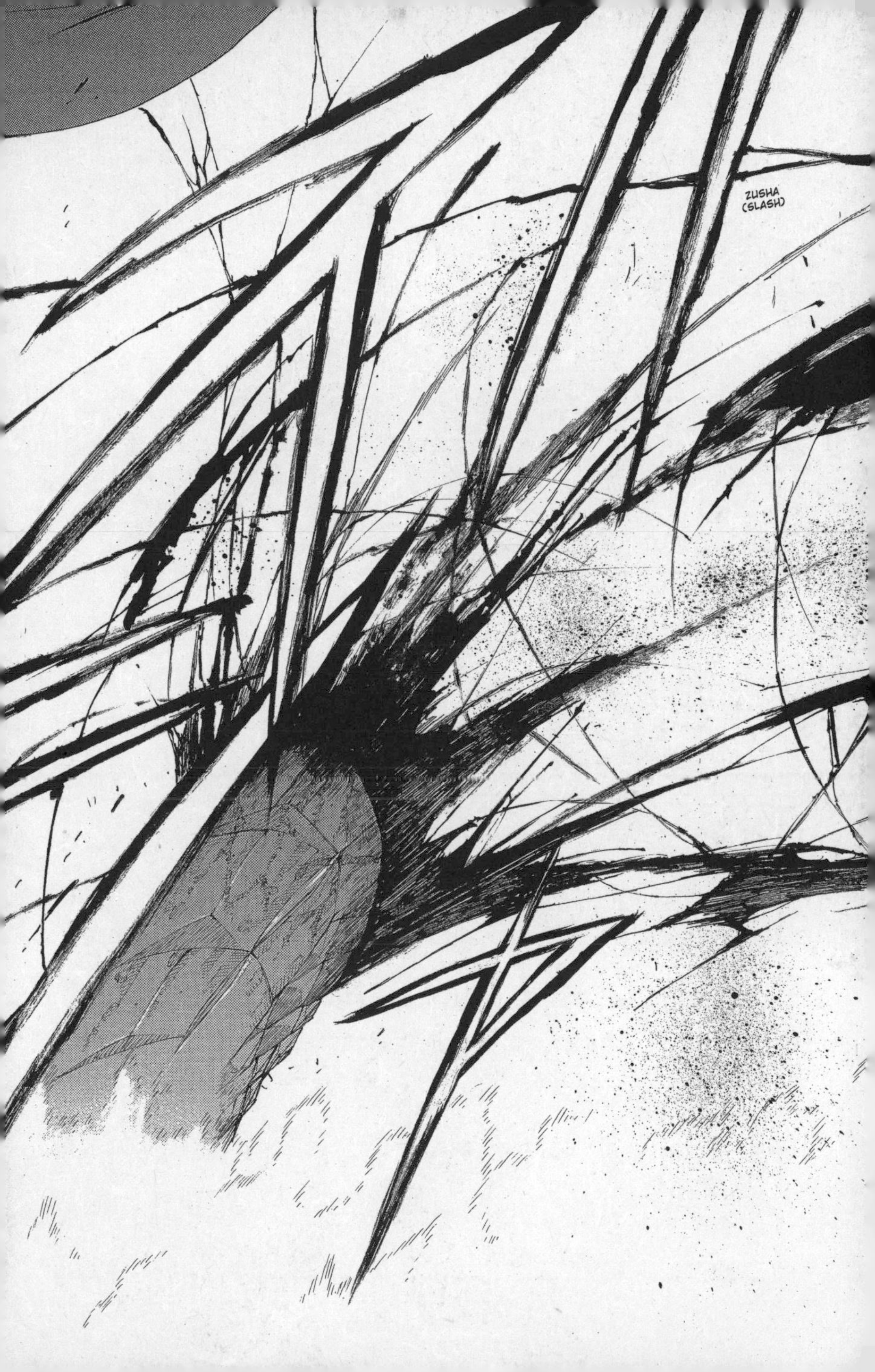
ZUSHA
(SLASH)

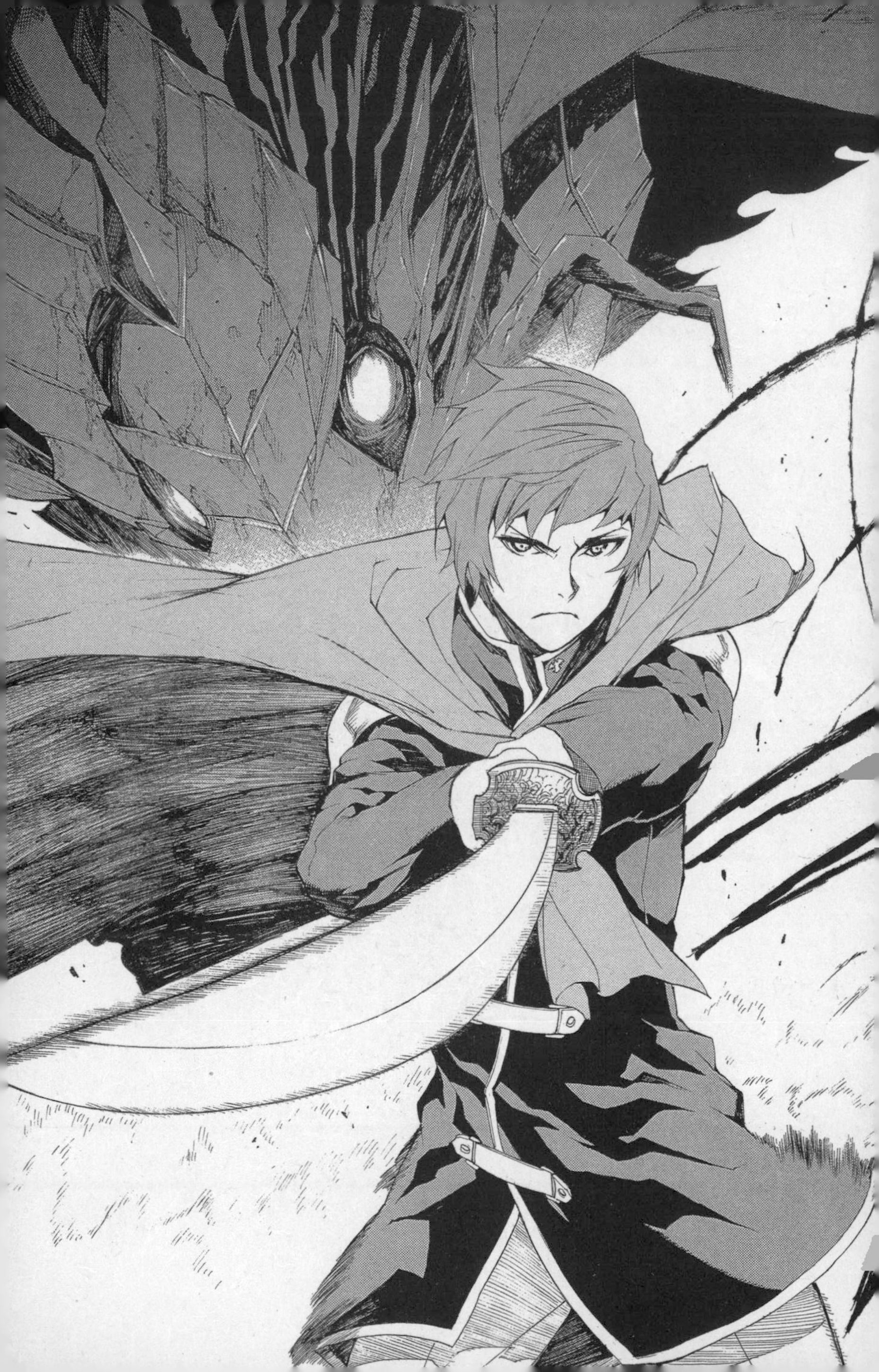

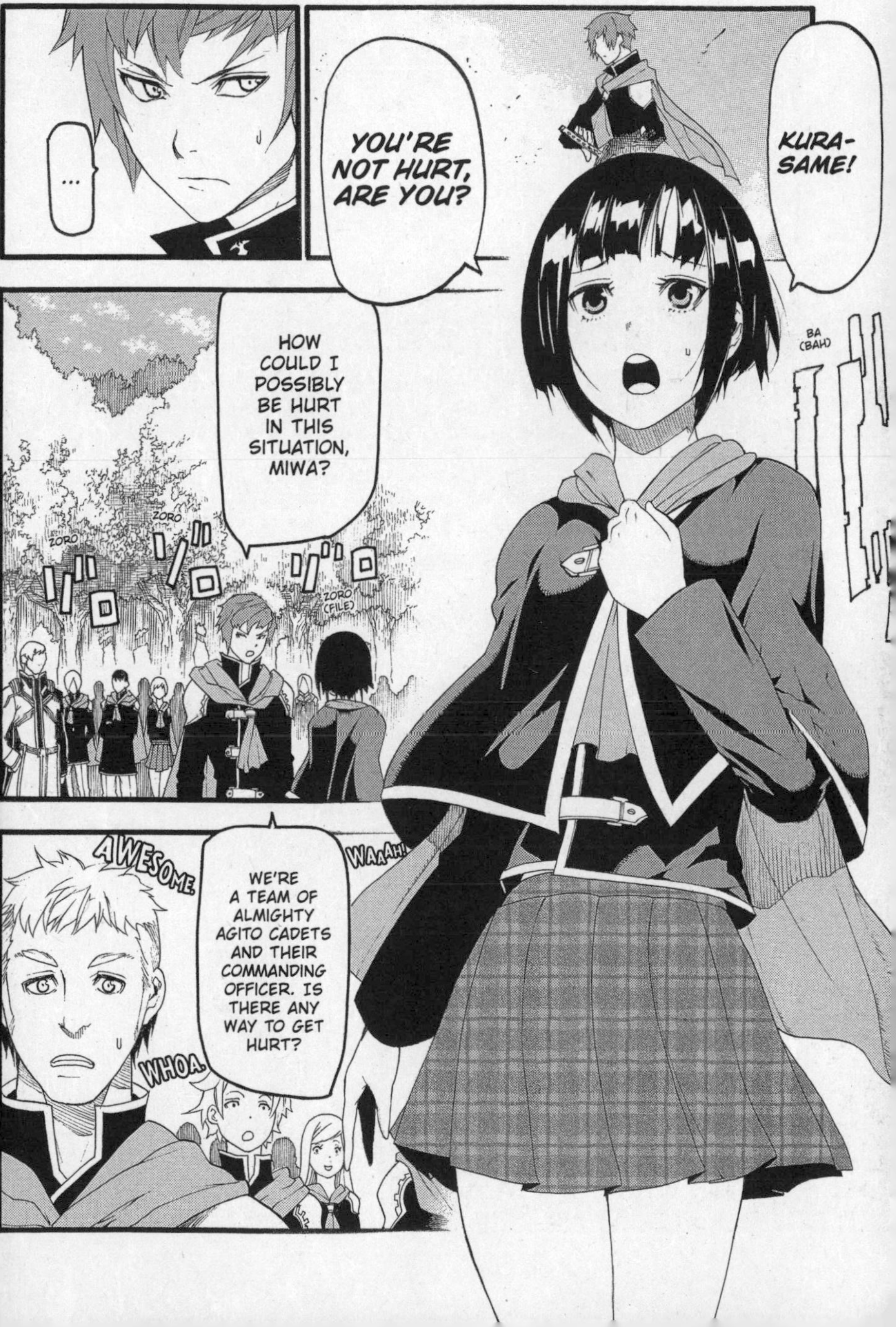
KURA-SAME!
YOU'RE NOT HURT, ARE YOU?
BA (BAH)
...
HOW COULD I POSSIBLY BE HURT IN THIS SITUATION, MIWA?
ZORO
ZORO
ZORO (FILE)
WAAAH!
WE'RE A TEAM OF ALMIGHTY AGITO CADETS AND THEIR COMMANDING OFFICER. IS THERE ANY WAY TO GET HURT?
AWESOME.
WHOA.

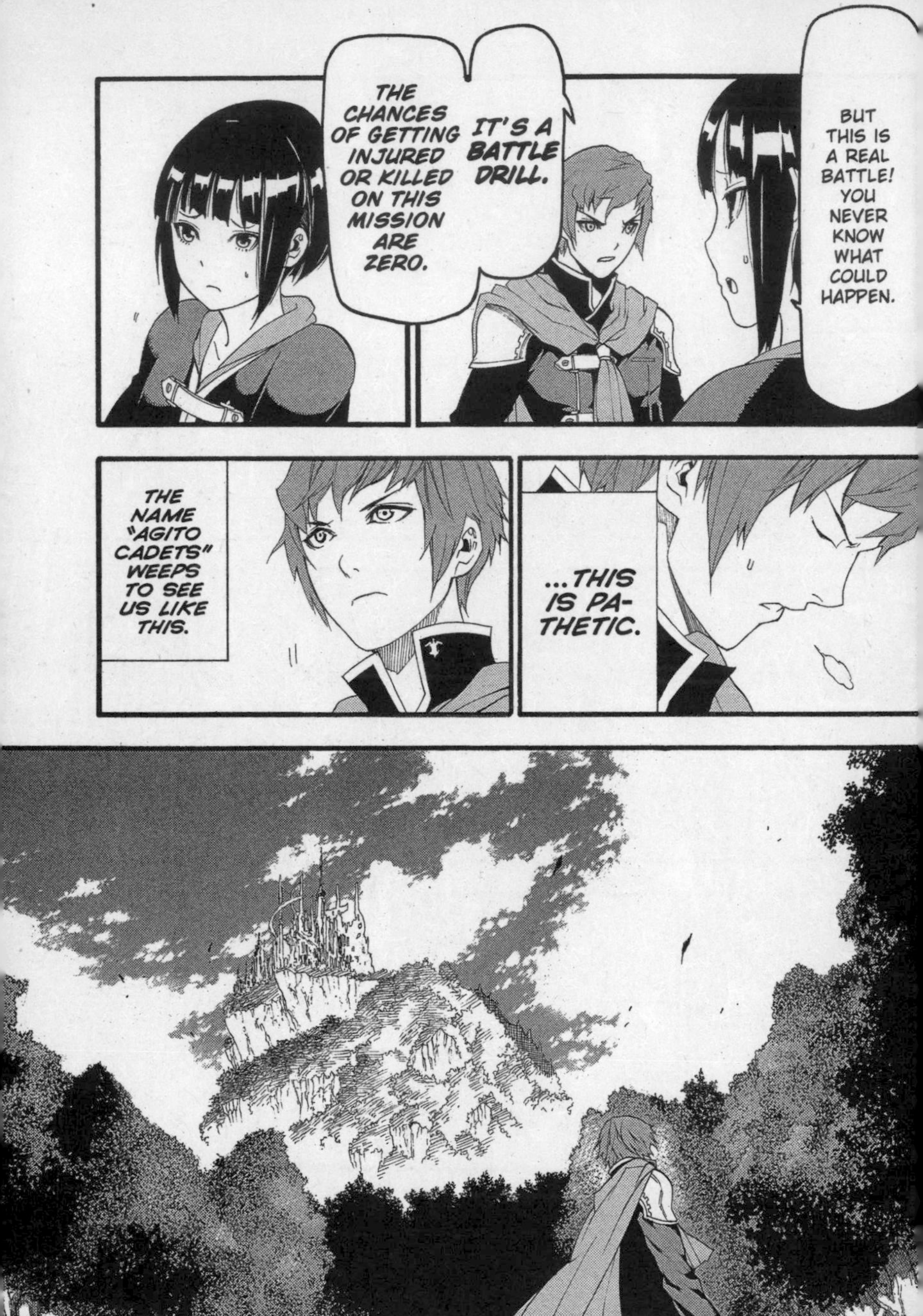
BUT THIS IS A REAL BATTLE! YOU NEVER KNOW WHAT COULD HAPPEN.
IT'S A BATTLE DRILL.
THE CHANCES OF GETTING INJURED OR KILLED ON THIS MISSION ARE ZERO.
...THIS IS PATHETIC.
THE NAME "AGITO CADETS" WEEPS TO SEE US LIKE THIS.

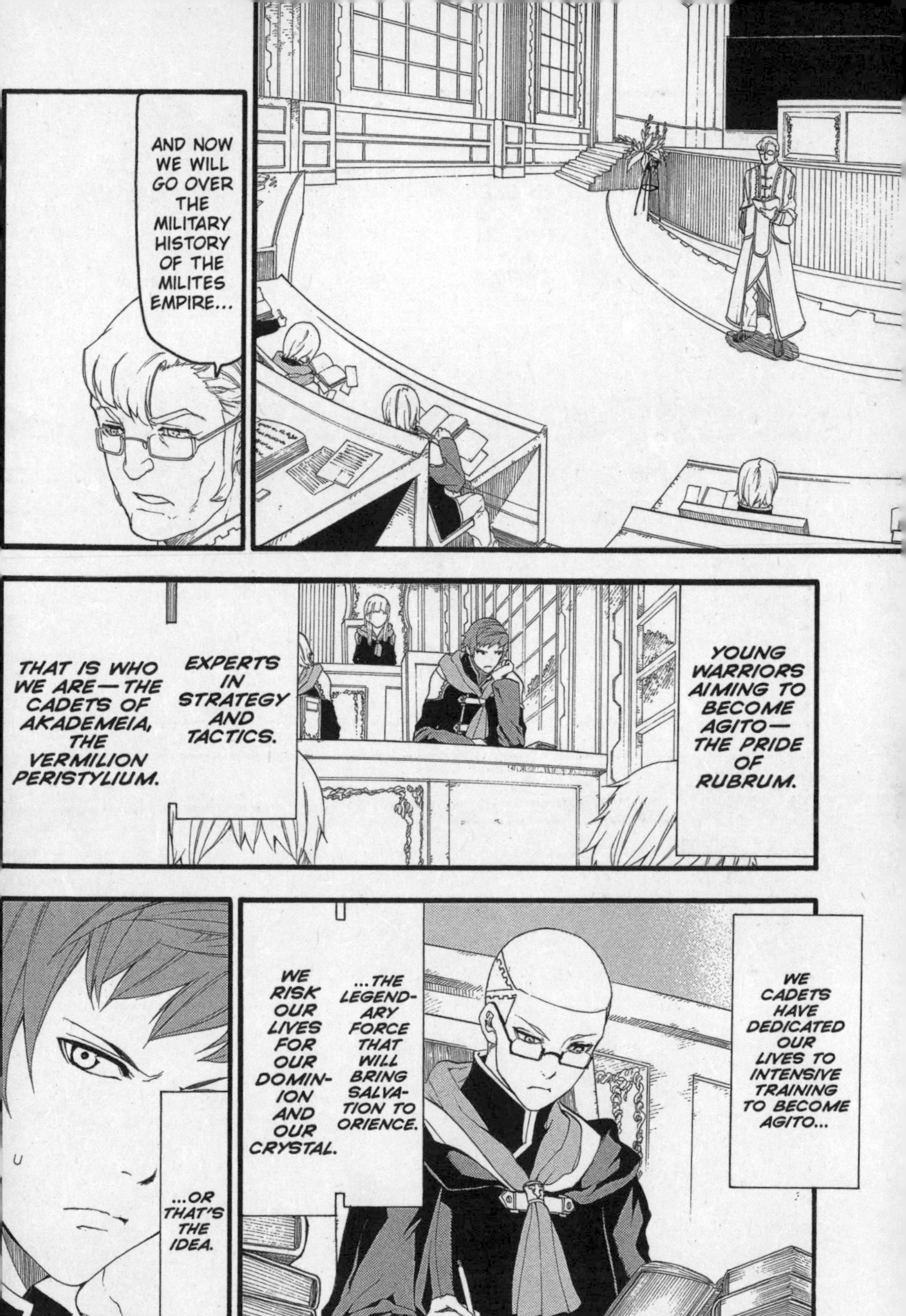
AND NOW WE WILL GO OVER THE MILITARY HISTORY OF THE MILITES EMPIRE...
YOUNG WARRIORS AIMING TO BECOME AGITO—THE PRIDE OF RUBRUM.
EXPERTS IN STRATEGY AND TACTICS.
THAT IS WHO WE ARE—THE CADETS OF AKADEMEIA, THE VERMILION PERISTYLIUM.
WE CADETS HAVE DEDICATED OUR LIVES TO INTENSIVE TRAINING TO BECOME AGITO...
...THE LEGENDARY FORCE THAT WILL BRING SALVATION TO ORIENCE.
WE RISK OUR LIVES FOR OUR DOMINION AND OUR CRYSTAL.
...OR THAT'S THE IDEA.

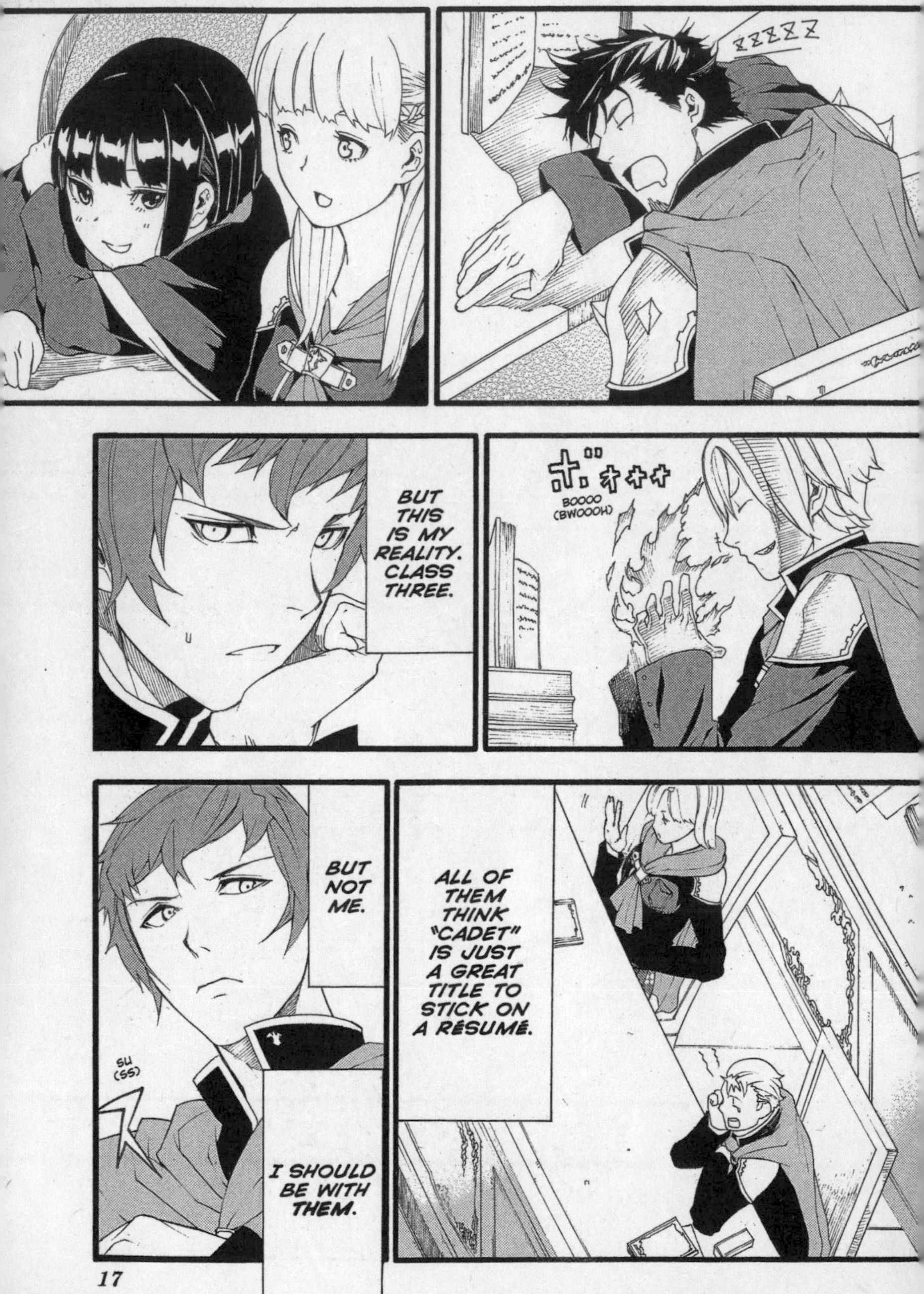
ZZZZZ
ボォォォ
BOOOO (BWOOOH)
BUT THIS IS MY REALITY. CLASS THREE.
ALL OF THEM THINK "CADET" IS JUST A GREAT TITLE TO STICK ON A RÉSUMÉ.
BUT NOT ME.
SU (SS)
I SHOULD BE WITH THEM.

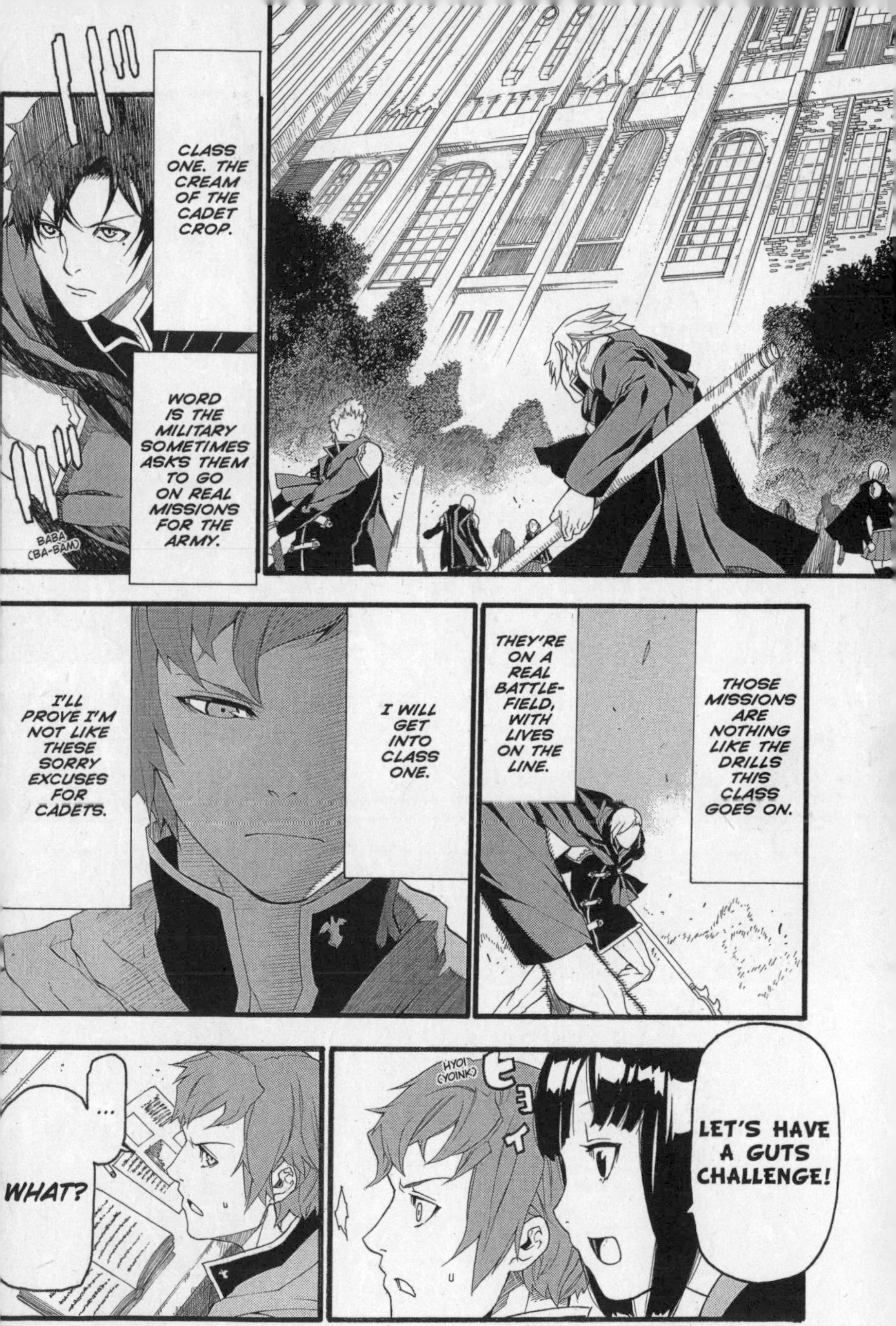
CLASS ONE. THE CREAM OF THE CADET CROP.
WORD IS THE MILITARY SOMETIMES ASKS THEM TO GO ON REAL MISSIONS FOR THE ARMY.
BABA (BA-BAM)
THOSE MISSIONS ARE NOTHING LIKE THE DRILLS THIS CLASS GOES ON.
THEY'RE ON A REAL BATTLEFIELD, WITH LIVES ON THE LINE.
I WILL GET INTO CLASS ONE.
I'LL PROVE I'M NOT LIKE THESE SORRY EXCUSES FOR CADETS.
LET'S HAVE A GUTS CHALLENGE!
HYOI (YOINK)
...
WHAT?

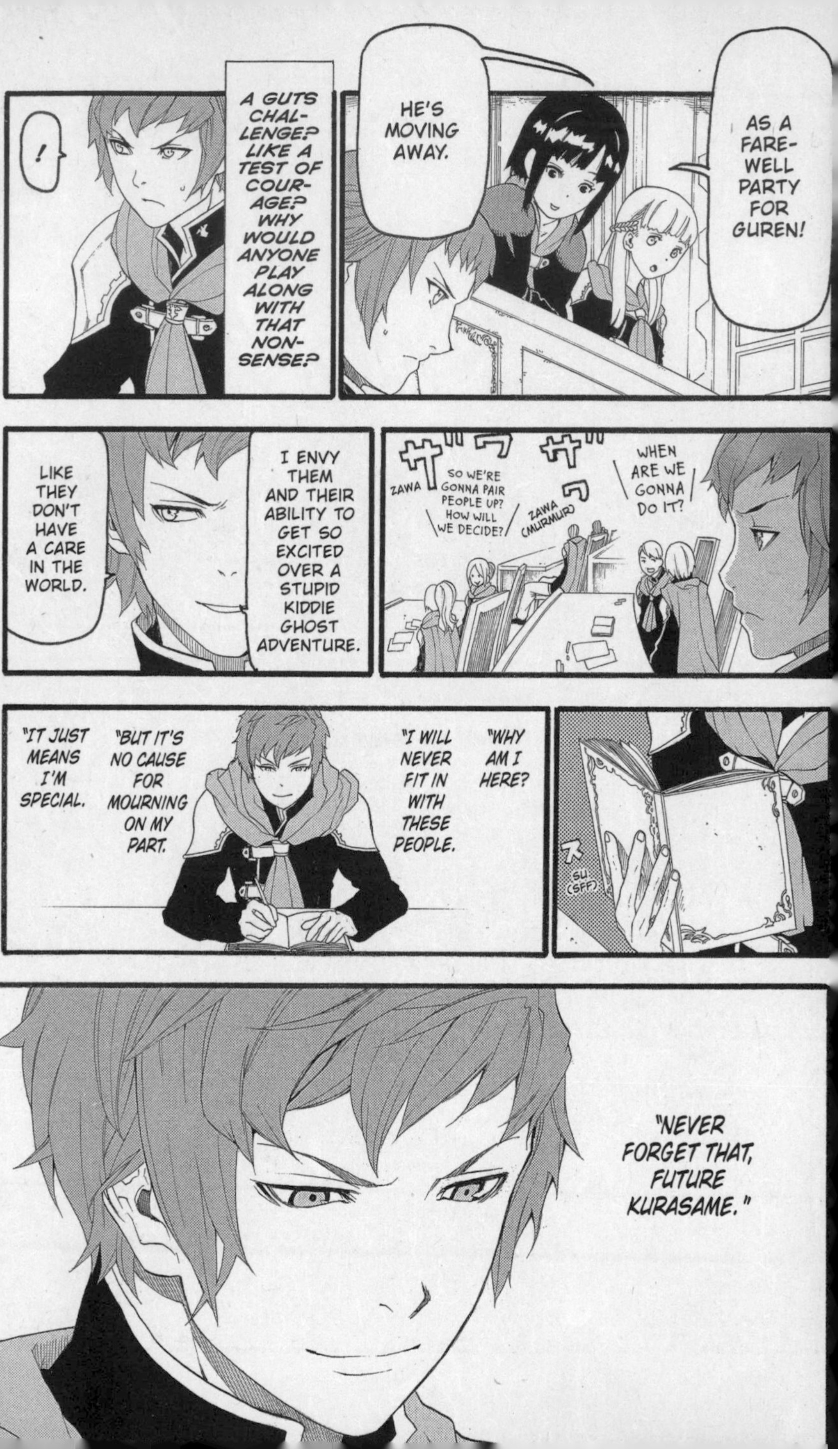
AS A FARE-WELL PARTY FOR GUREN!
HE'S MOVING AWAY.
A GUTS CHAL-LENGE? LIKE A TEST OF COUR-AGE? WHY WOULD ANYONE PLAY ALONG WITH THAT NON-SENSE?
!
WHEN ARE WE GONNA DO IT?
ZAWA (MURMUR)
SO WE'RE GONNA PAIR PEOPLE UP? HOW WILL WE DECIDE?
ZAWA
I ENVY THEM AND THEIR ABILITY TO GET SO EXCITED OVER A STUPID KIDDIE GHOST ADVENTURE.
LIKE THEY DON'T HAVE A CARE IN THE WORLD.
SU (SFF)
"WHY AM I HERE?
"I WILL NEVER FIT IN WITH THESE PEOPLE.
"BUT IT'S NO CAUSE FOR MOURNING ON MY PART.
"IT JUST MEANS I'M SPECIAL.
"NEVER FORGET THAT, FUTURE KURASAME."

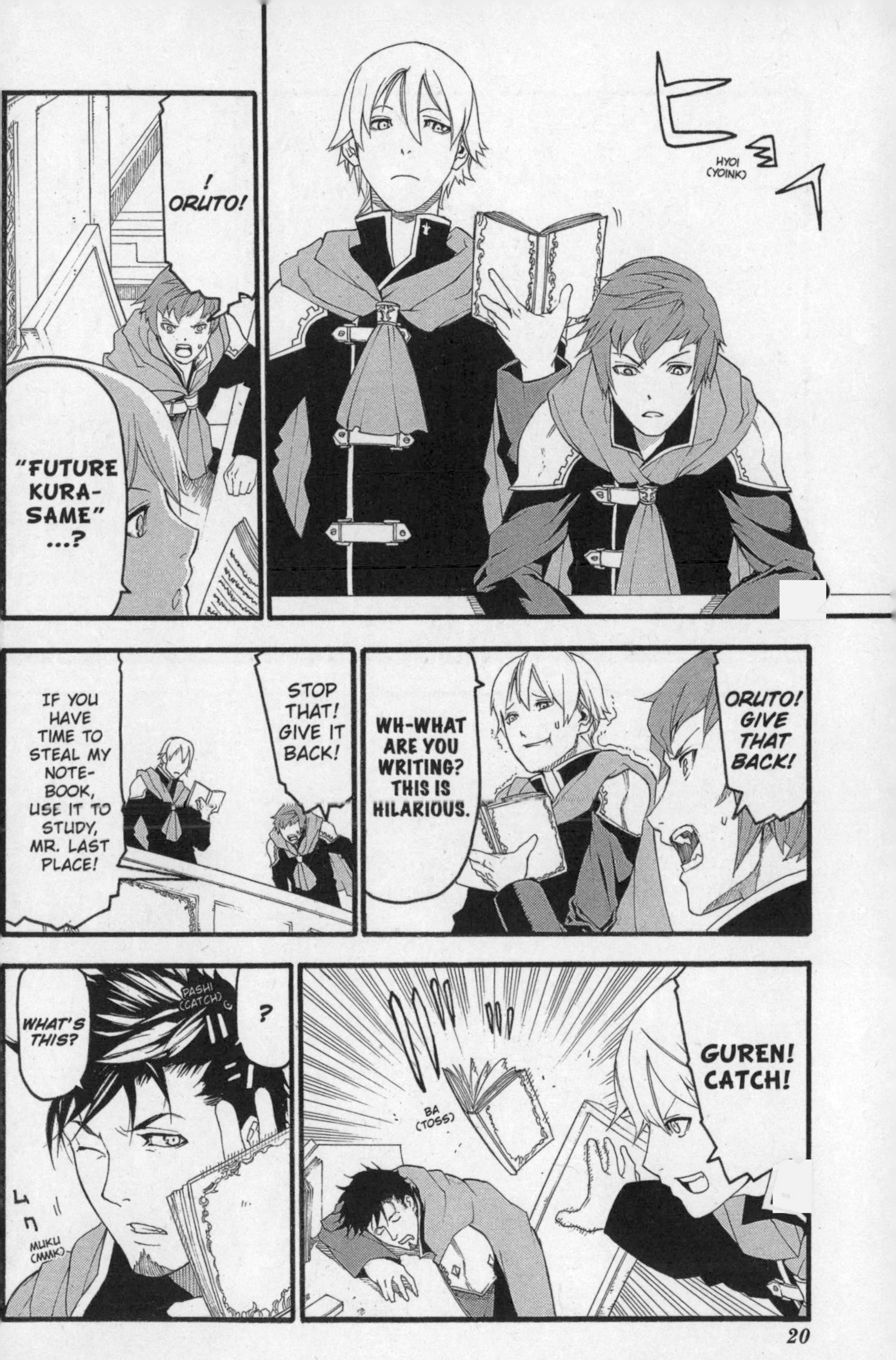
HYOI
(YOINK)
! ORUTO!
"FUTURE KURA-SAME" ...?
ORUTO! GIVE THAT BACK!
WH-WHAT ARE YOU WRITING? THIS IS HILARIOUS.
STOP THAT! GIVE IT BACK!
IF YOU HAVE TIME TO STEAL MY NOTE-BOOK, USE IT TO STUDY, MR. LAST PLACE!
GUREN! CATCH!
BA
(TOSS)
PASHI
(CATCH)
?
WHAT'S THIS?
MUKU
(MMK)

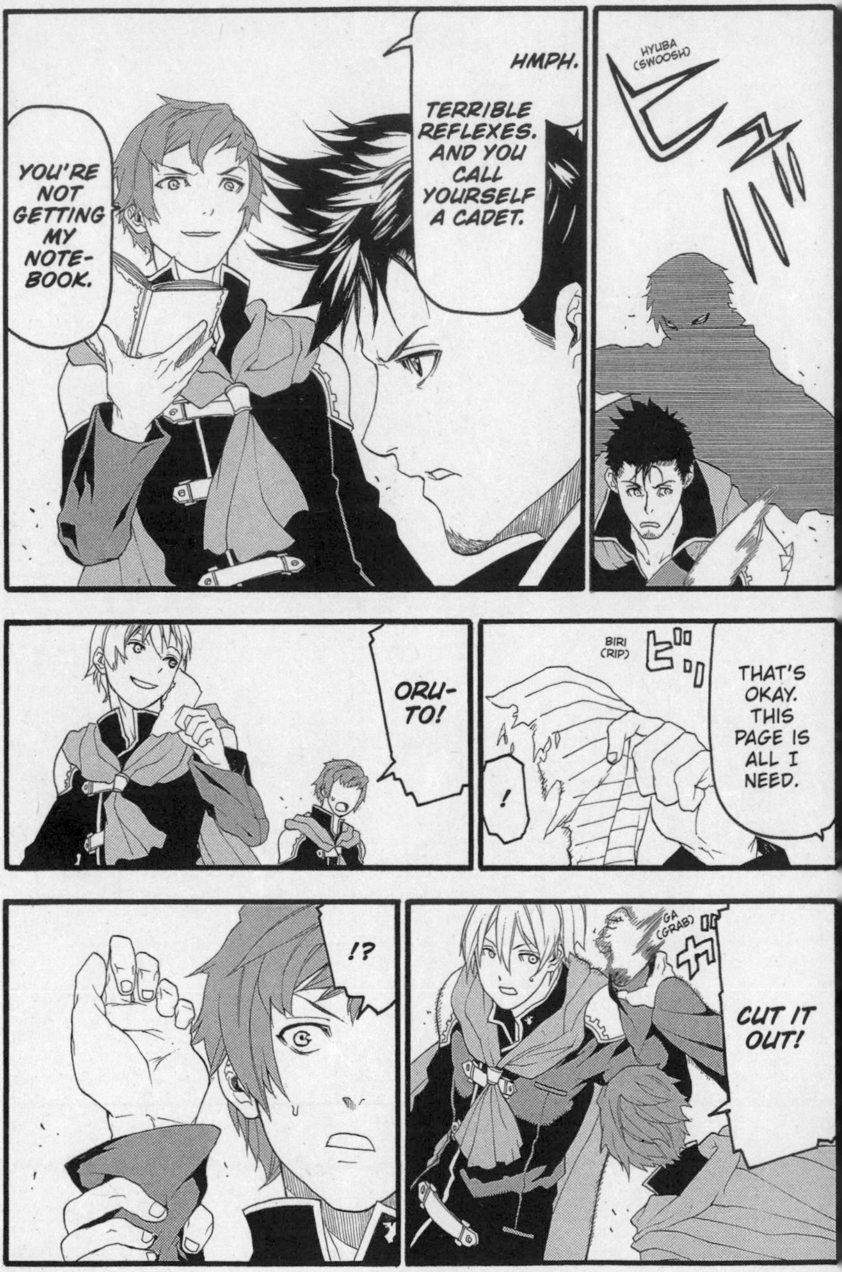
HYUBA (SWOOSH)
HMPH.
TERRIBLE REFLEXES. AND YOU CALL YOURSELF A CADET.
YOU'RE NOT GETTING MY NOTE-BOOK.
THAT'S OKAY. THIS PAGE IS ALL I NEED.
BIRI (RIP)
!
ORU-TO!
GA (GRAB)
CUT IT OUT!
!?

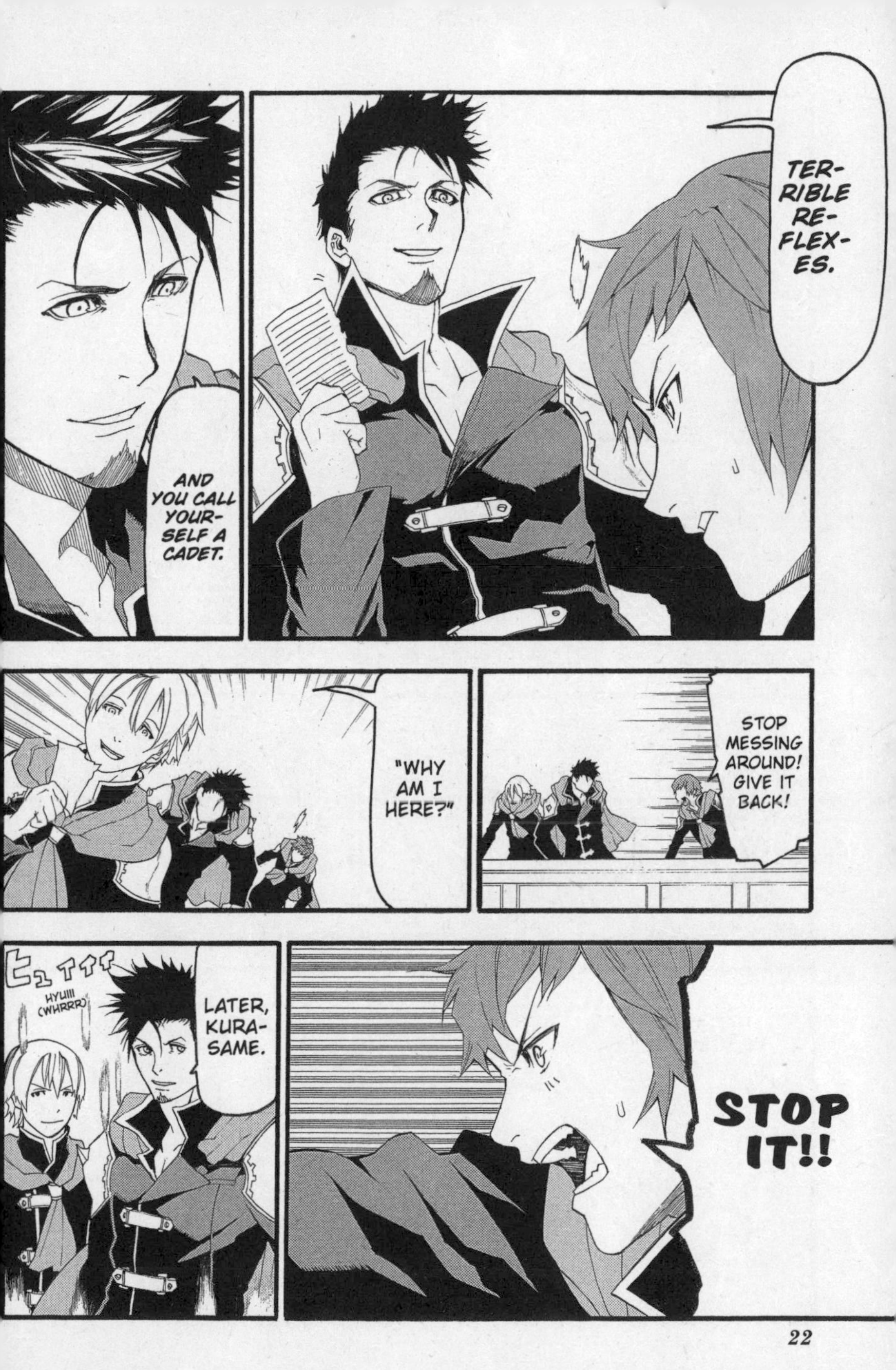
TER-RIBLE RE-FLEX-ES.
AND YOU CALL YOUR-SELF A CADET.
STOP MESSING AROUND! GIVE IT BACK!
"WHY AM I HERE?"
STOP IT!!
LATER, KURA-SAME.
HYUIII (WHRRR)

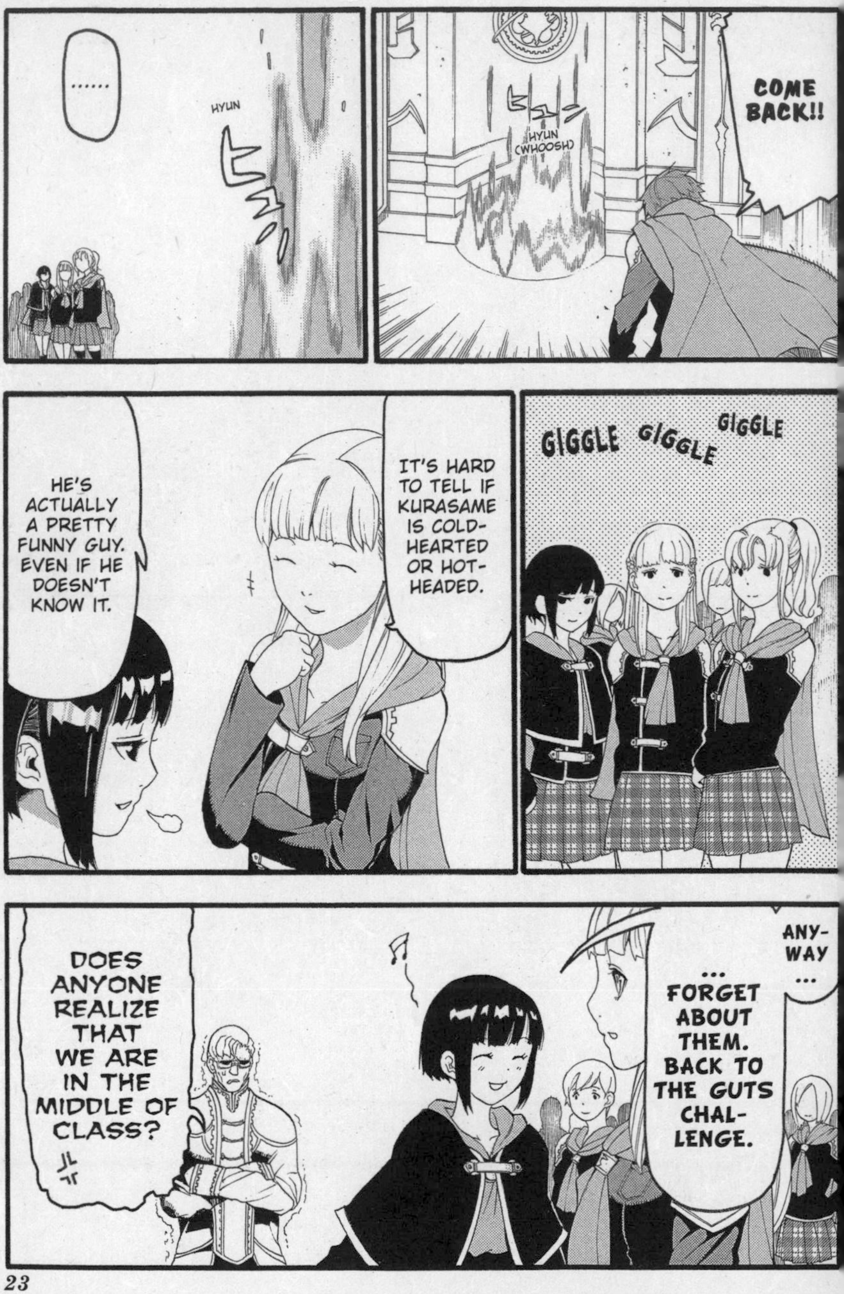
COME BACK!!
HYUN (WHOOSH)
HYUN
......
GIGGLE GIGGLE GIGGLE
IT'S HARD TO TELL IF KURASAME IS COLD-HEARTED OR HOT-HEADED.
HE'S ACTUALLY A PRETTY FUNNY GUY. EVEN IF HE DOESN'T KNOW IT.
ANYWAY ...
... FORGET ABOUT THEM. BACK TO THE GUTS CHALLENGE.
DOES ANYONE REALIZE THAT WE ARE IN THE MIDDLE OF CLASS?

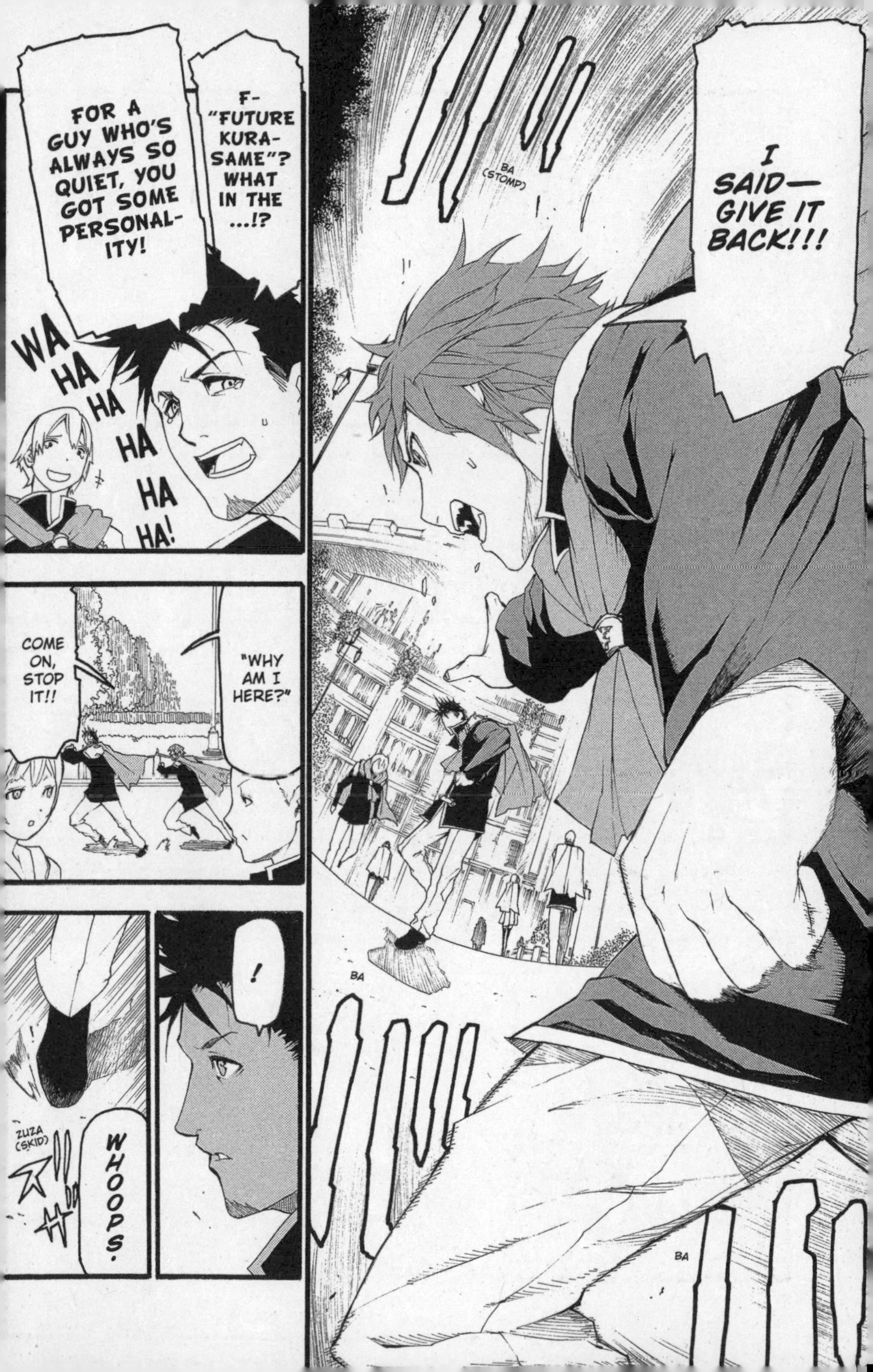
I SAID— GIVE IT BACK!!!
BA (STOMP)
BA
BA
F- "FUTURE KURA-SAME"? WHAT IN THE ...!?
FOR A GUY WHO'S ALWAYS SO QUIET, YOU GOT SOME PERSONAL-ITY!
WA HA HA HA HA HA!
"WHY AM I HERE?"
COME ON, STOP IT!!
!
WHOOPS.
ZUZA (SKID)

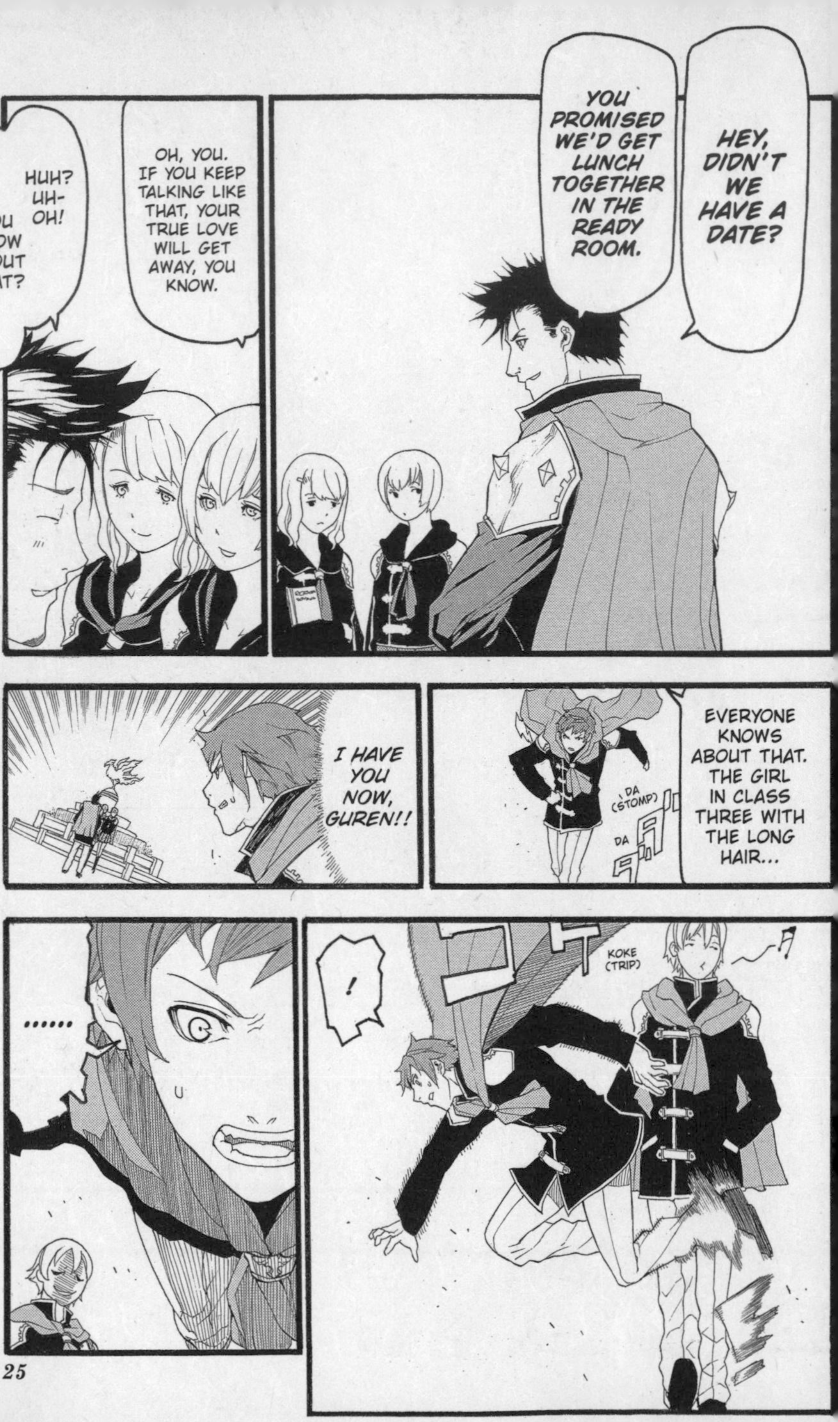
HEY, DIDN'T WE HAVE A DATE?
YOU PROMISED WE'D GET LUNCH TOGETHER IN THE READY ROOM.
OH, YOU. IF YOU KEEP TALKING LIKE THAT, YOUR TRUE LOVE WILL GET AWAY, YOU KNOW.
HUH? UH-OH!
YOU KNOW ABOUT THAT?
EVERYONE KNOWS ABOUT THAT. THE GIRL IN CLASS THREE WITH THE LONG HAIR...
DA (STOMP)
DA
I HAVE YOU NOW, GUREN!!
!
KOKE (TRIP)
......

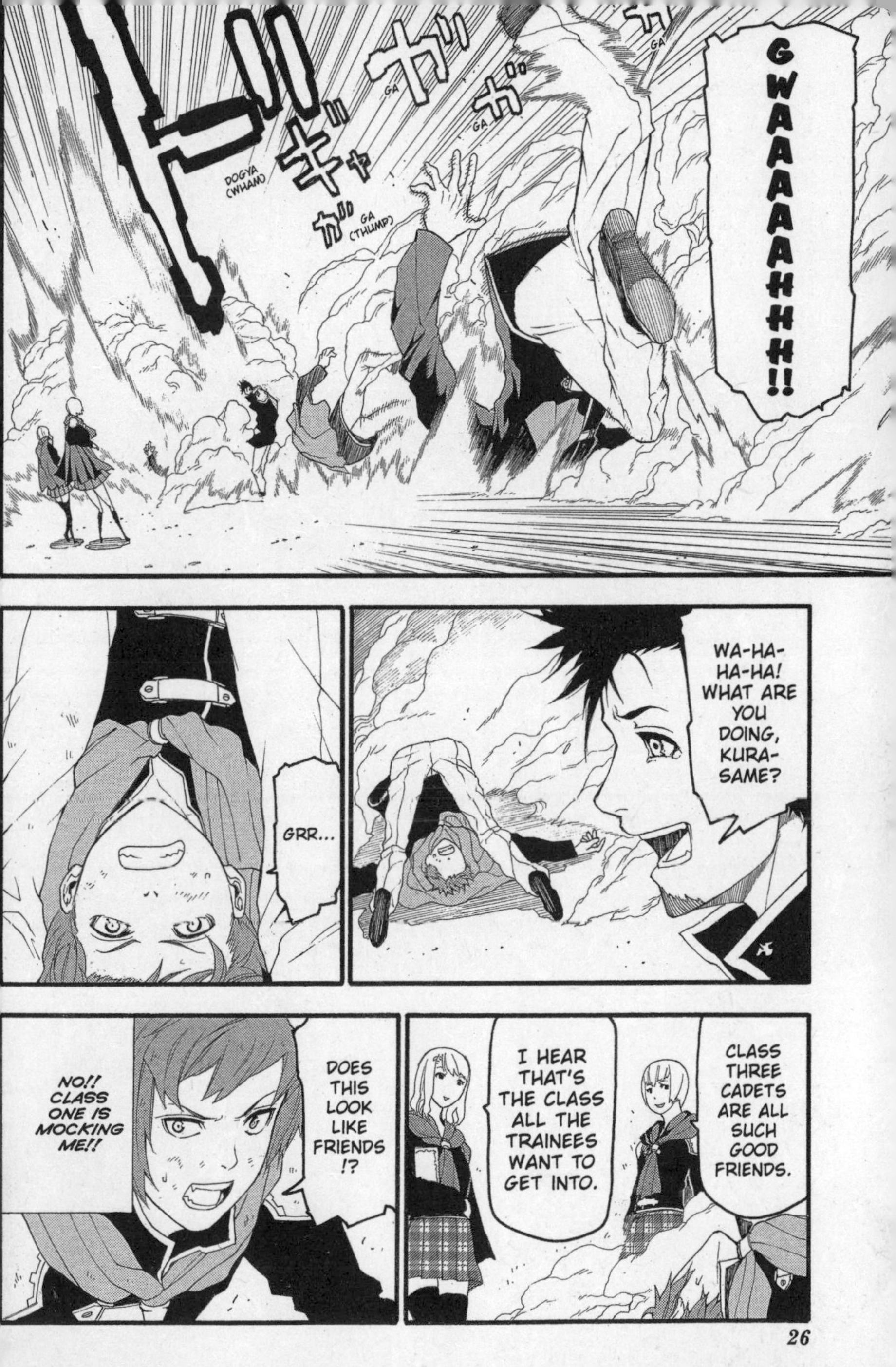
GWAAAAAHHHH!!
GA
GA
GA
DOGYA (WHAM)
GA (THUMP)
WA-HA-HA-HA! WHAT ARE YOU DOING, KURA-SAME?
GRR...
CLASS THREE CADETS ARE ALL SUCH GOOD FRIENDS.
I HEAR THAT'S THE CLASS ALL THE TRAINEES WANT TO GET INTO.
DOES THIS LOOK LIKE FRIENDS!?
NO!! CLASS ONE IS MOCKING ME!!

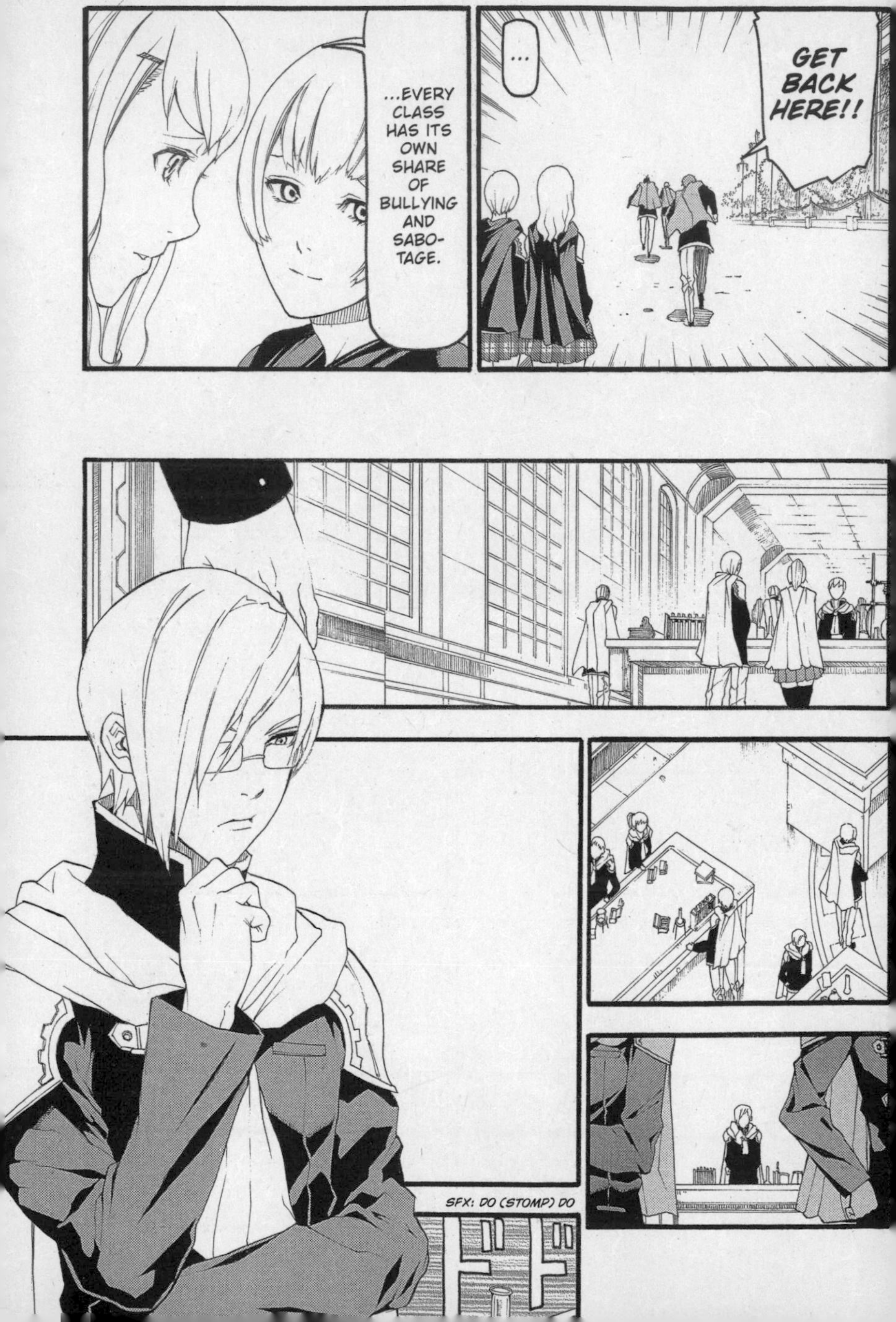
GET BACK HERE!!
...
...EVERY CLASS HAS ITS OWN SHARE OF BULLYING AND SABOTAGE.
SFX: DO (STOMP) DO

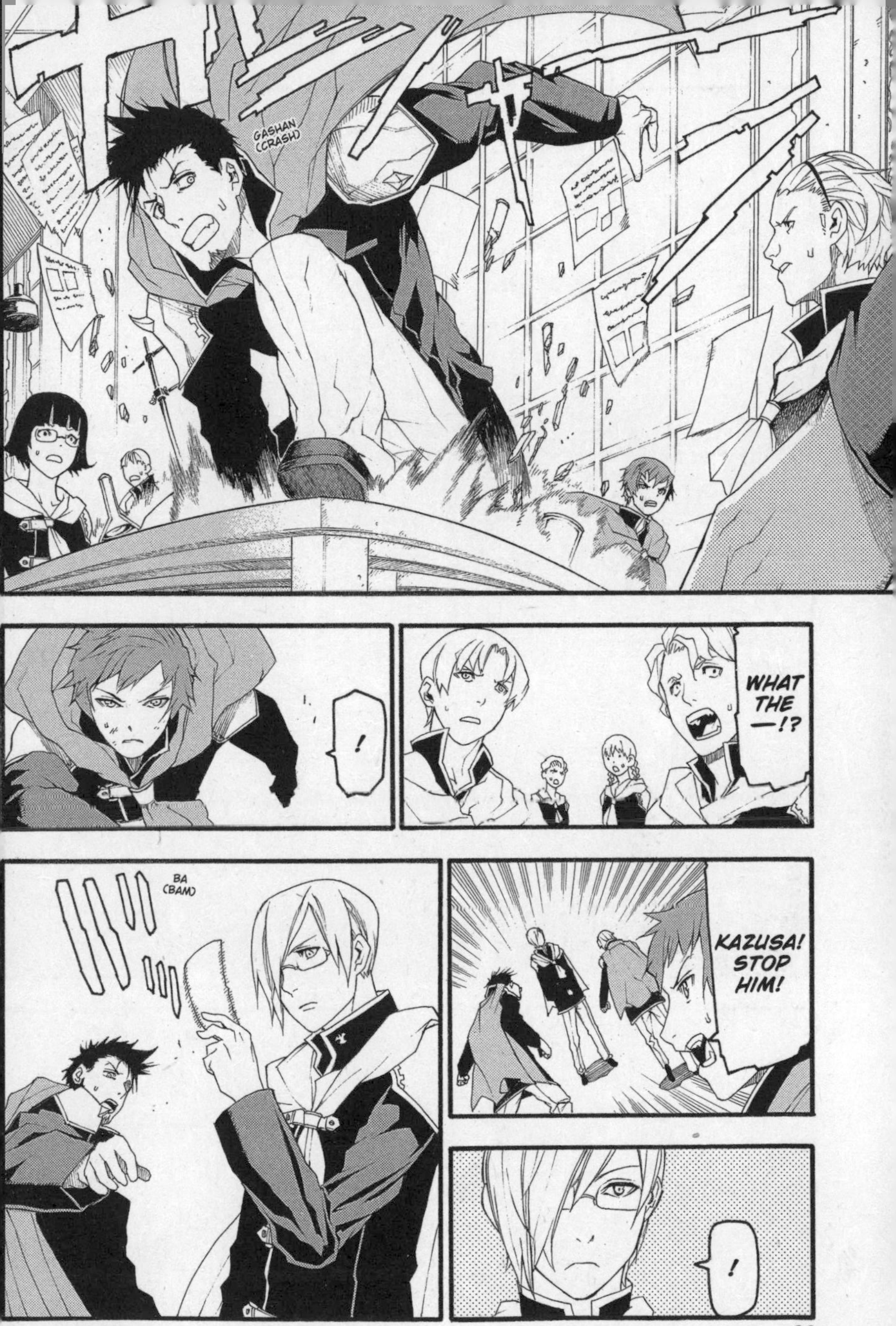
GASHAN (CRASH)
WHAT THE—!?
!
KAZUSA! STOP HIM!
!
BA (BAM)

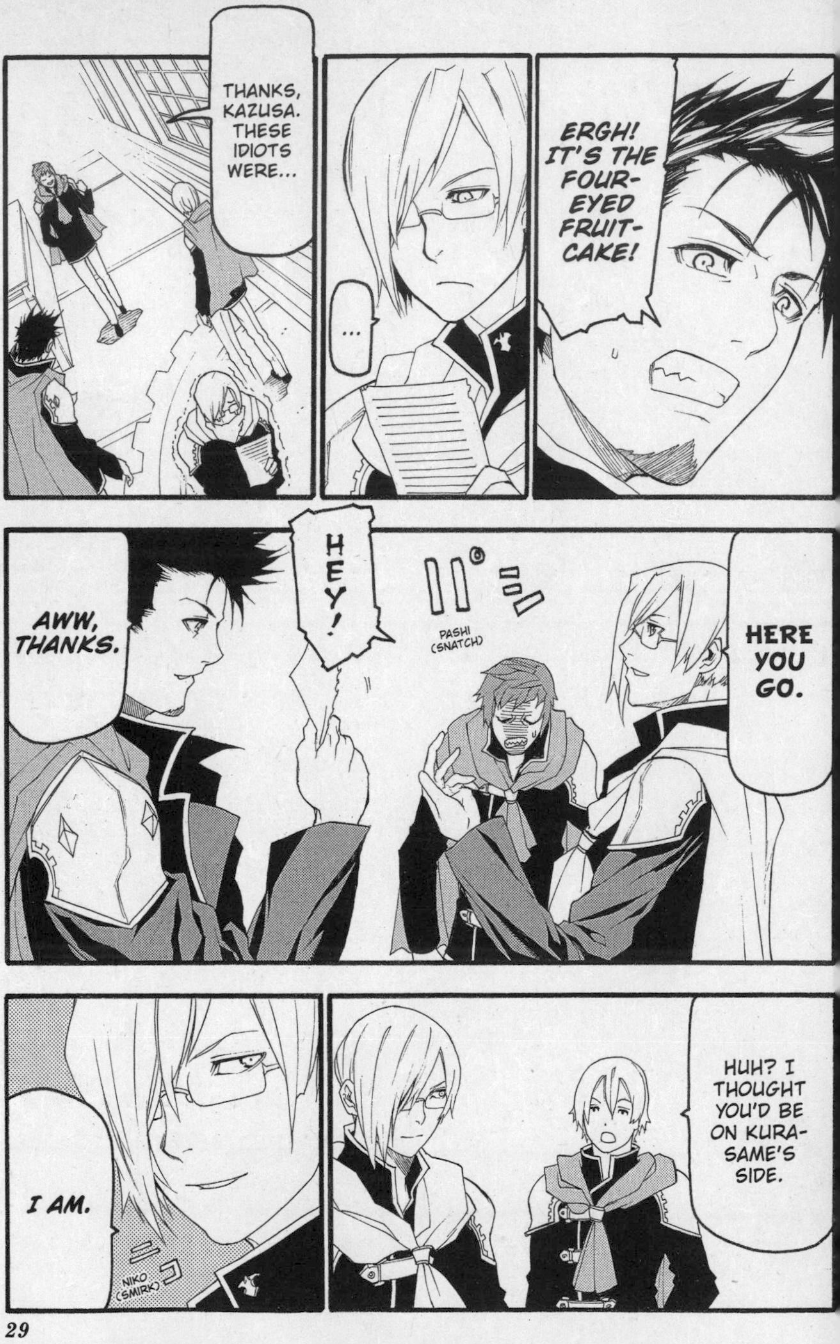
ERGH! IT'S THE FOUR-EYED FRUIT-CAKE!
...
THANKS, KAZUSA. THESE IDIOTS WERE...
HERE YOU GO.
PASHI (SNATCH)
HEY!
AWW, THANKS.
HUH? I THOUGHT YOU'D BE ON KURA-SAME'S SIDE.
I AM.
NIKO (SMIRK)

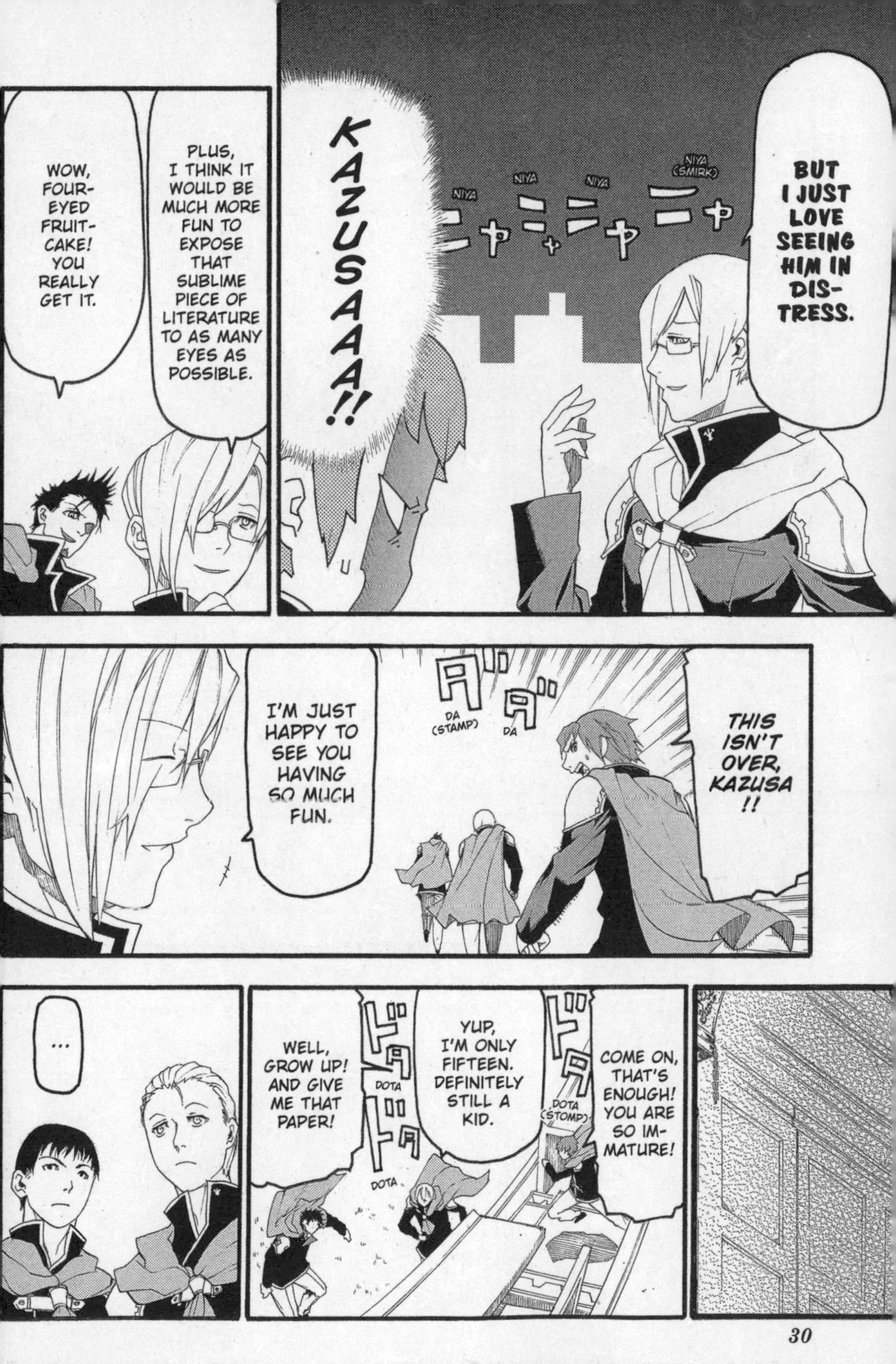
BUT I JUST LOVE SEEING HIM IN DISTRESS.
NIYA (SMIRK)
NIYA
NIYA
NIYA
KAZUSAAAA!!
PLUS, I THINK IT WOULD BE MUCH MORE FUN TO EXPOSE THAT SUBLIME PIECE OF LITERATURE TO AS MANY EYES AS POSSIBLE.
WOW, FOUR-EYED FRUITCAKE! YOU REALLY GET IT.
THIS ISN'T OVER, KAZUSA!!
DA
DA (STAMP)
I'M JUST HAPPY TO SEE YOU HAVING SO MUCH FUN.
COME ON, THAT'S ENOUGH! YOU ARE SO IMMATURE!
DOTA (STOMP)
YUP, I'M ONLY FIFTEEN. DEFINITELY STILL A KID.
DOTA
WELL, GROW UP! AND GIVE ME THAT PAPER!
DOTA
...

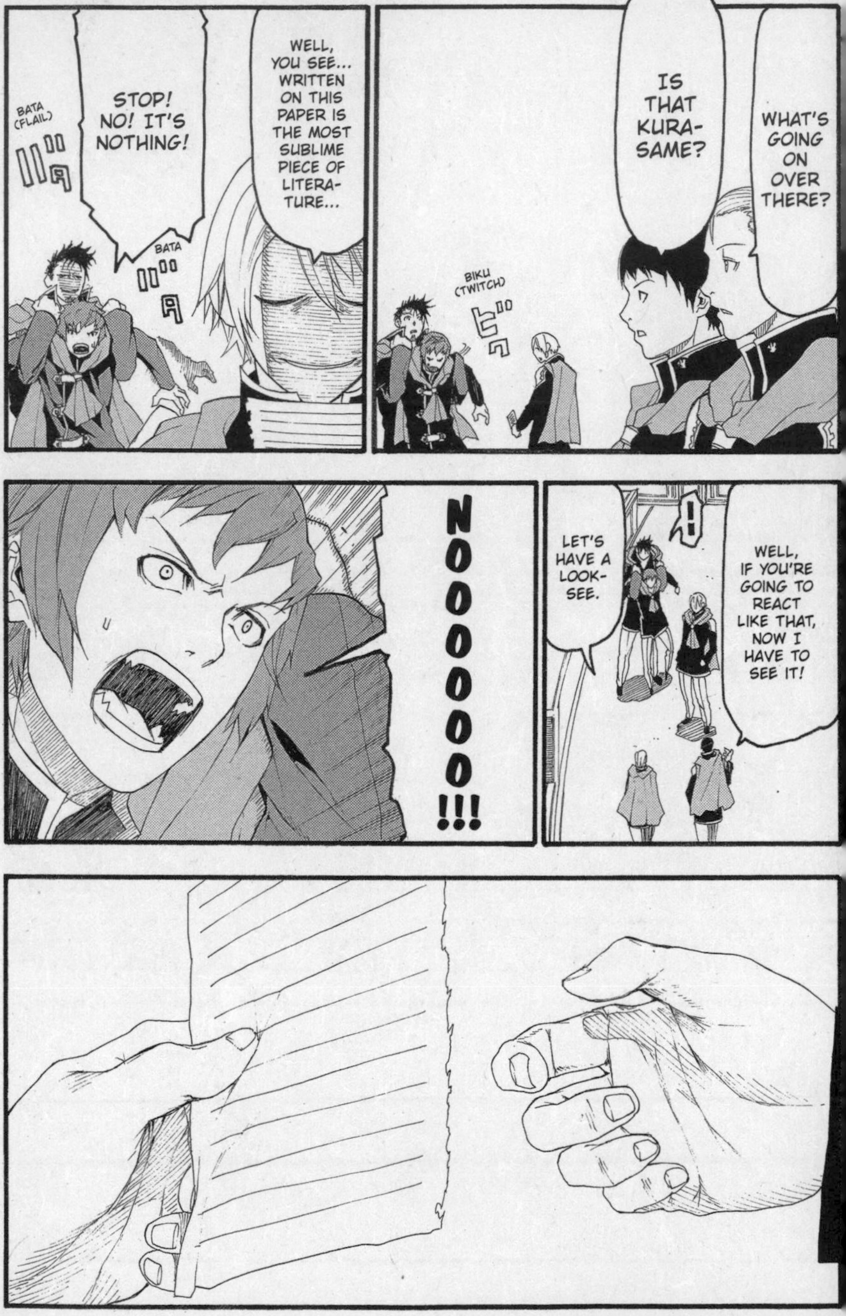
WHAT'S GOING ON OVER THERE?
IS THAT KURA-SAME?
BIKU (TWITCH)
WELL, YOU SEE... WRITTEN ON THIS PAPER IS THE MOST SUBLIME PIECE OF LITERA-TURE...
STOP! NO! IT'S NOTHING!
BATA (FLAIL)
BATA
WELL, IF YOU'RE GOING TO REACT LIKE THAT, NOW I HAVE TO SEE IT!
!
LET'S HAVE A LOOK-SEE.
NOOOOOOO!!!

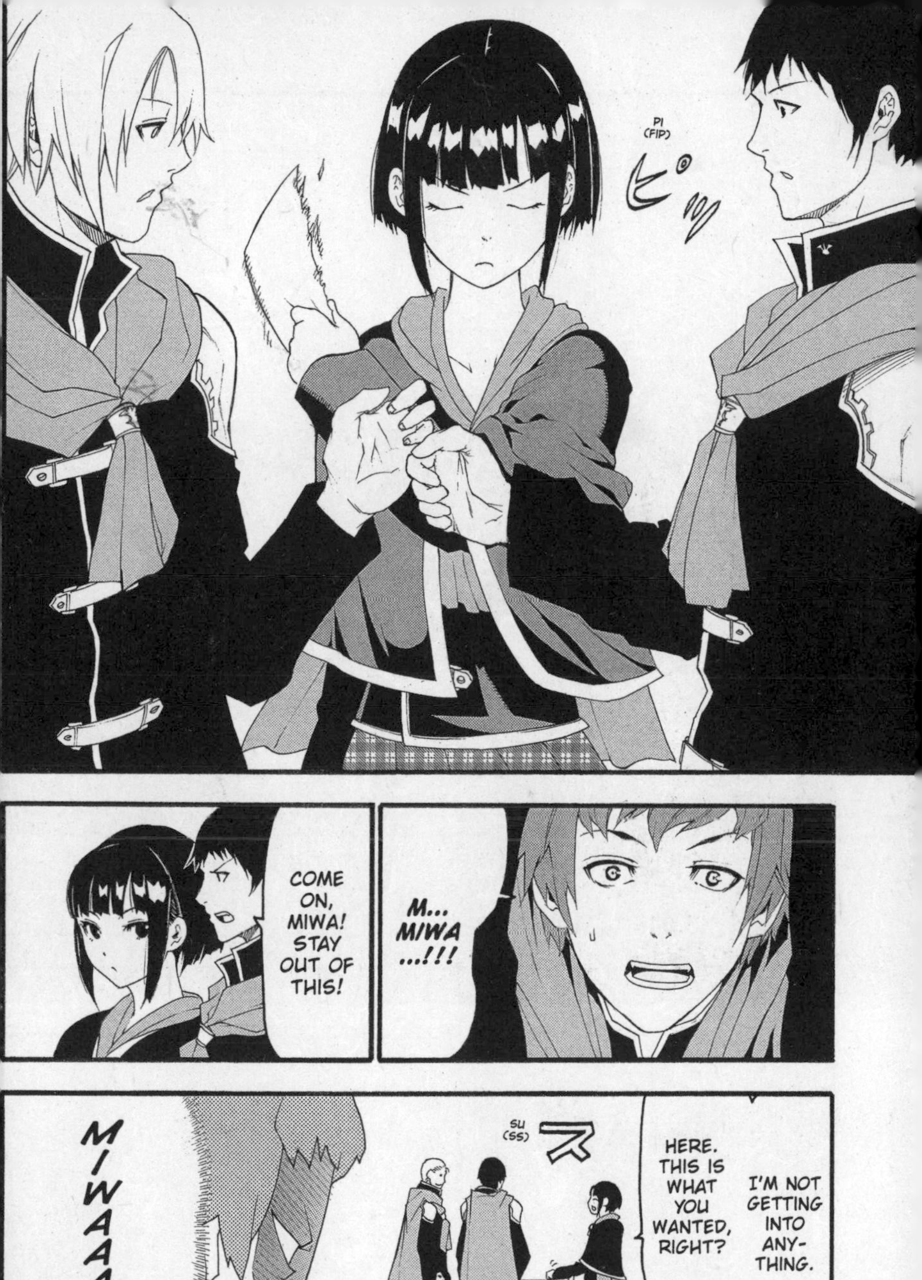
PI
(FIP)
M... MIWA ...!!!
COME ON, MIWA! STAY OUT OF THIS!
I'M NOT GETTING INTO ANY-THING.
HERE. THIS IS WHAT YOU WANTED, RIGHT?
SU
(SS)
MIWAAAA!!!

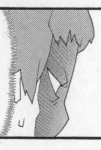

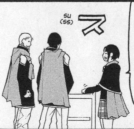

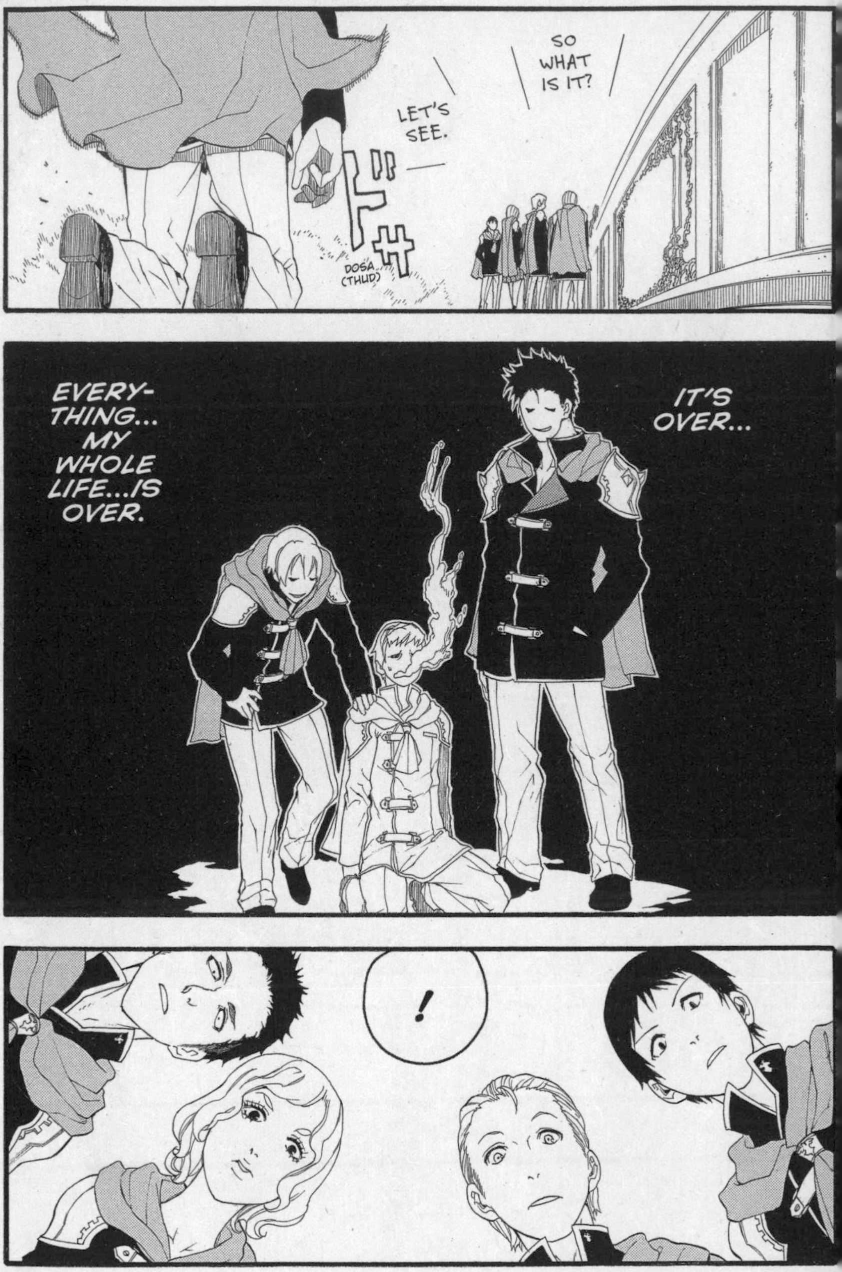
SO WHAT IS IT?
LET'S SEE.
DOSA (THUD)
IT'S OVER...
EVERY-THING... MY WHOLE LIFE...IS OVER.
!

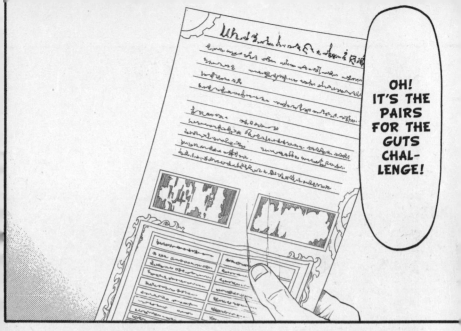

OH! IT'S THE PAIRS FOR THE GUTS CHALLENGE!

SUTA (SKFF)

SUTA

...

...

WHAT? LET ME SEE!

......

......

KI (GLARE)

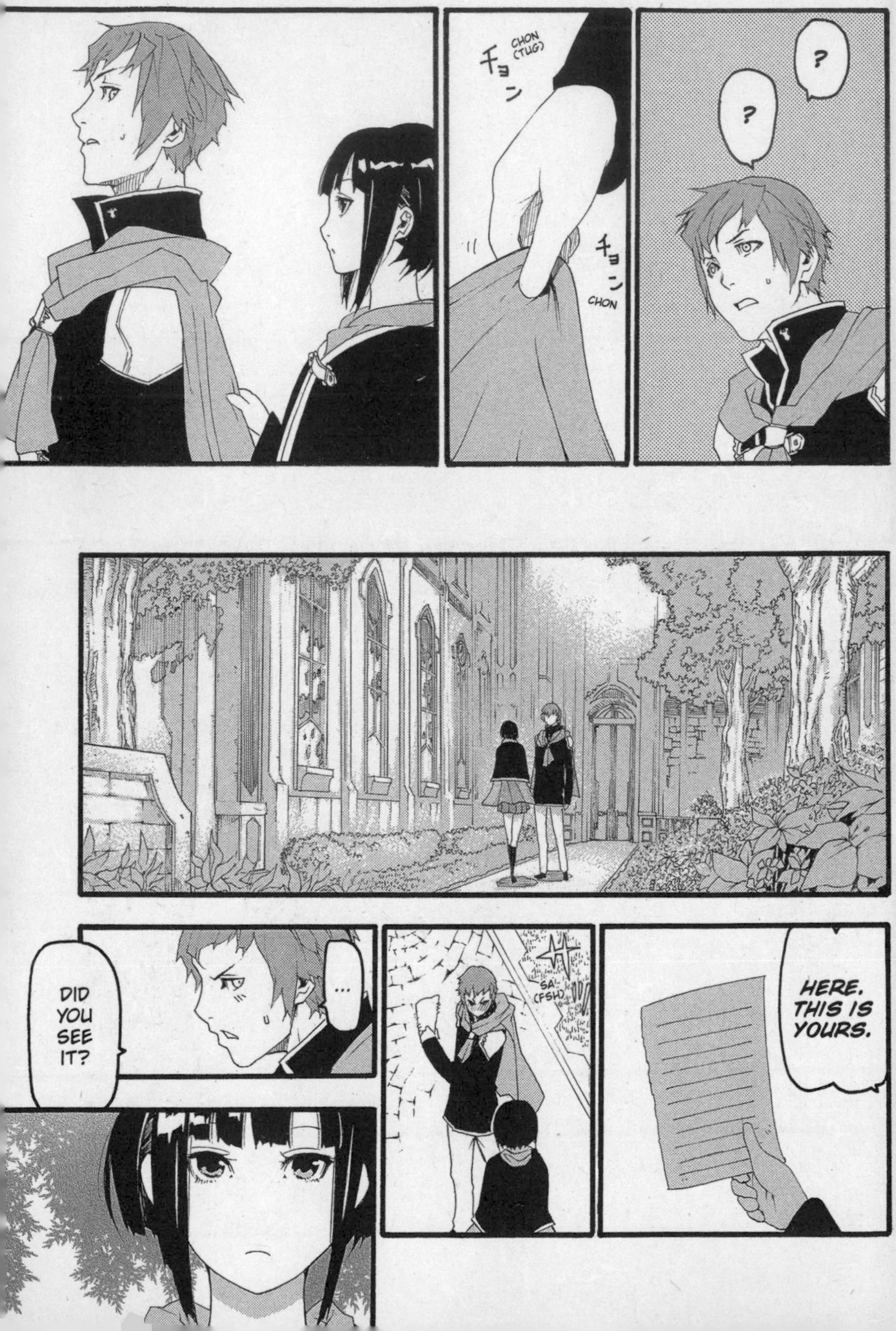
?
?
チョン
CHON (TUG)
チョン
CHON
HERE. THIS IS YOURS.
SA (FSH)
...
DID YOU SEE IT?

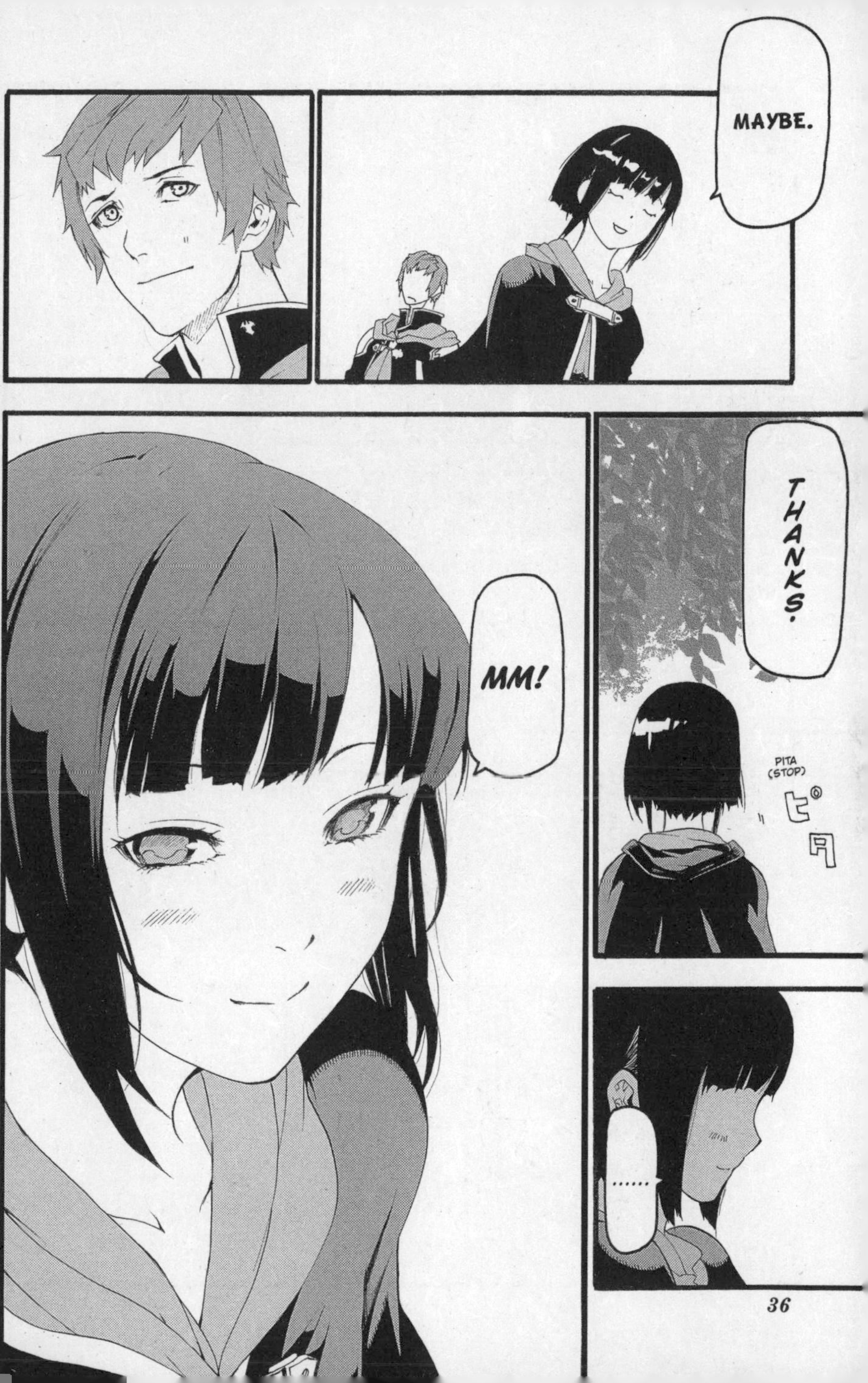
MAYBE.
THANKS.
PITA (STOP)
ピタ
......
MM!

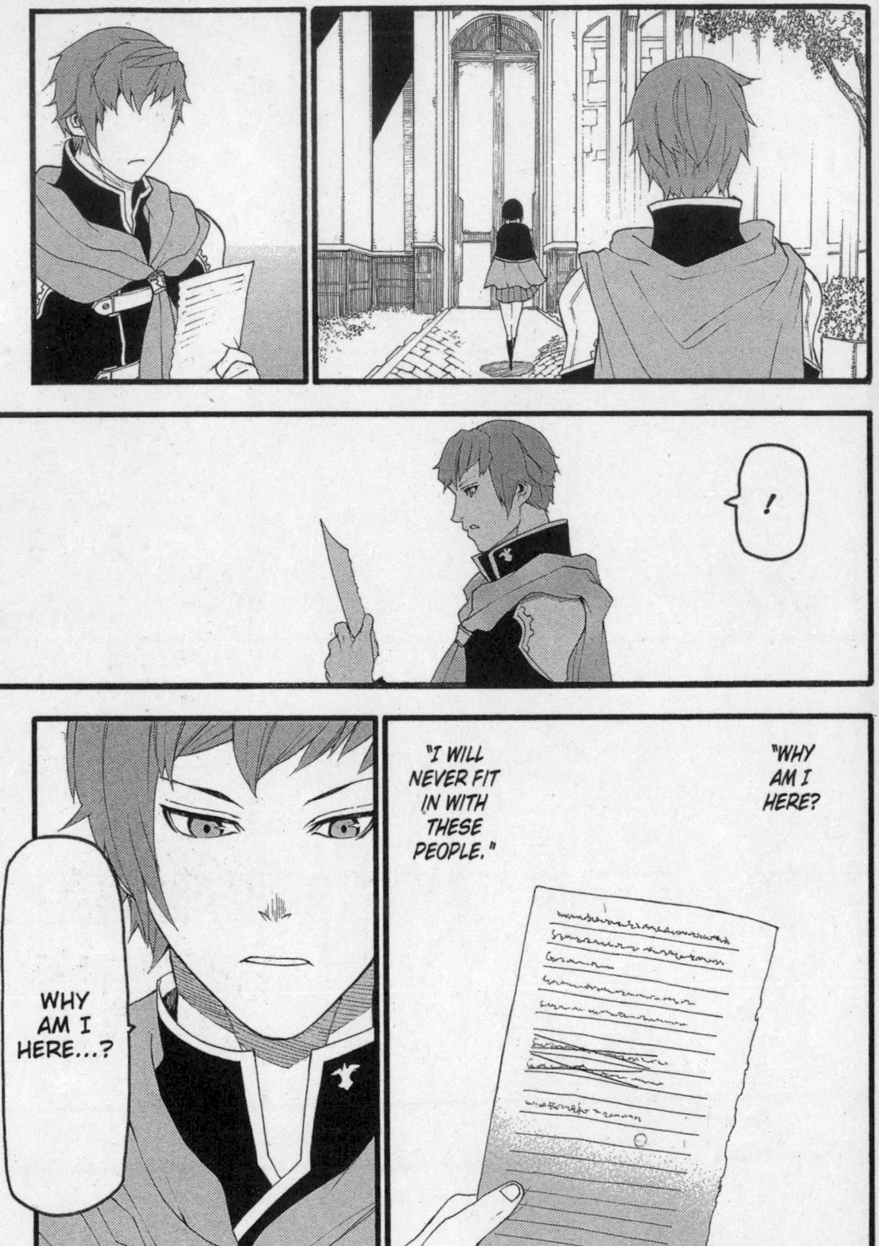
!
"WHY AM I HERE?
"I WILL NEVER FIT IN WITH THESE PEOPLE."
WHY AM I HERE...?

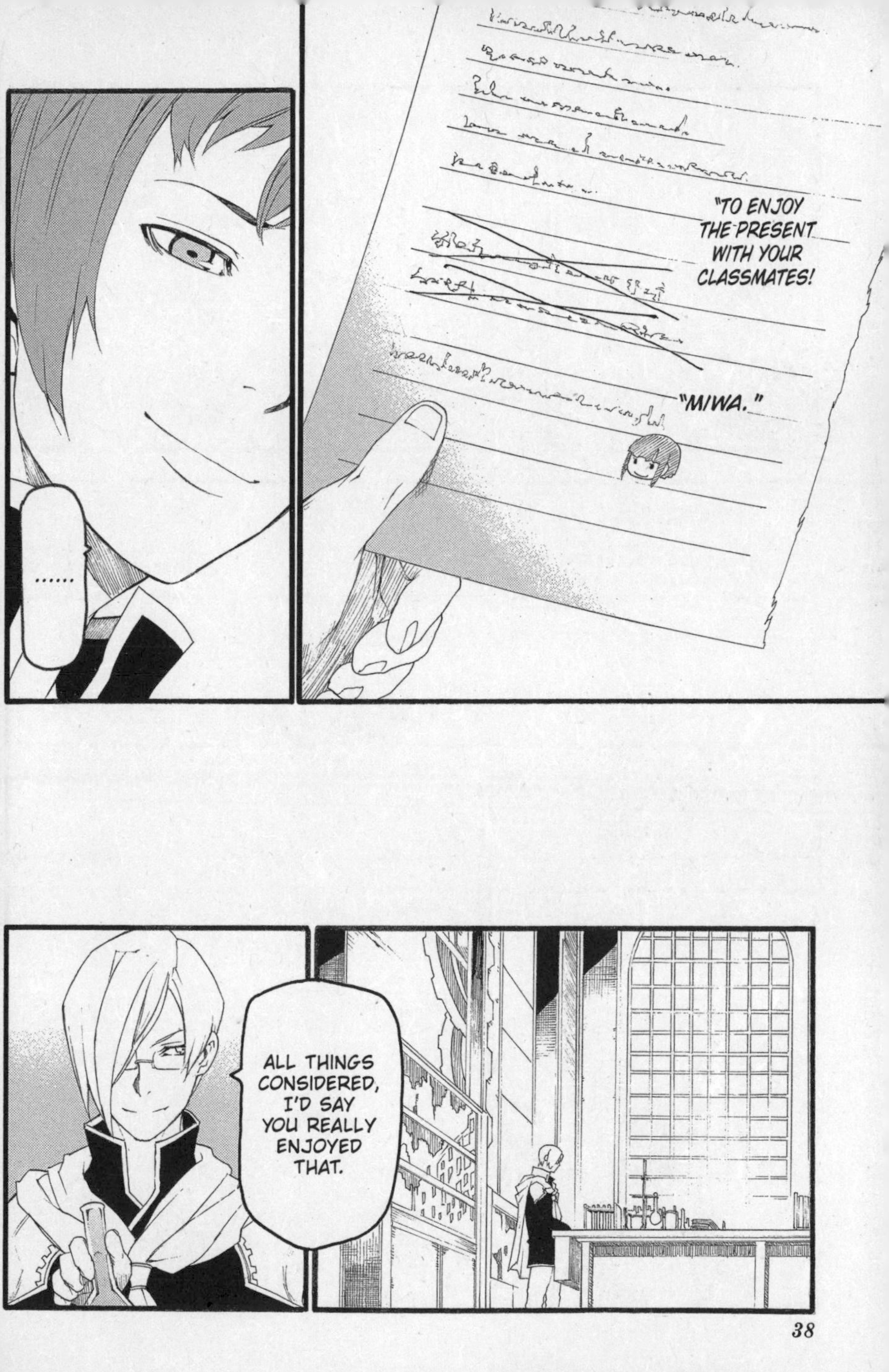
"TO ENJOY THE PRESENT WITH YOUR CLASSMATES!
"MIWA."
......
ALL THINGS CONSIDERED, I'D SAY YOU REALLY ENJOYED THAT.

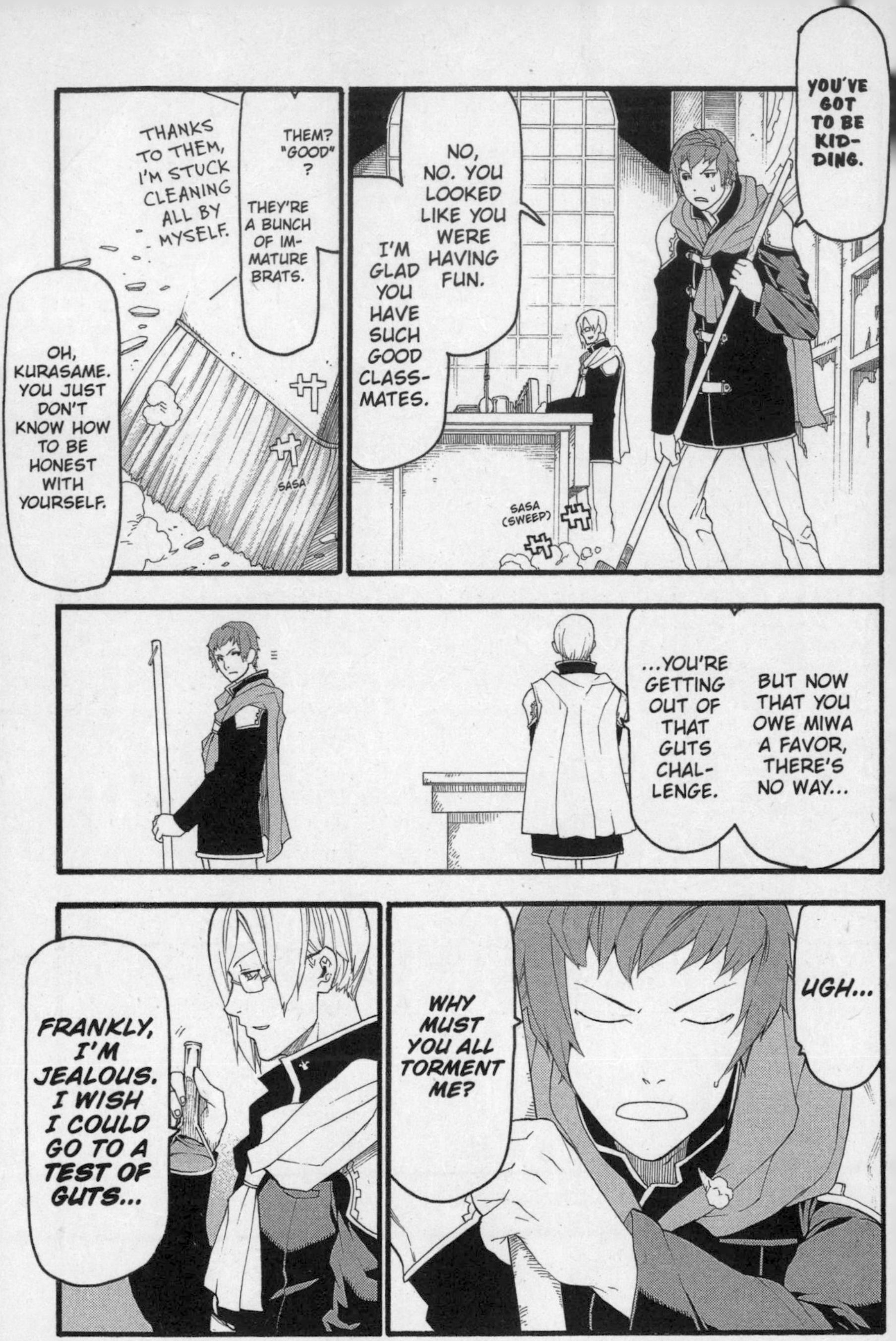
YOU'VE GOT TO BE KID-DING.
NO, NO. YOU LOOKED LIKE YOU WERE HAVING FUN.
I'M GLAD YOU HAVE SUCH GOOD CLASS-MATES.
SASA (SWEEP)
THEM? "GOOD"?
THEY'RE A BUNCH OF IM-MATURE BRATS.
THANKS TO THEM, I'M STUCK CLEANING ALL BY MYSELF.
SASA
OH, KURASAME. YOU JUST DON'T KNOW HOW TO BE HONEST WITH YOURSELF.
BUT NOW THAT YOU OWE MIWA A FAVOR, THERE'S NO WAY...
...YOU'RE GETTING OUT OF THAT GUTS CHAL-LENGE.
UGH...
WHY MUST YOU ALL TORMENT ME?
FRANKLY, I'M JEALOUS. I WISH I COULD GO TO A TEST OF GUTS...

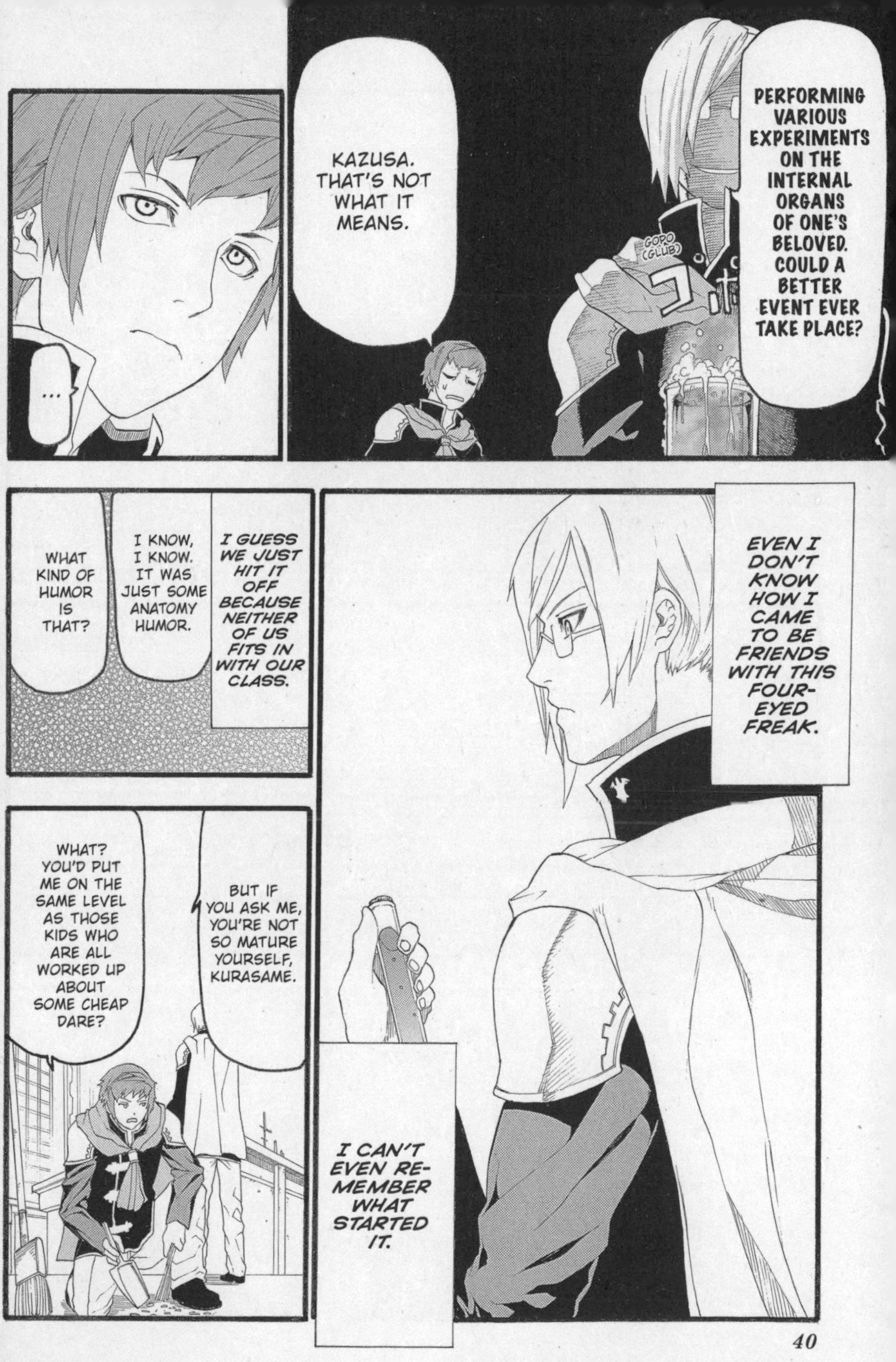

PERFORMING VARIOUS EXPERIMENTS ON THE INTERNAL ORGANS OF ONE'S BELOVED. COULD A BETTER EVENT EVER TAKE PLACE?
GOPO (GLUB)
KAZUSA. THAT'S NOT WHAT IT MEANS.
...
EVEN I DON'T KNOW HOW I CAME TO BE FRIENDS WITH THIS FOUR-EYED FREAK.
I CAN'T EVEN RE-MEMBER WHAT STARTED IT.
I GUESS WE JUST HIT IT OFF BECAUSE NEITHER OF US FITS IN WITH OUR CLASS.
I KNOW, I KNOW. IT WAS JUST SOME ANATOMY HUMOR.
WHAT KIND OF HUMOR IS THAT?
BUT IF YOU ASK ME, YOU'RE NOT SO MATURE YOURSELF, KURASAME.
WHAT? YOU'D PUT ME ON THE SAME LEVEL AS THOSE KIDS WHO ARE ALL WORKED UP ABOUT SOME CHEAP DARE?

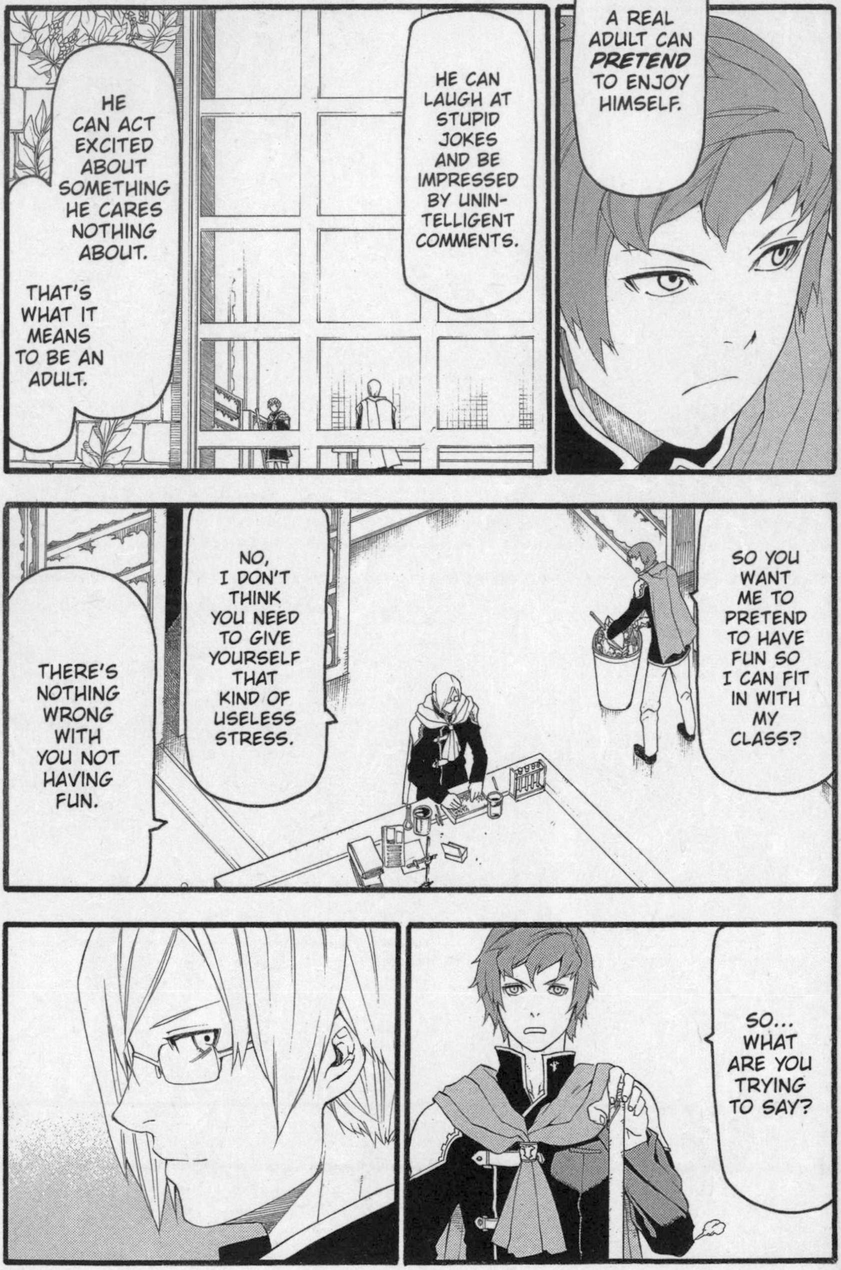
A REAL ADULT CAN *PRETEND* TO ENJOY HIMSELF.
HE CAN LAUGH AT STUPID JOKES AND BE IMPRESSED BY UNIN-TELLIGENT COMMENTS.
HE CAN ACT EXCITED ABOUT SOMETHING HE CARES NOTHING ABOUT.
THAT'S WHAT IT MEANS TO BE AN ADULT.
SO YOU WANT ME TO PRETEND TO HAVE FUN SO I CAN FIT IN WITH MY CLASS?
NO, I DON'T THINK YOU NEED TO GIVE YOURSELF THAT KIND OF USELESS STRESS.
THERE'S NOTHING WRONG WITH YOU NOT HAVING FUN.
SO... WHAT ARE YOU TRYING TO SAY?

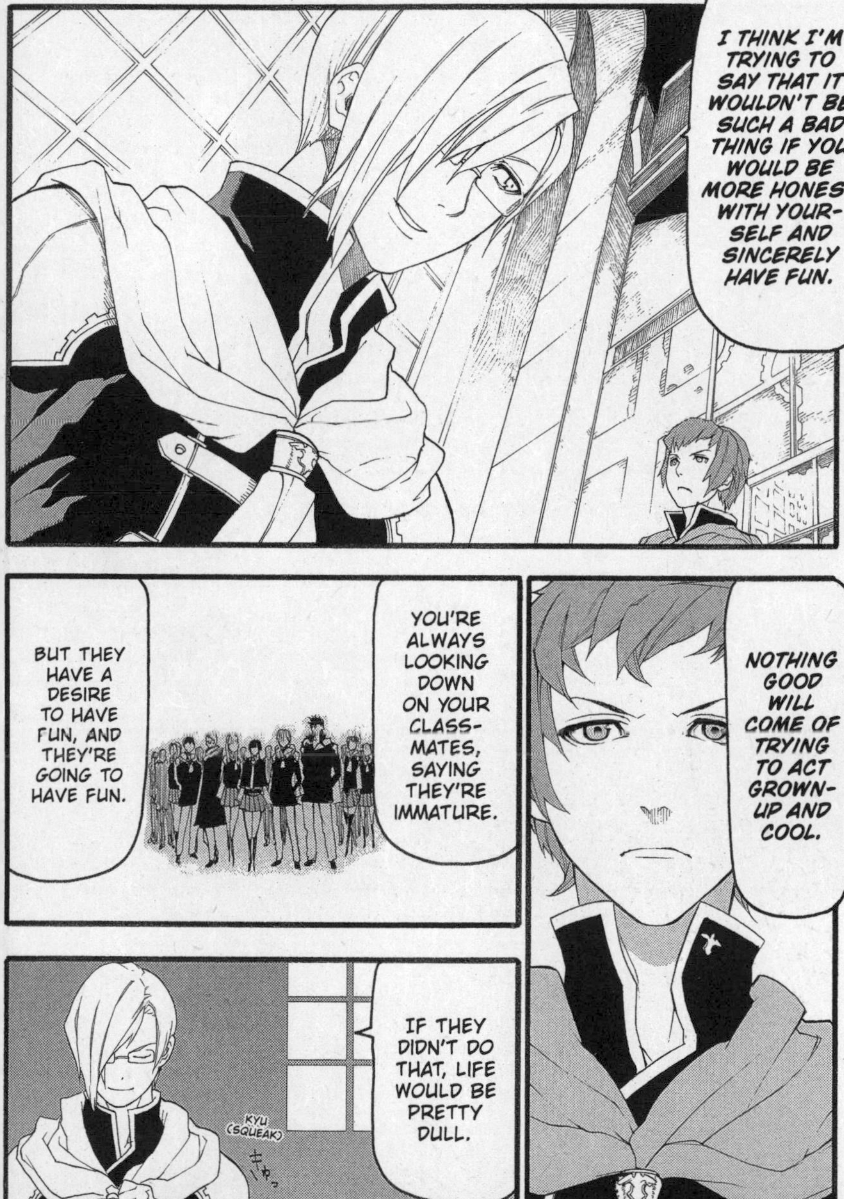
I THINK I'M TRYING TO SAY THAT IT WOULDN'T BE SUCH A BAD THING IF YOU WOULD BE MORE HONEST WITH YOURSELF AND SINCERELY HAVE FUN.
NOTHING GOOD WILL COME OF TRYING TO ACT GROWN-UP AND COOL.
YOU'RE ALWAYS LOOKING DOWN ON YOUR CLASSMATES, SAYING THEY'RE IMMATURE.
BUT THEY HAVE A DESIRE TO HAVE FUN, AND THEY'RE GOING TO HAVE FUN.
IF THEY DIDN'T DO THAT, LIFE WOULD BE PRETTY DULL.
KYU (SQUEAK)
KYU

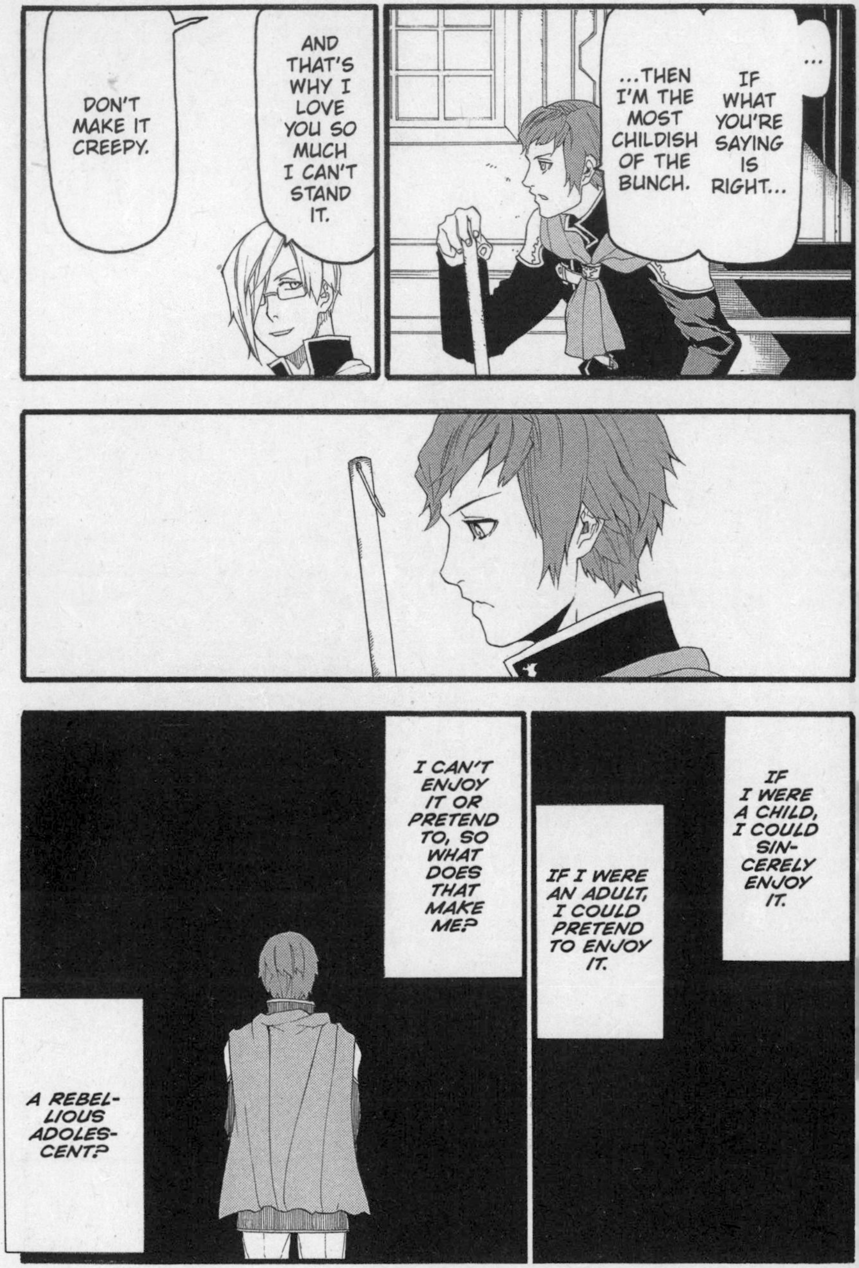
...
IF WHAT YOU'RE SAYING IS RIGHT...
...THEN I'M THE MOST CHILDISH OF THE BUNCH.
AND THAT'S WHY I LOVE YOU SO MUCH I CAN'T STAND IT.
DON'T MAKE IT CREEPY.
IF I WERE A CHILD, I COULD SINCERELY ENJOY IT.
IF I WERE AN ADULT, I COULD PRETEND TO ENJOY IT.
I CAN'T ENJOY IT OR PRETEND TO, SO WHAT DOES THAT MAKE ME?
A REBELLIOUS ADOLESCENT?

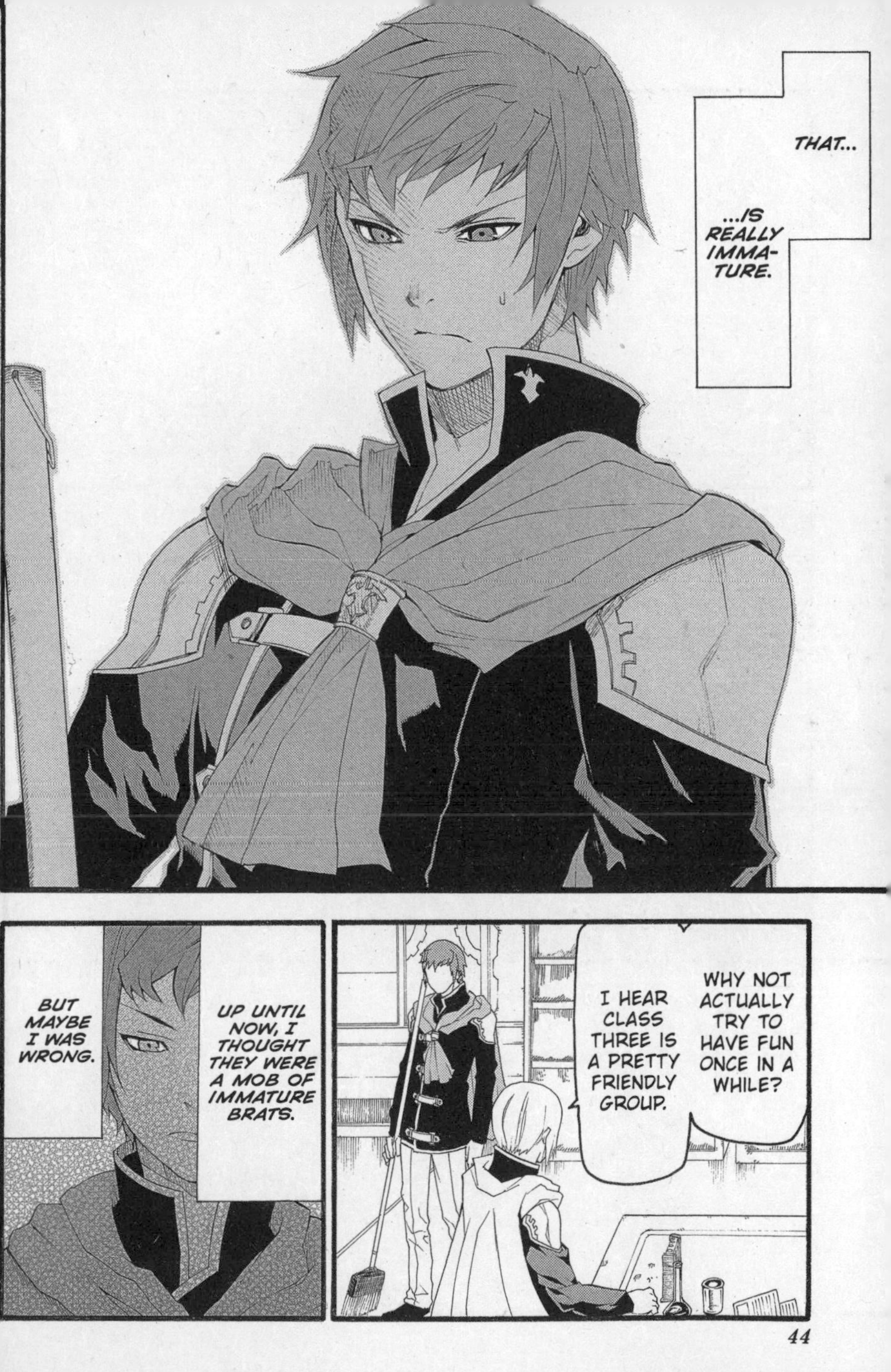
THAT...
...IS REALLY IMMATURE.
I HEAR CLASS THREE IS A PRETTY FRIENDLY GROUP.
WHY NOT ACTUALLY TRY TO HAVE FUN ONCE IN A WHILE?
UP UNTIL NOW, I THOUGHT THEY WERE A MOB OF IMMATURE BRATS.
BUT MAYBE I WAS WRONG.

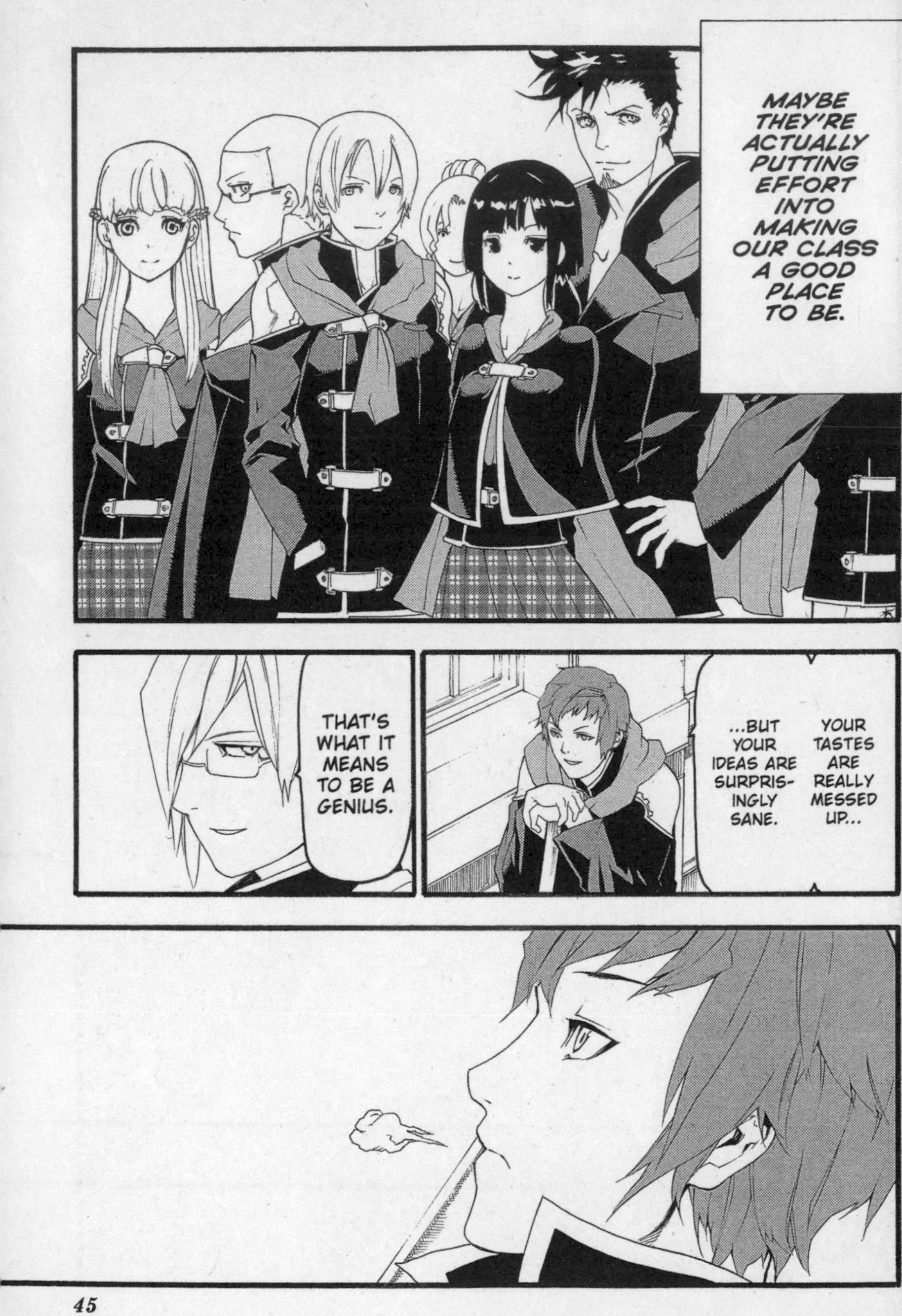
MAYBE THEY'RE ACTUALLY PUTTING EFFORT INTO MAKING OUR CLASS A GOOD PLACE TO BE.
YOUR TASTES ARE REALLY MESSED UP...
...BUT YOUR IDEAS ARE SURPRIS-INGLY SANE.
THAT'S WHAT IT MEANS TO BE A GENIUS.

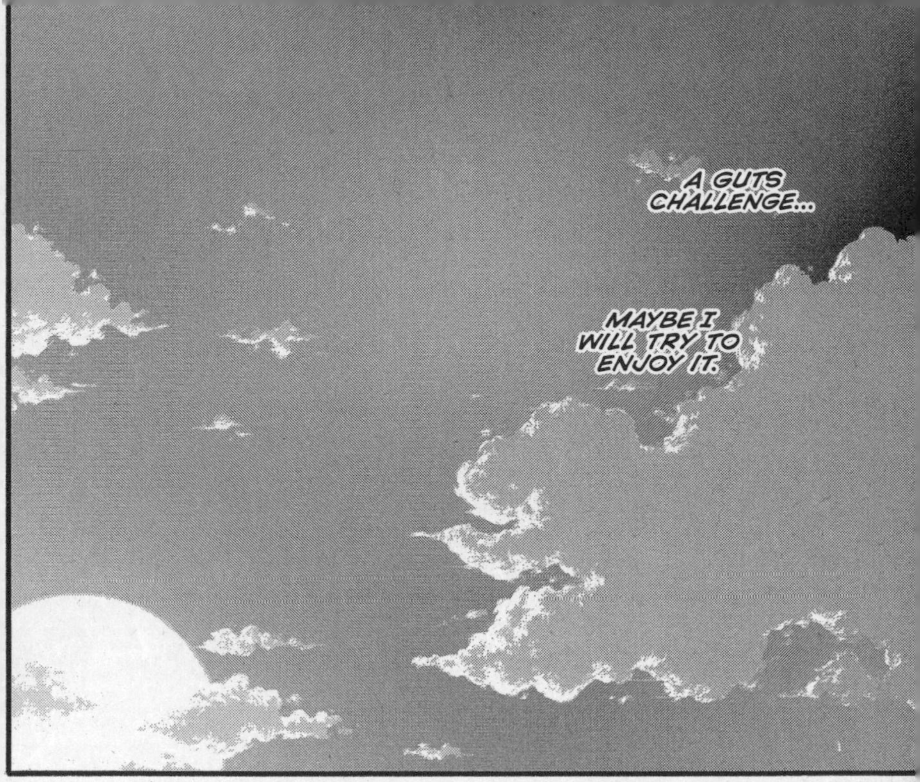
A GUTS CHALLENGE...
MAYBE I WILL TRY TO ENJOY IT.

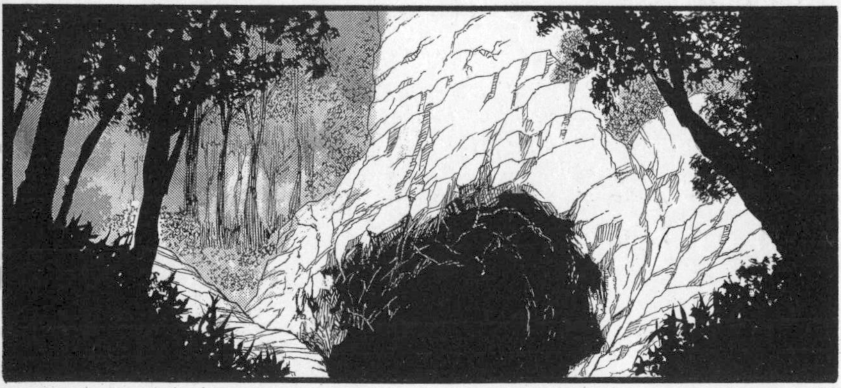

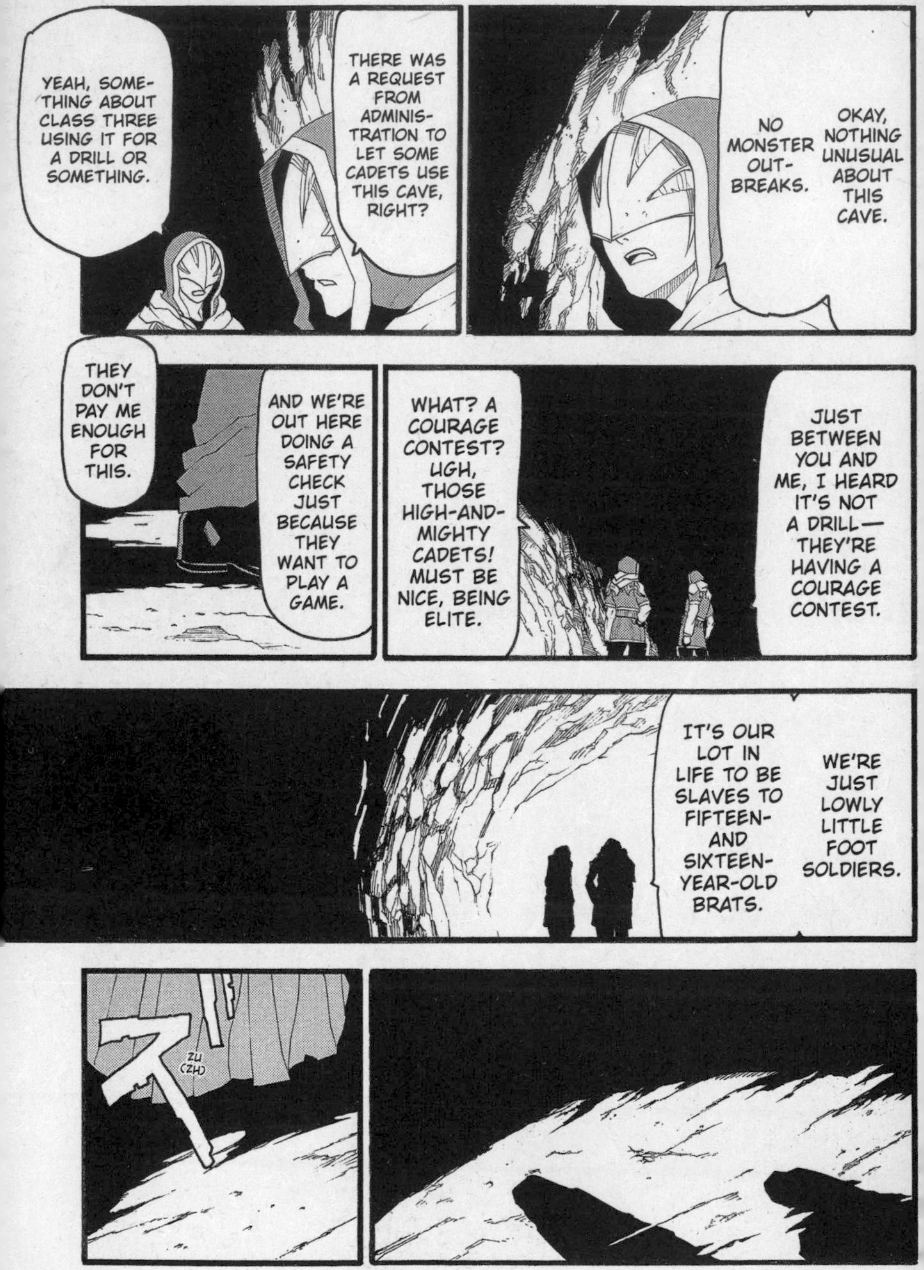
OKAY, NOTHING UNUSUAL ABOUT THIS CAVE.
NO MONSTER OUTBREAKS.
THERE WAS A REQUEST FROM ADMINISTRATION TO LET SOME CADETS USE THIS CAVE, RIGHT?
YEAH, SOMETHING ABOUT CLASS THREE USING IT FOR A DRILL OR SOMETHING.
JUST BETWEEN YOU AND ME, I HEARD IT'S NOT A DRILL—THEY'RE HAVING A COURAGE CONTEST.
WHAT? A COURAGE CONTEST? UGH, THOSE HIGH-AND-MIGHTY CADETS! MUST BE NICE, BEING ELITE.
AND WE'RE OUT HERE DOING A SAFETY CHECK JUST BECAUSE THEY WANT TO PLAY A GAME.
THEY DON'T PAY ME ENOUGH FOR THIS.
WE'RE JUST LOWLY LITTLE FOOT SOLDIERS.
IT'S OUR LOT IN LIFE TO BE SLAVES TO FIFTEEN- AND SIXTEEN-YEAR-OLD BRATS.
ZU (ZH)

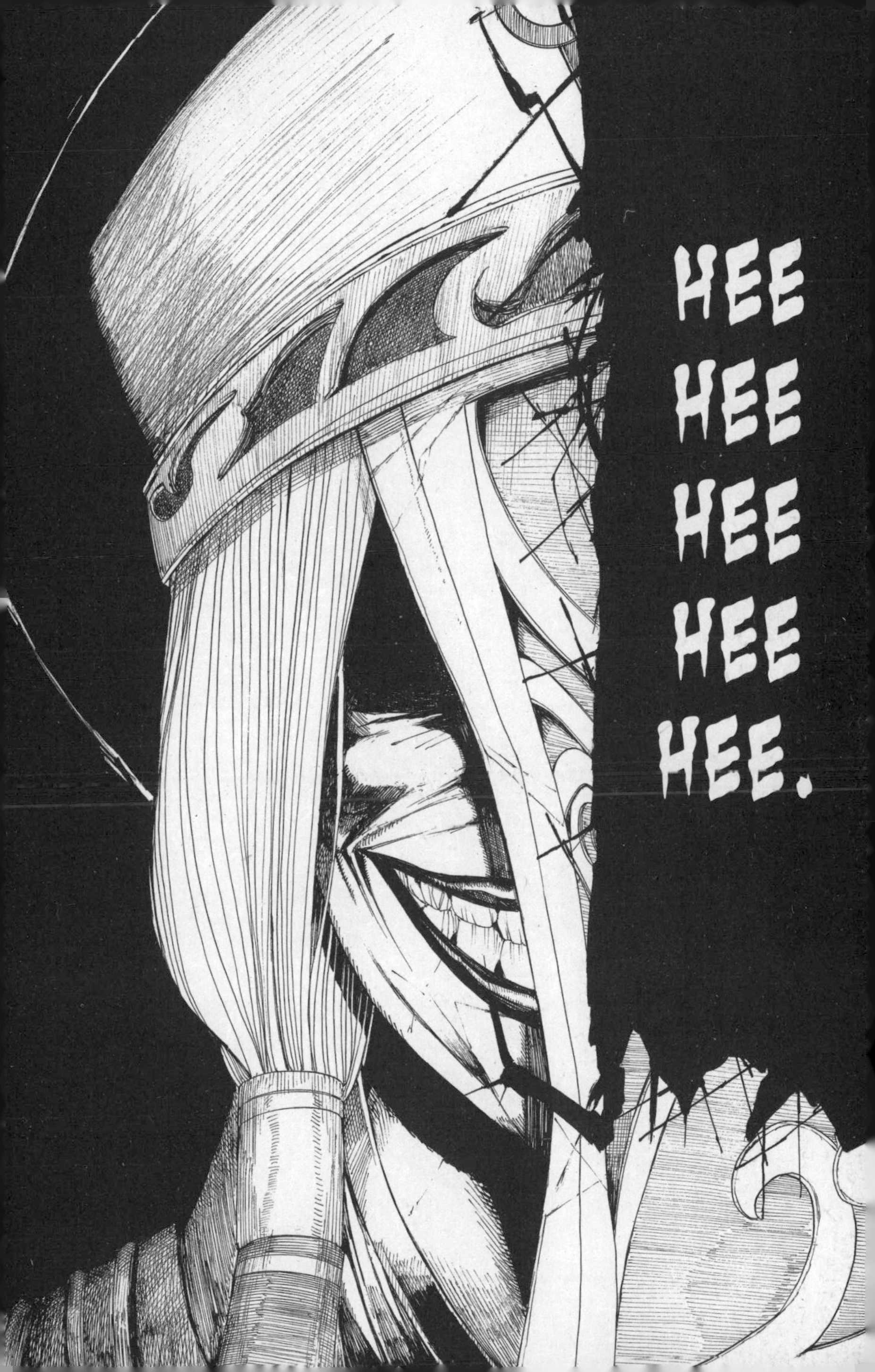
HEE HEE HEE HEE HEE.

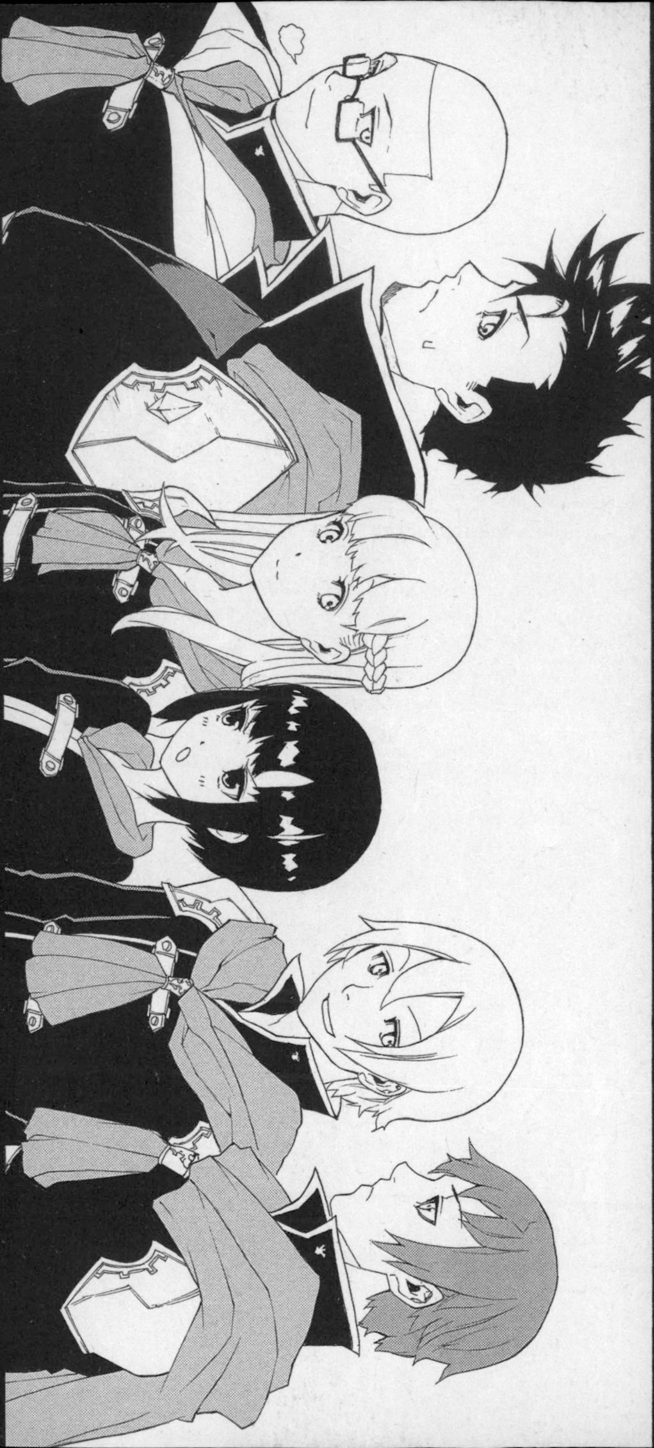

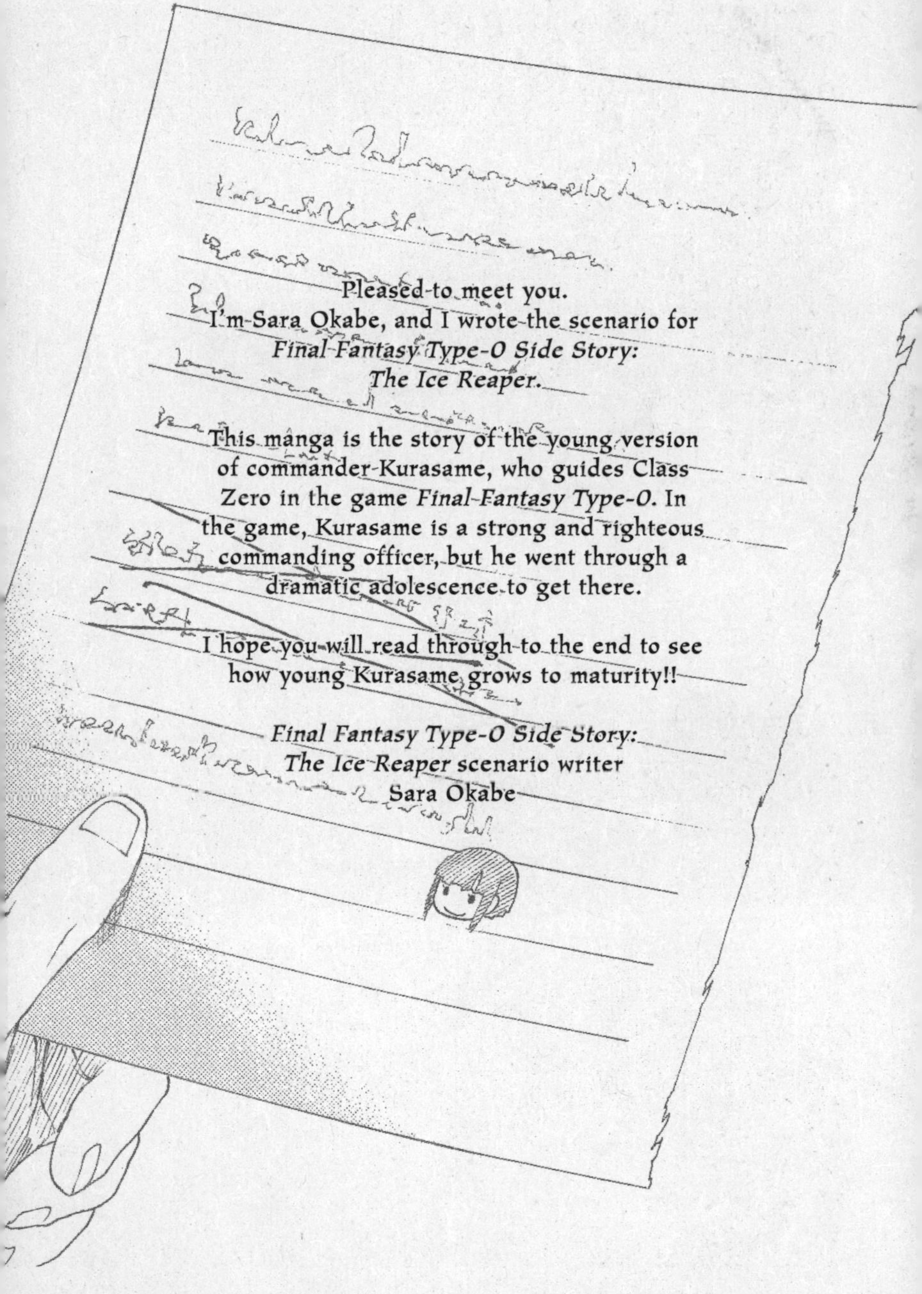

Pleased to meet you.
I'm Sara Okabe, and I wrote the scenario for *Final Fantasy Type-0 Side Story: The Ice Reaper.*
This manga is the story of the young version of commander Kurasame, who guides Class Zero in the game *Final Fantasy Type-0.* In the game, Kurasame is a strong and righteous commanding officer, but he went through a dramatic adolescence to get there.
I hope you will read through to the end to see how young Kurasame grows to maturity!!
Final Fantasy Type-0 Side Story: The Ice Reaper scenario writer
Sara Okabe

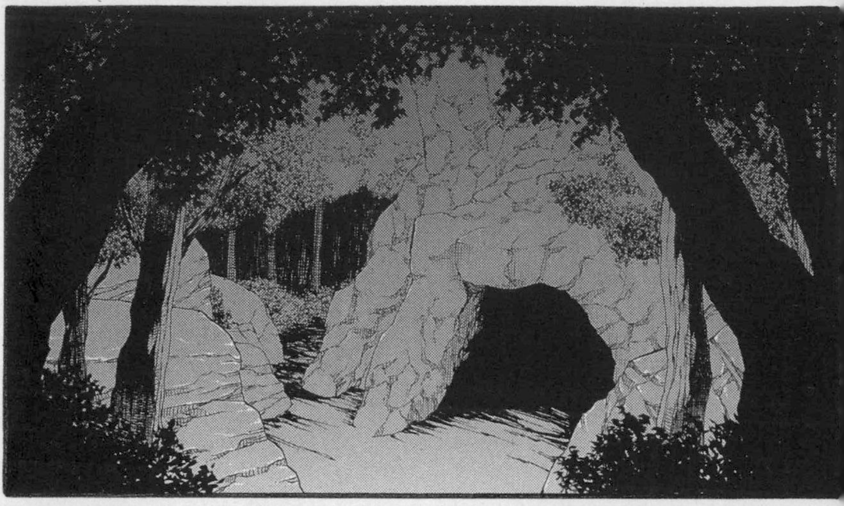

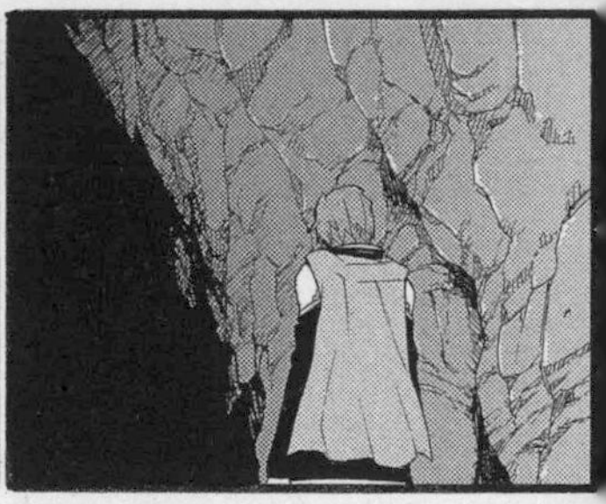

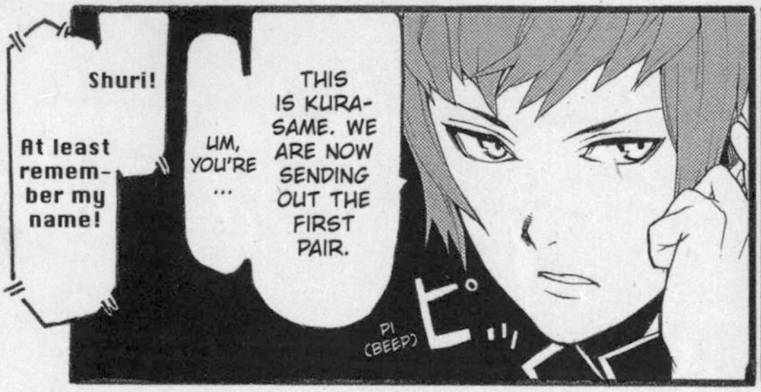
THIS IS KURA-SAME. WE ARE NOW SENDING OUT THE FIRST PAIR.
UM, YOU'RE ...
Shuri! At least remem-ber my name!
PI (BEEP)

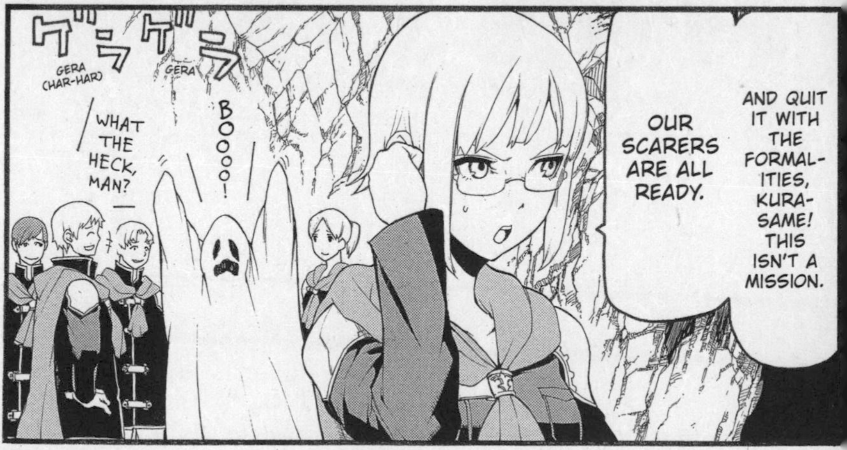
AND QUIT IT WITH THE FORMAL-ITIES, KURA-SAME! THIS ISN'T A MISSION.
OUR SCARERS ARE ALL READY.
BOOOOO!
WHAT THE HECK, MAN?
GERA GERA (HAR-HAR)

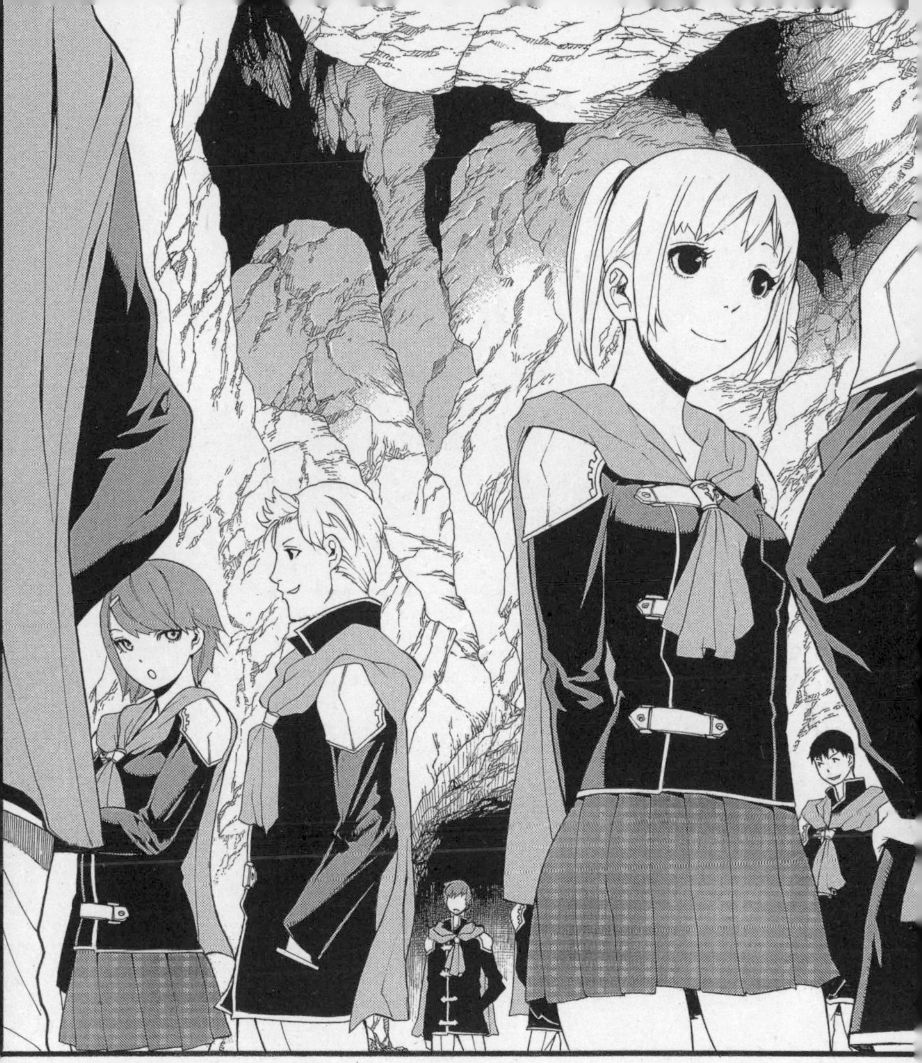

CHAPTER 2: IN THE DARKNESS

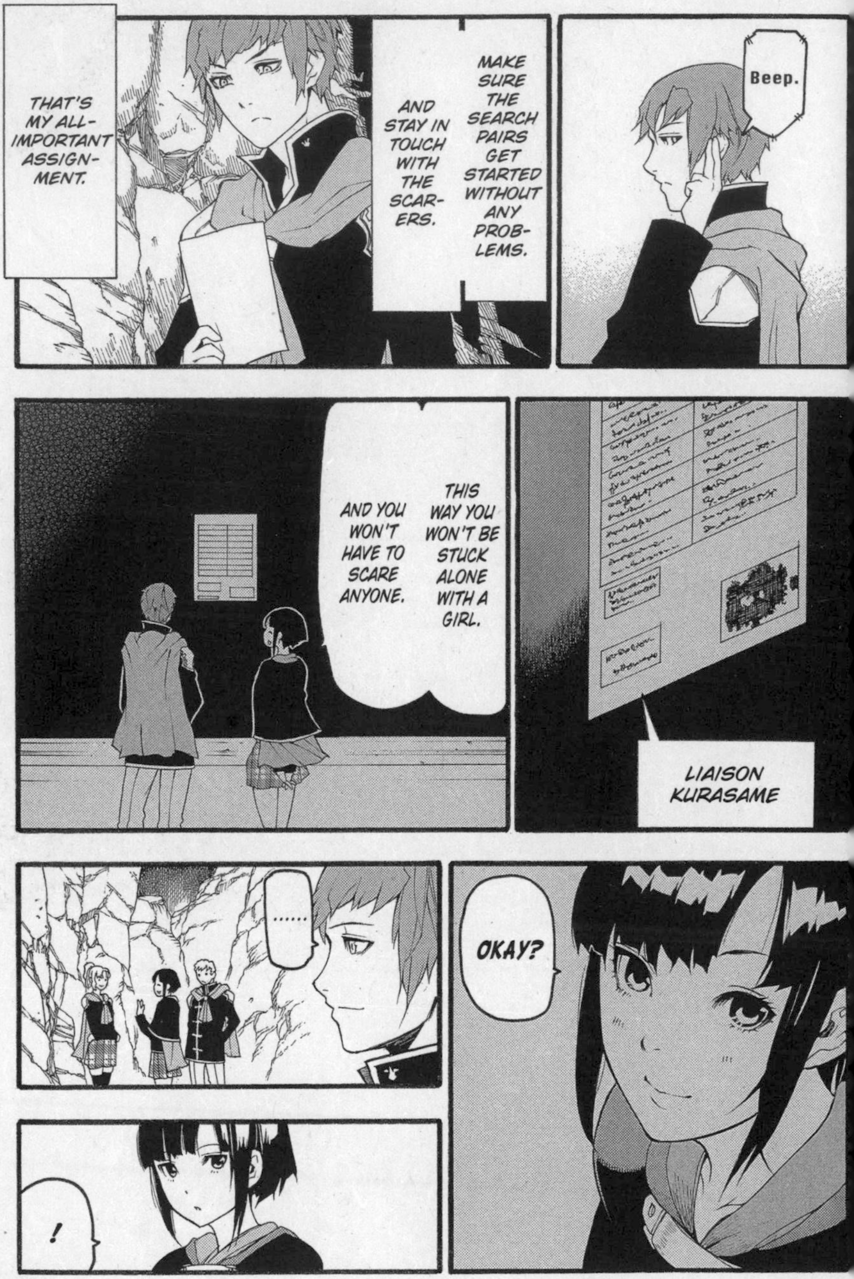
Beep.
MAKE SURE THE SEARCH PAIRS GET STARTED WITHOUT ANY PROB-LEMS.
AND STAY IN TOUCH WITH THE SCAR-ERS.
THAT'S MY ALL-IMPORTANT ASSIGN-MENT.
LIAISON KURASAME
THIS WAY YOU WON'T BE STUCK ALONE WITH A GIRL.
AND YOU WON'T HAVE TO SCARE ANYONE.
OKAY?
......
!

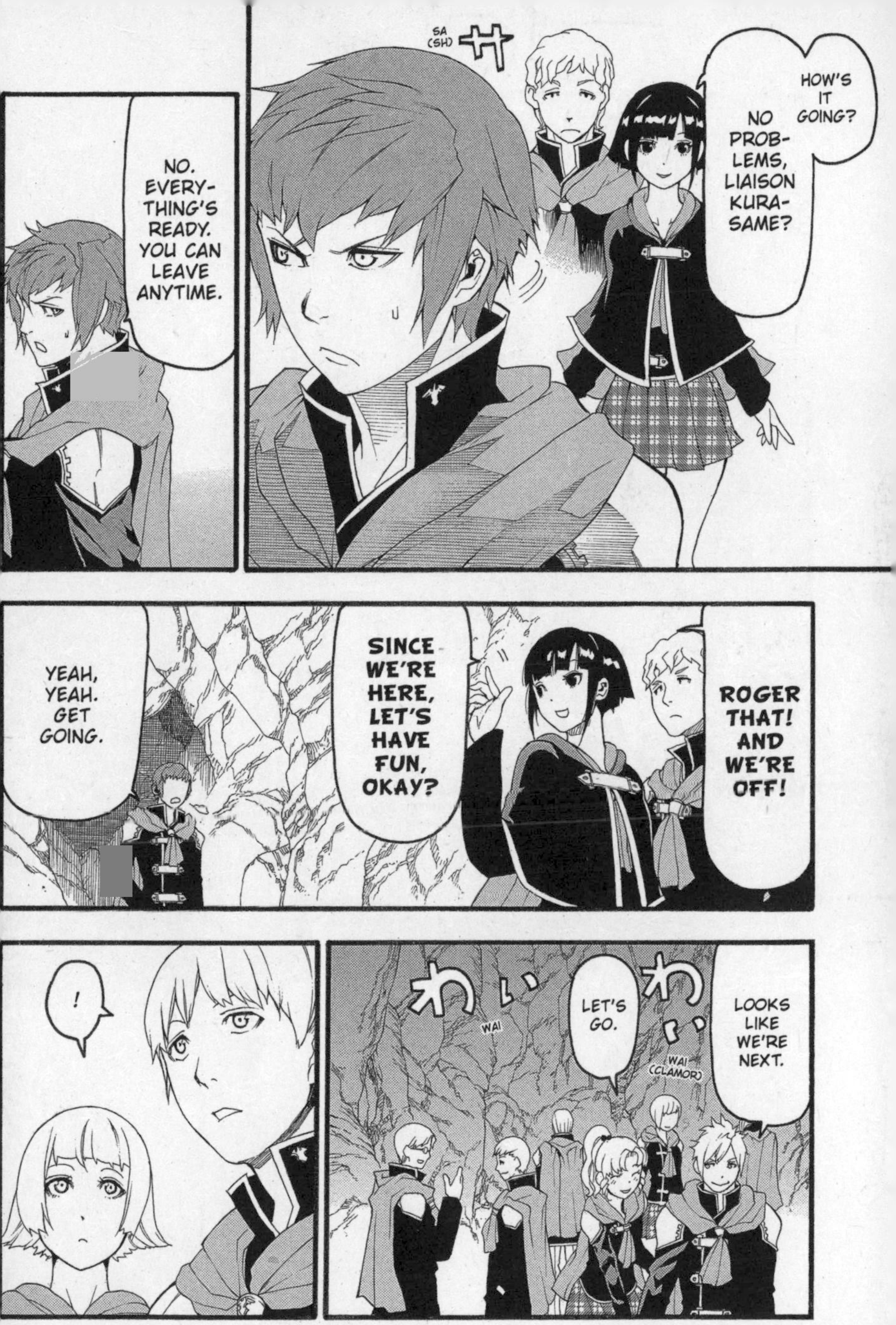
SA (SH)
HOW'S IT GOING?
NO PROB-LEMS, LIAISON KURA-SAME?
NO. EVERY-THING'S READY. YOU CAN LEAVE ANYTIME.
ROGER THAT! AND WE'RE OFF!
SINCE WE'RE HERE, LET'S HAVE FUN, OKAY?
YEAH, YEAH. GET GOING.
LOOKS LIKE WE'RE NEXT.
WAI (CLAMOR)
LET'S GO.
WAI
!

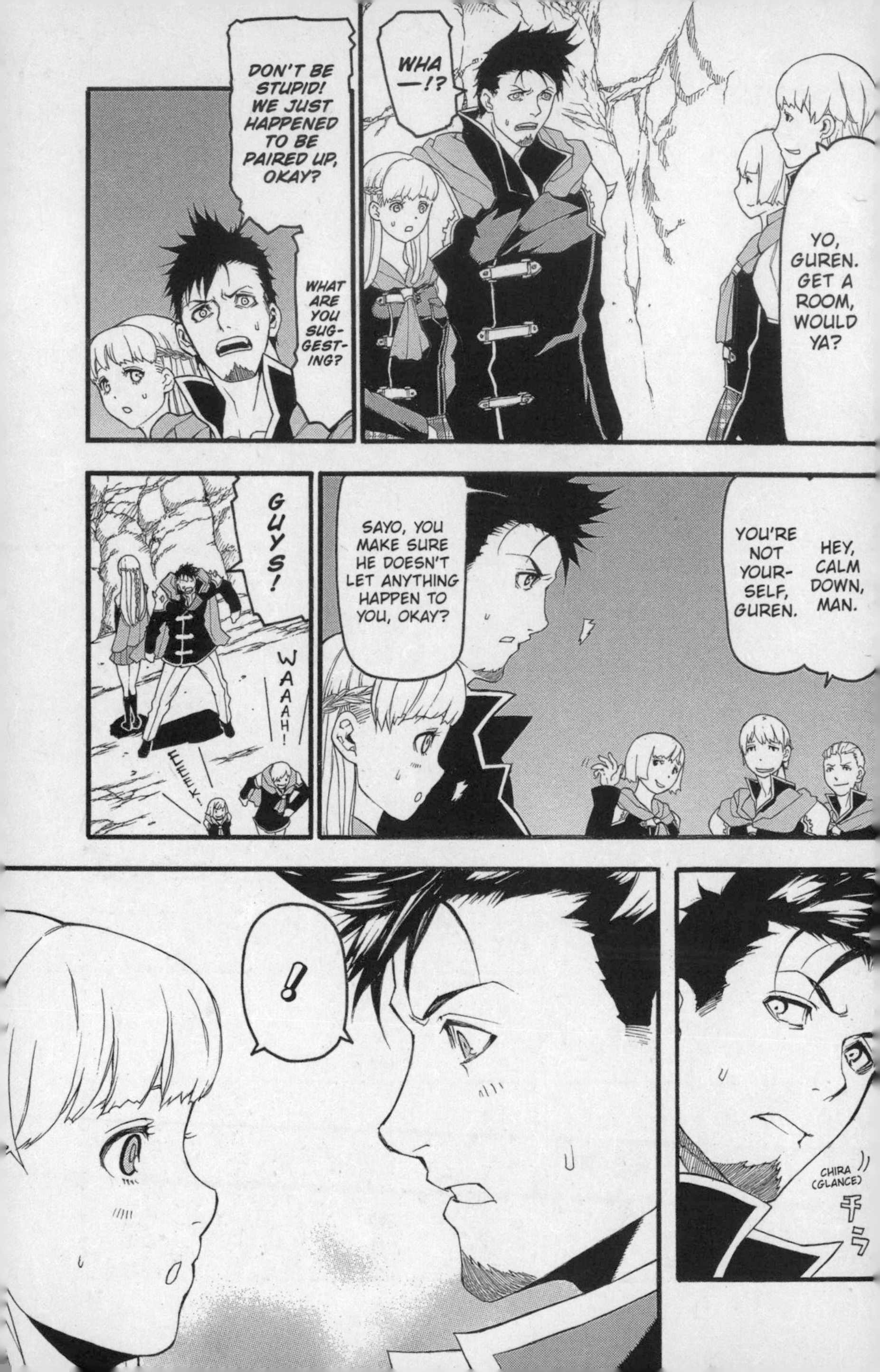
YO, GUREN. GET A ROOM, WOULD YA?
WHA—!?
DON'T BE STUPID! WE JUST HAPPENED TO BE PAIRED UP, OKAY?
WHAT ARE YOU SUG-GEST-ING?
HEY, CALM DOWN, MAN.
YOU'RE NOT YOUR-SELF, GUREN.
SAYO, YOU MAKE SURE HE DOESN'T LET ANYTHING HAPPEN TO YOU, OKAY?
GUYS!
WAAAAH!
EEEK!
CHIRA (GLANCE)
チラ
!

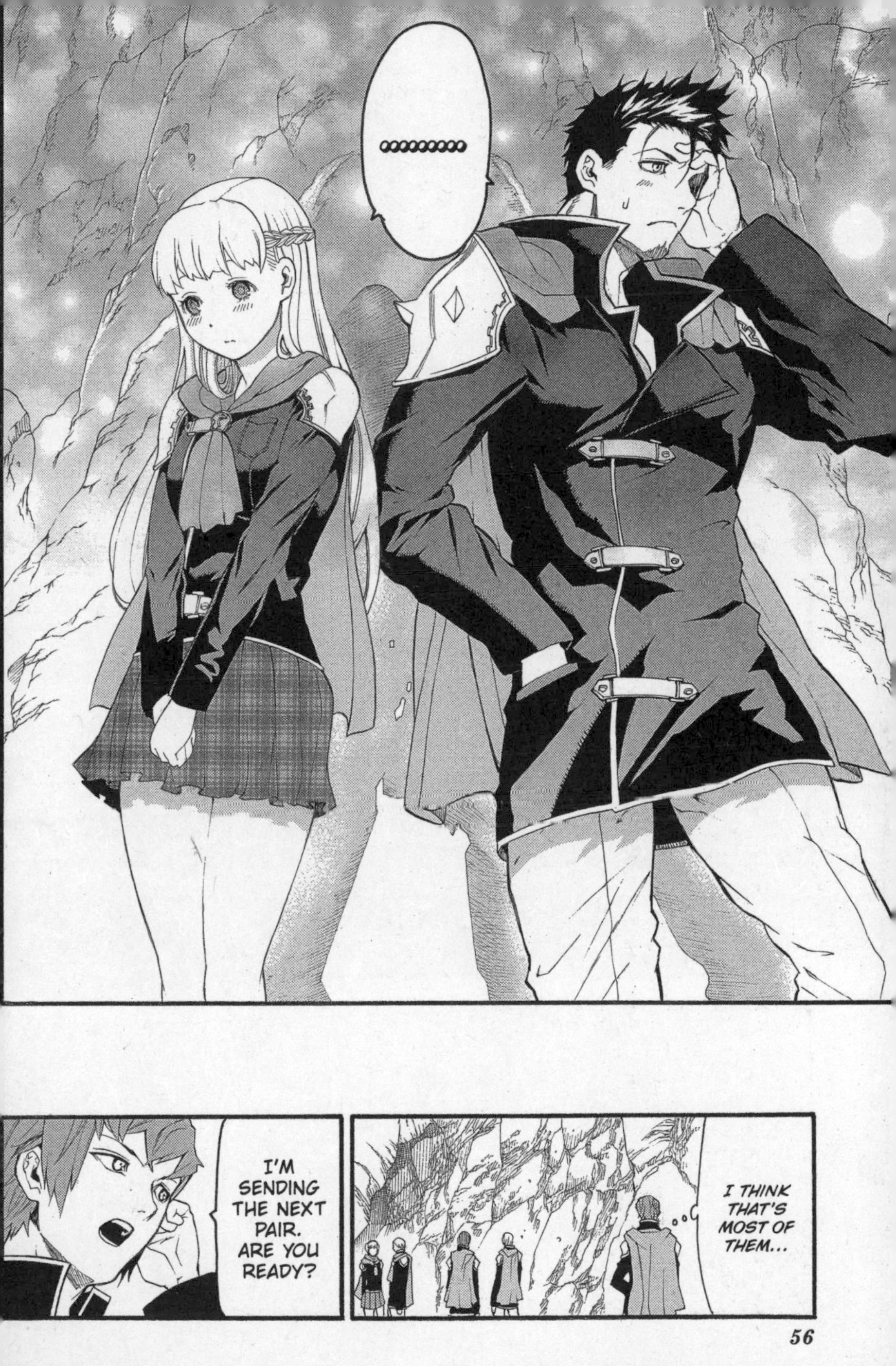
....
I THINK THAT'S MOST OF THEM...
I'M SENDING THE NEXT PAIR. ARE YOU READY?

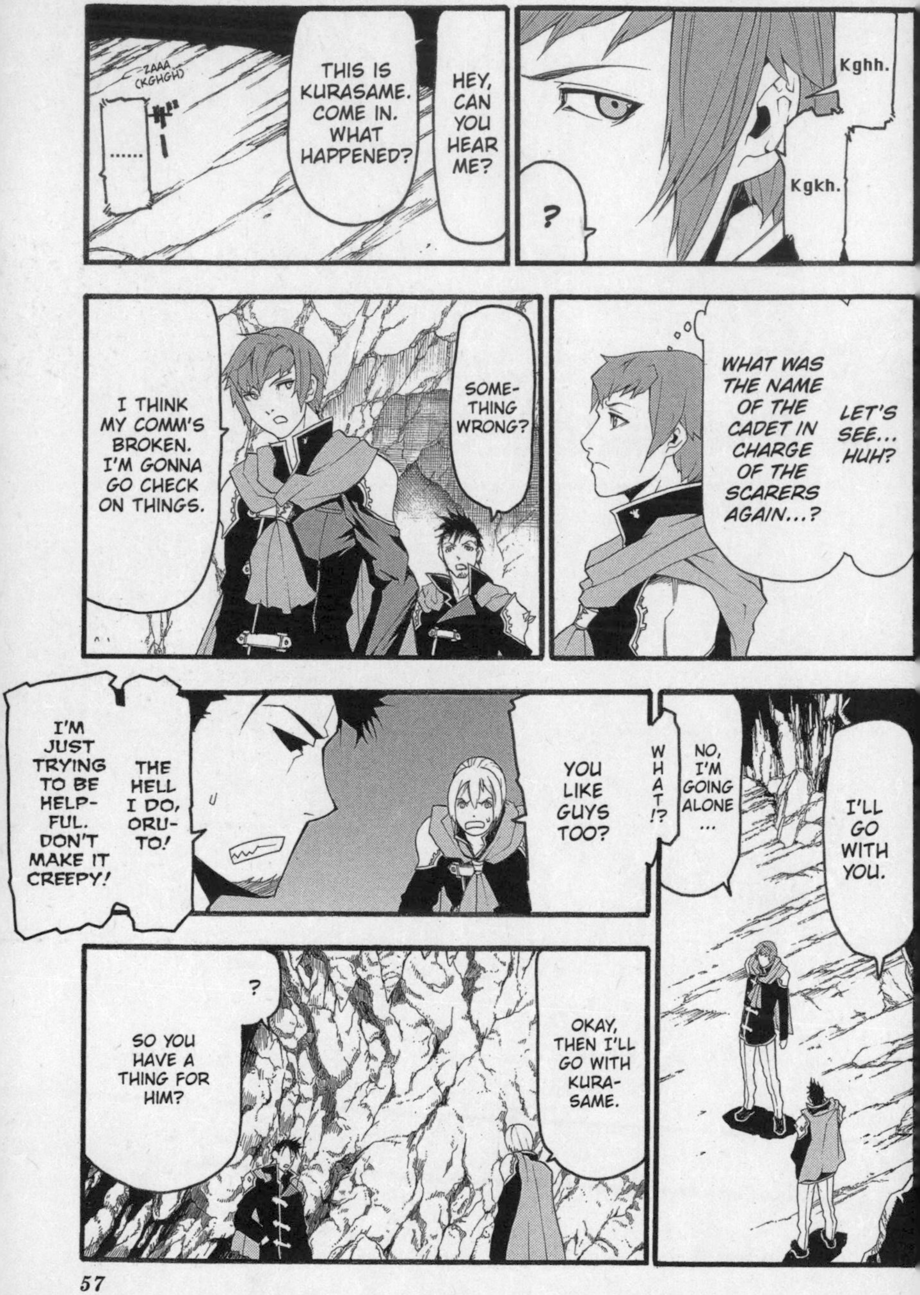
Kghh.
Kgkh.
?
HEY, CAN YOU HEAR ME?
THIS IS KURASAME. COME IN. WHAT HAPPENED?
ZAAA (KGHGH)
......
LET'S SEE... HUH?
WHAT WAS THE NAME OF THE CADET IN CHARGE OF THE SCARERS AGAIN...?
SOME-THING WRONG?
I THINK MY COMM'S BROKEN. I'M GONNA GO CHECK ON THINGS.
I'LL GO WITH YOU.
NO, I'M GOING ALONE...
WHAT!?
YOU LIKE GUYS TOO?
THE HELL I DO, ORU-TO!
I'M JUST TRYING TO BE HELP-FUL. DON'T MAKE IT CREEPY!
OKAY, THEN I'LL GO WITH KURA-SAME.
?
SO YOU HAVE A THING FOR HIM?

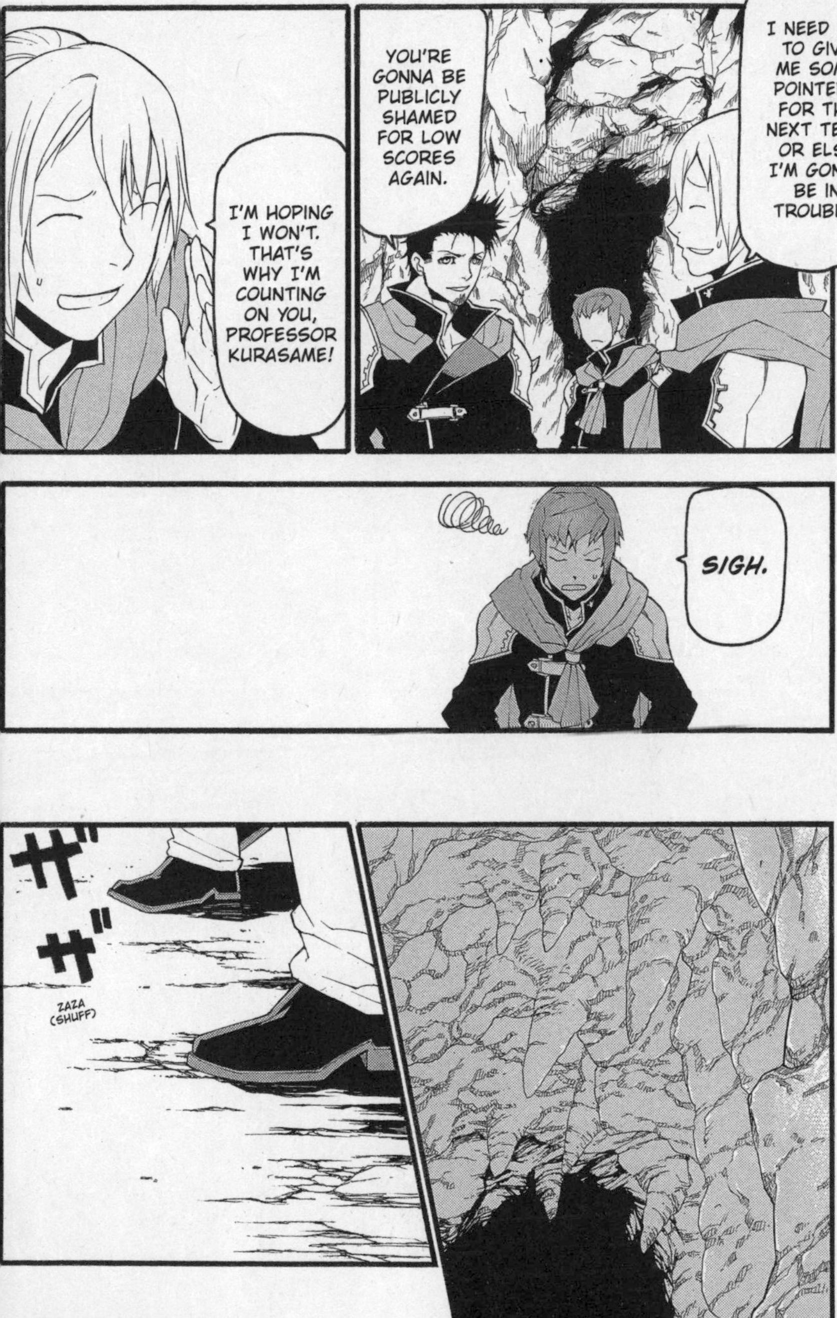
I NEED HIM TO GIVE ME SOME POINTERS FOR THE NEXT TEST, OR ELSE I'M GONNA BE IN TROUBLE.
YOU'RE GONNA BE PUBLICLY SHAMED FOR LOW SCORES AGAIN.
I'M HOPING I WON'T. THAT'S WHY I'M COUNTING ON YOU, PROFESSOR KURASAME!
SIGH.
ZAZA (SHUFF)

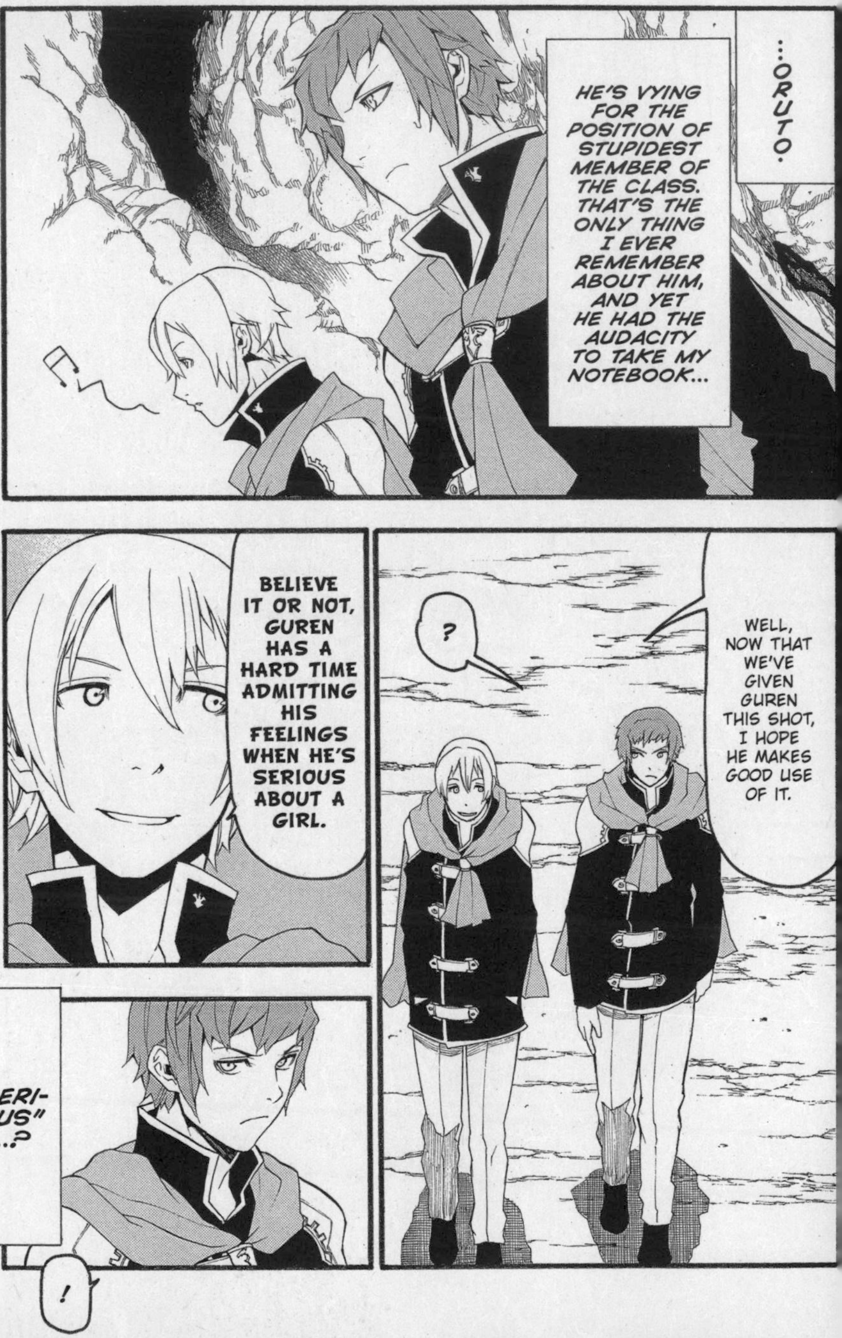
...ORUTO.
HE'S VYING FOR THE POSITION OF STUPIDEST MEMBER OF THE CLASS. THAT'S THE ONLY THING I EVER REMEMBER ABOUT HIM, AND YET HE HAD THE AUDACITY TO TAKE MY NOTEBOOK...
WELL, NOW THAT WE'VE GIVEN GUREN THIS SHOT, I HOPE HE MAKES GOOD USE OF IT.
?
BELIEVE IT OR NOT, GUREN HAS A HARD TIME ADMITTING HIS FEELINGS WHEN HE'S SERIOUS ABOUT A GIRL.
"SERI-OUS" ...?
!

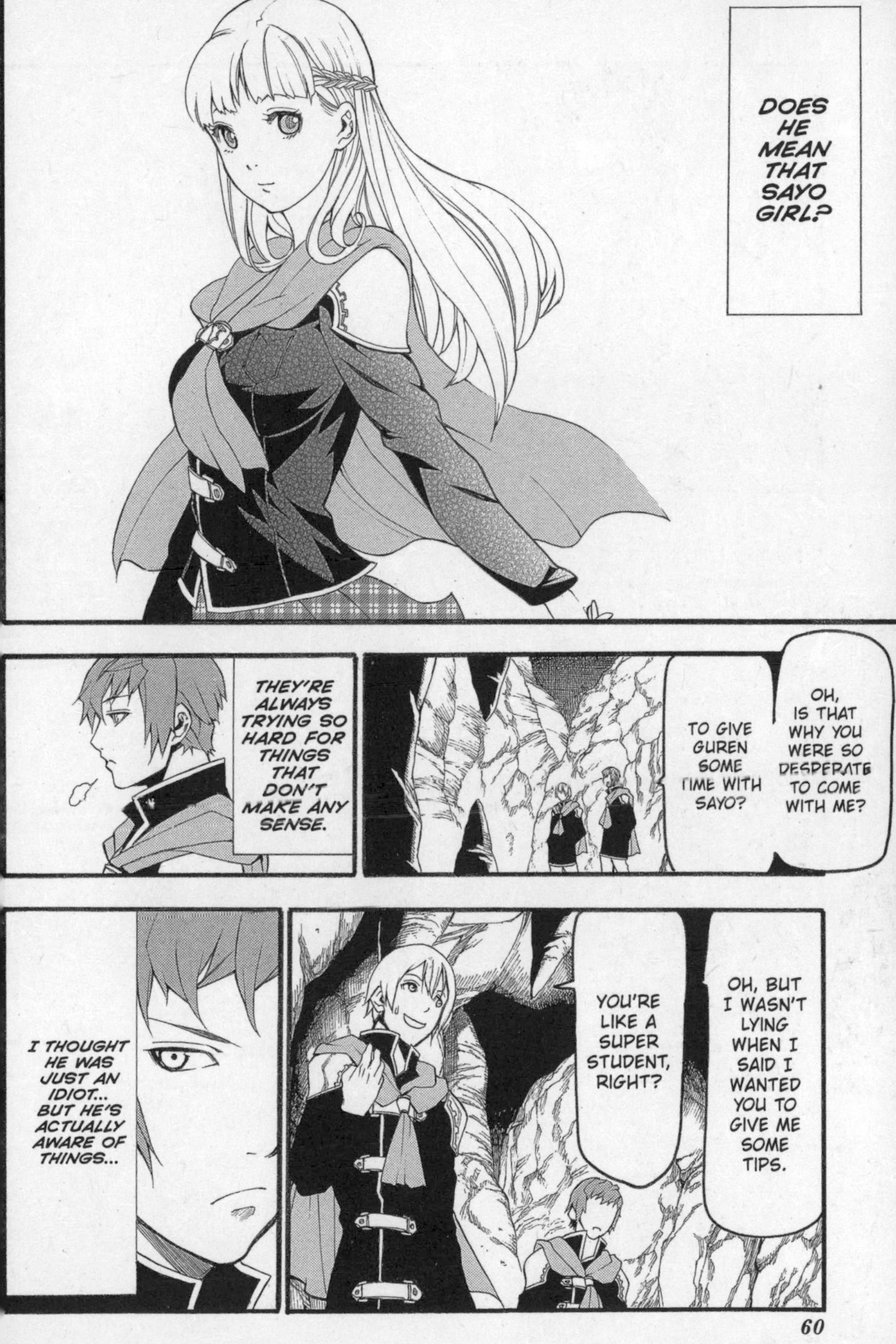
DOES HE MEAN THAT SAYO GIRL?
OH, IS THAT WHY YOU WERE SO DESPERATE TO COME WITH ME?
TO GIVE GUREN SOME TIME WITH SAYO?
THEY'RE ALWAYS TRYING SO HARD FOR THINGS THAT DON'T MAKE ANY SENSE.
OH, BUT I WASN'T LYING WHEN I SAID I WANTED YOU TO GIVE ME SOME TIPS.
YOU'RE LIKE A SUPER STUDENT, RIGHT?
I THOUGHT HE WAS JUST AN IDIOT... BUT HE'S ACTUALLY AWARE OF THINGS...

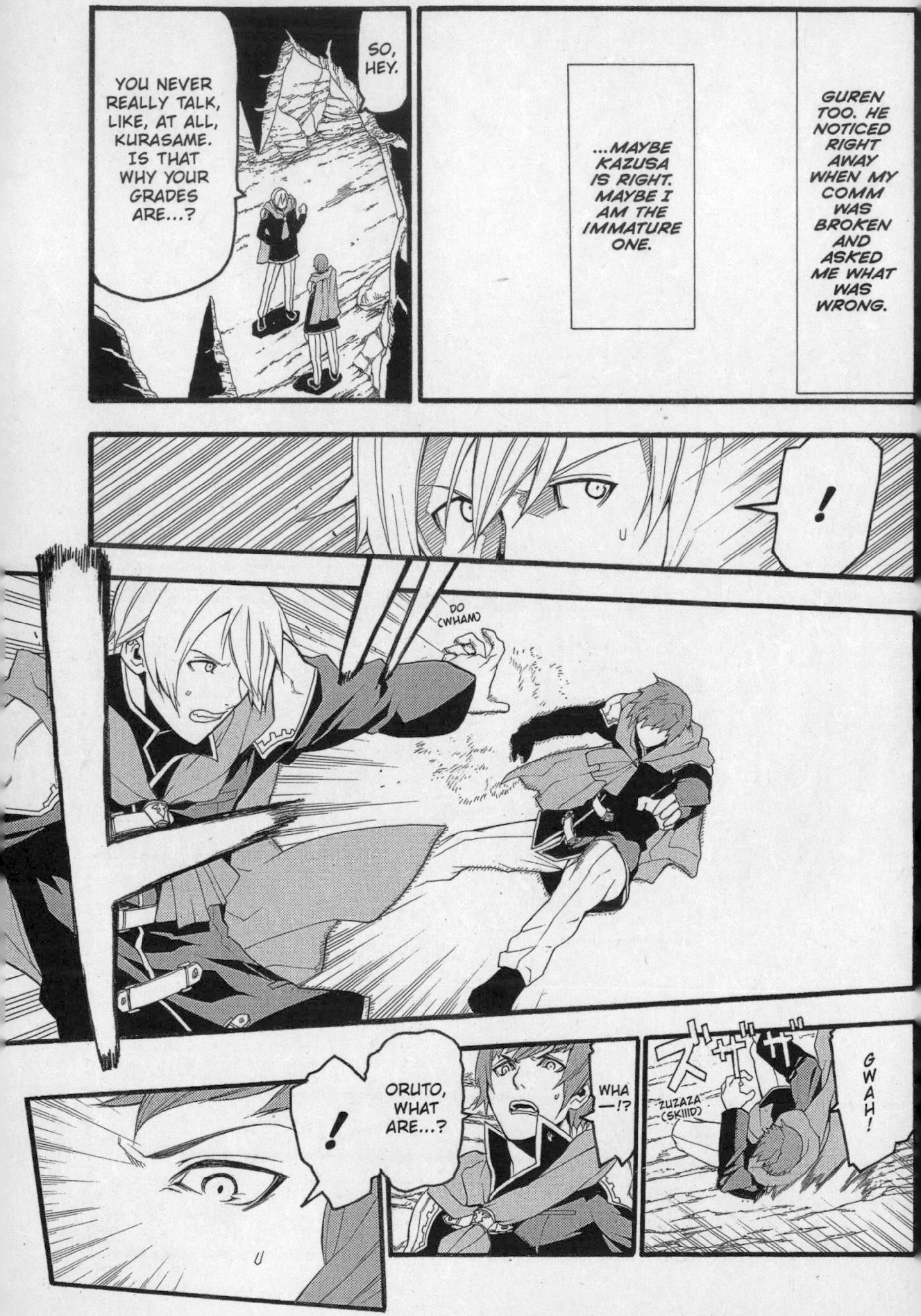
GUREN TOO. HE NOTICED RIGHT AWAY WHEN MY COMM WAS BROKEN AND ASKED ME WHAT WAS WRONG.
...MAYBE KAZUSA IS RIGHT. MAYBE I AM THE IMMATURE ONE.
SO, HEY.
YOU NEVER REALLY TALK, LIKE, AT ALL, KURASAME. IS THAT WHY YOUR GRADES ARE...?
!
DO (WHAM)
GWAH!
ZUZAZA (SKIIID)
WHA—!?
ORUTO, WHAT ARE...?
!

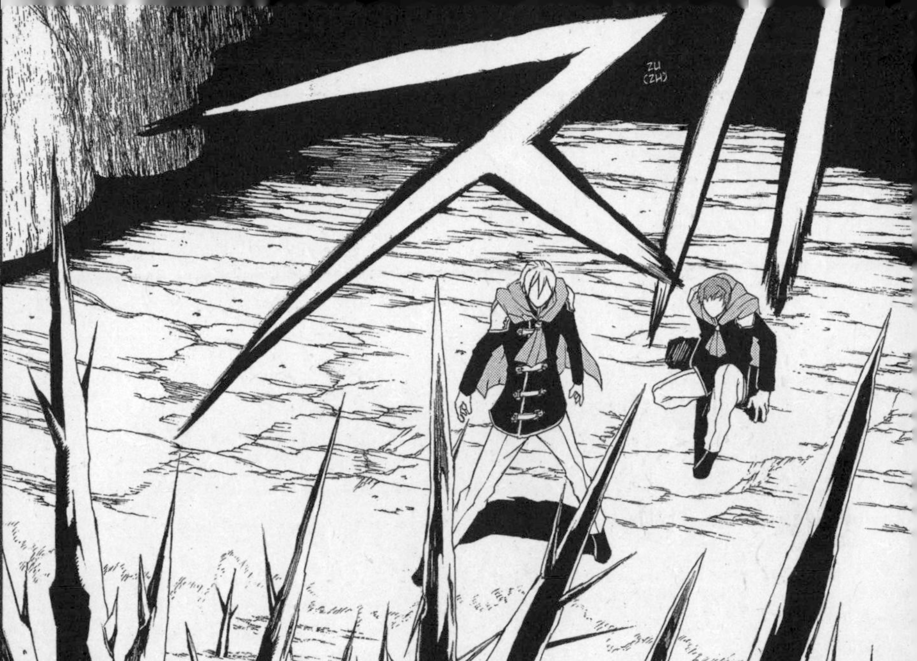
ZU
(ZH)
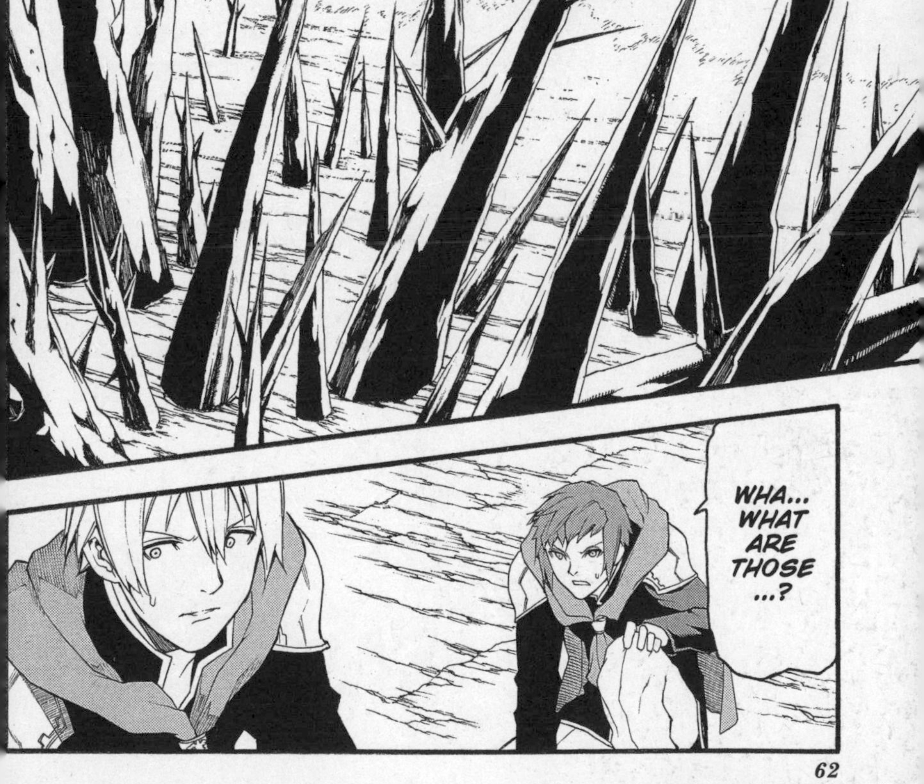
WHA... WHAT ARE THOSE ...?

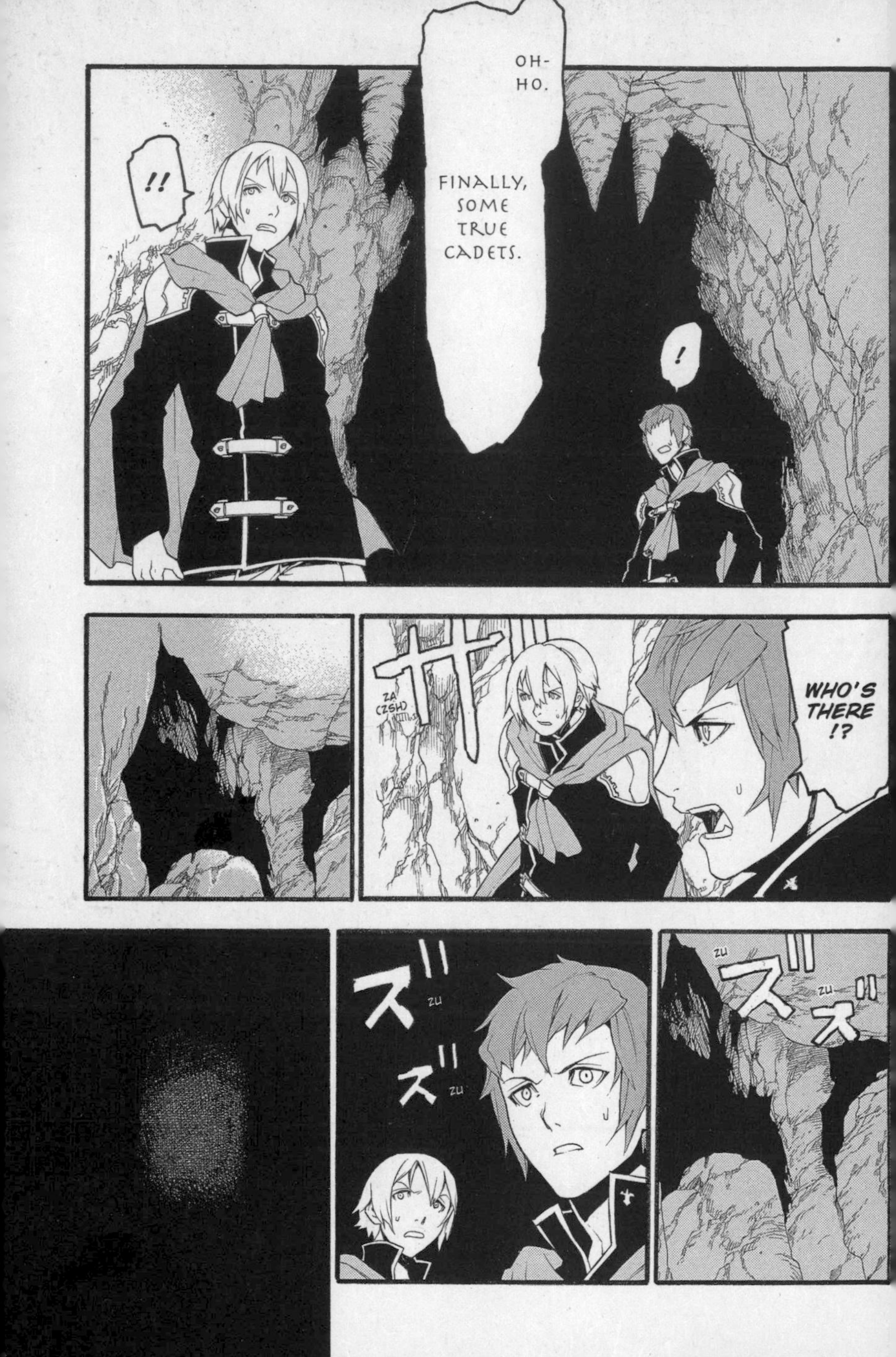
OH-HO.
FINALLY, SOME TRUE CADETS.
!
!!
WHO'S THERE !?
ZA (ZSH)
zu
zu
zu
zu

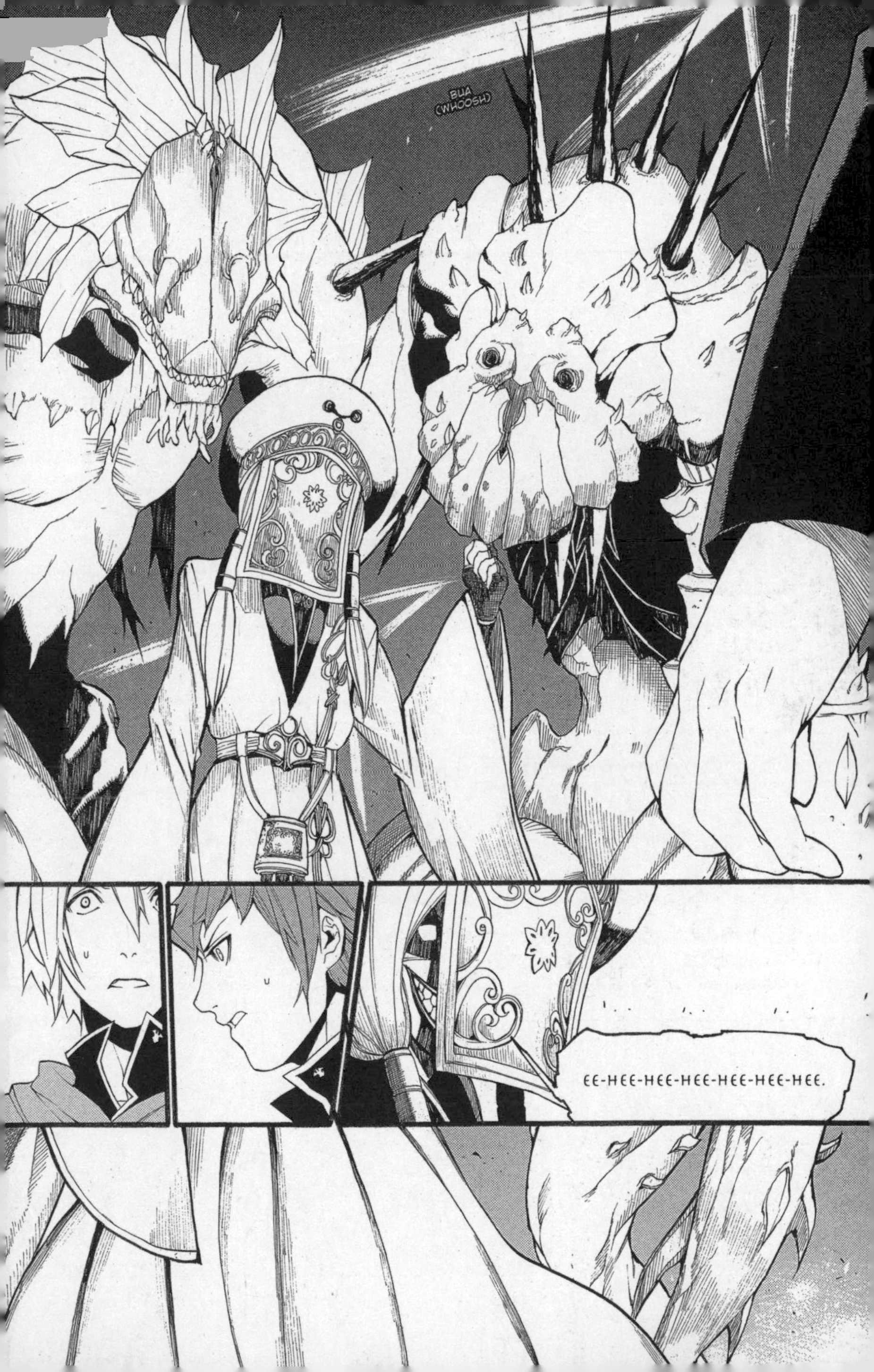
BUA (WHOOSH)
...
...
...
EE-HEE-HEE-HEE-HEE-HEE-HEE.

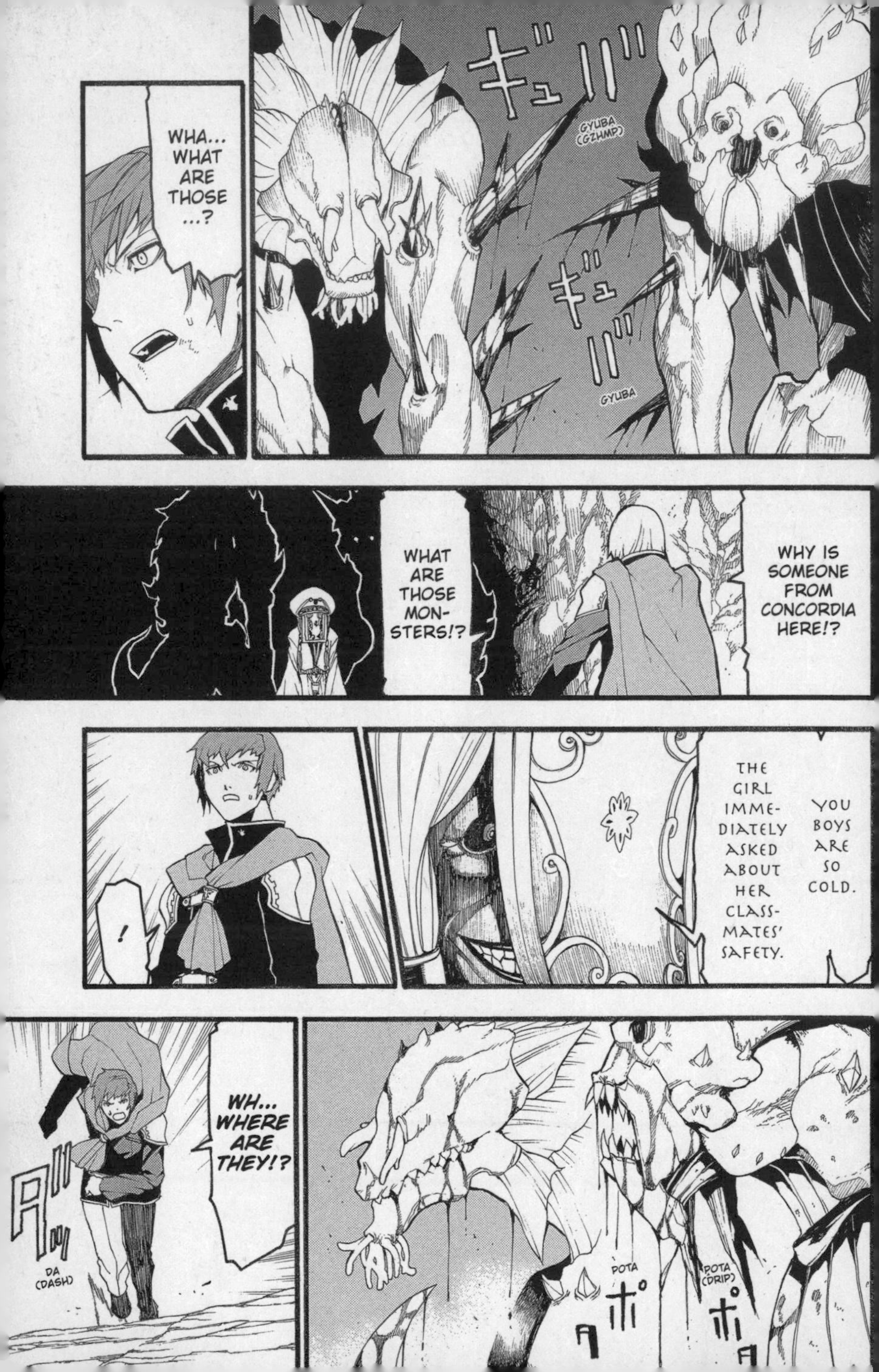
GYUBA (GZHMP)
GYUBA
WHA... WHAT ARE THOSE ...?
WHY IS SOMEONE FROM CONCORDIA HERE!?
WHAT ARE THOSE MON-STERS!?
YOU BOYS ARE SO COLD.
THE GIRL IMME-DIATELY ASKED ABOUT HER CLASS-MATES' SAFETY.
!
POTA (DRIP)
POTA
WH... WHERE ARE THEY!?
DA (DASH)

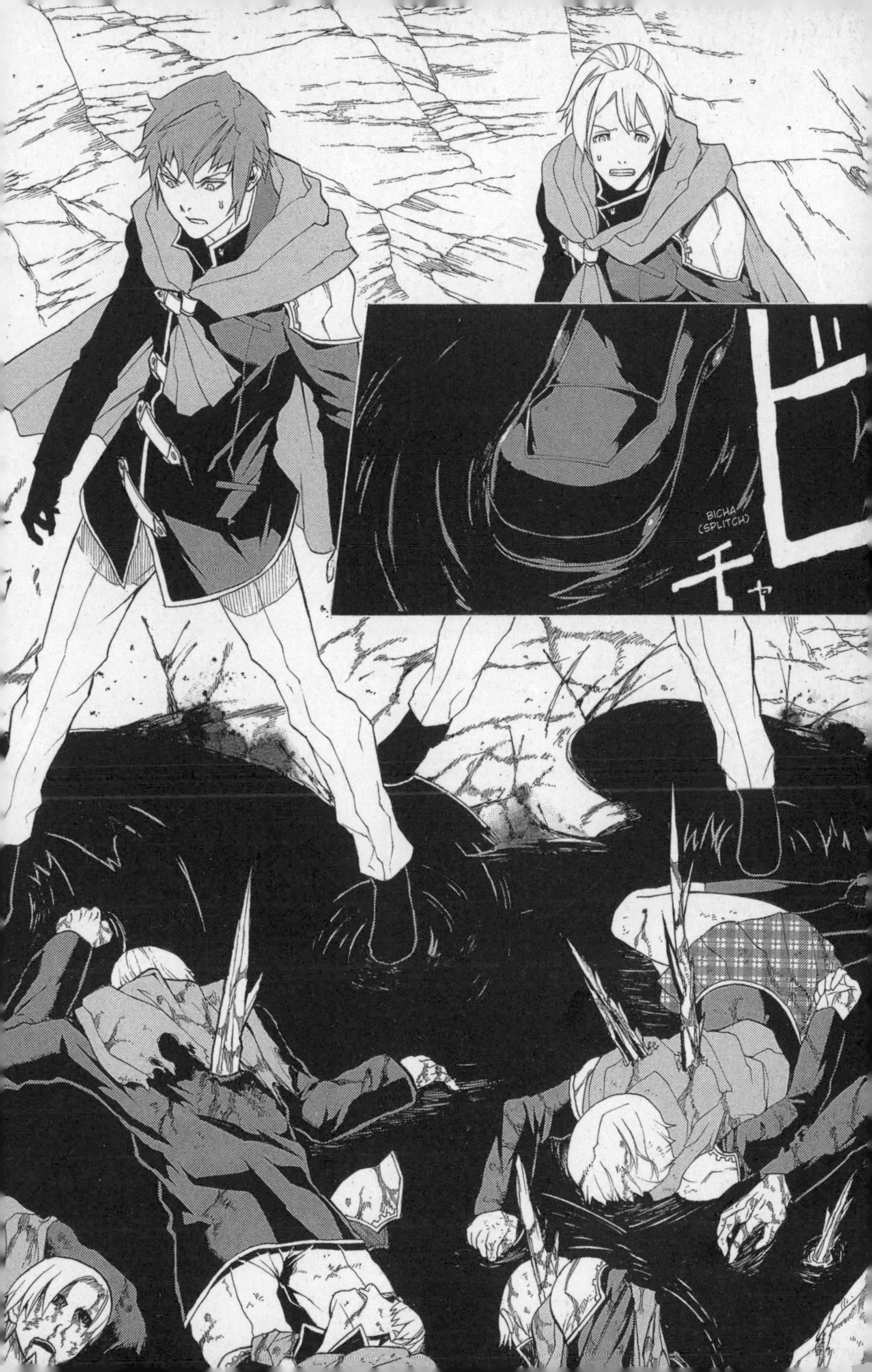
ビチャ
BICHA
(SPLITCH)

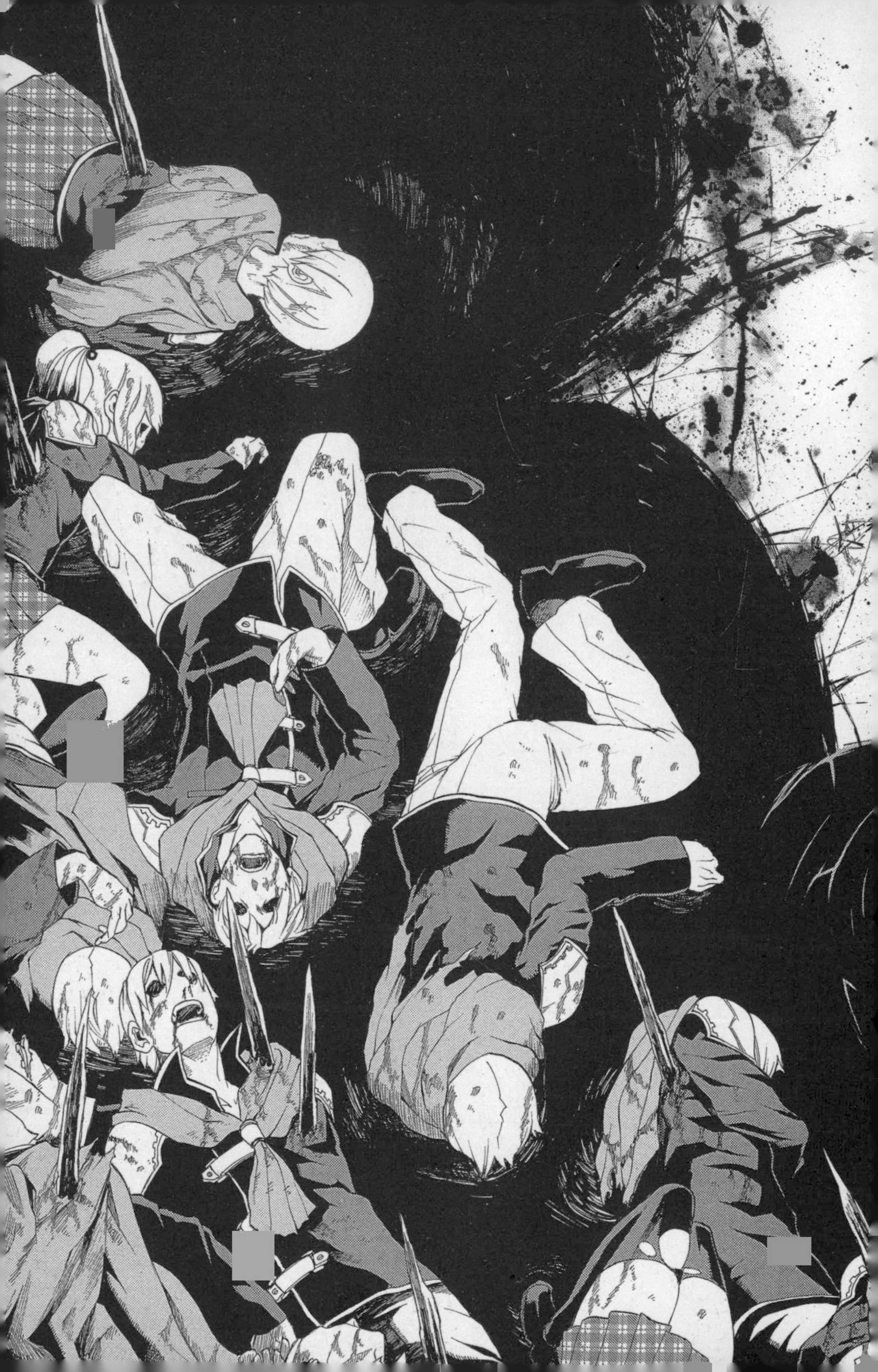

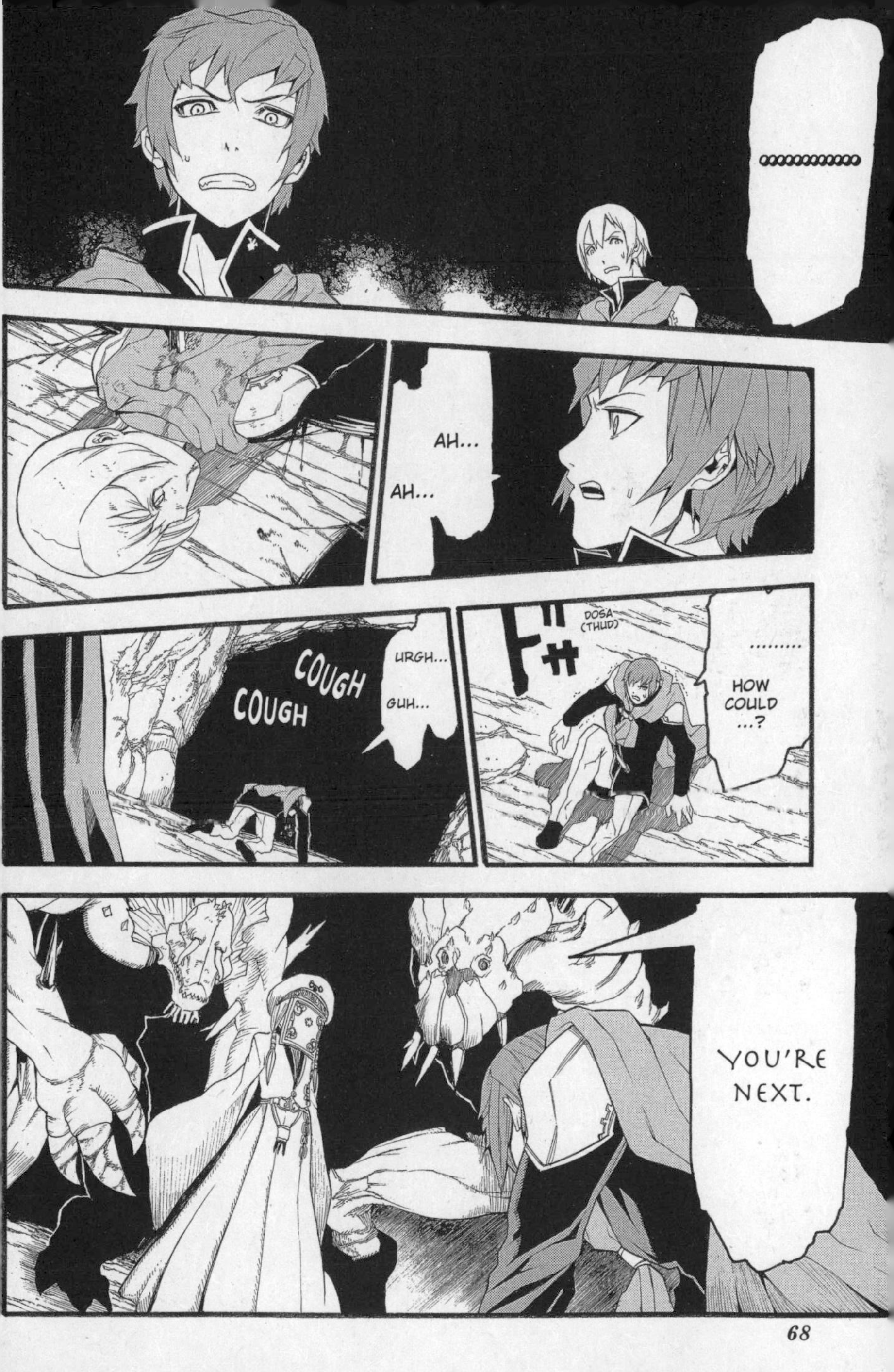

oooooooooooo
AH... AH...
DOSA (THUD)
....
HOW COULD ...?
URGH... GUH...
COUGH COUGH
YOU'RE NEXT.

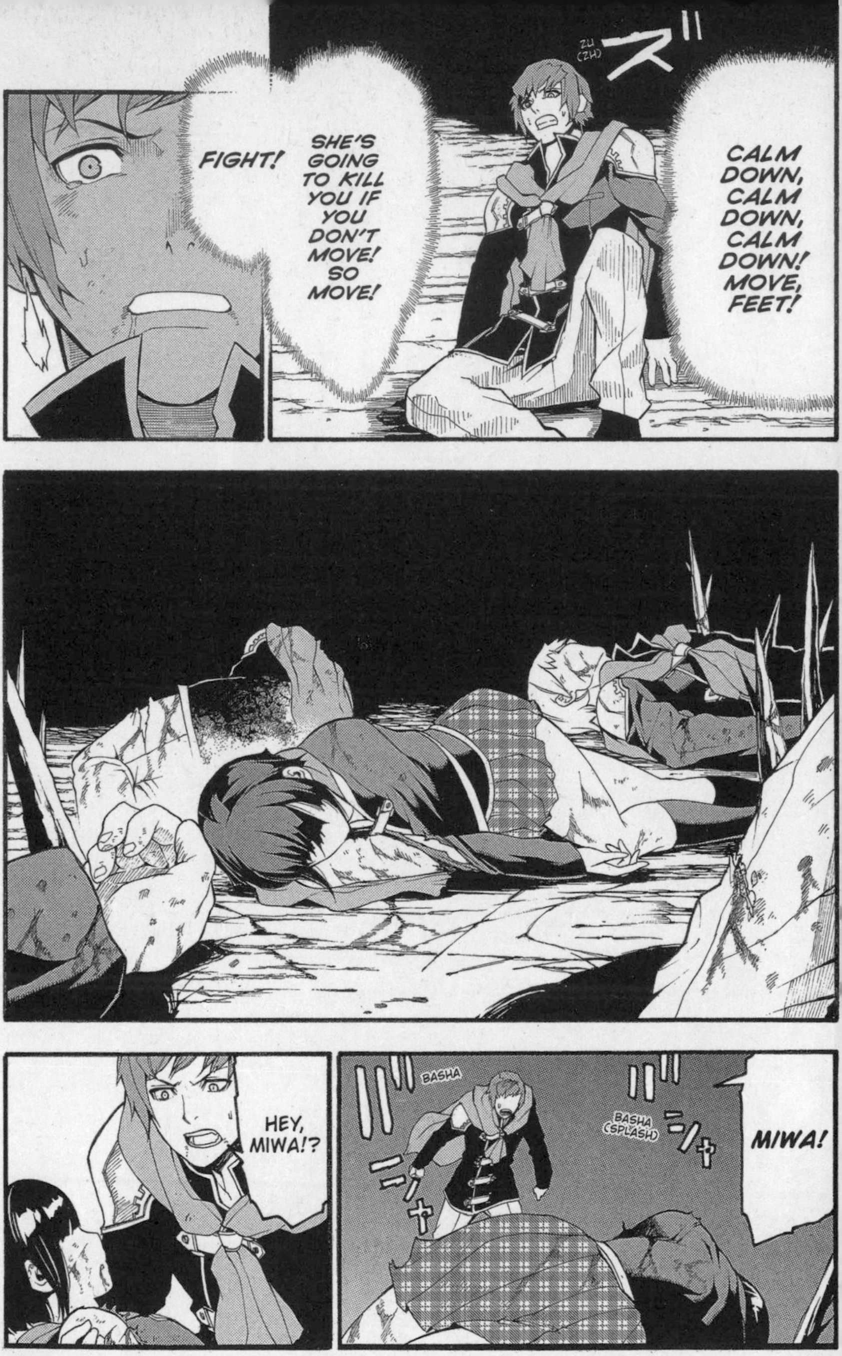
ZU (ZH)
CALM DOWN, CALM DOWN, CALM DOWN! MOVE, FEET!
SHE'S GOING TO KILL YOU IF YOU DON'T MOVE! SO MOVE!
FIGHT!
MIWA!
BASHA (SPLASH)
BASHA
HEY, MIWA!?

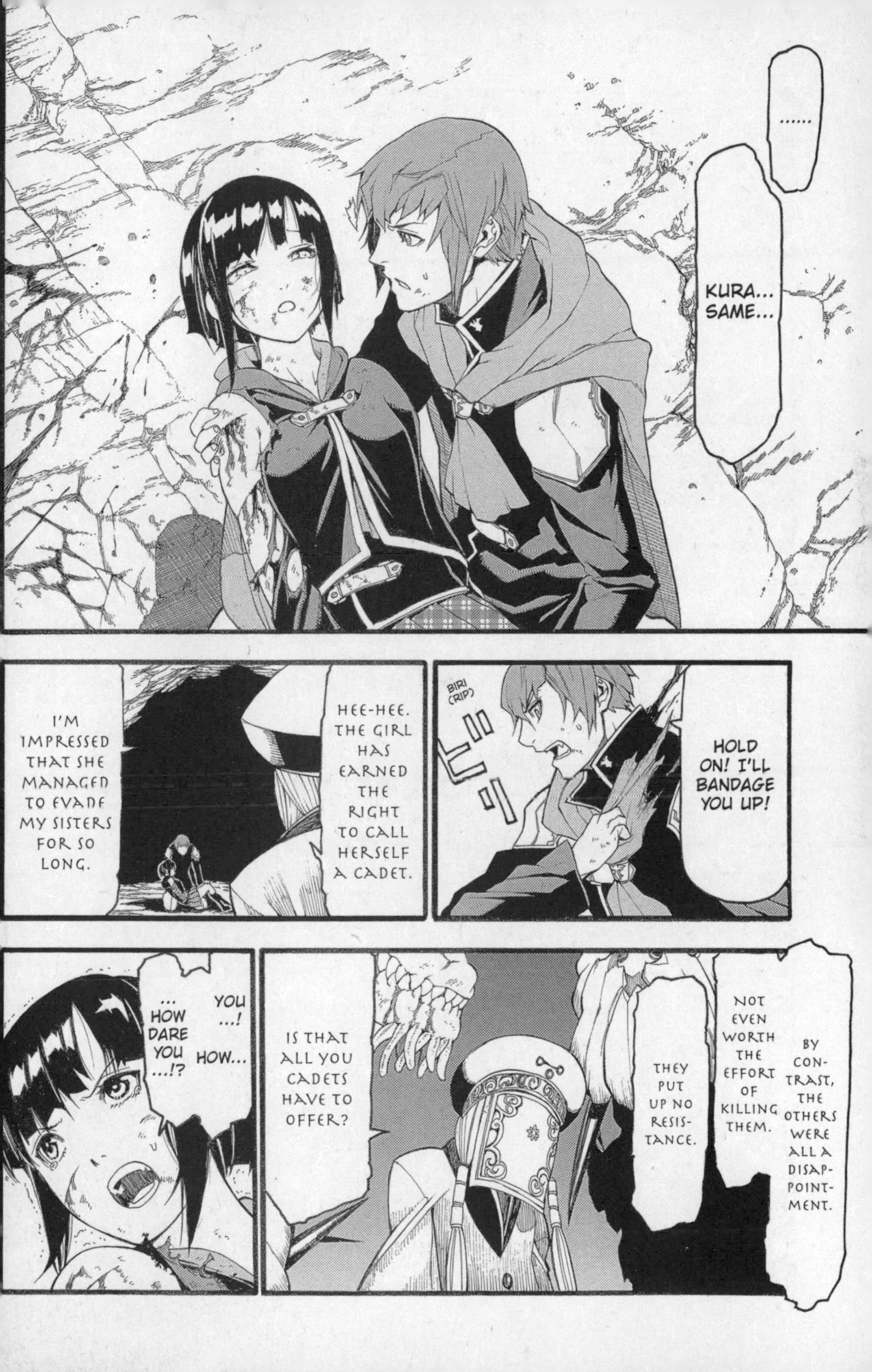
......
KURA... SAME...
BIRI (RIP)
HOLD ON! I'LL BANDAGE YOU UP!
HEE-HEE. THE GIRL HAS EARNED THE RIGHT TO CALL HERSELF A CADET.
I'M IMPRESSED THAT SHE MANAGED TO EVADE MY SISTERS FOR SO LONG.
BY CONTRAST, THE OTHERS WERE ALL A DISAPPOINTMENT.
NOT EVEN WORTH THE EFFORT OF KILLING THEM.
THEY PUT UP NO RESISTANCE.
IS THAT ALL YOU CADETS HAVE TO OFFER?
YOU...! HOW...
...HOW DARE YOU...!?

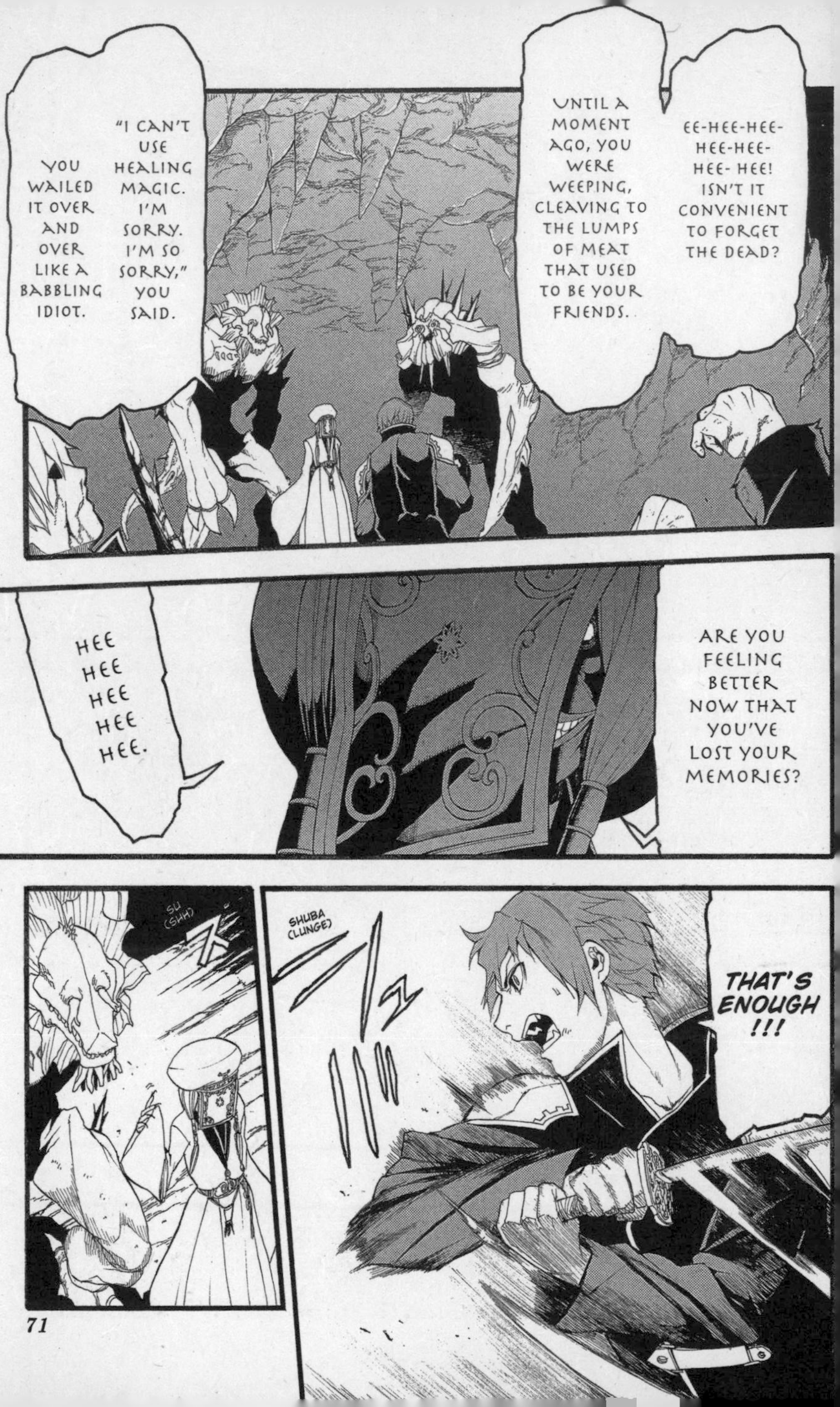
EE-HEE-HEE-HEE-HEE-HEE- HEE! ISN'T IT CONVENIENT TO FORGET THE DEAD?
UNTIL A MOMENT AGO, YOU WERE WEEPING, CLEAVING TO THE LUMPS OF MEAT THAT USED TO BE YOUR FRIENDS.
"I CAN'T USE HEALING MAGIC. I'M SORRY. I'M SO SORRY," YOU SAID.
YOU WAILED IT OVER AND OVER LIKE A BABBLING IDIOT.
ARE YOU FEELING BETTER NOW THAT YOU'VE LOST YOUR MEMORIES?
HEE HEE HEE HEE HEE.
THAT'S ENOUGH!!!
SHUBA (LUNGE)
SU (SHH)

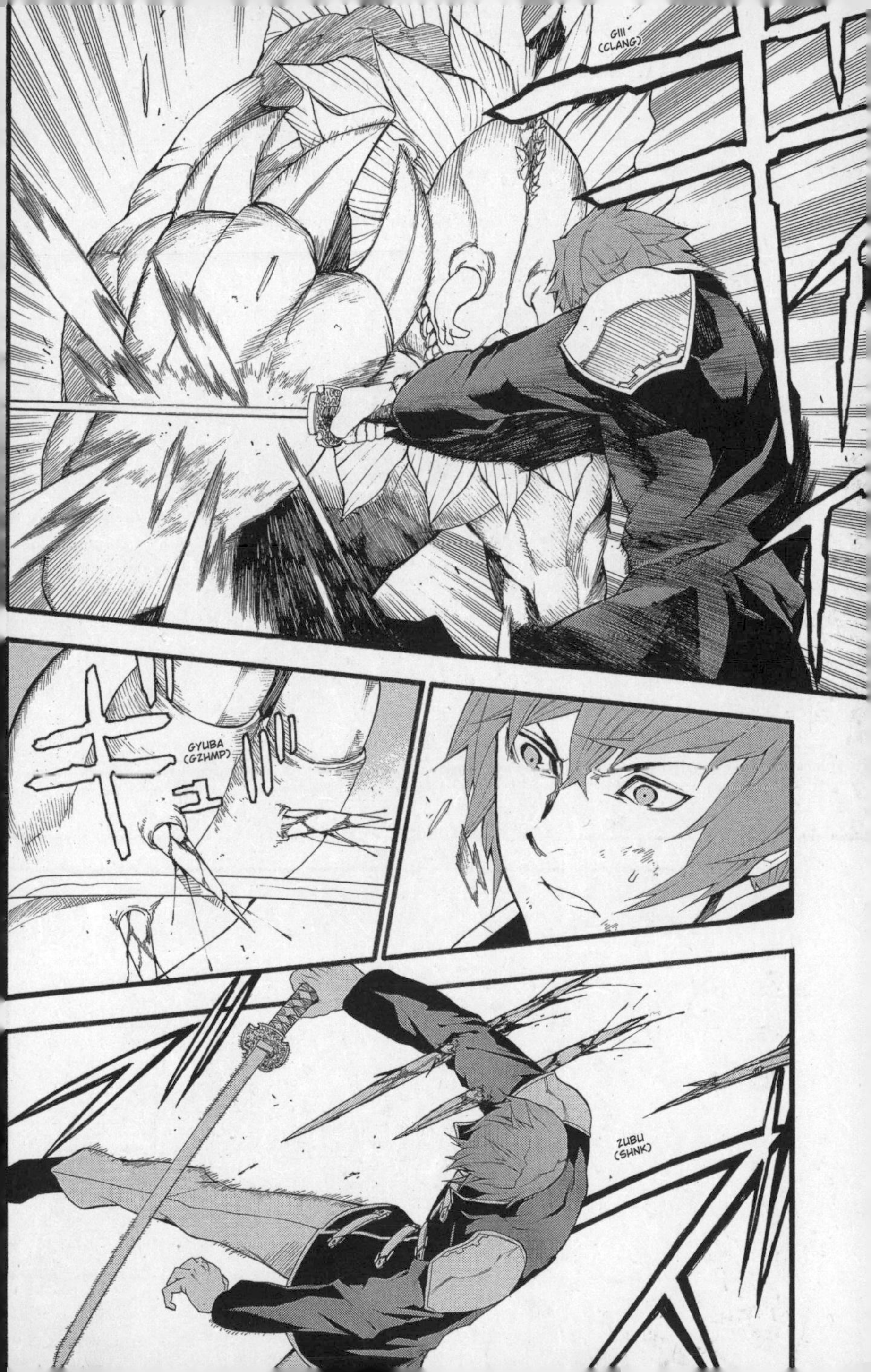
GIII
(CLANG)
GYUBA
(GZHMP)
ZUBU
(SHNK)

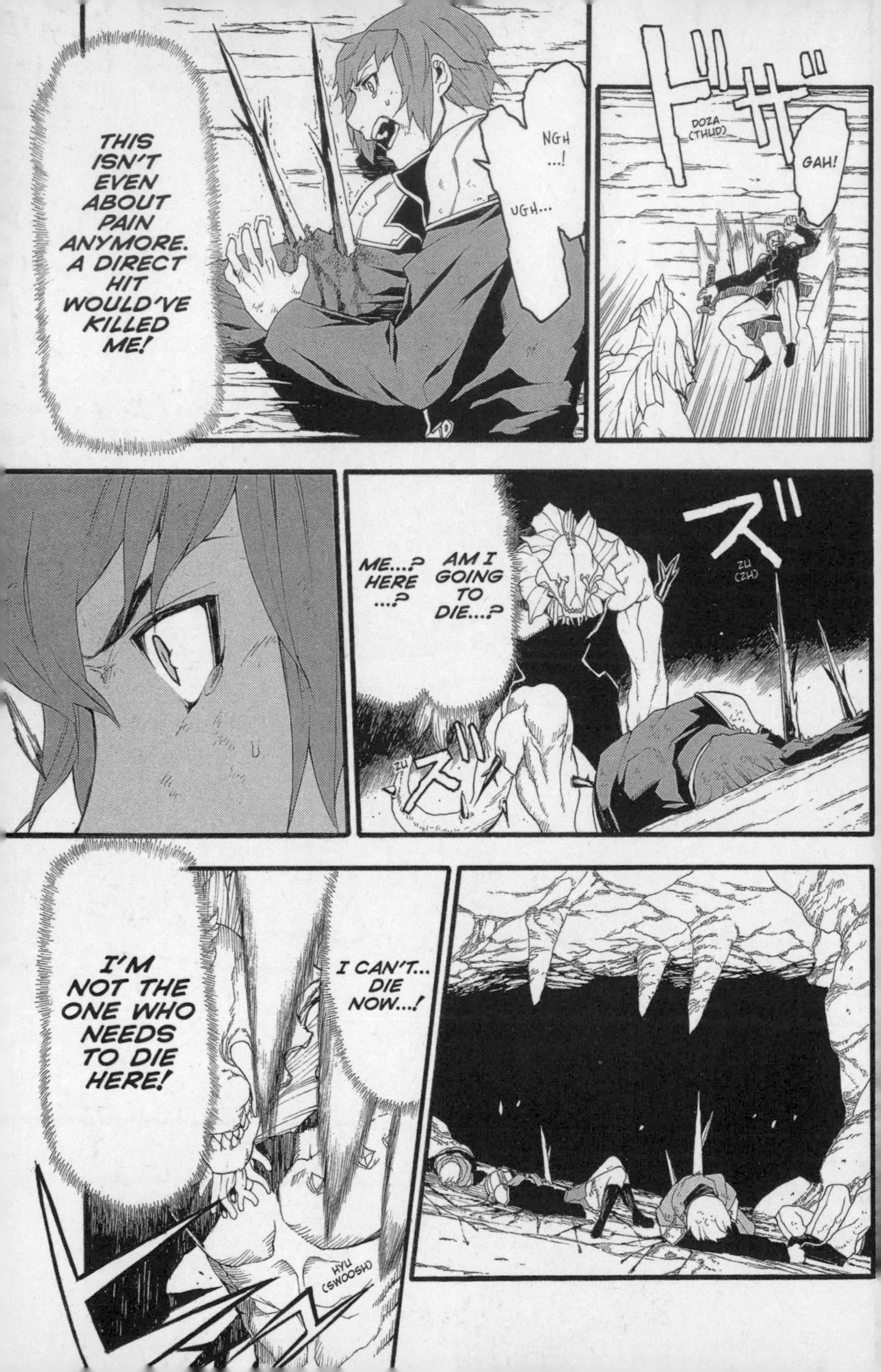
ドザ
DOZA (THUD)
GAH!
NGH ...!
UGH...
THIS ISN'T EVEN ABOUT PAIN ANYMORE. A DIRECT HIT WOULD'VE KILLED ME!
ズ
ZU (ZH)
AM I GOING TO DIE...?
ME...? HERE ...?
ズ
ZU
I CAN'T... DIE NOW...!
I'M NOT THE ONE WHO NEEDS TO DIE HERE!
HYU (SWOOSH)

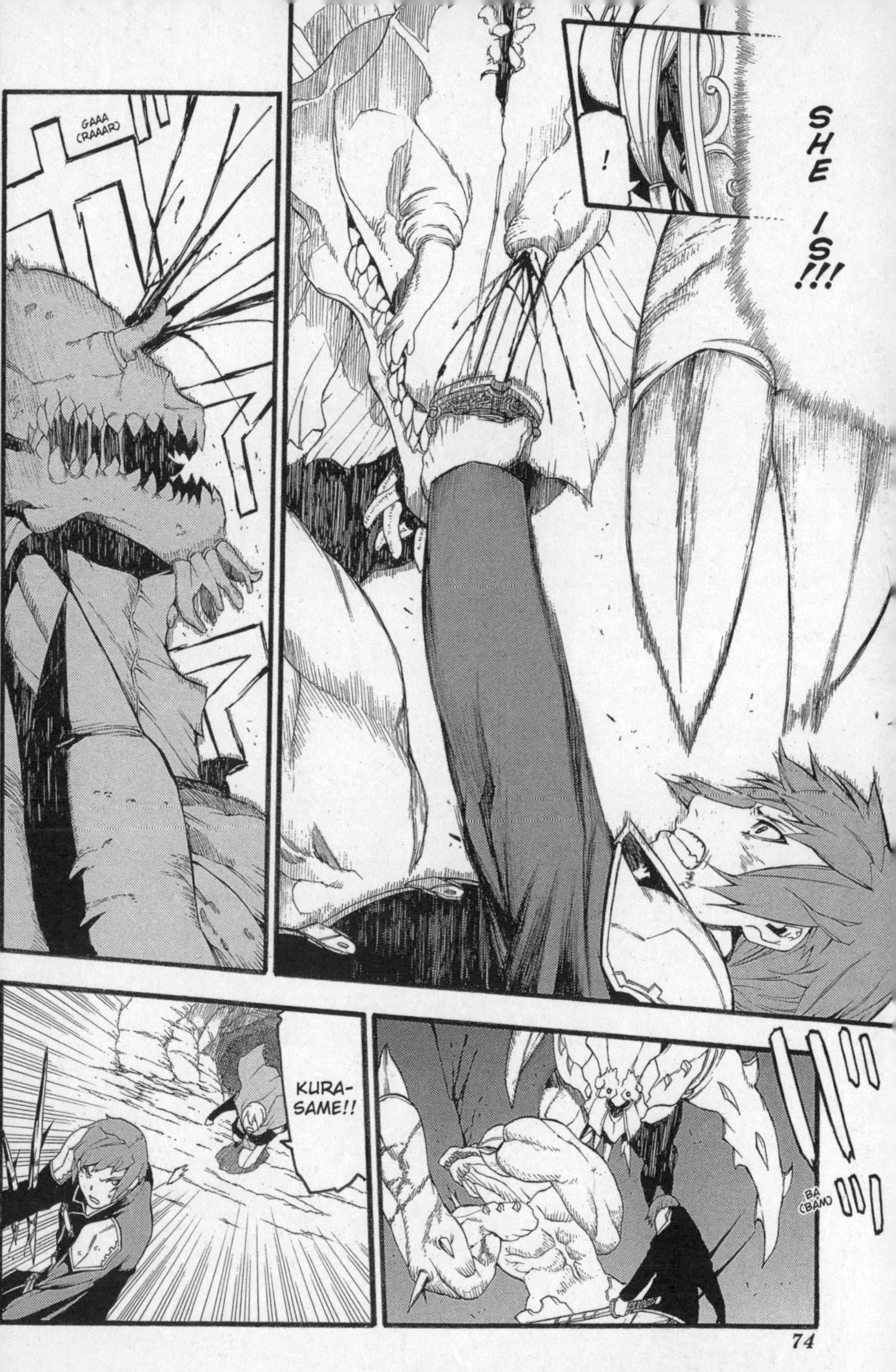
!
SHE IS!!!
GAAA (RAAAR)
BA (BAM)
KURA-SAME!!

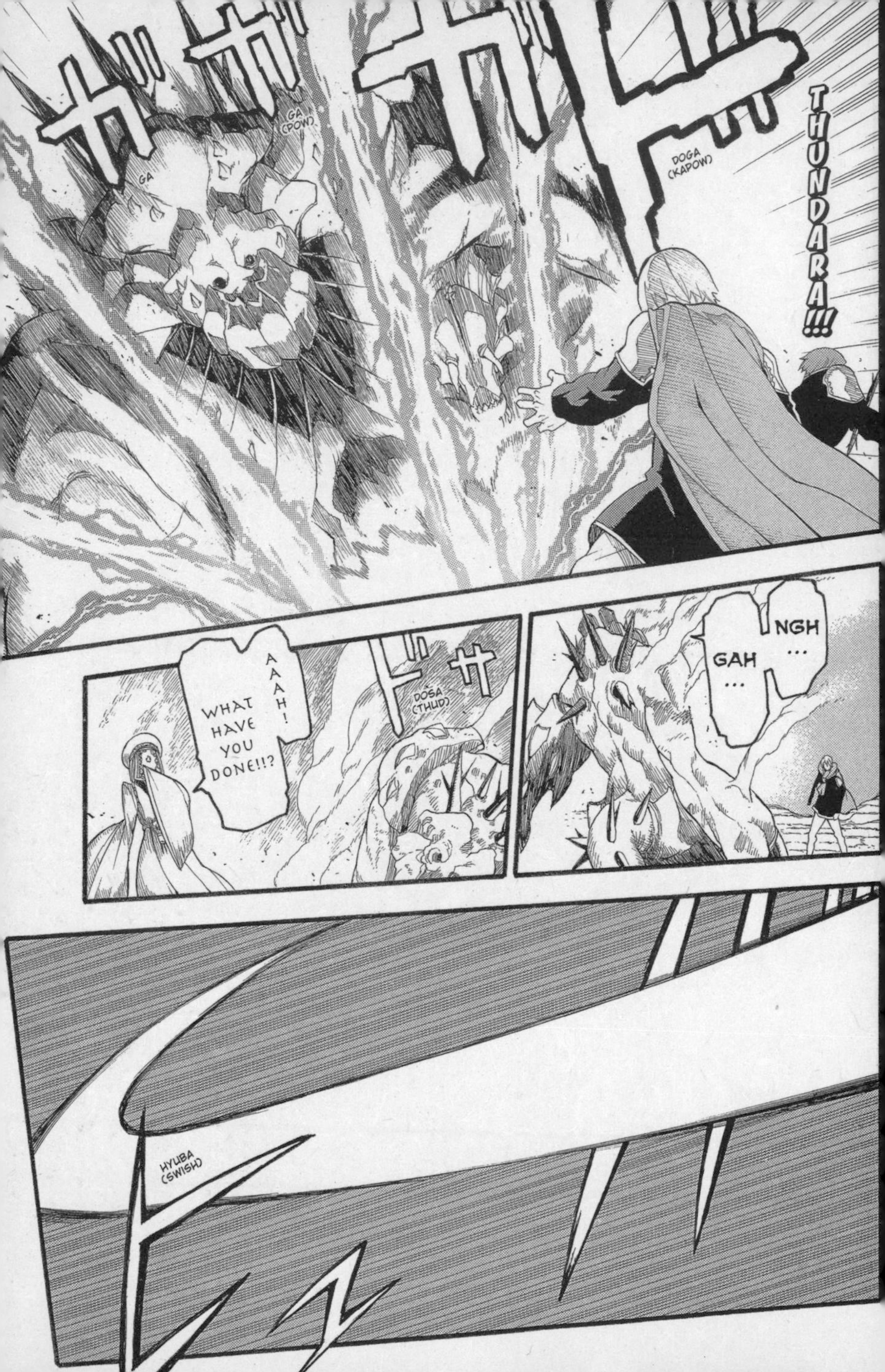
THUNDARA!!!
DOGA (KAPOW)
GA (POW)
GA
NGH... GAH...
DOSA (THUD)
AAAH! WHAT HAVE YOU DONE!!?
HYUBA (SWISH)

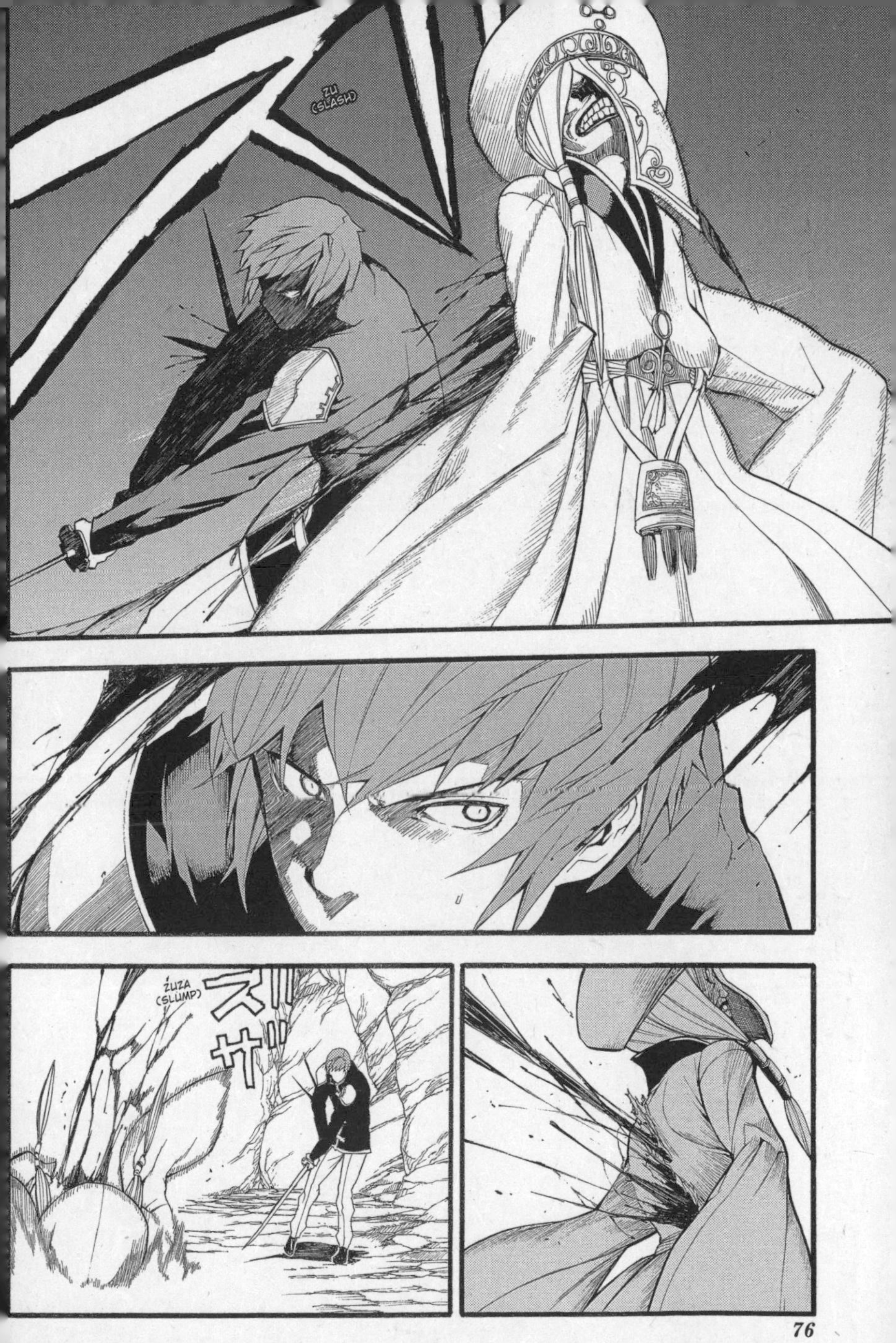
ZU (SLASH)
ZUZA (SLUMP)

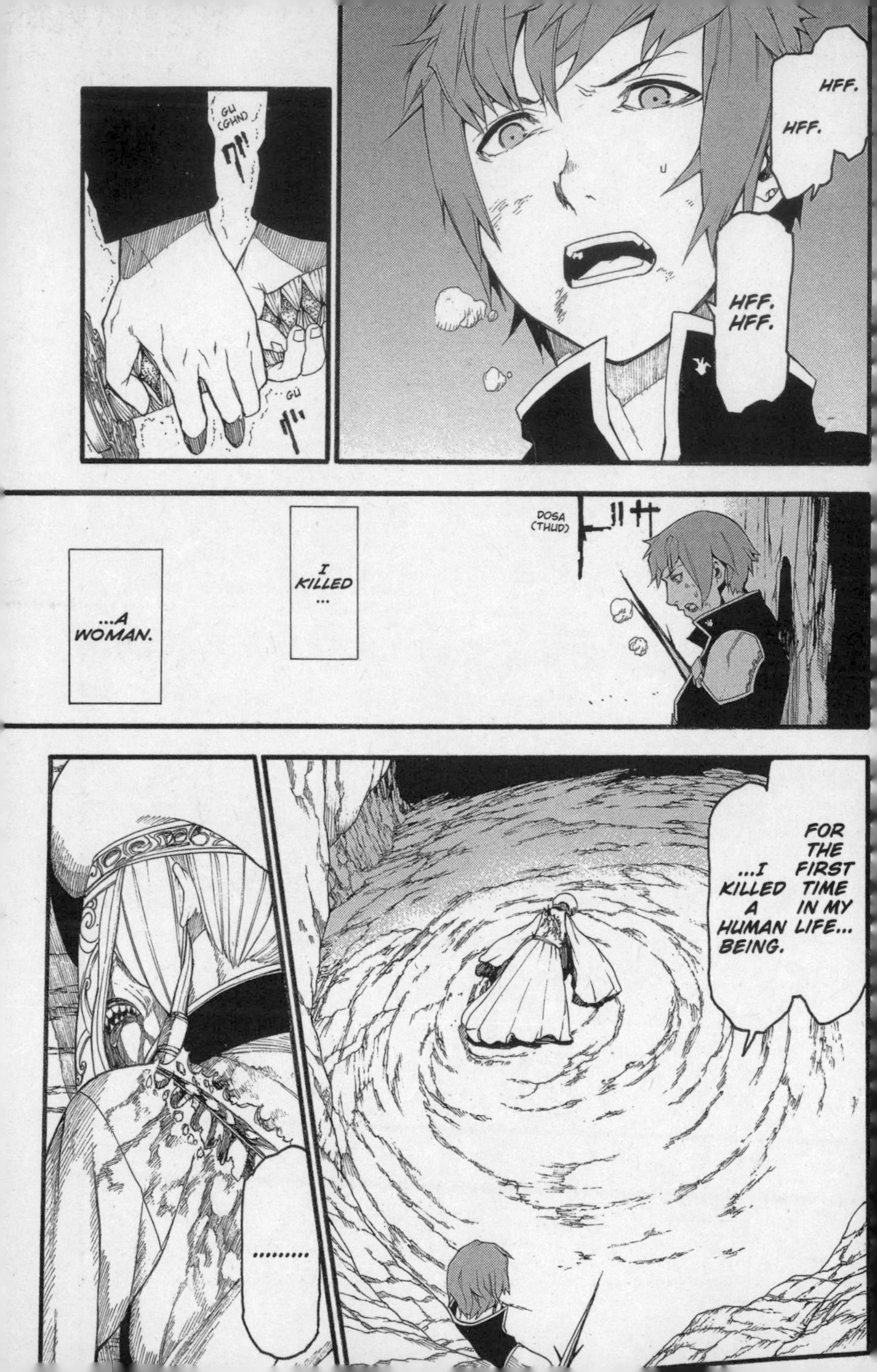
HFF.
HFF.
HFF. HFF.
GU (GHN)
GU
DOSA (THUD)
I KILLED...
...A WOMAN.
FOR THE FIRST TIME IN MY LIFE...
...I KILLED A HUMAN BEING.
....

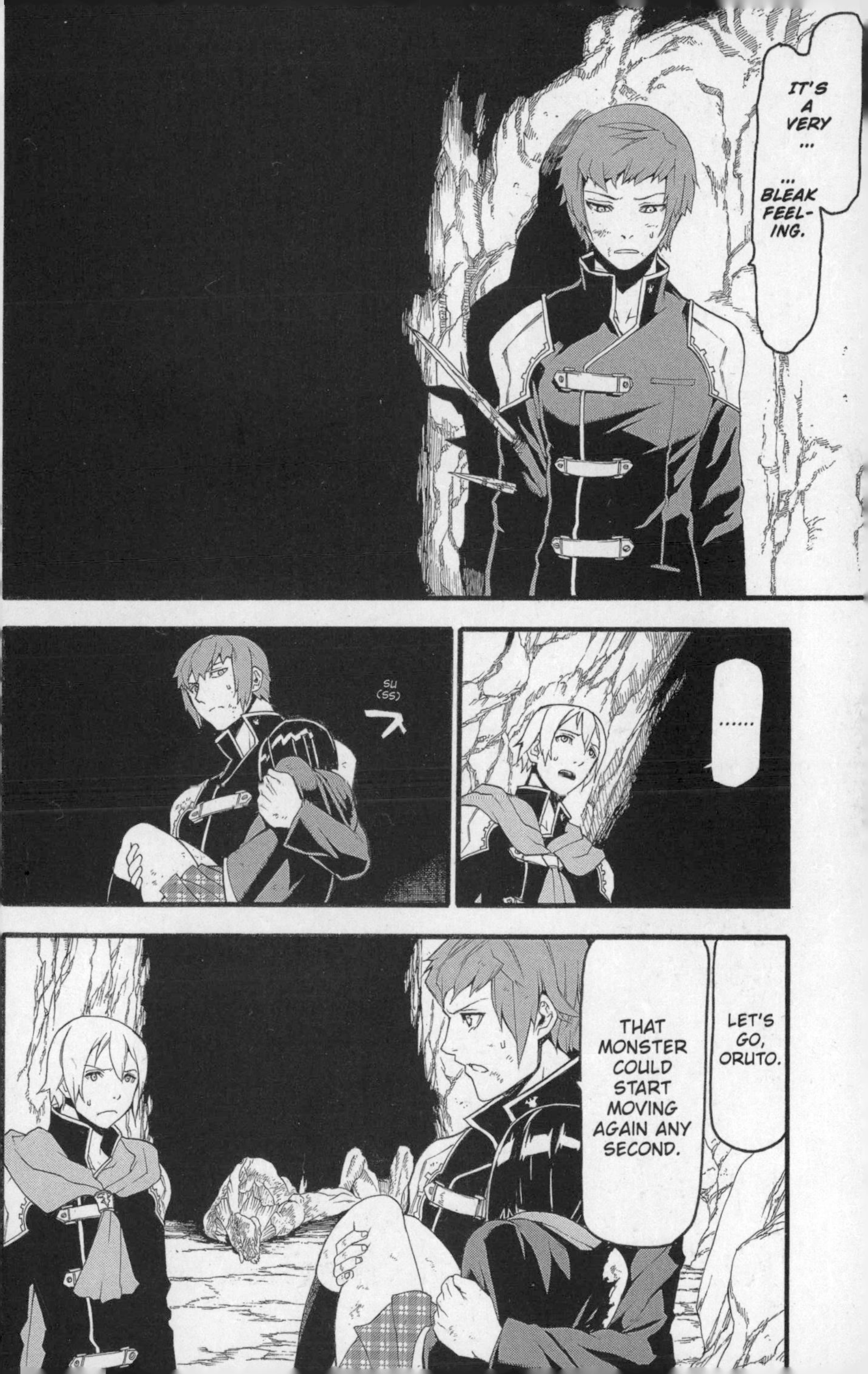
IT'S A VERY ... ... BLEAK FEELING.
......
SU (SS)
LET'S GO, ORUTO.
THAT MONSTER COULD START MOVING AGAIN ANY SECOND.

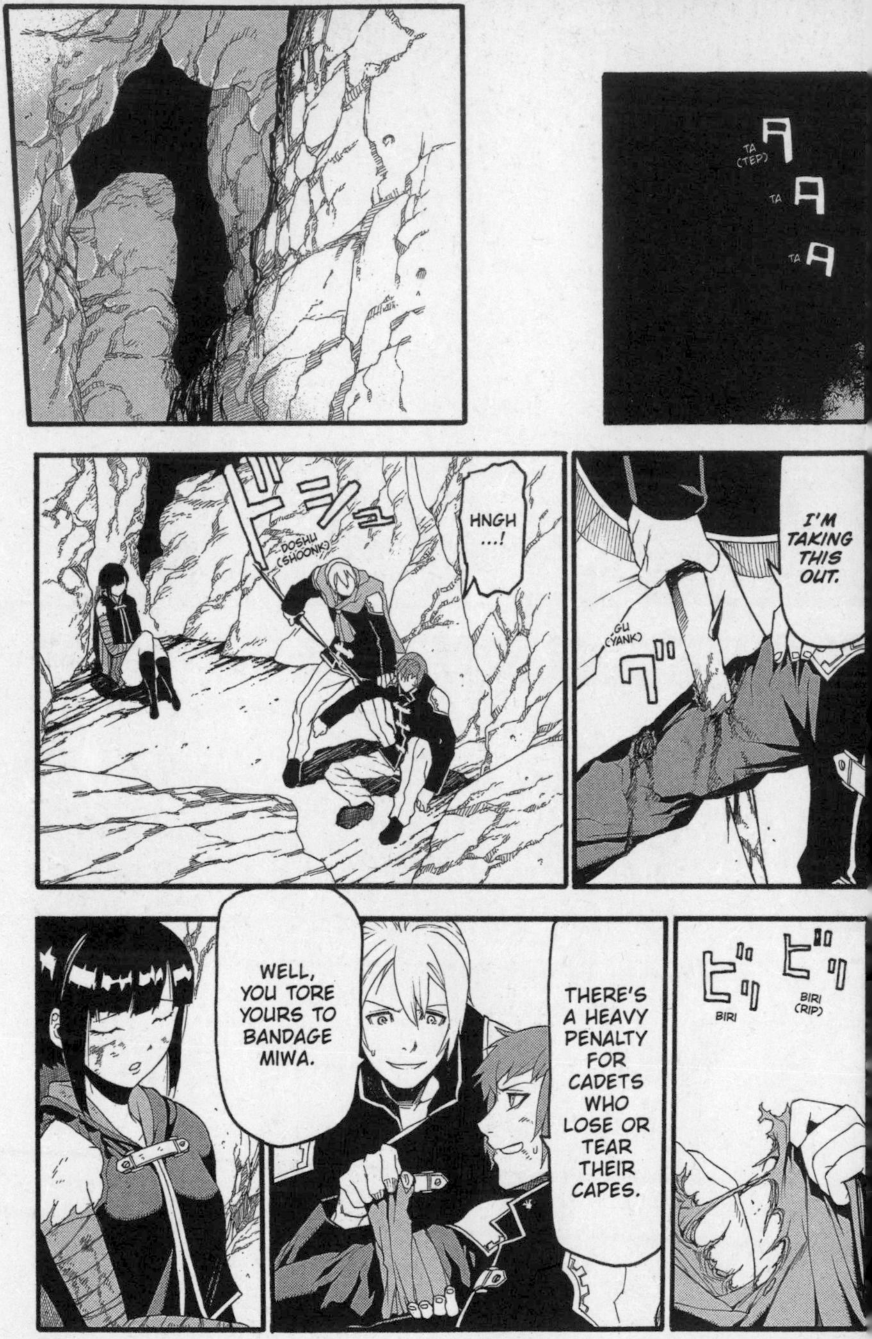
TA (TEP)
TA
TA
I'M TAKING THIS OUT.
GU (YANK)
HNGH ...!
DOSHU (SHOONK)
BIRI
BIRI (RIP)
THERE'S A HEAVY PENALTY FOR CADETS WHO LOSE OR TEAR THEIR CAPES.
WELL, YOU TORE YOURS TO BANDAGE MIWA.

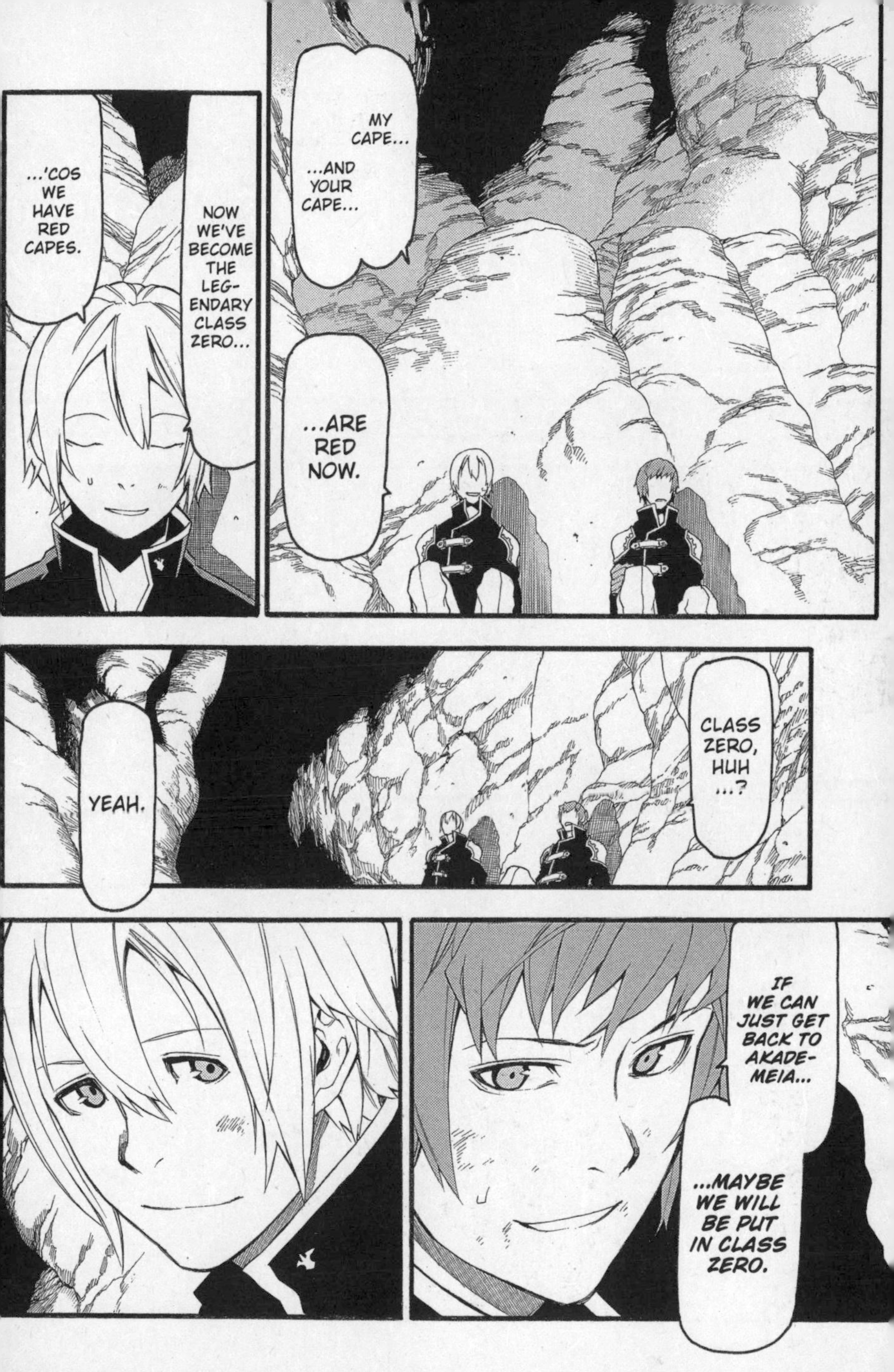
MY CAPE...
...AND YOUR CAPE...
...ARE RED NOW.
NOW WE'VE BECOME THE LEG-ENDARY CLASS ZERO...
...'COS WE HAVE RED CAPES.
CLASS ZERO, HUH ...?
YEAH.
IF WE CAN JUST GET BACK TO AKADE-MEIA...
...MAYBE WE WILL BE PUT IN CLASS ZERO.

MIWA... ARE YOU OKAY?

MM... NN...

TSU (DRIP)

. . . .

. . .

...

MIWA ...?

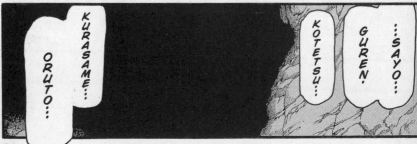

ORUTO...

KURASAME...

KOTETSU...

GUREN!

...SAYO...

81

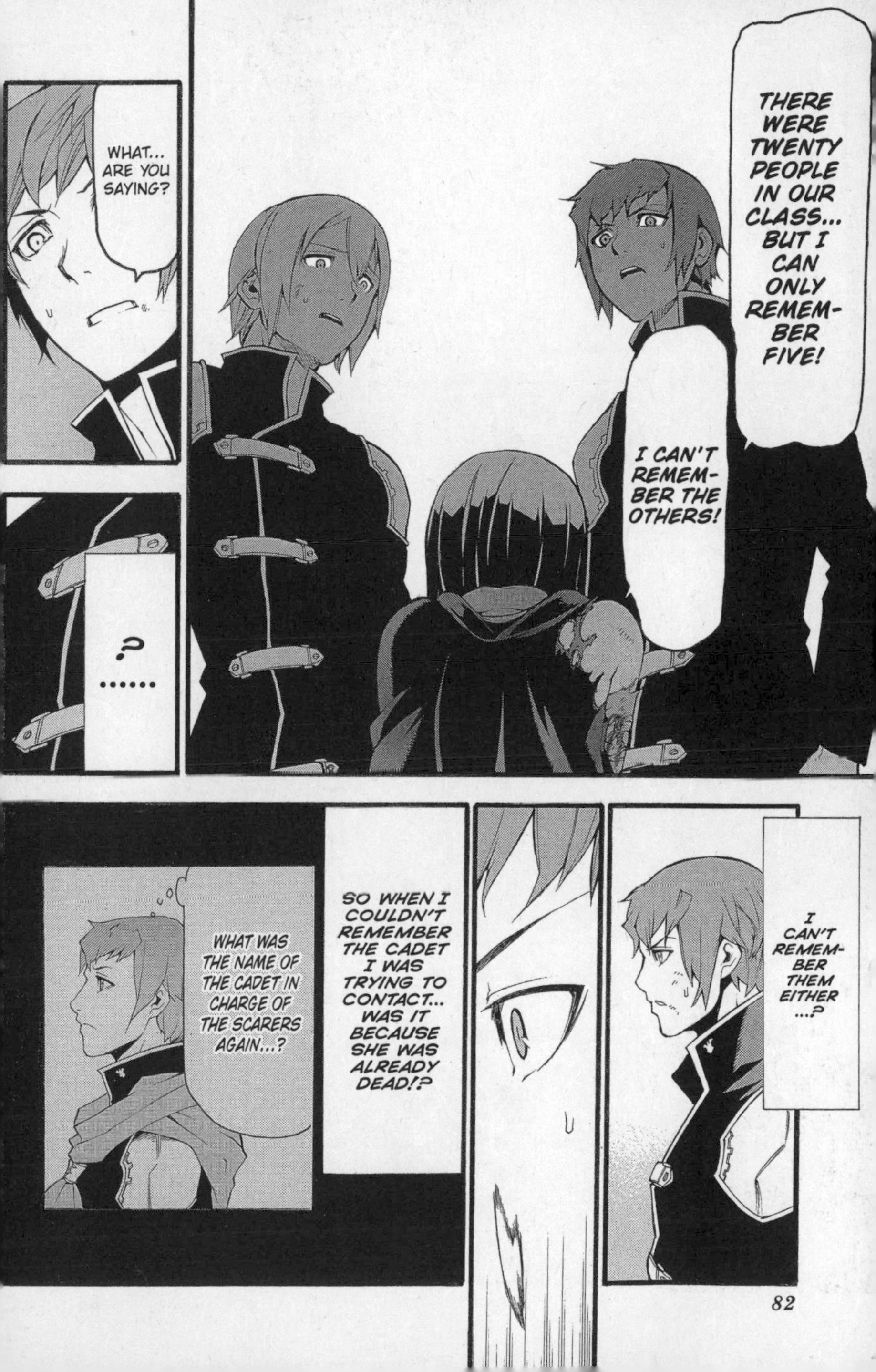
THERE WERE TWENTY PEOPLE IN OUR CLASS... BUT I CAN ONLY REMEMBER FIVE!
I CAN'T REMEMBER THE OTHERS!
WHAT... ARE YOU SAYING?
?
......
I CAN'T REMEMBER THEM EITHER ...?
SO WHEN I COULDN'T REMEMBER THE CADET I WAS TRYING TO CONTACT... WAS IT BECAUSE SHE WAS ALREADY DEAD!?
WHAT WAS THE NAME OF THE CADET IN CHARGE OF THE SCARERS AGAIN...?

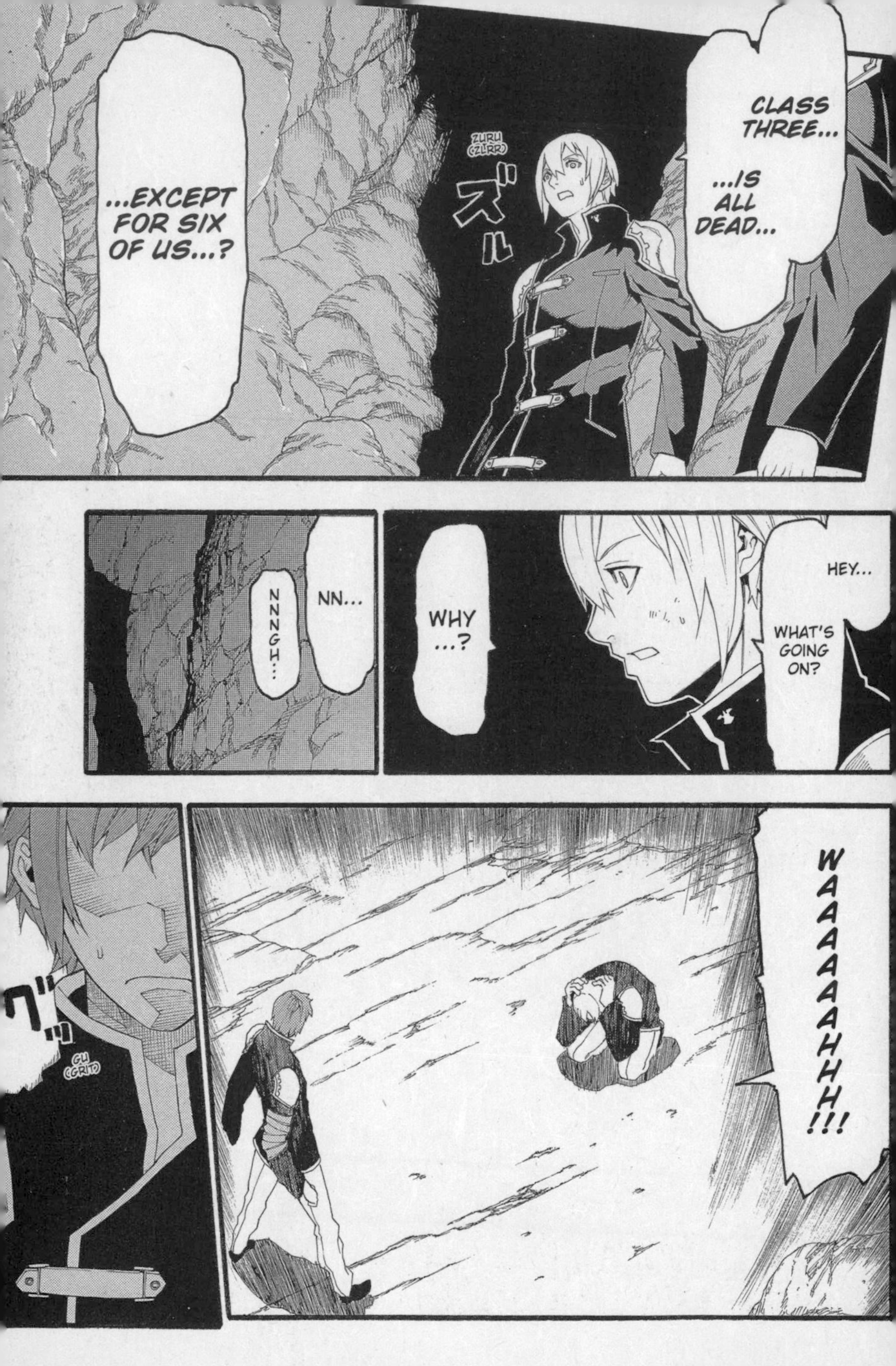
CLASS THREE...
...IS ALL DEAD...
ZURU (ZLRR)
ズル
...EXCEPT FOR SIX OF US...?
HEY...
WHAT'S GOING ON?
WHY ...?
NN...
NNNGH...
WAAAAAAAHHH!!!
グッ
GU (GRIT)

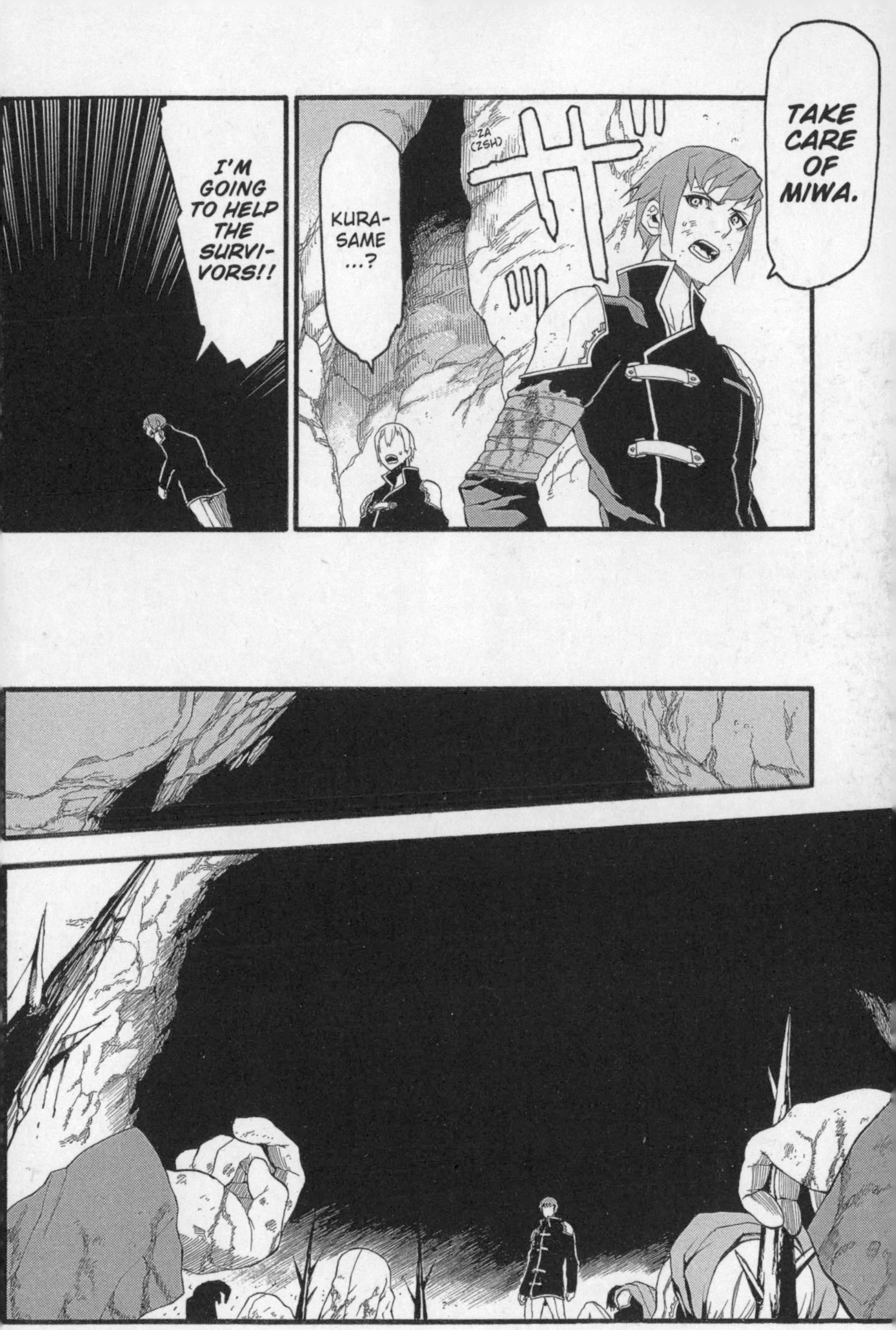
TAKE CARE OF MIWA.
ZA (ZSH)
KURA-SAME ...?
I'M GOING TO HELP THE SURVI-VORS!!

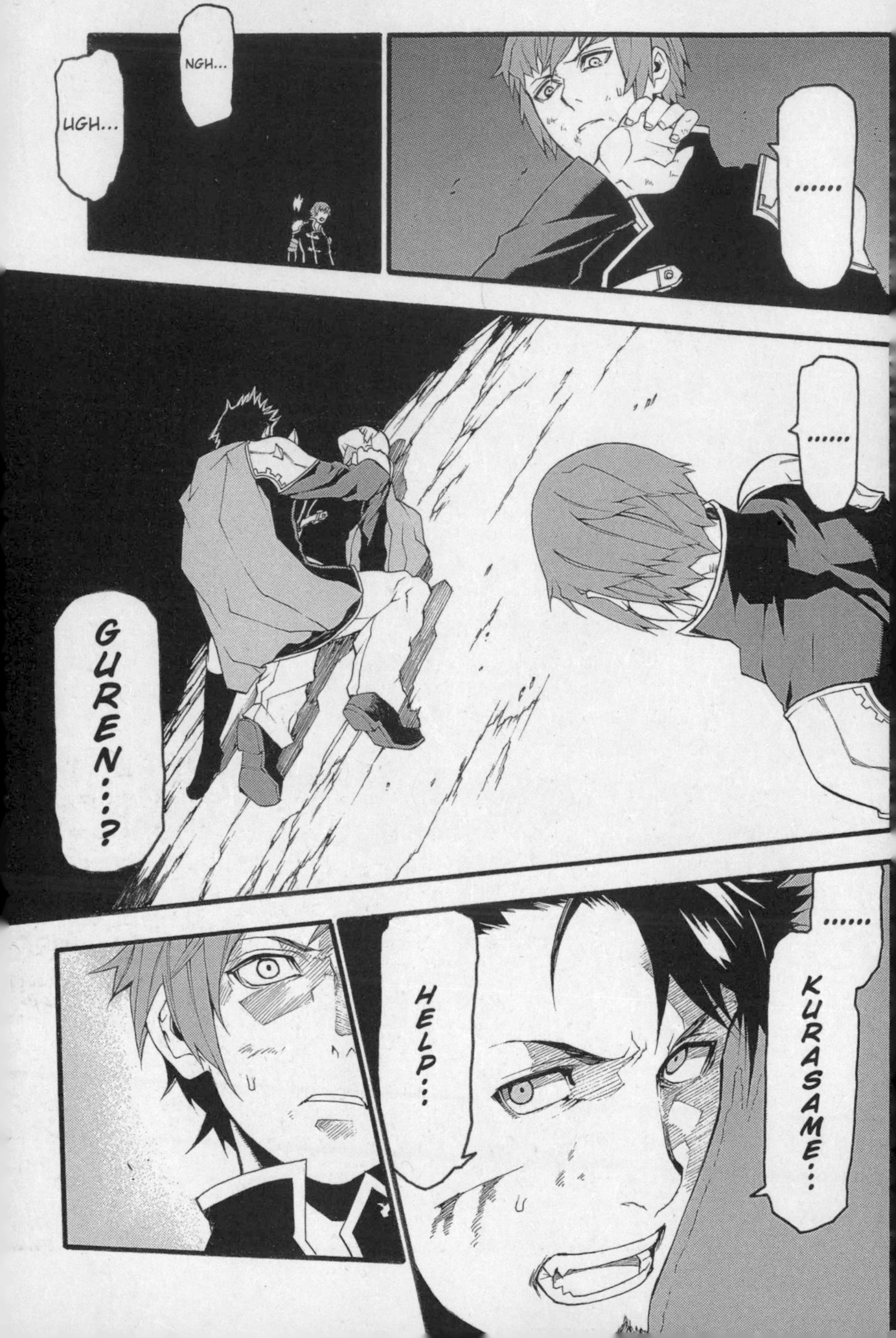
......
NGH...
UGH...
......
GUREN...?
......
KURASAME...
HELP...

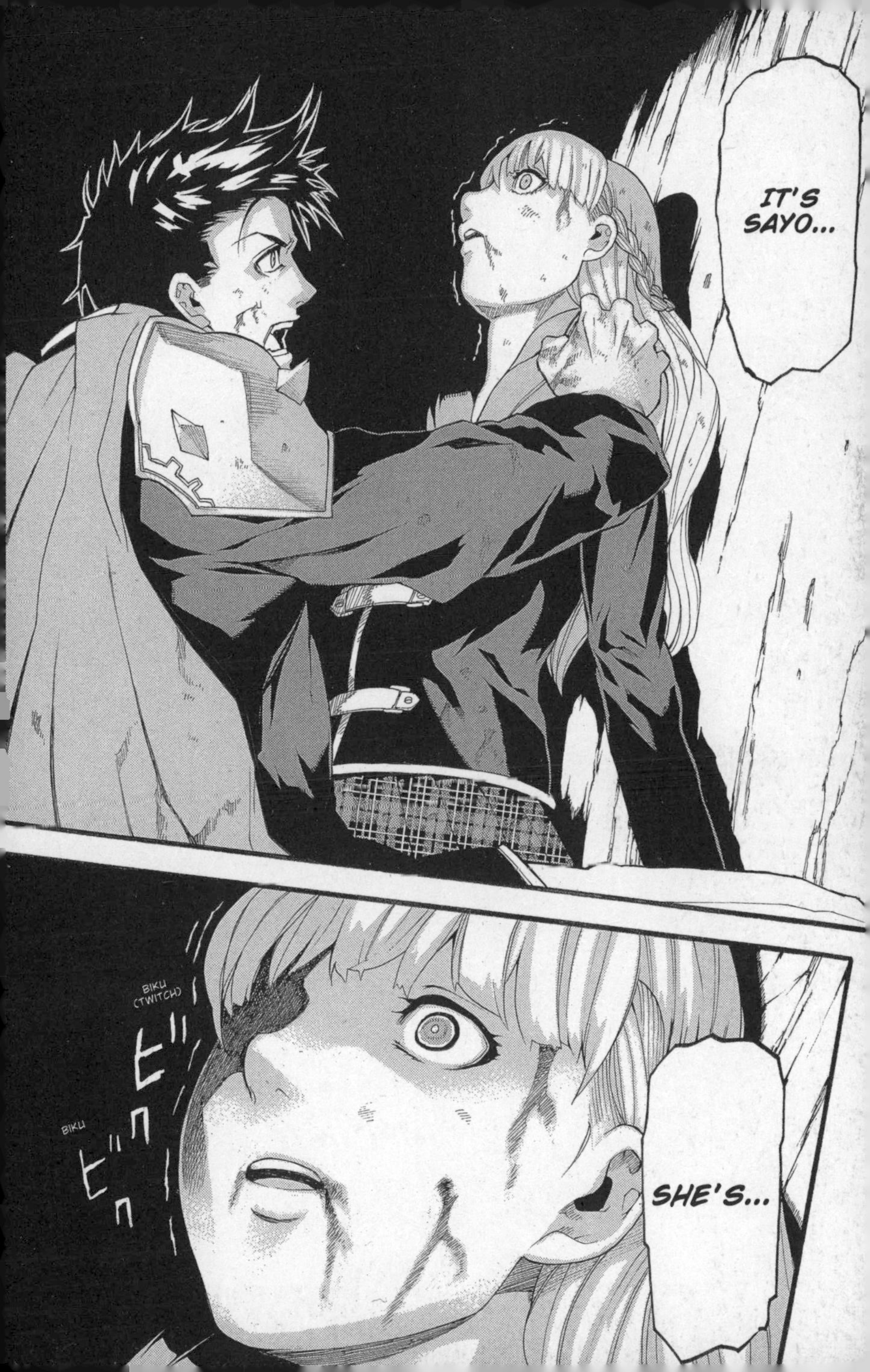
IT'S SAYO...
SHE'S...
BIKU (TWITCH)
BIKU

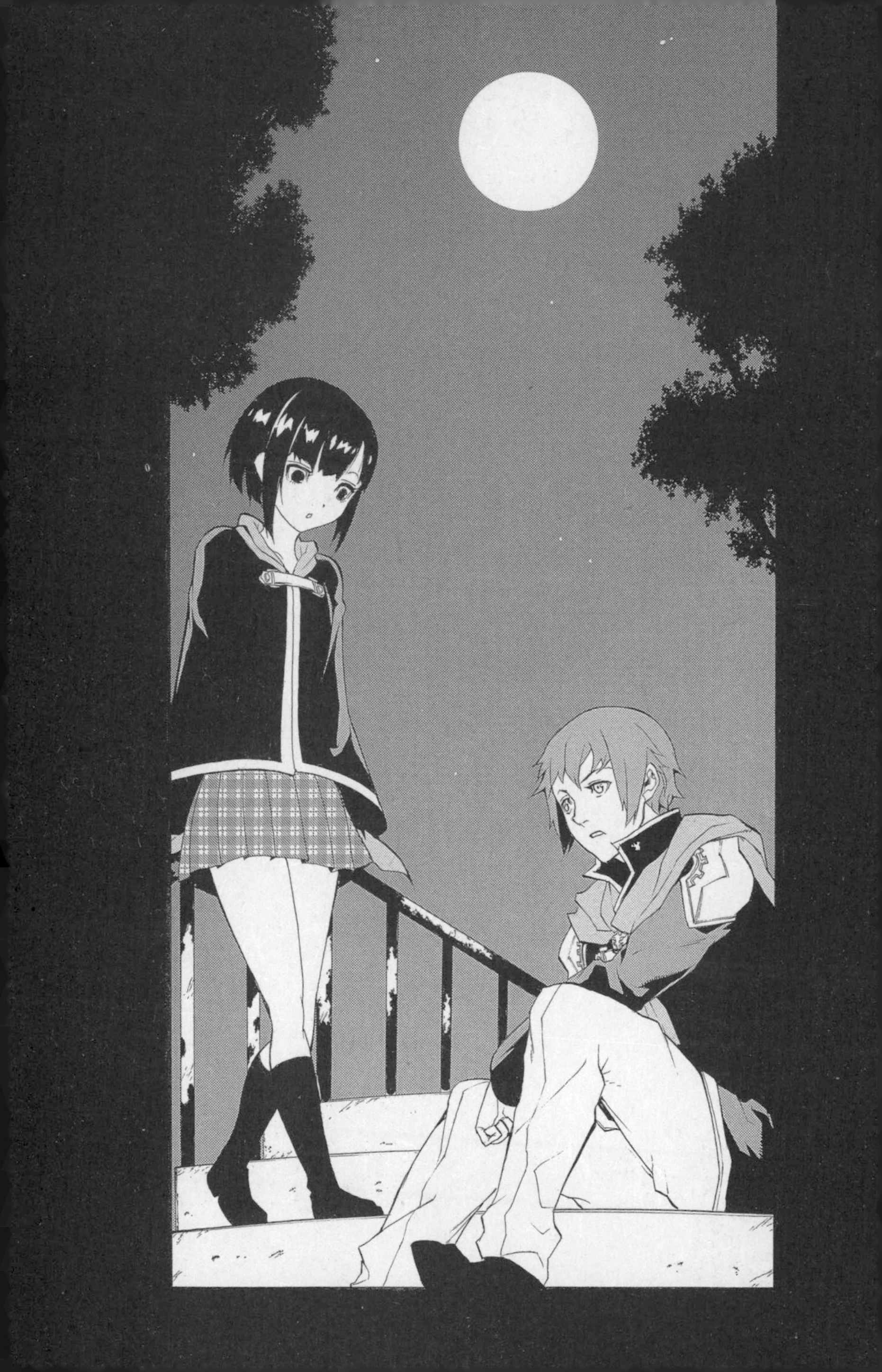

Congratulations on the release of
Side Story, Volume 1.

The tale of young Kurasame.

And...

We see a different piece of the game world,
a world where death and oblivion go hand in
hand, depicted boldly with the delicate touch
of Shiozawa-sensei.

That being the case, I am thoroughly enjoying it as
a reader myself.

May the crystal guide Kurasame and his friends
on their path, as well as all of you who have picked
up this book!

Final Fantasy Type-0
Co-Art Director, Yusaku Nakaaki

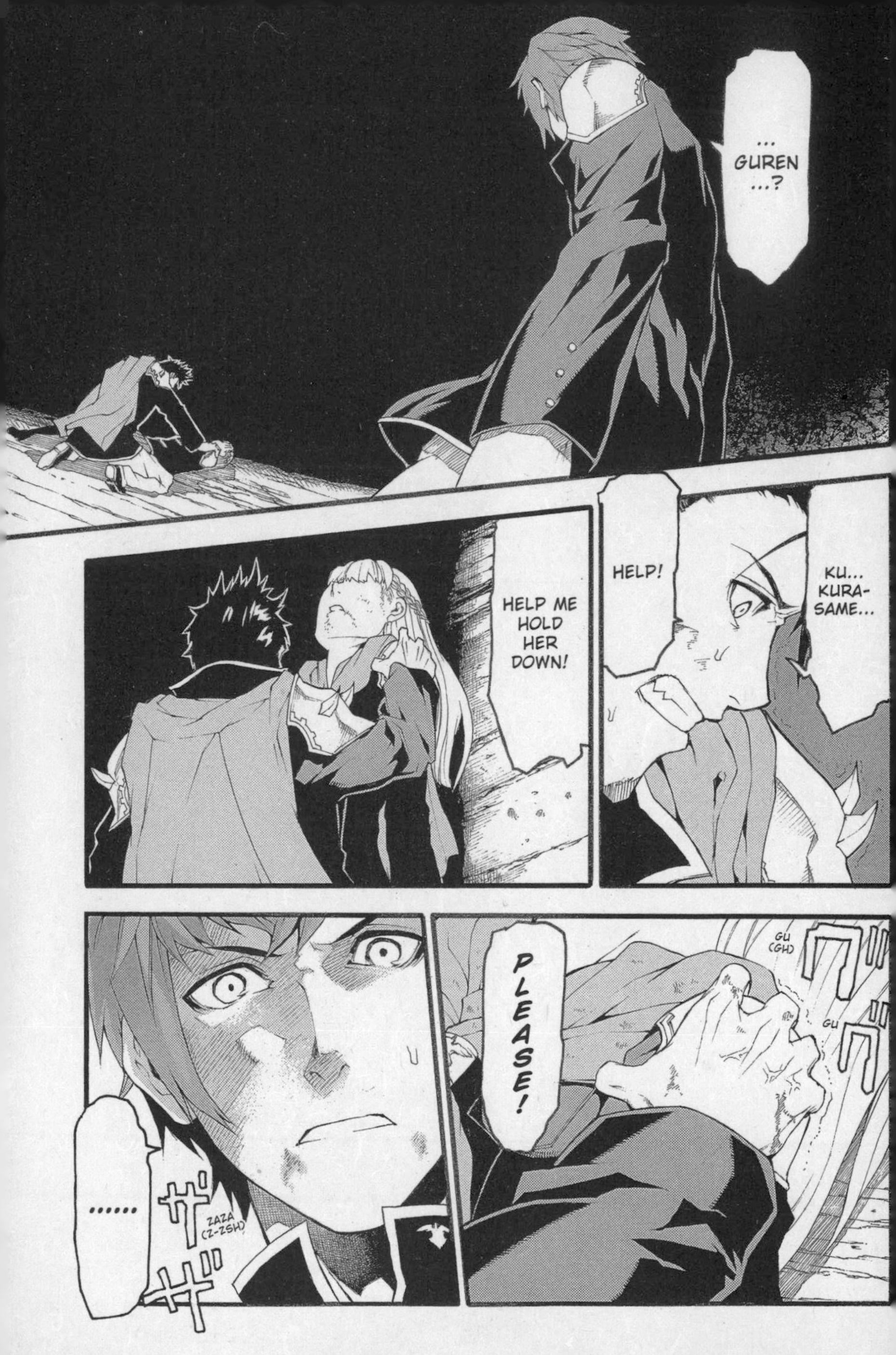
... GUREN ...?
KU... KURA-SAME...
HELP!
HELP ME HOLD HER DOWN!
GU (GH)
PLEASE!
GU
......
ZAZA (Z-ZSH)

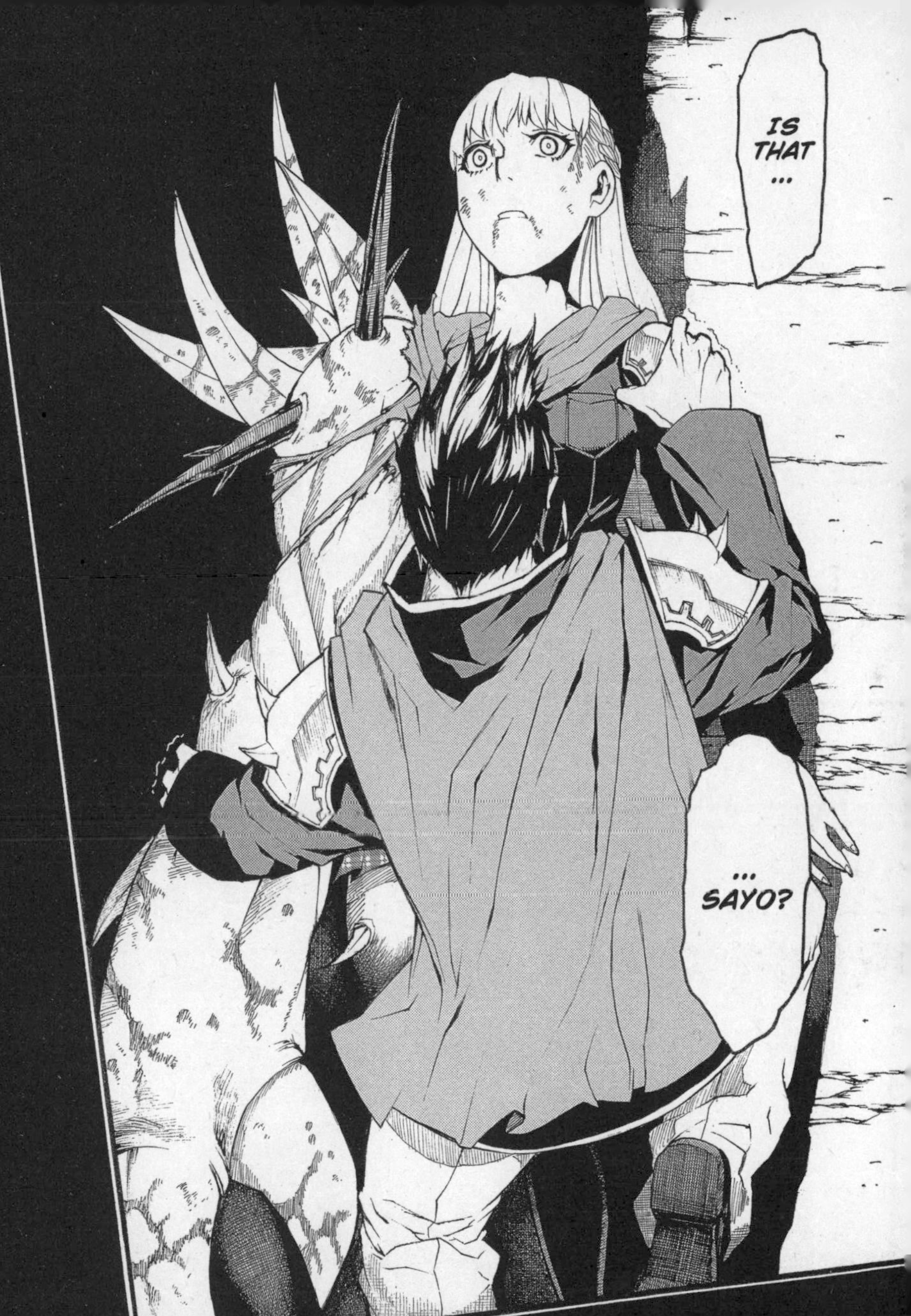
IS THAT ...
... SAYO?

CHAPTER 3: LOST AND FORGOTTEN

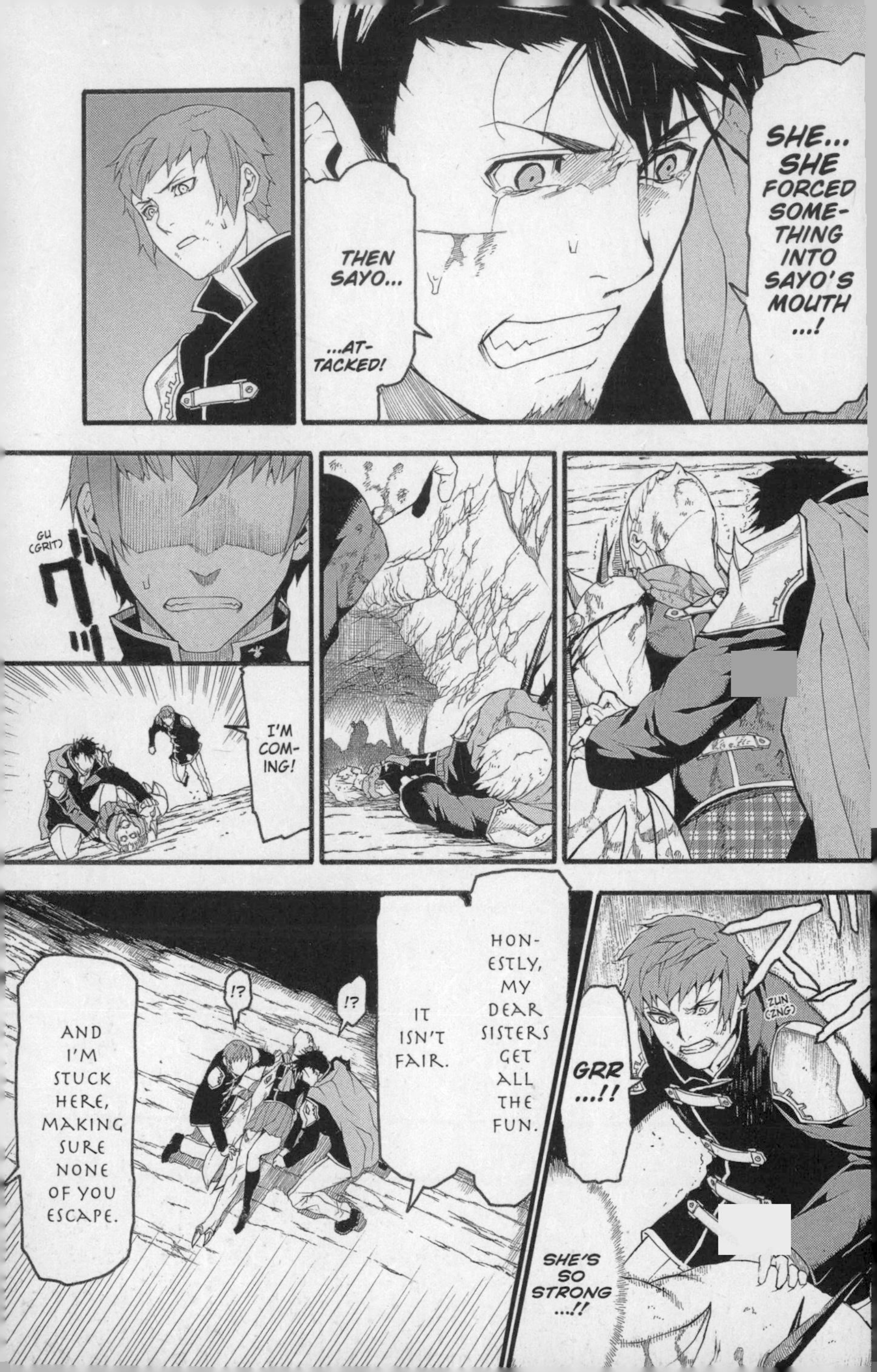
SHE... SHE FORCED SOME-THING INTO SAYO'S MOUTH ...!
THEN SAYO...
...AT-TACKED!
GU (GRIT)
I'M COM-ING!
ZUN (ZNG)
GRR ...!!
SHE'S SO STRONG ...!!
HON-ESTLY, MY DEAR SISTERS GET ALL THE FUN.
IT ISN'T FAIR.
!?
!?
AND I'M STUCK HERE, MAKING SURE NONE OF YOU ESCAPE.

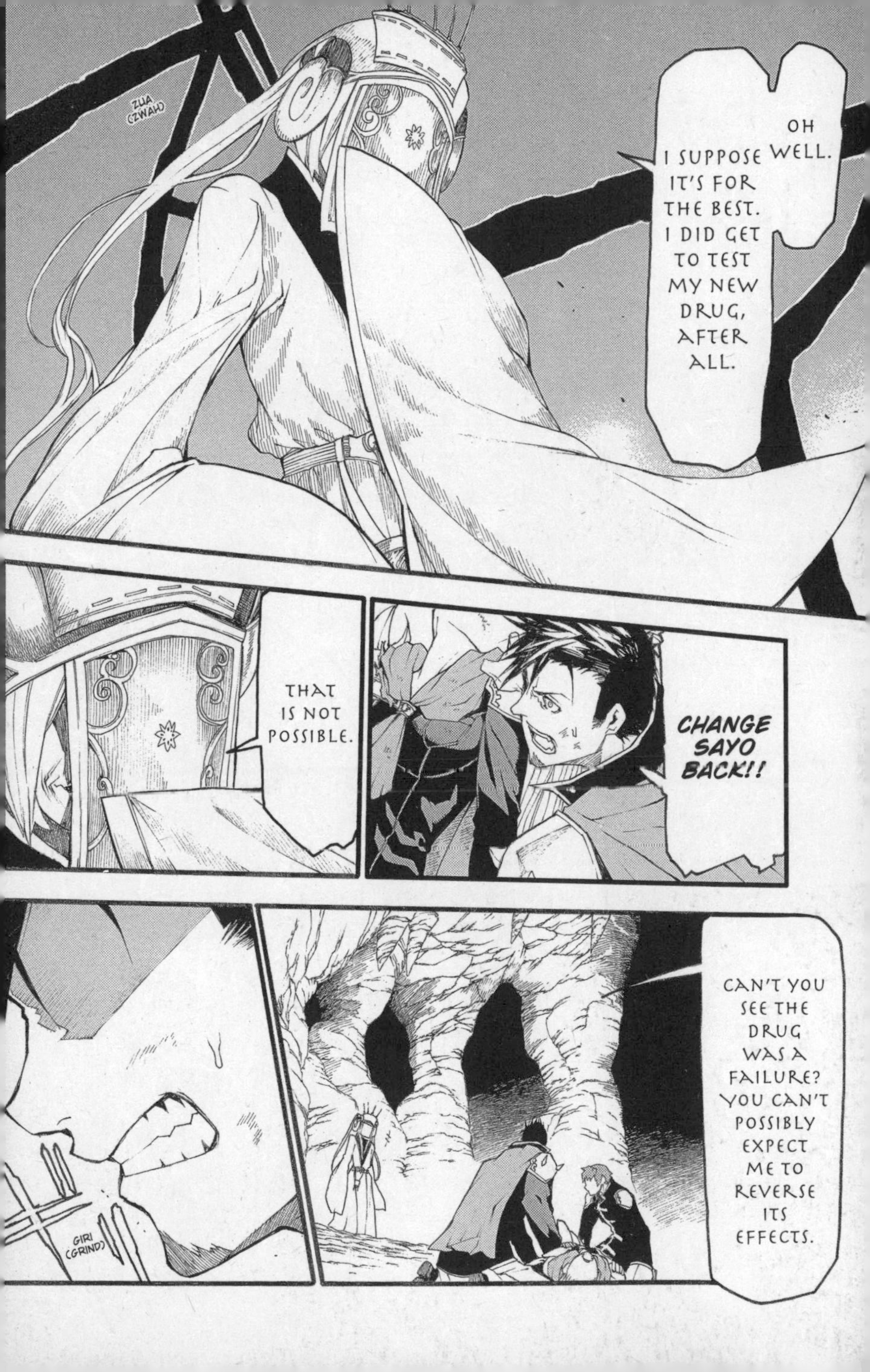
OH WELL.
I SUPPOSE IT'S FOR THE BEST. I DID GET TO TEST MY NEW DRUG, AFTER ALL.
ZUA (ZWAH)
CHANGE SAYO BACK!!
THAT IS NOT POSSIBLE.
CAN'T YOU SEE THE DRUG WAS A FAILURE? YOU CAN'T POSSIBLY EXPECT ME TO REVERSE ITS EFFECTS.
GIRI (GRIND)

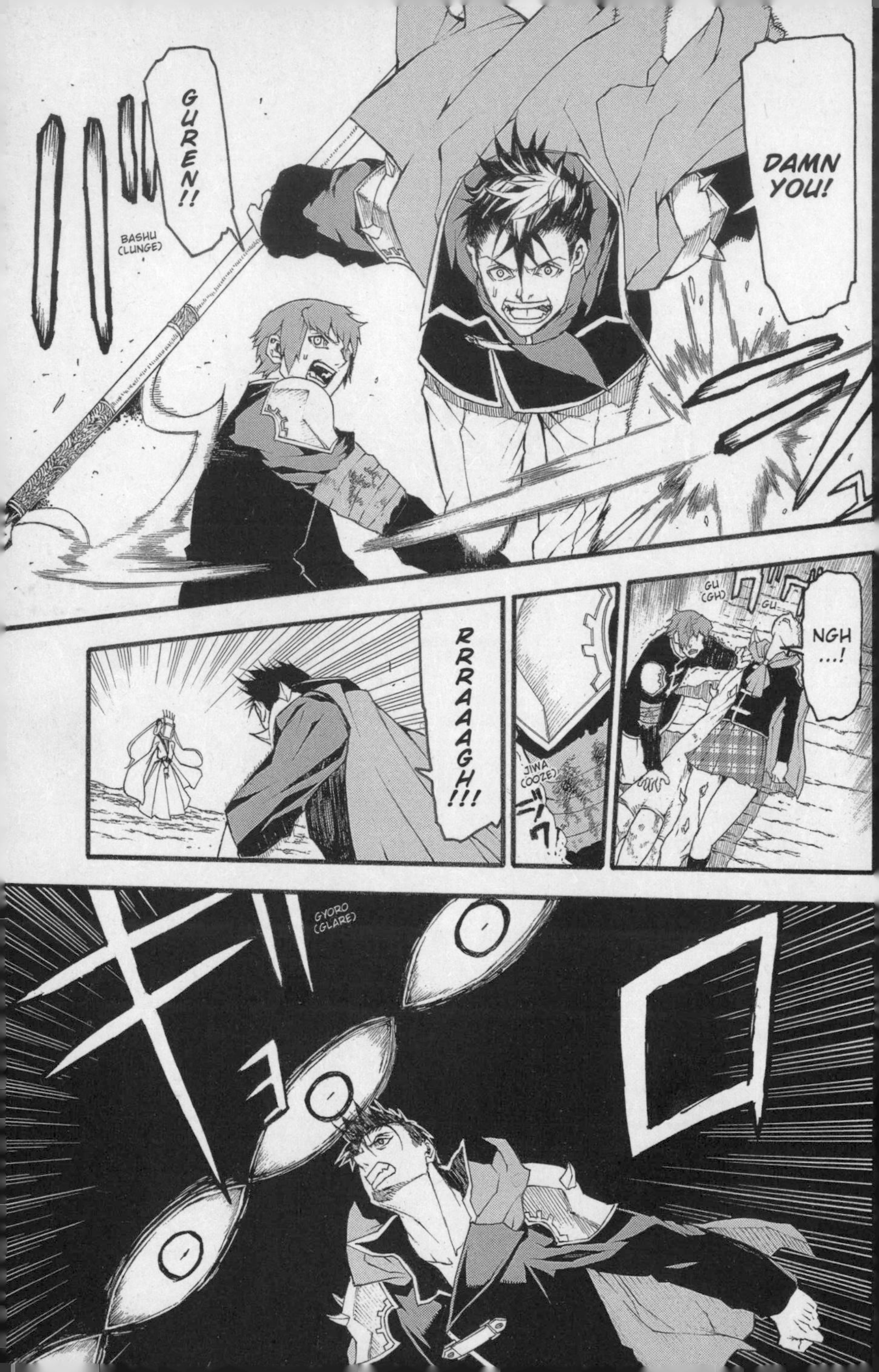
DAMN YOU!
GUREN!!
BASHU (LUNGE)
GU (GH)
GU
NGH ...!
JIWA (OOZE)
RRRAAAAGH!!!
GYORO (GLARE)

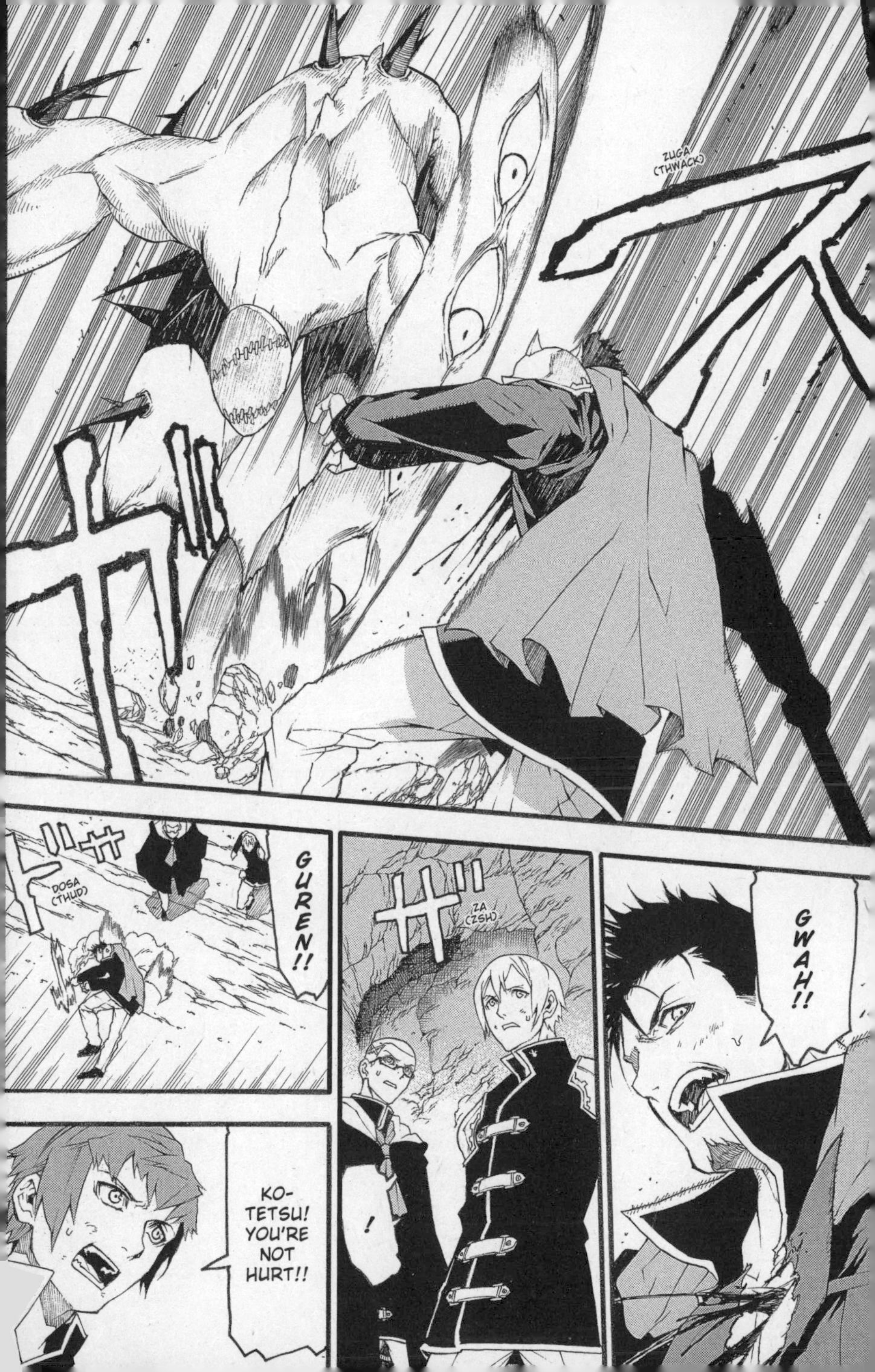
ZUGA (THWACK)
GWAH!!
ZA (ZSH)
!
GUREN!!
DOSA (THUD)
KO-TETSU! YOU'RE NOT HURT!!

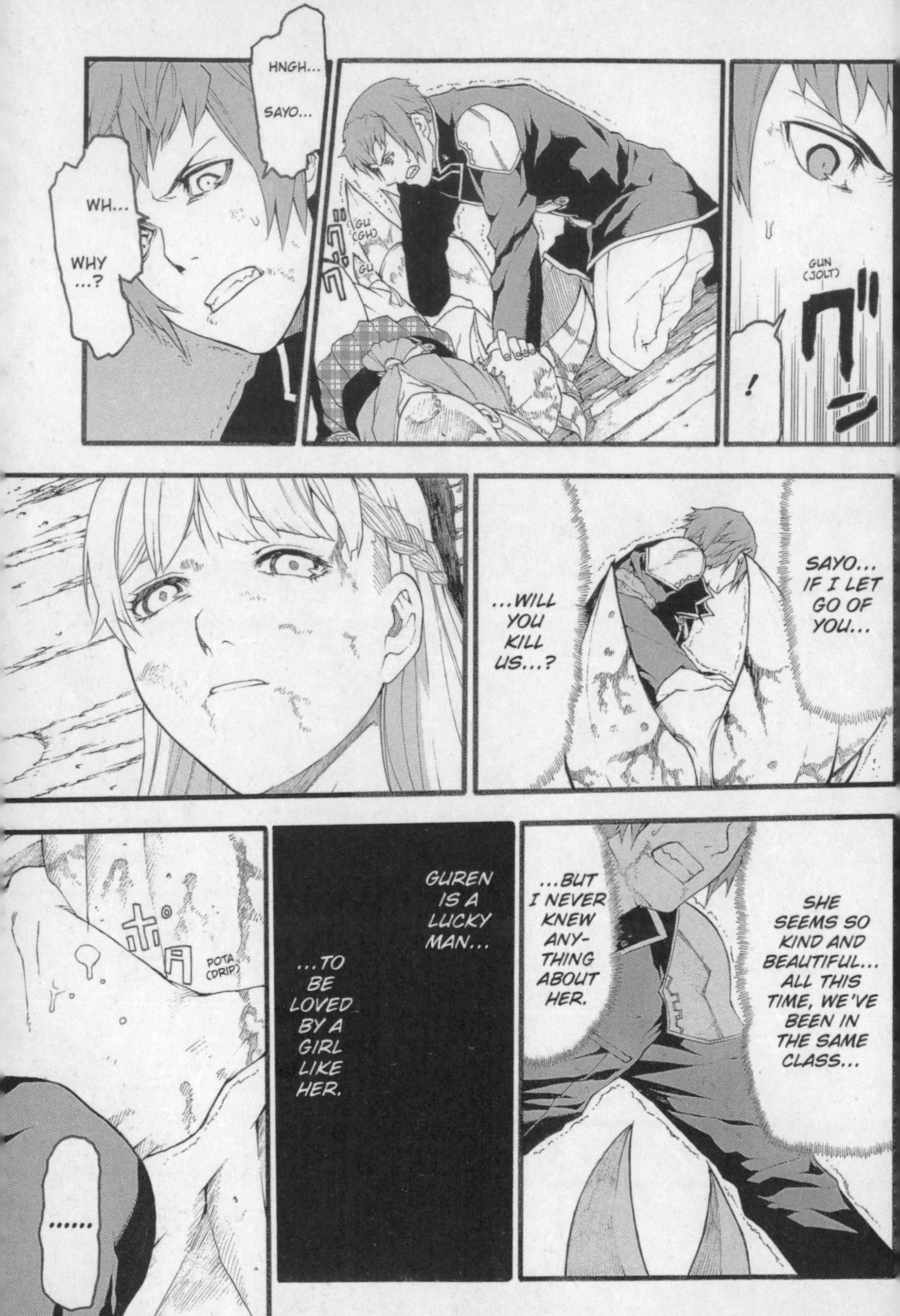
GUN (JOLT)
!
GU (GH)
GU
HNGH...
SAYO...
WH...
WHY ...?
SAYO... IF I LET GO OF YOU...
...WILL YOU KILL US...?
SHE SEEMS SO KIND AND BEAUTIFUL... ALL THIS TIME, WE'VE BEEN IN THE SAME CLASS...
...BUT I NEVER KNEW ANY-THING ABOUT HER.
GUREN IS A LUCKY MAN...
...TO BE LOVED BY A GIRL LIKE HER.
POTA (DRIP)
......

HNGH...

NNNGH...

...

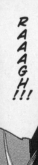

RAAAGH!!!

SHUBA (SHOOM)

GU CGHND

KO- TETSU ...?

...

SU (SS)

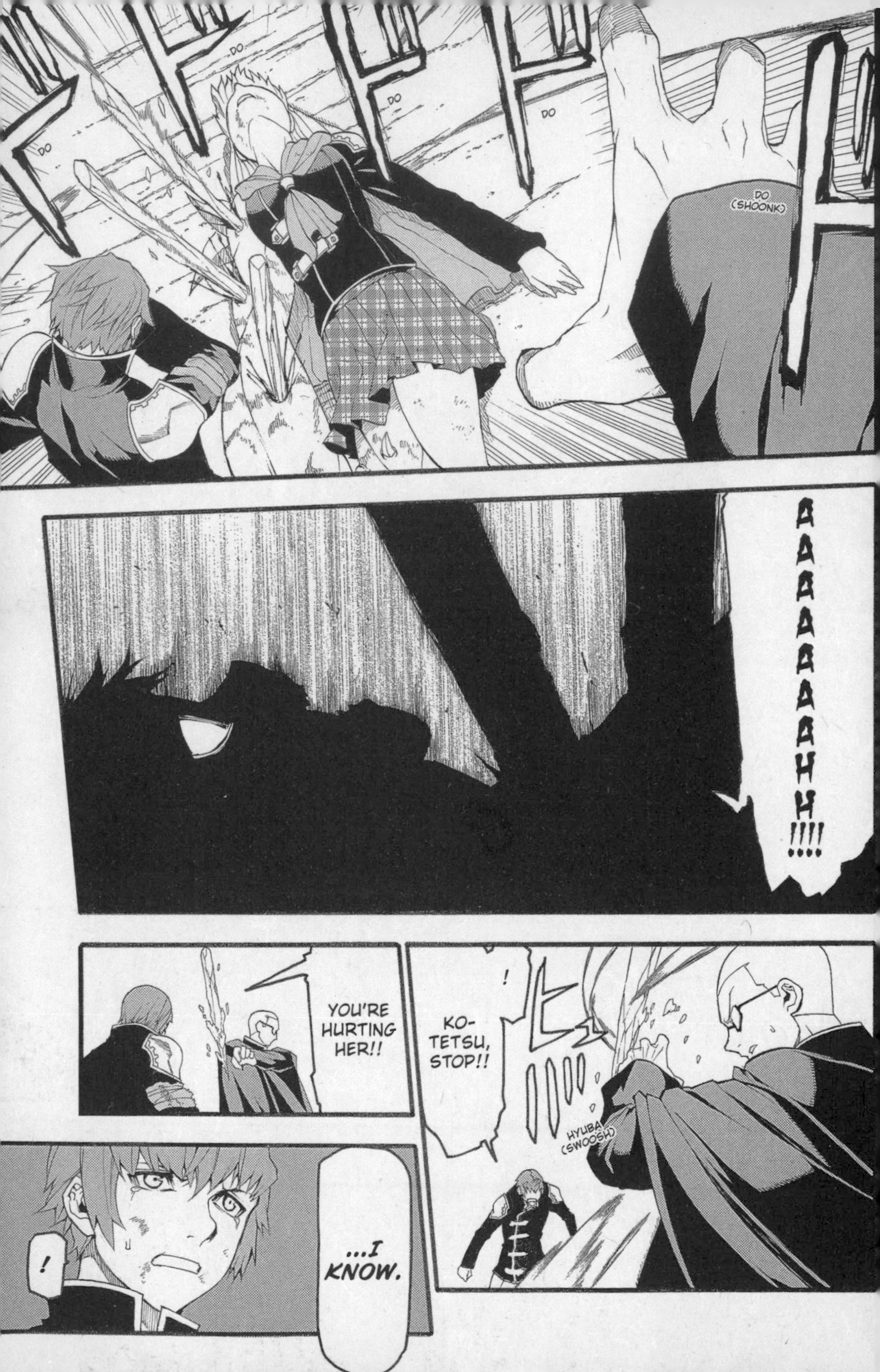

DO (SHOONK)
DO
DO
DO
DO
AAAAAAAAH!!!!
!
KO-TETSU, STOP!!
HYUBA (SWOOSH)
YOU'RE HURTING HER!!
!
...I KNOW.

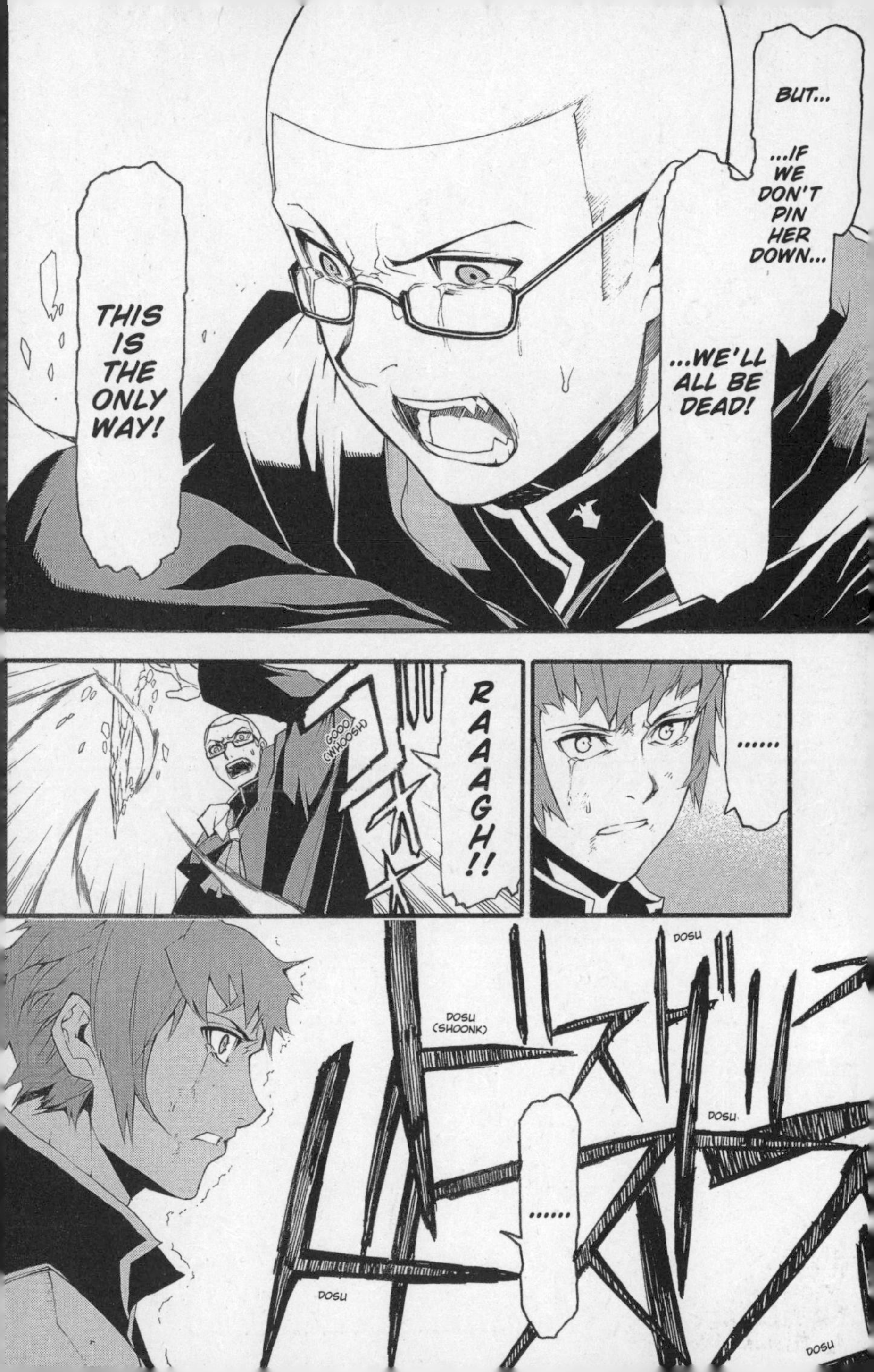
BUT...
...IF WE DON'T PIN HER DOWN...
...WE'LL ALL BE DEAD!
THIS IS THE ONLY WAY!
......
RAAAGH!!
GOOO (WHOOSH)
DOSU
DOSU (SHOONK)
DOSU
......
DOSU
DOSU

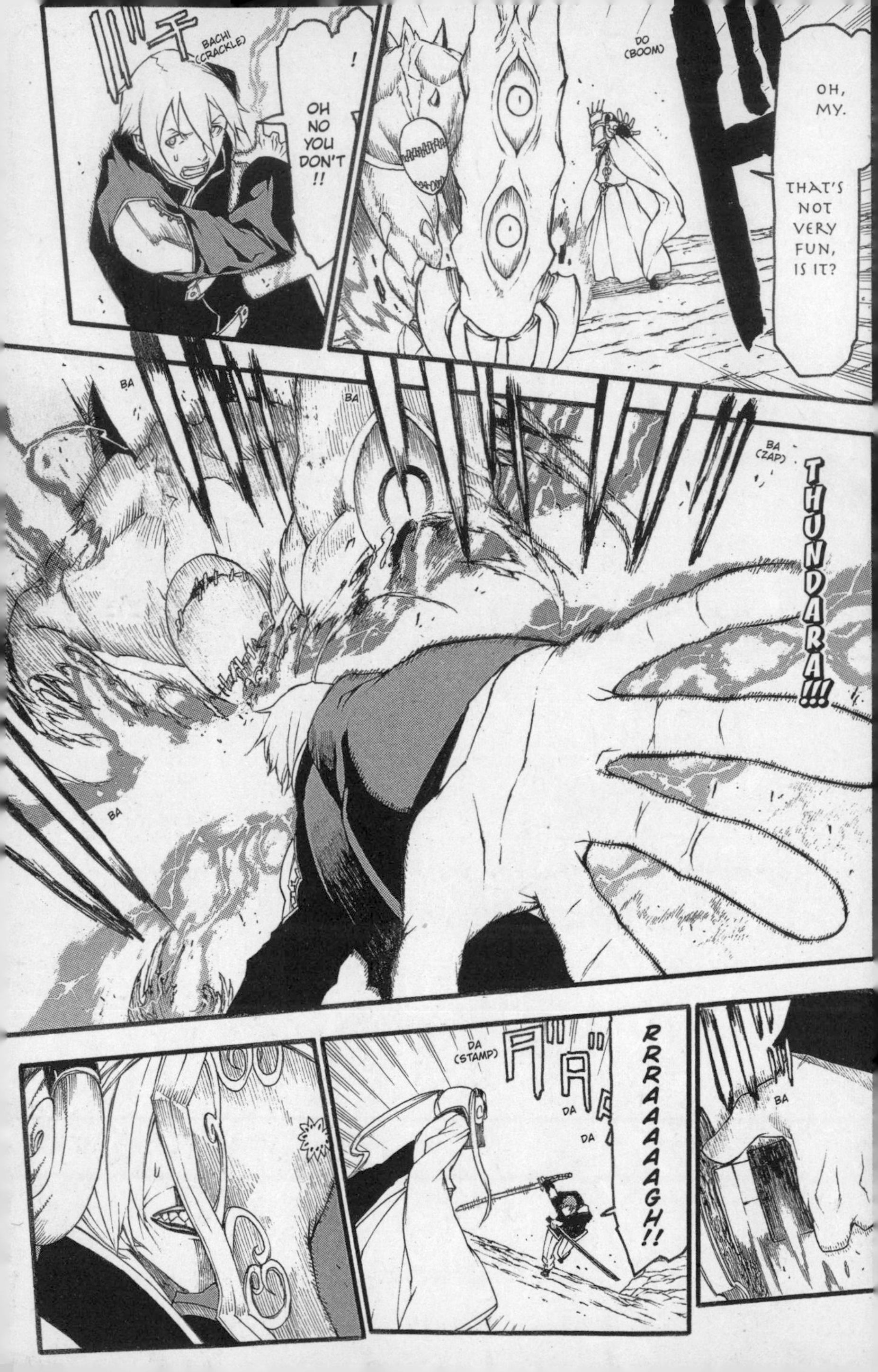
OH, MY.
THAT'S NOT VERY FUN, IS IT?
DO (BOOM)
!
OH NO YOU DON'T !!
BACHI (CRACKLE)
BA (ZAP)
THUNDARA!!!
BA
BA
BA
BA
RRRAAAAAAGH!!
DA (STAMP)
DA
DA

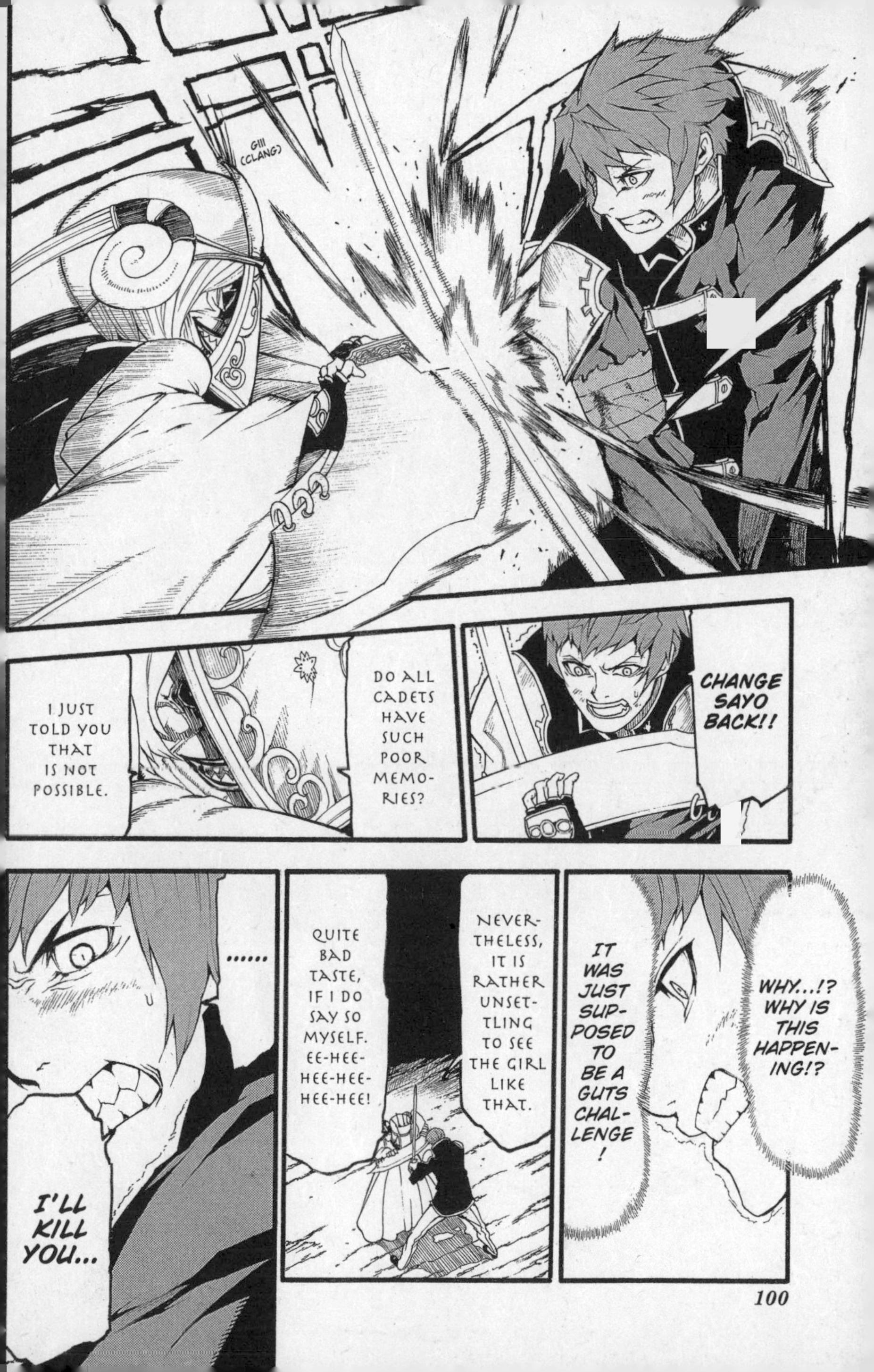
GIII
(CLANG)
CHANGE SAYO BACK!!
DO ALL CADETS HAVE SUCH POOR MEMORIES?
I JUST TOLD YOU THAT IS NOT POSSIBLE.
WHY...!? WHY IS THIS HAPPENING!?
IT WAS JUST SUPPOSED TO BE A GUTS CHALLENGE!
NEVERTHELESS, IT IS RATHER UNSETTLING TO SEE THE GIRL LIKE THAT.
QUITE BAD TASTE, IF I DO SAY SO MYSELF. EE-HEE-HEE-HEE-HEE-HEE!
......
I'LL KILL YOU...

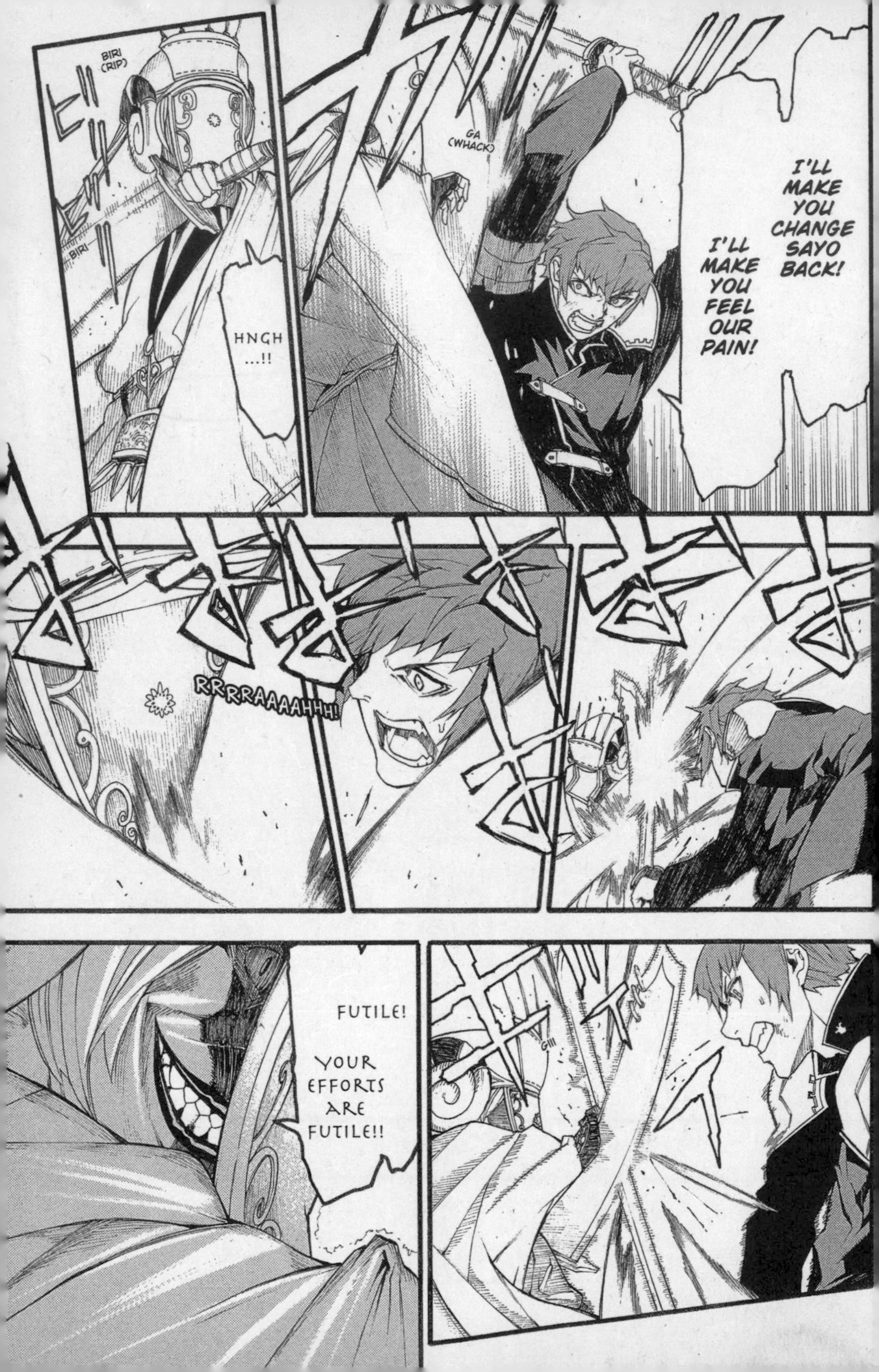
I'LL MAKE YOU CHANGE SAYO BACK!
I'LL MAKE YOU FEEL OUR PAIN!
GA (WHACK)
HNGH ...!!
BIRI (RIP)
BIRI
RRRRAAAAHHH!
GIII
FUTILE!
YOUR EFFORTS ARE FUTILE!!

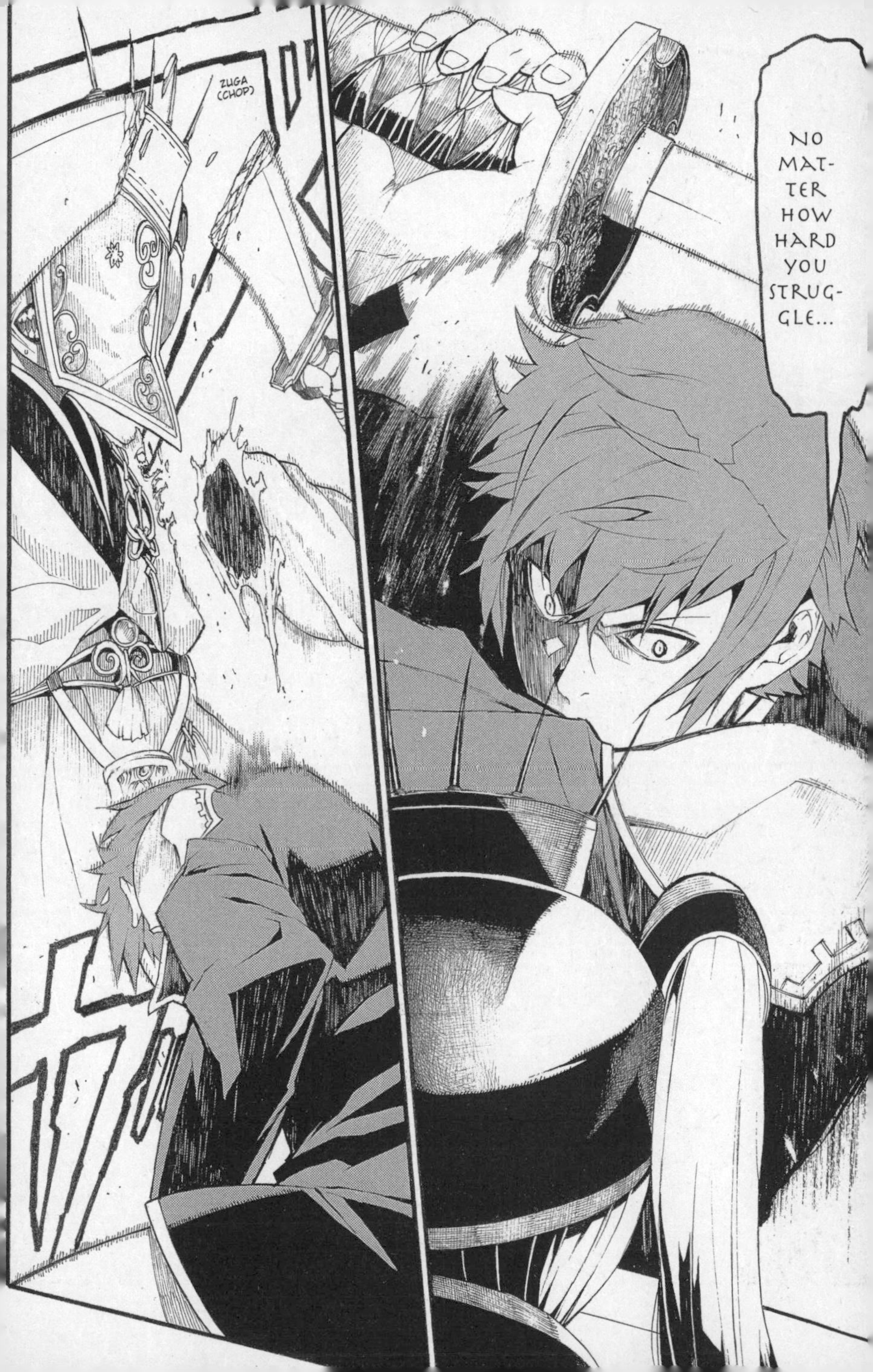
NO MATTER HOW HARD YOU STRUGGLE...
ZUGA (CHOP)

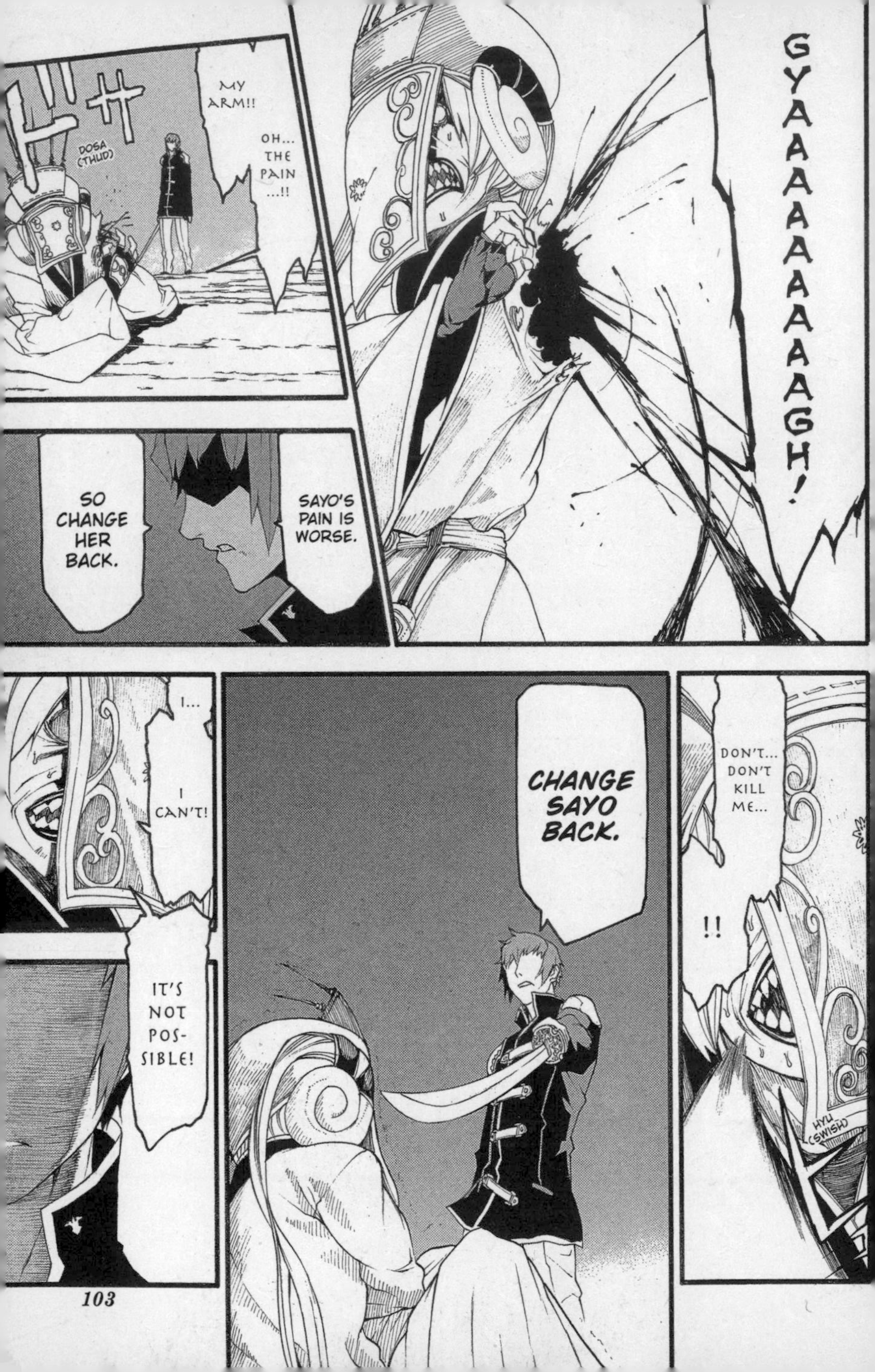
GYAAAAAAAAAGH!
MY ARM!!
OH... THE PAIN ...!!
DOSA (THUD)
SAYO'S PAIN IS WORSE.
SO CHANGE HER BACK.
DON'T... DON'T KILL ME...
!!
HYU (SWISH)
CHANGE SAYO BACK.
I...
I CAN'T!
IT'S NOT POS-SIBLE!

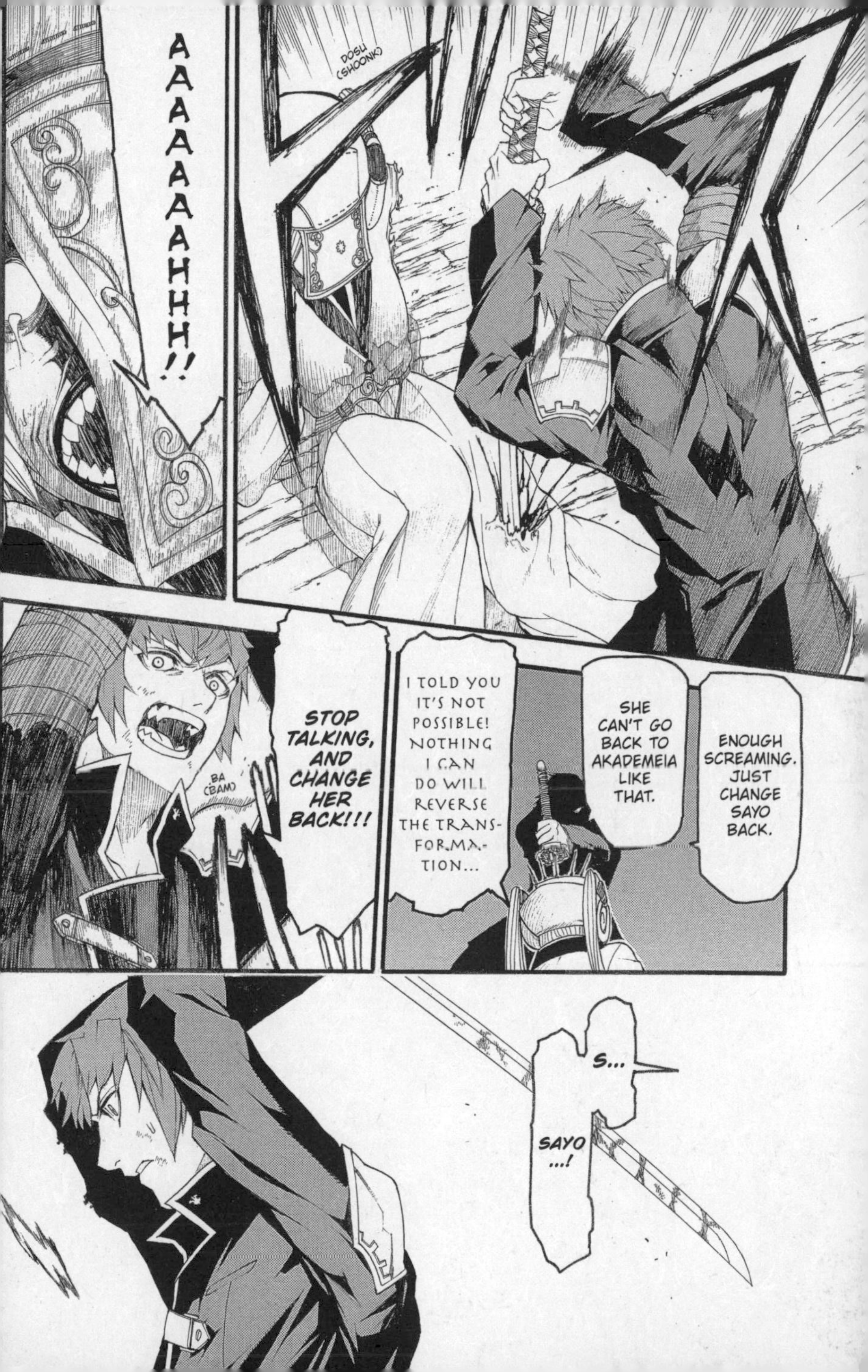
DOSU (SHOONK)
AAAAAAAHHH!!
ENOUGH SCREAMING. JUST CHANGE SAYO BACK.
SHE CAN'T GO BACK TO AKADEMEIA LIKE THAT.
I TOLD YOU IT'S NOT POSSIBLE! NOTHING I CAN DO WILL REVERSE THE TRANS-FORMA-TION...
STOP TALKING, AND CHANGE HER BACK!!!
BA (BAM)
S...
SAYO ...!

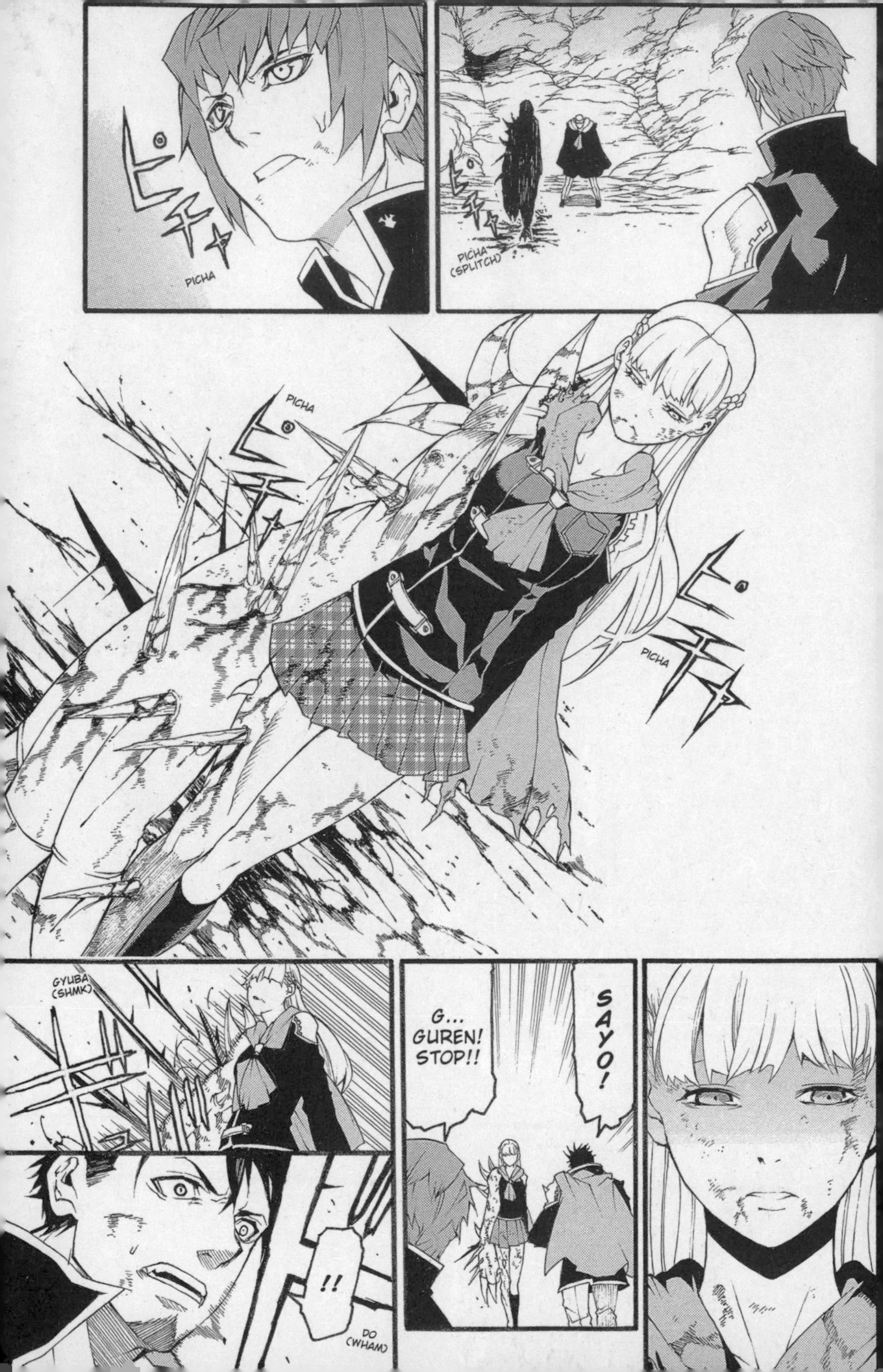

ピチャ
PICHA (SPLITCH)
ピチャ
PICHA
ピチャ
PICHA
ピチャ
PICHA
SAYO!
G... GUREN! STOP!!
GYUBA (SHMK)
!!
DO (WHAM)

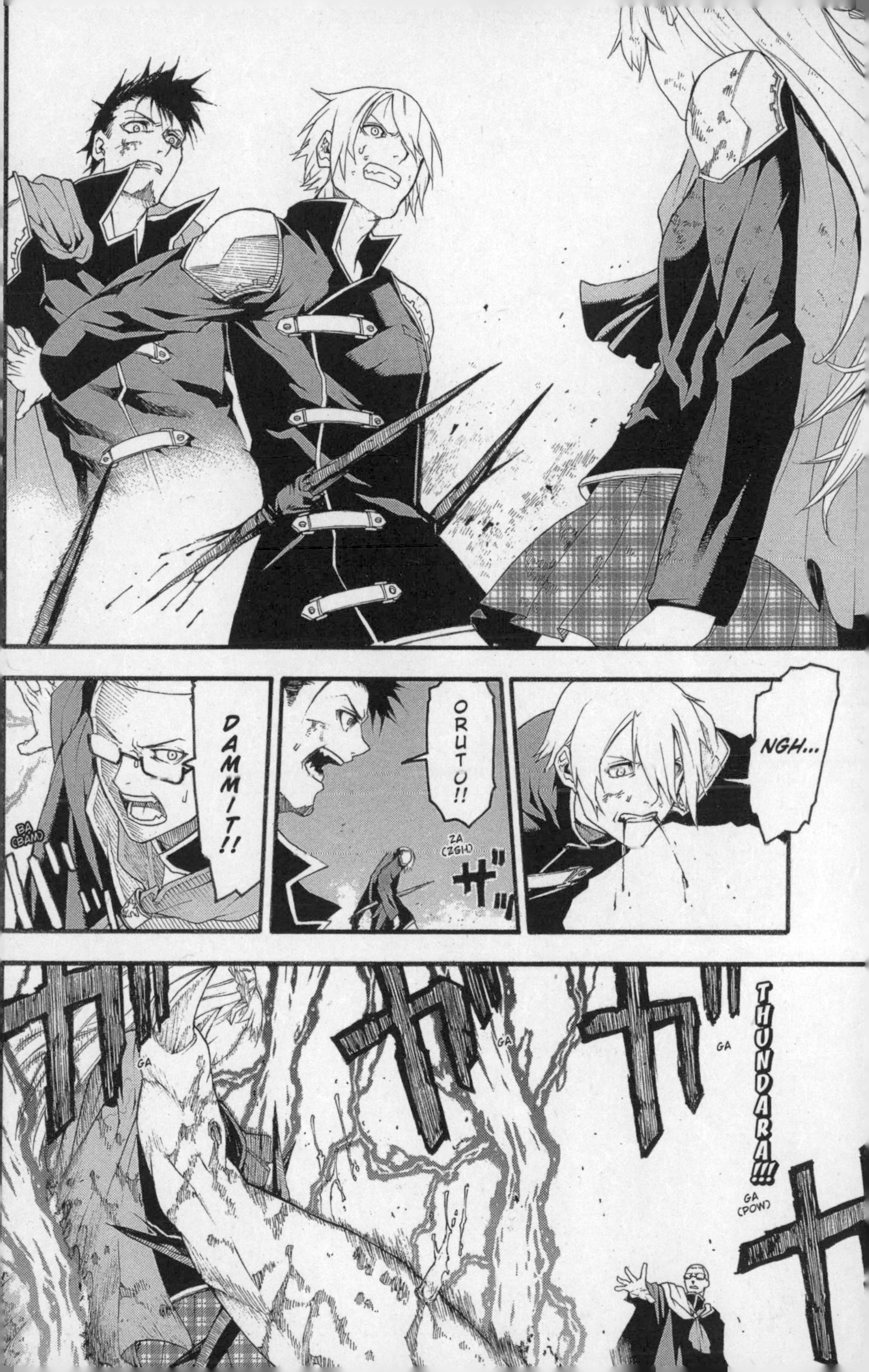
NGH...
ORUTO!!
ZA (ZGH)
DAMMIT!!
BA (BAM)
THUNDARA!!!
GA
GA (POW)
GA
GA

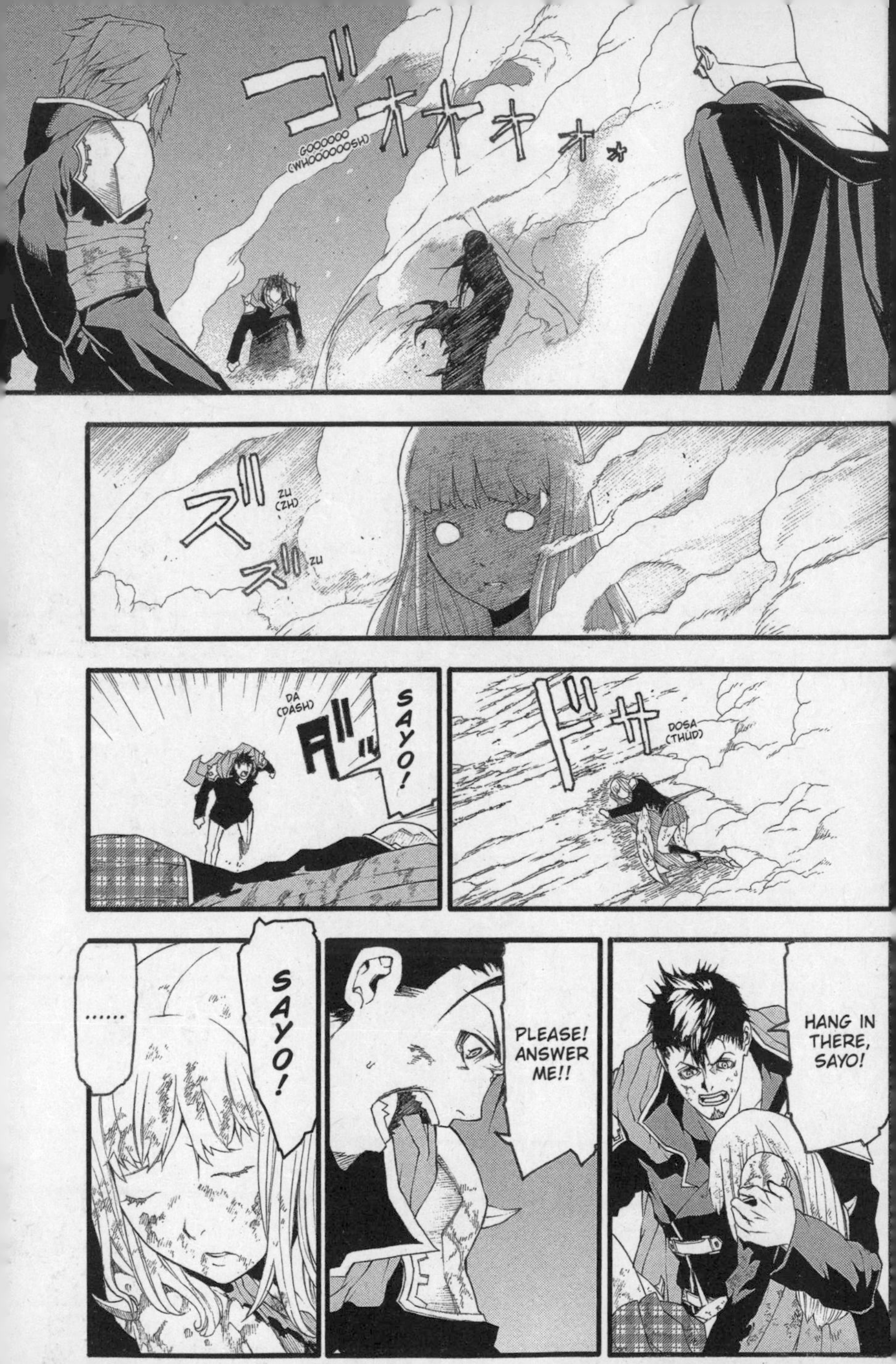
ゴオオオオォ
GOOOOOO (WHOOOOOOSH)
ズズ
ZU (ZH)
ZU
ドサ
DOSA (THUD)
SAYO!
ダッ
DA (DASH)
HANG IN THERE, SAYO!
PLEASE! ANSWER ME!!
SAYO!
......

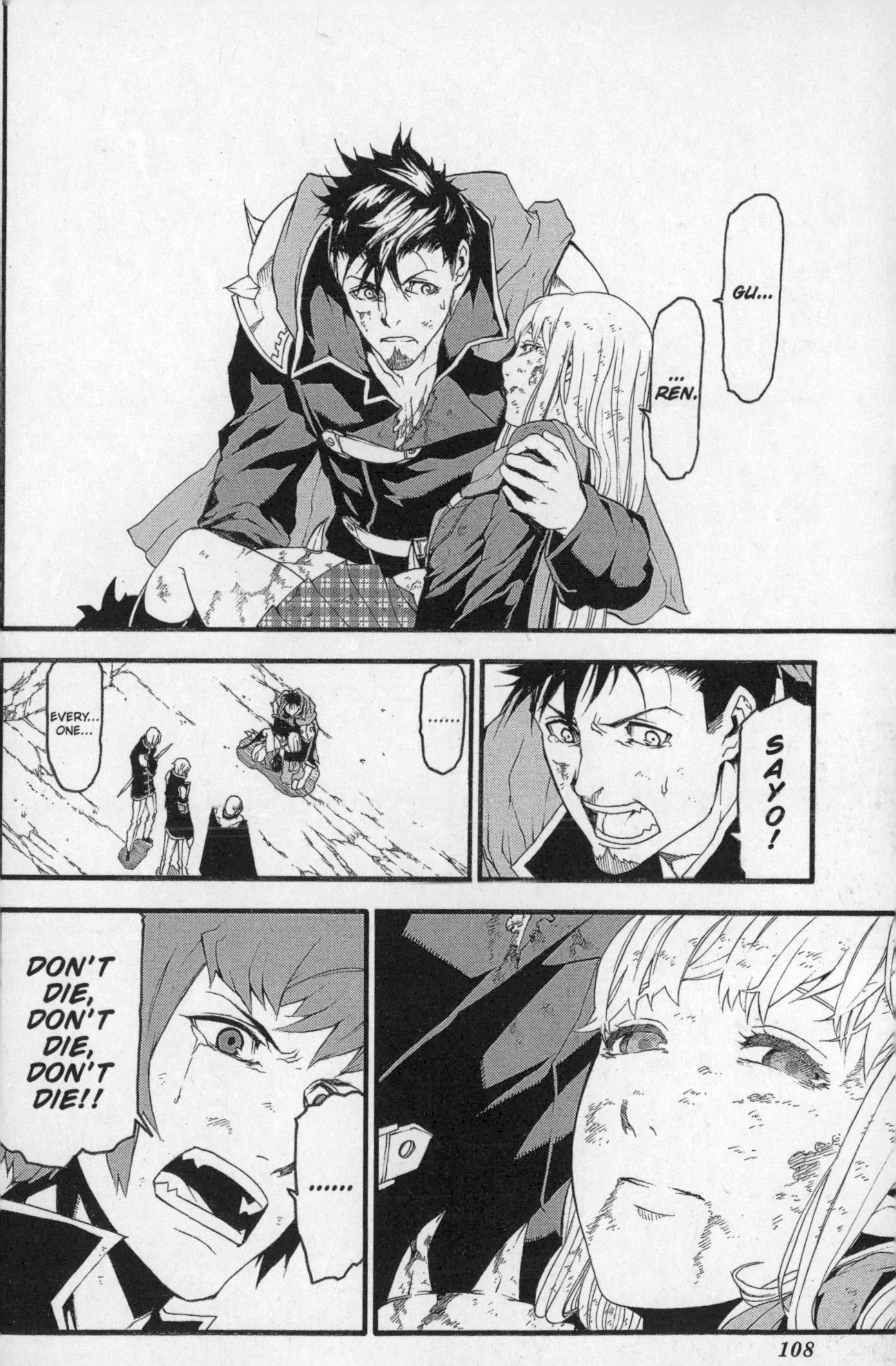
GU...
...REN.
SAYO!
......
EVERY... ONE...
DON'T DIE, DON'T DIE, DON'T DIE!!
......

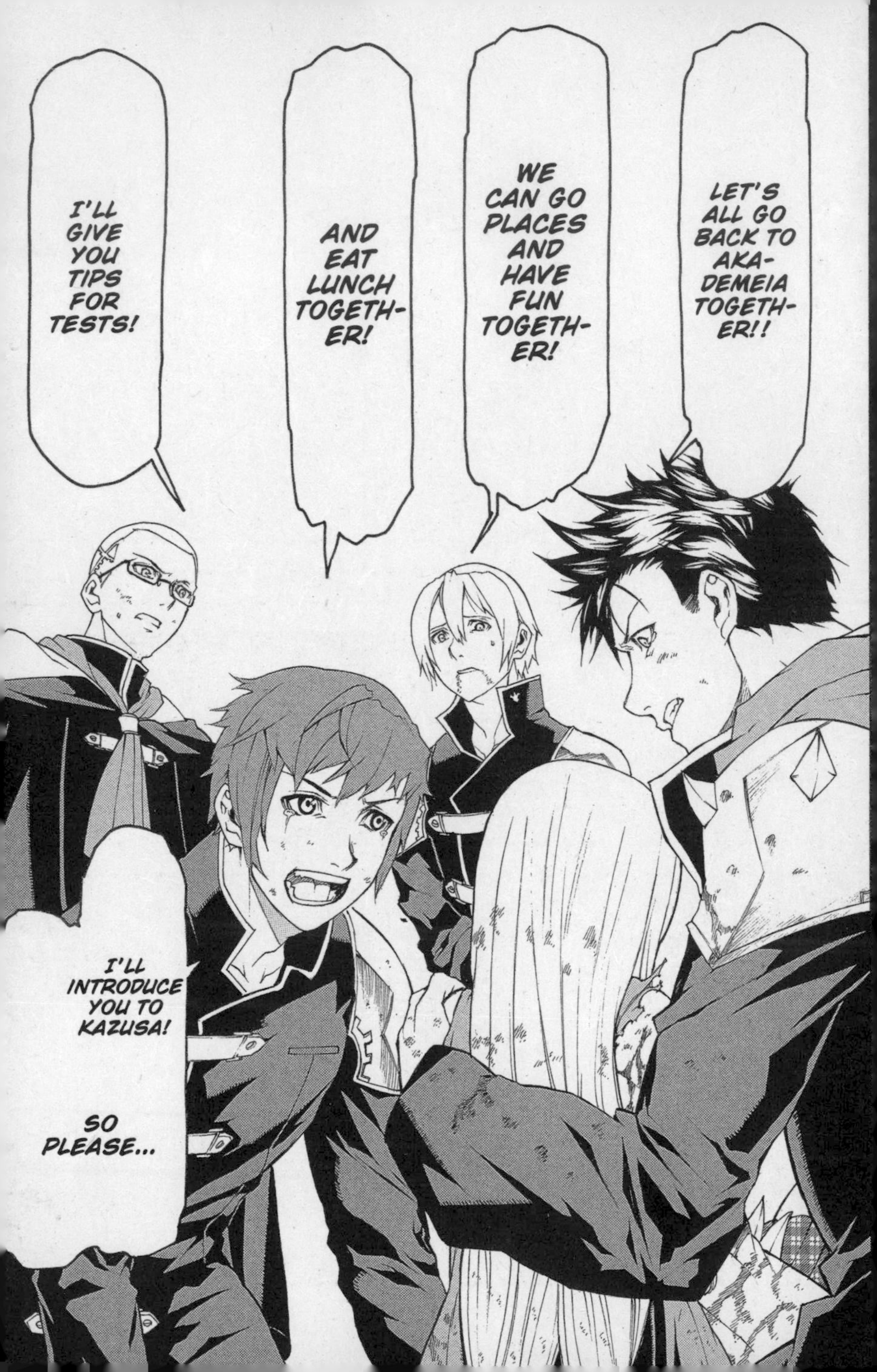
LET'S ALL GO BACK TO AKA-DEMEIA TOGETH-ER!!
WE CAN GO PLACES AND HAVE FUN TOGETH-ER!
AND EAT LUNCH TOGETH-ER!
I'LL GIVE YOU TIPS FOR TESTS!
I'LL INTRODUCE YOU TO KAZUSA!
SO PLEASE...

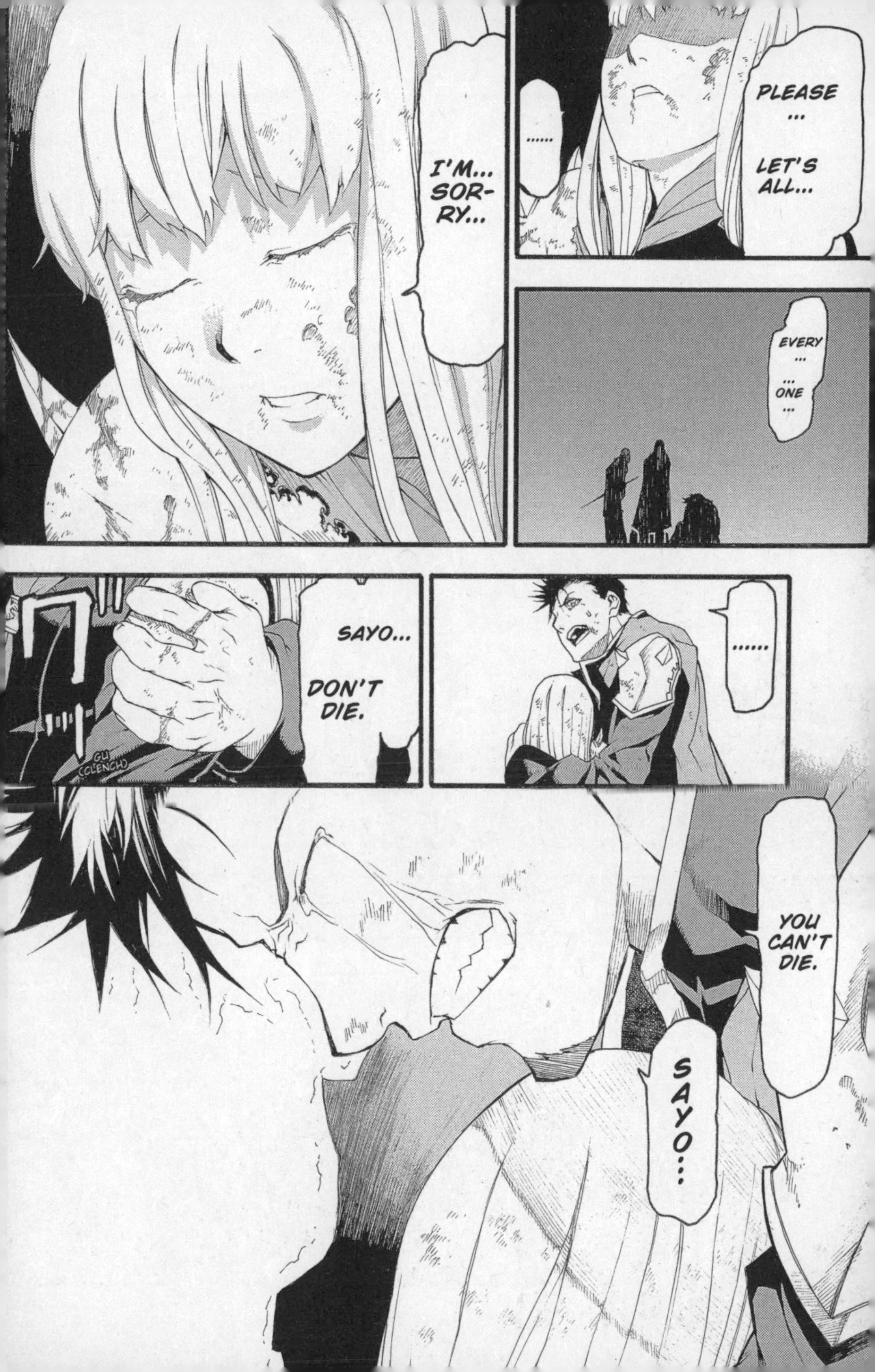
PLEASE ... LET'S ALL...
......
EVERY... ...ONE...
I'M... SORRY...
......
SAYO...
DON'T DIE.
GU (CLENCH)
YOU CAN'T DIE.
SAYO...

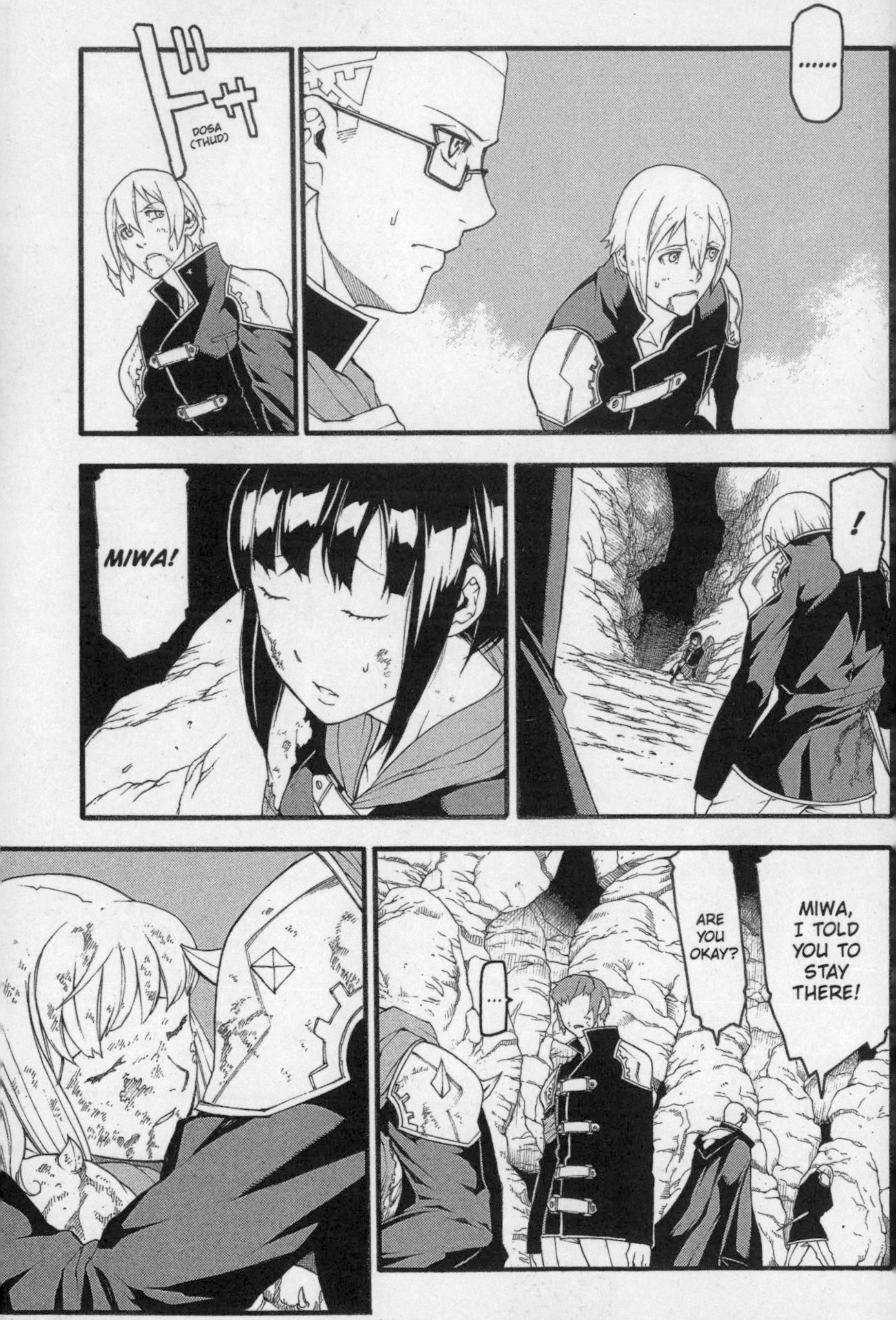
……
ドサ
DOSA (THUD)
!
MIWA!
MIWA, I TOLD YOU TO STAY THERE!
ARE YOU OKAY?
…

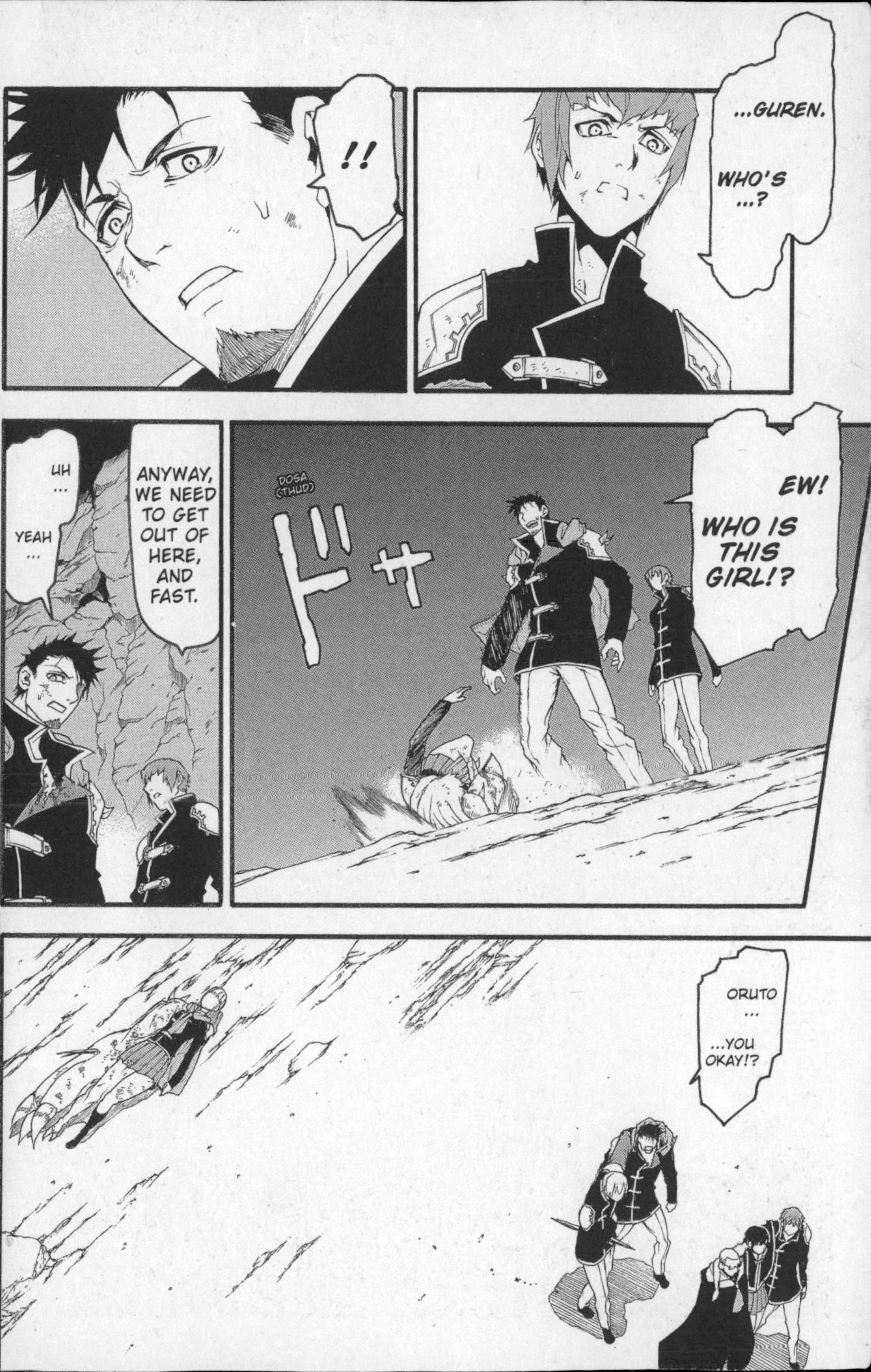
...GUREN.
WHO'S ...?
!!
EW!
WHO IS THIS GIRL!?
DOSA (THUD)
ドサ
ANYWAY, WE NEED TO GET OUT OF HERE, AND FAST.
UH ... YEAH ...
ORUTO ...
...YOU OKAY!?
...

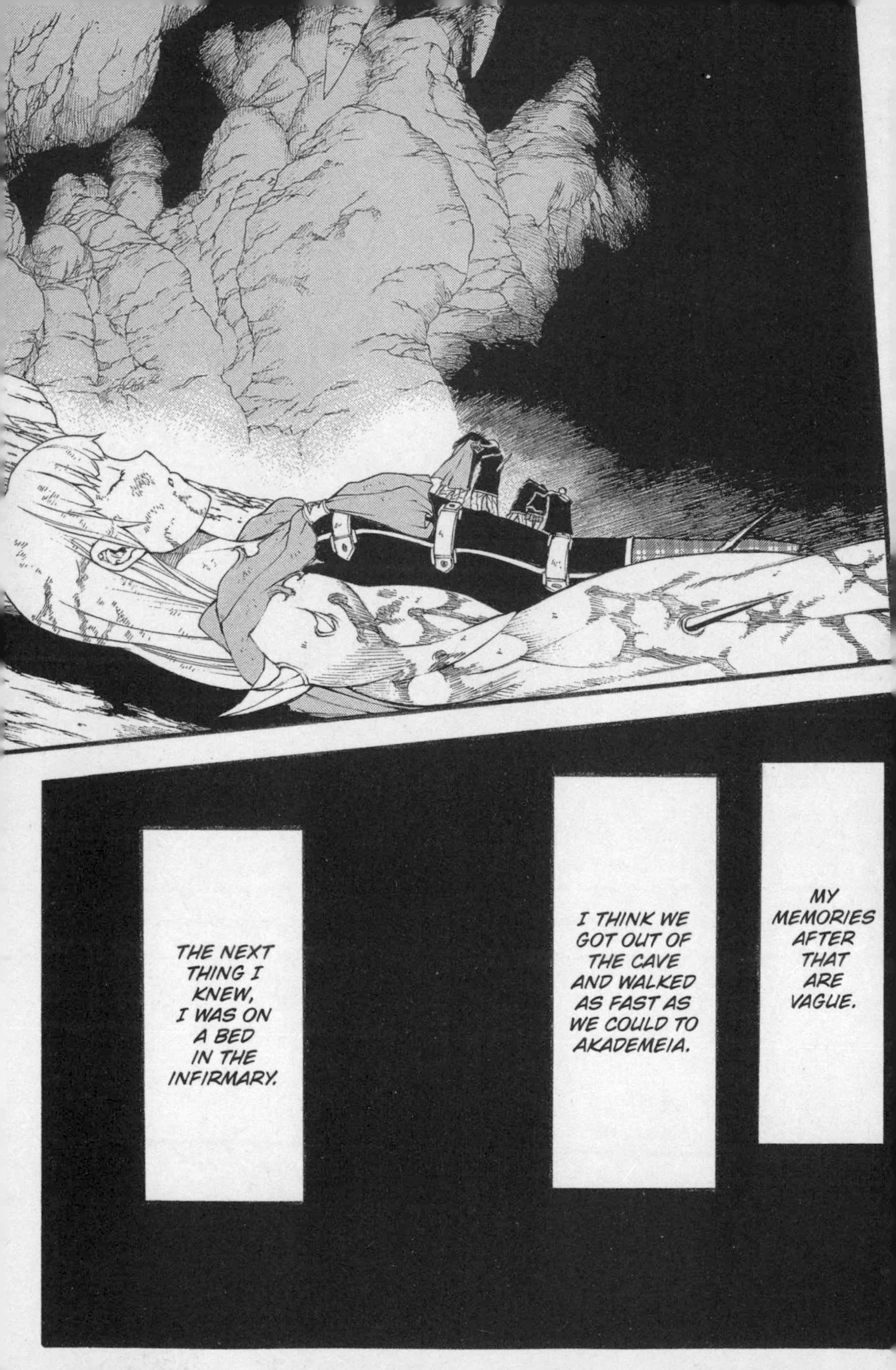
MY MEMORIES AFTER THAT ARE VAGUE.
I THINK WE GOT OUT OF THE CAVE AND WALKED AS FAST AS WE COULD TO AKADEMEIA.
THE NEXT THING I KNEW, I WAS ON A BED IN THE INFIRMARY.

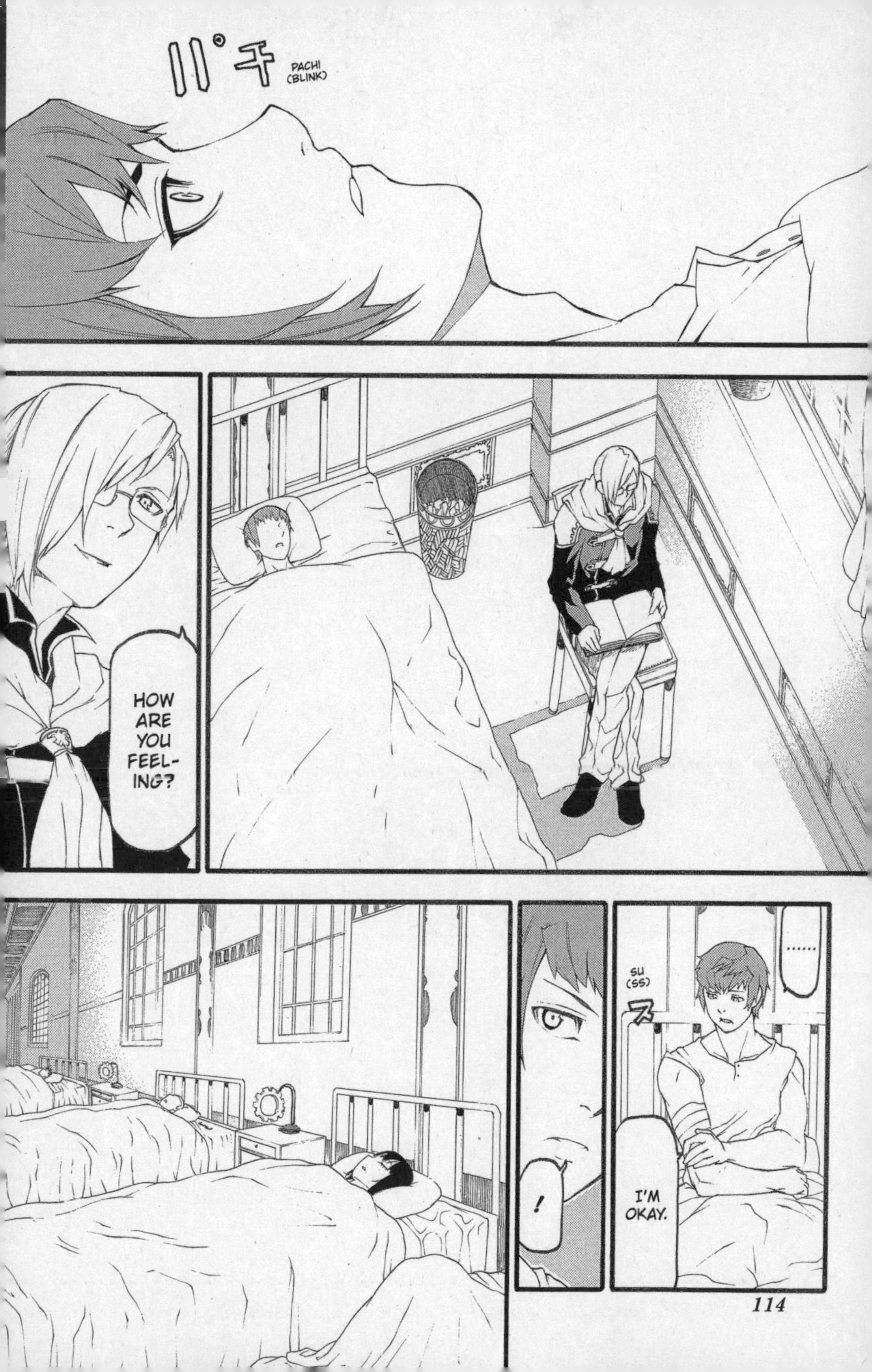
パチ
PACHI (BLINK)
HOW ARE YOU FEEL-ING?
......
ス
SU (SS)
I'M OKAY.
!

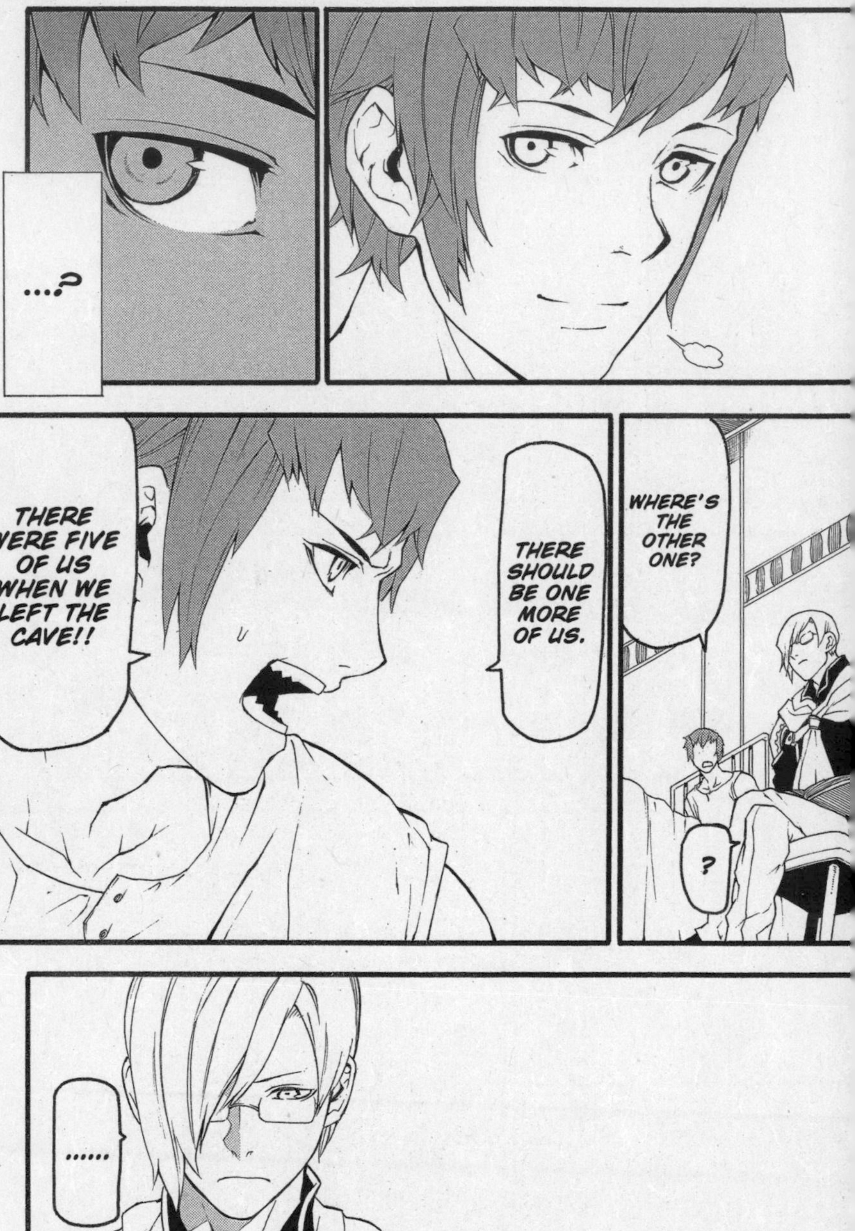
...?
WHERE'S THE OTHER ONE?
?
THERE SHOULD BE ONE MORE OF US.
THERE WERE FIVE OF US WHEN WE LEFT THE CAVE!!
......

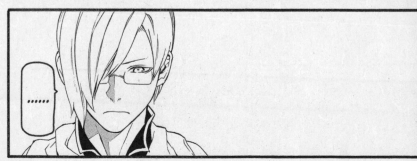

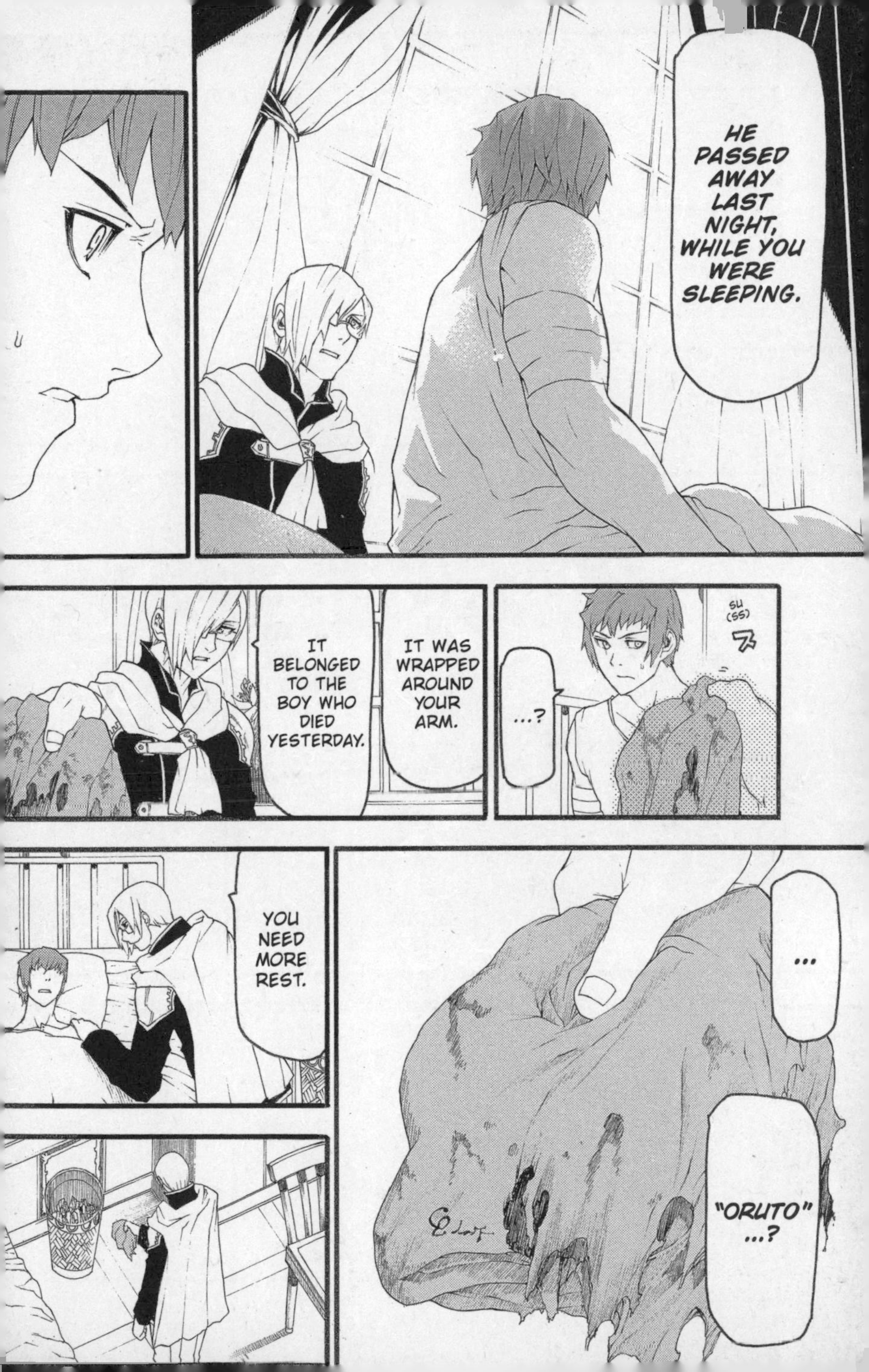
HE PASSED AWAY LAST NIGHT, WHILE YOU WERE SLEEPING.
SU (SS)
...?
IT WAS WRAPPED AROUND YOUR ARM.
IT BELONGED TO THE BOY WHO DIED YESTERDAY.
...
"ORUTO" ...?
YOU NEED MORE REST.

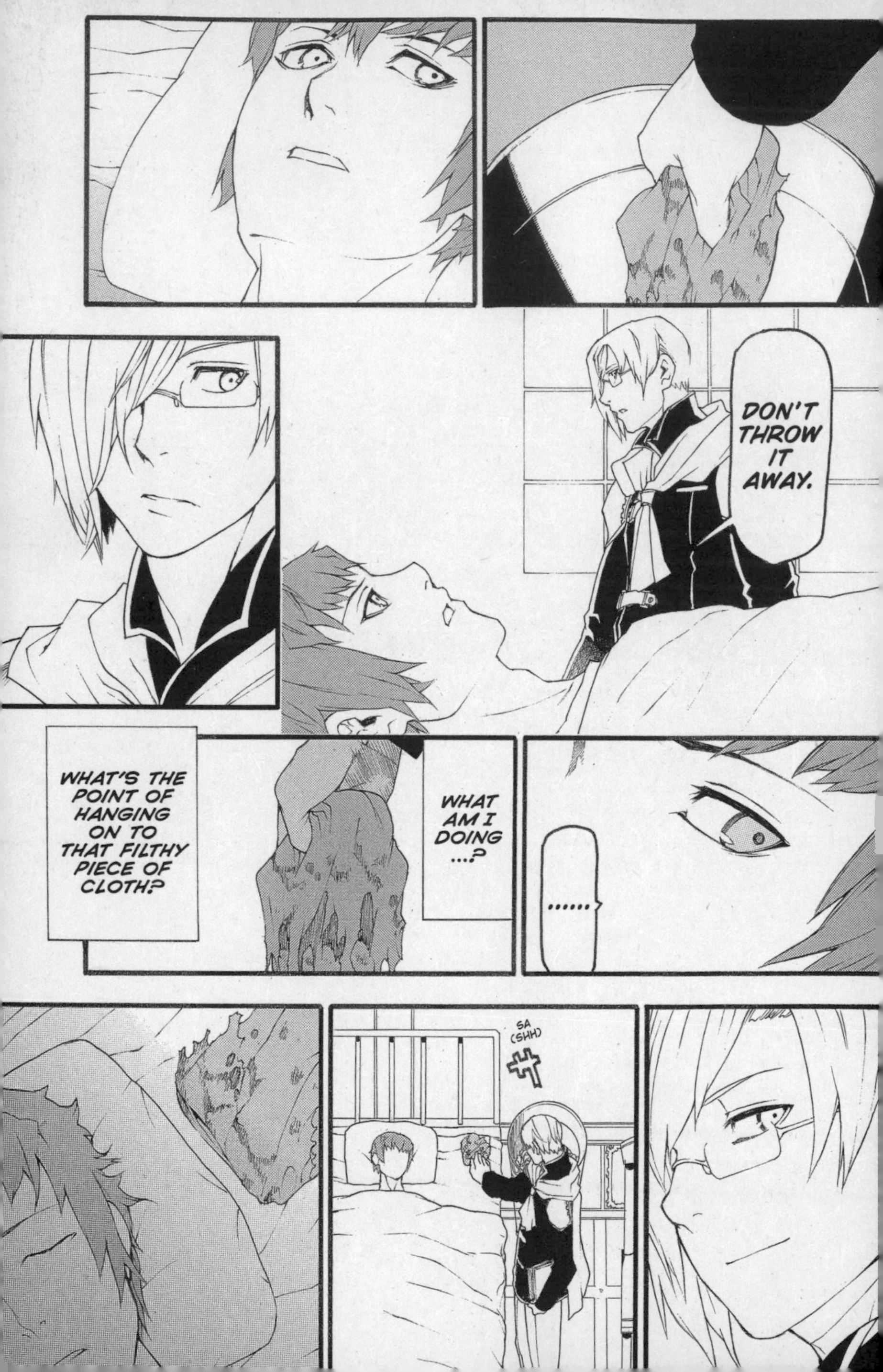
DON'T THROW IT AWAY.
......
WHAT AM I DOING ...?
WHAT'S THE POINT OF HANGING ON TO THAT FILTHY PIECE OF CLOTH?
SA (SHH)

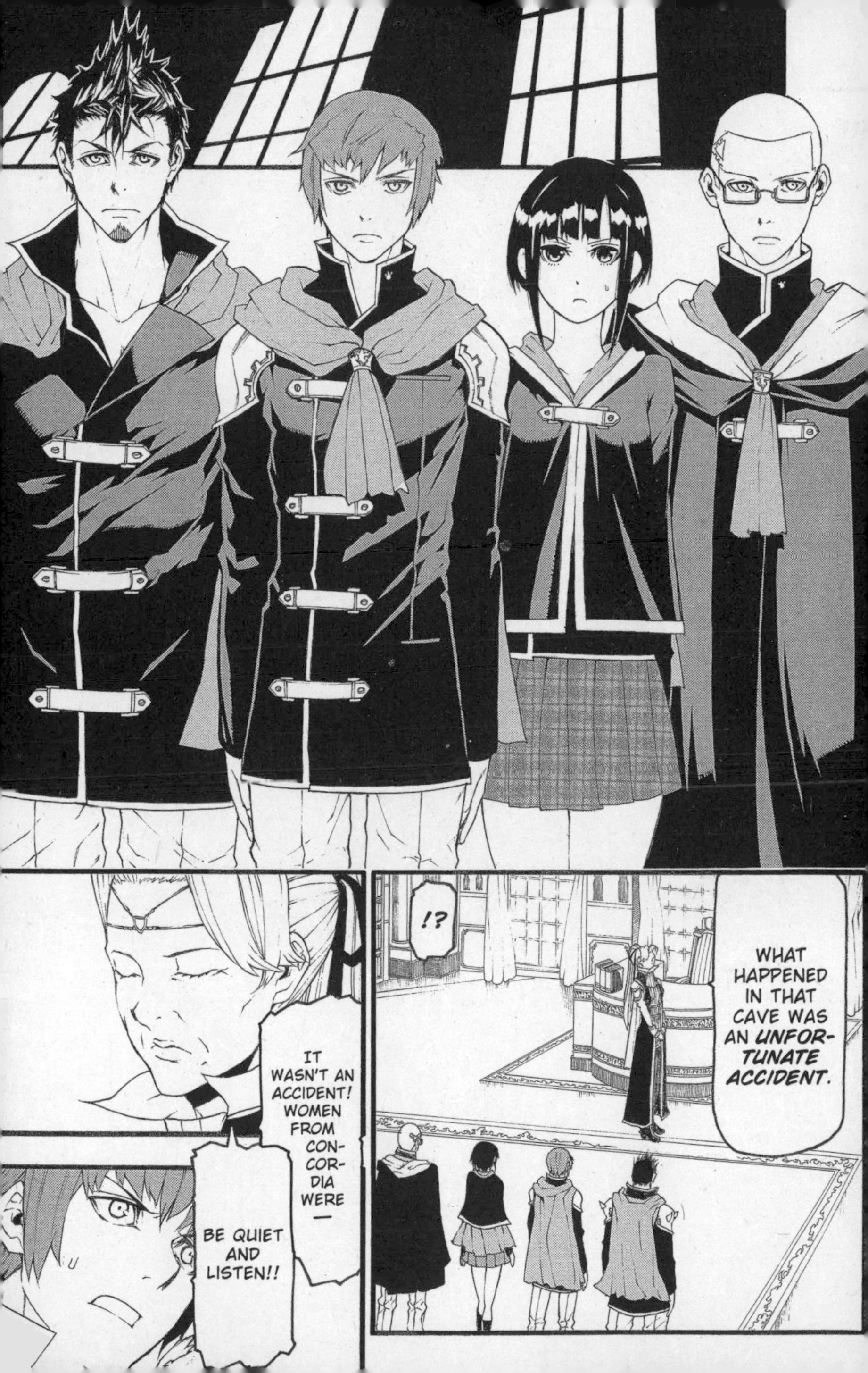
WHAT HAPPENED IN THAT CAVE WAS AN UNFORTUNATE ACCIDENT.
!?
IT WASN'T AN ACCIDENT! WOMEN FROM CONCORDIA WERE—
BE QUIET AND LISTEN!!

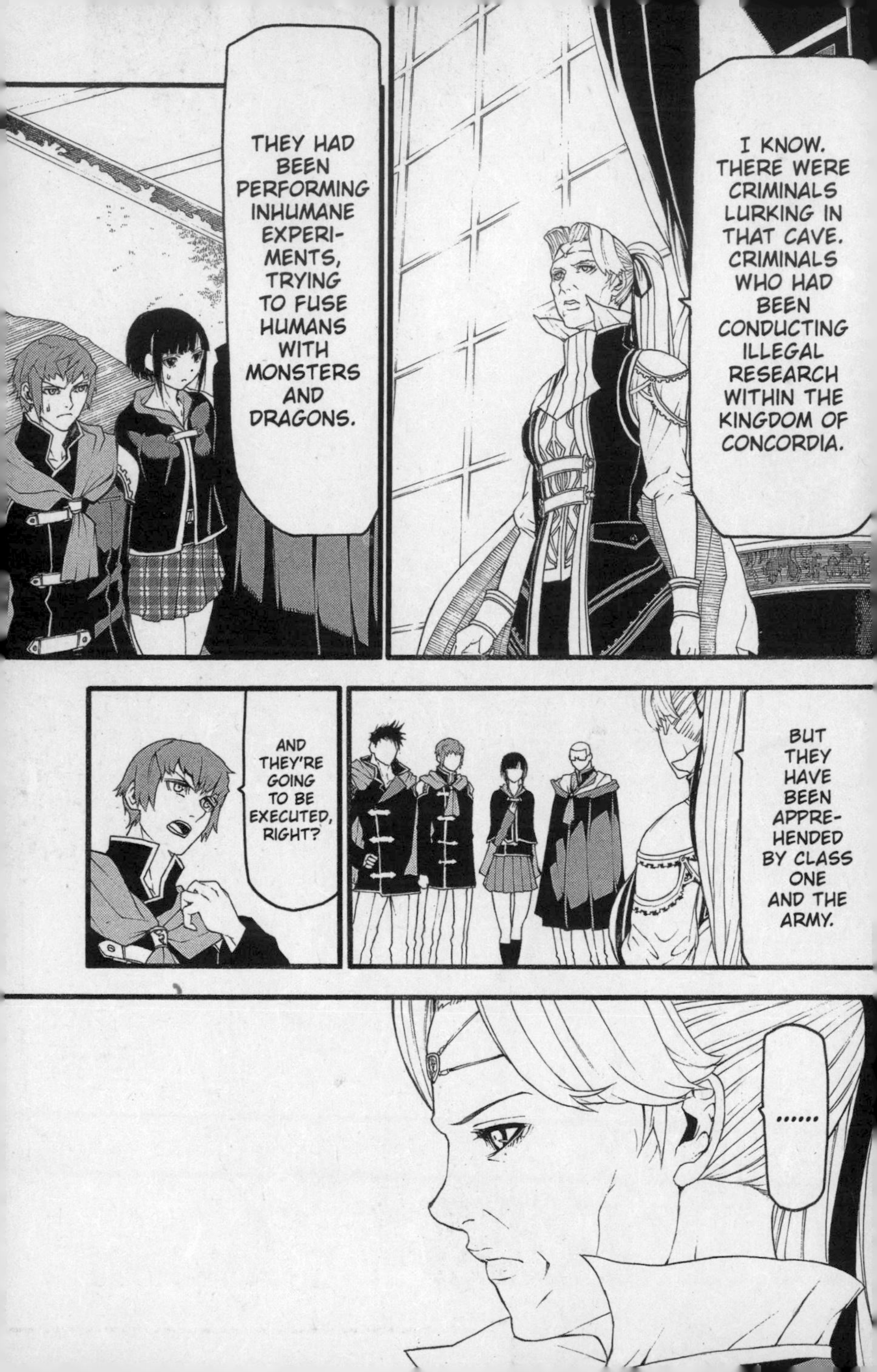
I KNOW. THERE WERE CRIMINALS LURKING IN THAT CAVE. CRIMINALS WHO HAD BEEN CONDUCTING ILLEGAL RESEARCH WITHIN THE KINGDOM OF CONCORDIA.
THEY HAD BEEN PERFORMING INHUMANE EXPERI-MENTS, TRYING TO FUSE HUMANS WITH MONSTERS AND DRAGONS.
BUT THEY HAVE BEEN APPRE-HENDED BY CLASS ONE AND THE ARMY.
AND THEY'RE GOING TO BE EXECUTED, RIGHT?
......

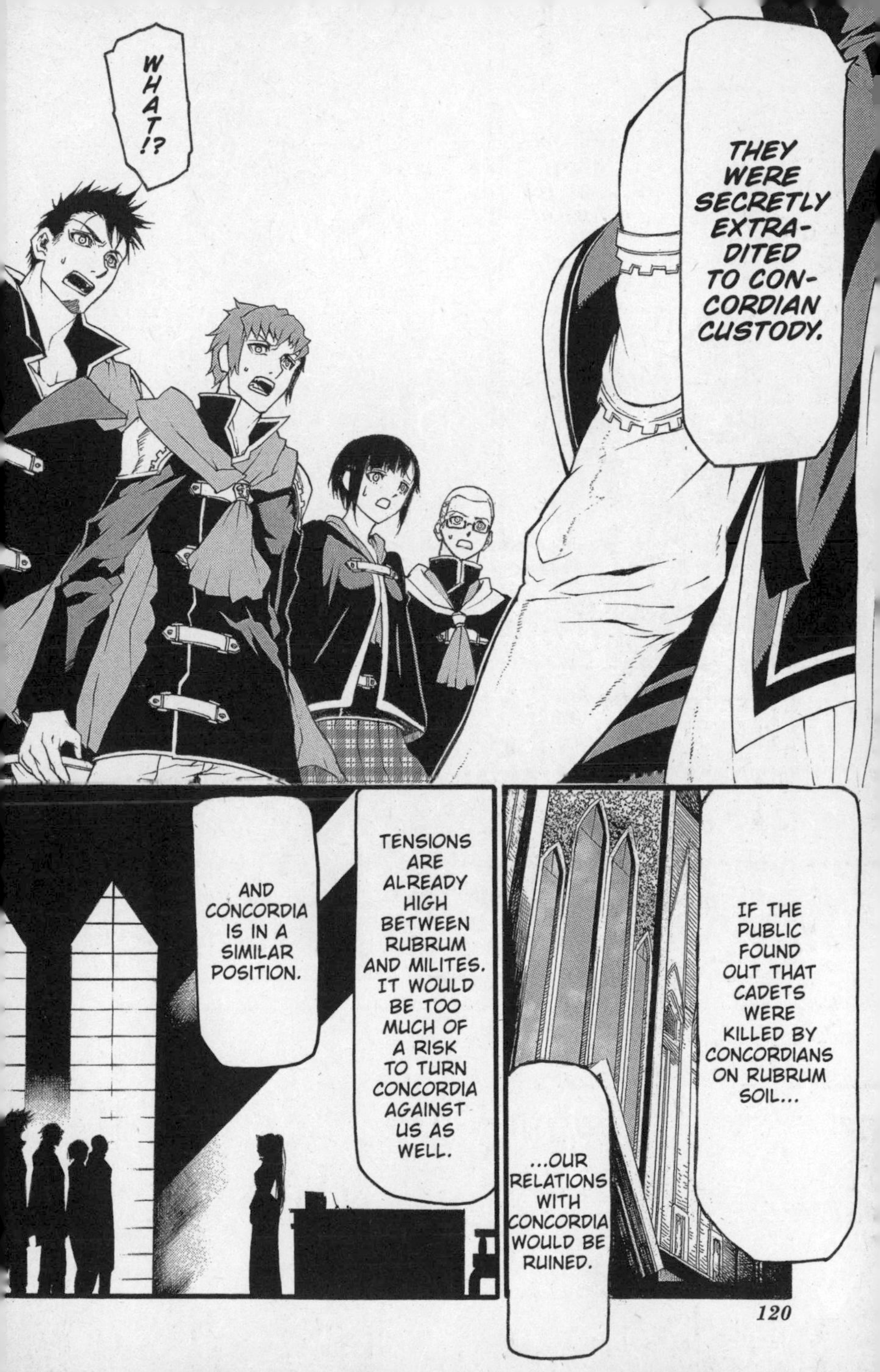
THEY WERE SECRETLY EXTRA-DITED TO CON-CORDIAN CUSTODY.
WHAT!?
IF THE PUBLIC FOUND OUT THAT CADETS WERE KILLED BY CONCORDIANS ON RUBRUM SOIL...
...OUR RELATIONS WITH CONCORDIA WOULD BE RUINED.
TENSIONS ARE ALREADY HIGH BETWEEN RUBRUM AND MILITES. IT WOULD BE TOO MUCH OF A RISK TO TURN CONCORDIA AGAINST US AS WELL.
AND CONCORDIA IS IN A SIMILAR POSITION.

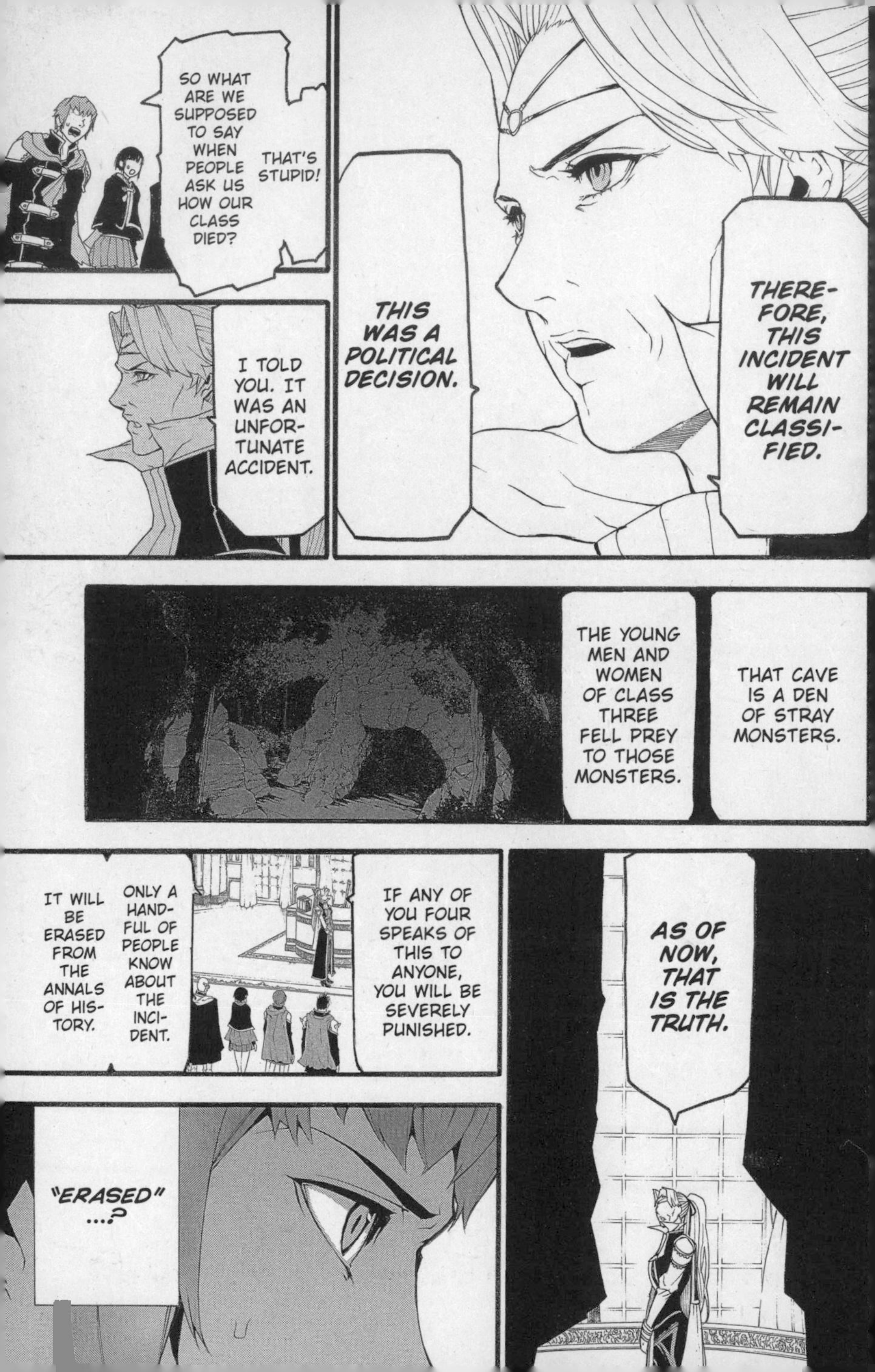
THEREFORE, THIS INCIDENT WILL REMAIN CLASSIFIED.
THIS WAS A POLITICAL DECISION.
SO WHAT ARE WE SUPPOSED TO SAY WHEN PEOPLE ASK US HOW OUR CLASS DIED?
THAT'S STUPID!
I TOLD YOU. IT WAS AN UNFORTUNATE ACCIDENT.
THAT CAVE IS A DEN OF STRAY MONSTERS.
THE YOUNG MEN AND WOMEN OF CLASS THREE FELL PREY TO THOSE MONSTERS.
AS OF NOW, THAT IS THE TRUTH.
IF ANY OF YOU FOUR SPEAKS OF THIS TO ANYONE, YOU WILL BE SEVERELY PUNISHED.
ONLY A HANDFUL OF PEOPLE KNOW ABOUT THE INCIDENT.
IT WILL BE ERASED FROM THE ANNALS OF HISTORY.
"ERASED" ...?

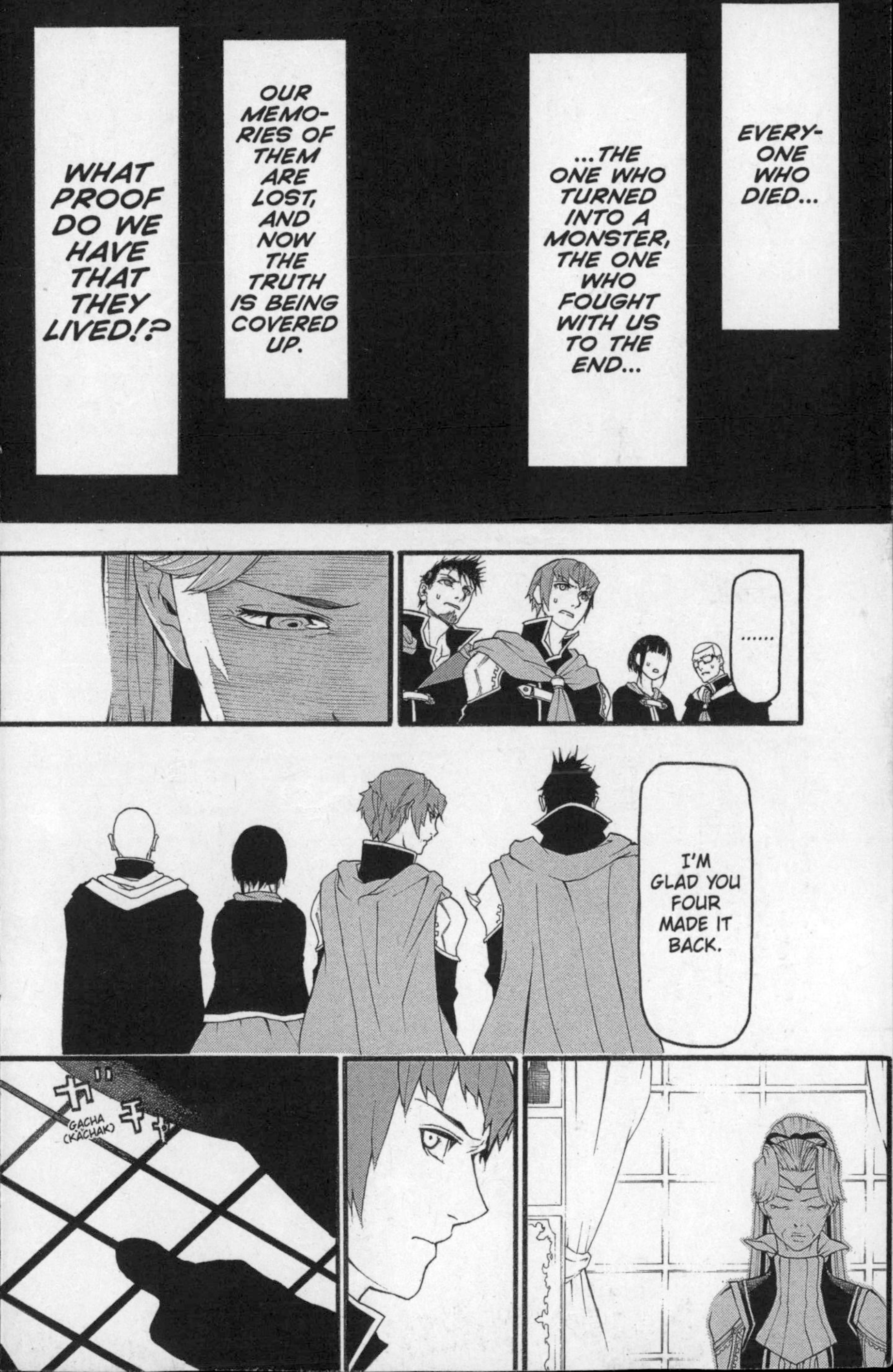
EVERY-ONE WHO DIED...
...THE ONE WHO TURNED INTO A MONSTER, THE ONE WHO FOUGHT WITH US TO THE END...
OUR MEMORIES OF THEM ARE LOST, AND NOW THE TRUTH IS BEING COVERED UP.
WHAT PROOF DO WE HAVE THAT THEY LIVED!?
......
I'M GLAD YOU FOUR MADE IT BACK.
GACHA (KACHAK)

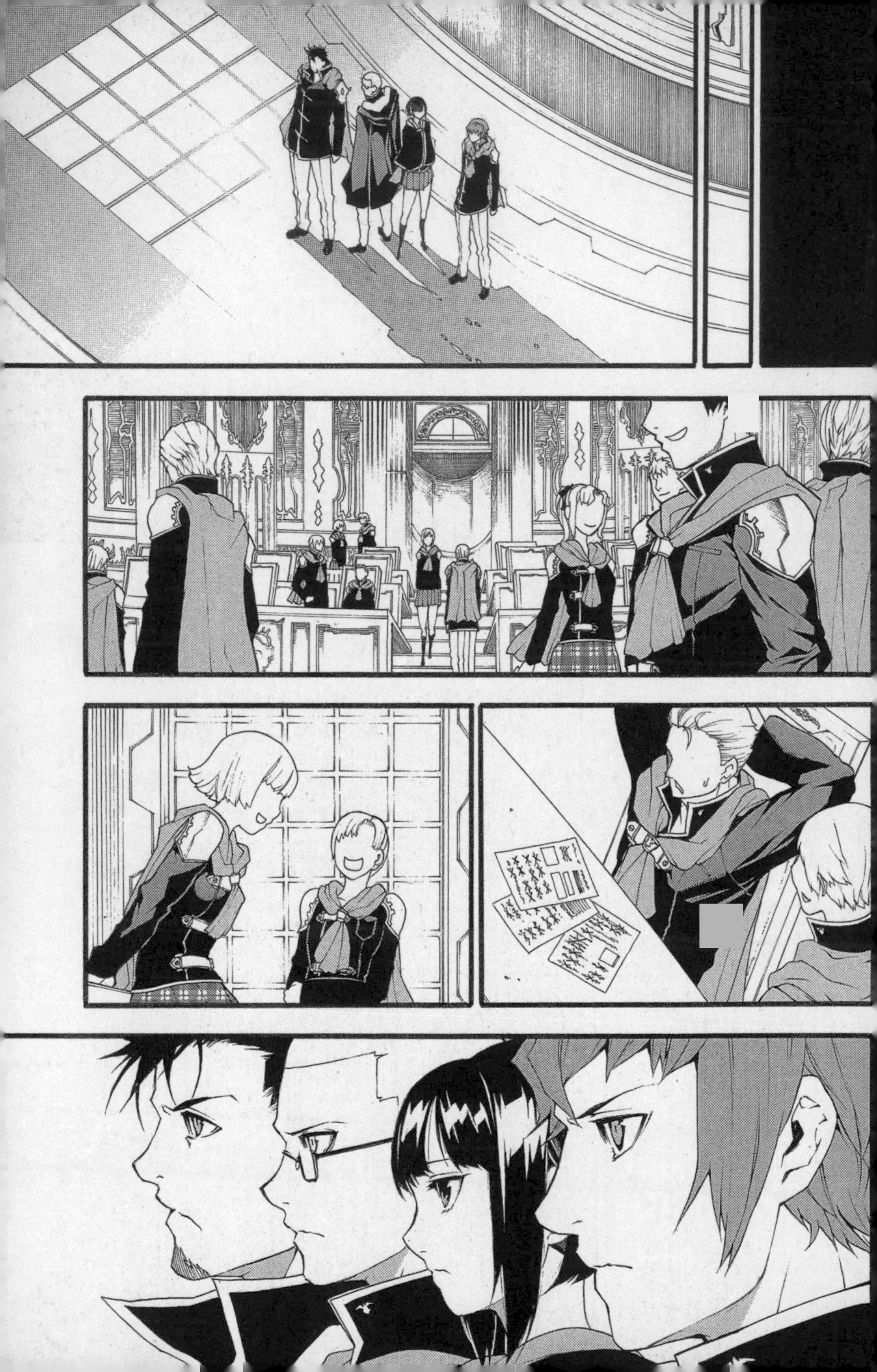

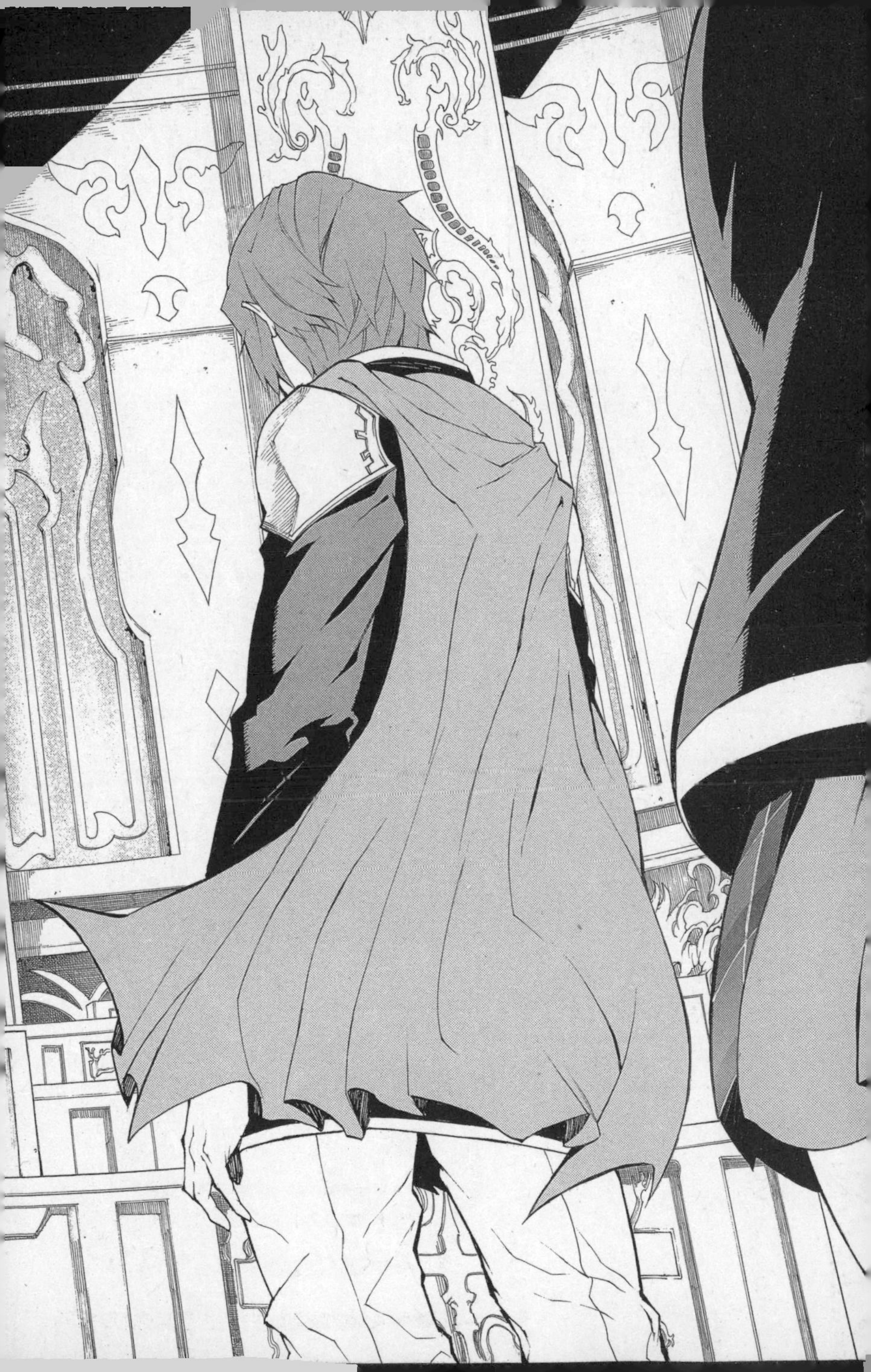

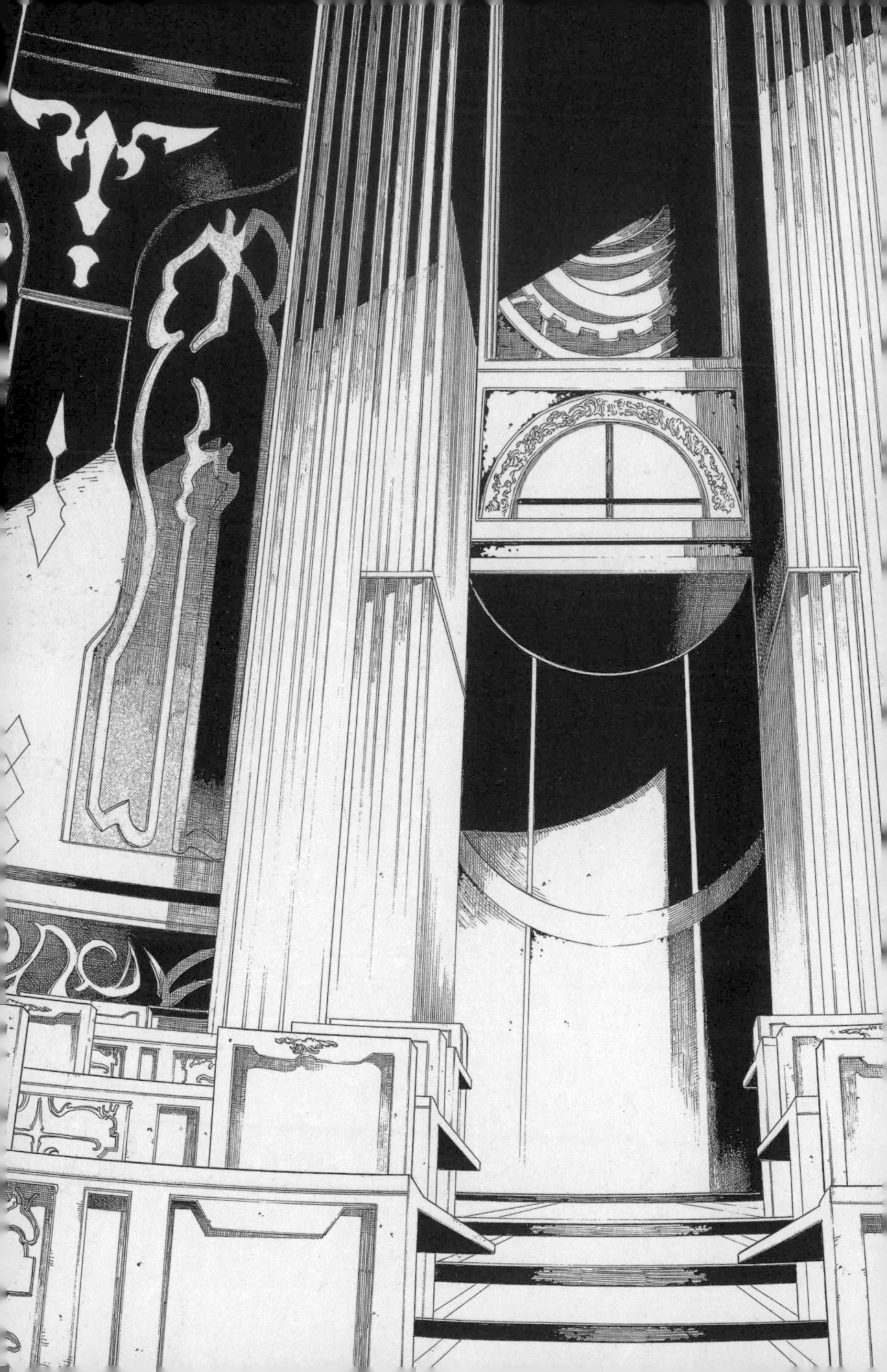

KURA-
SAME...

ㅠ TA
(TMP)

ズ SU
(SS)

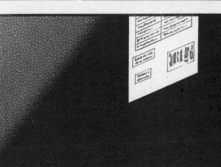

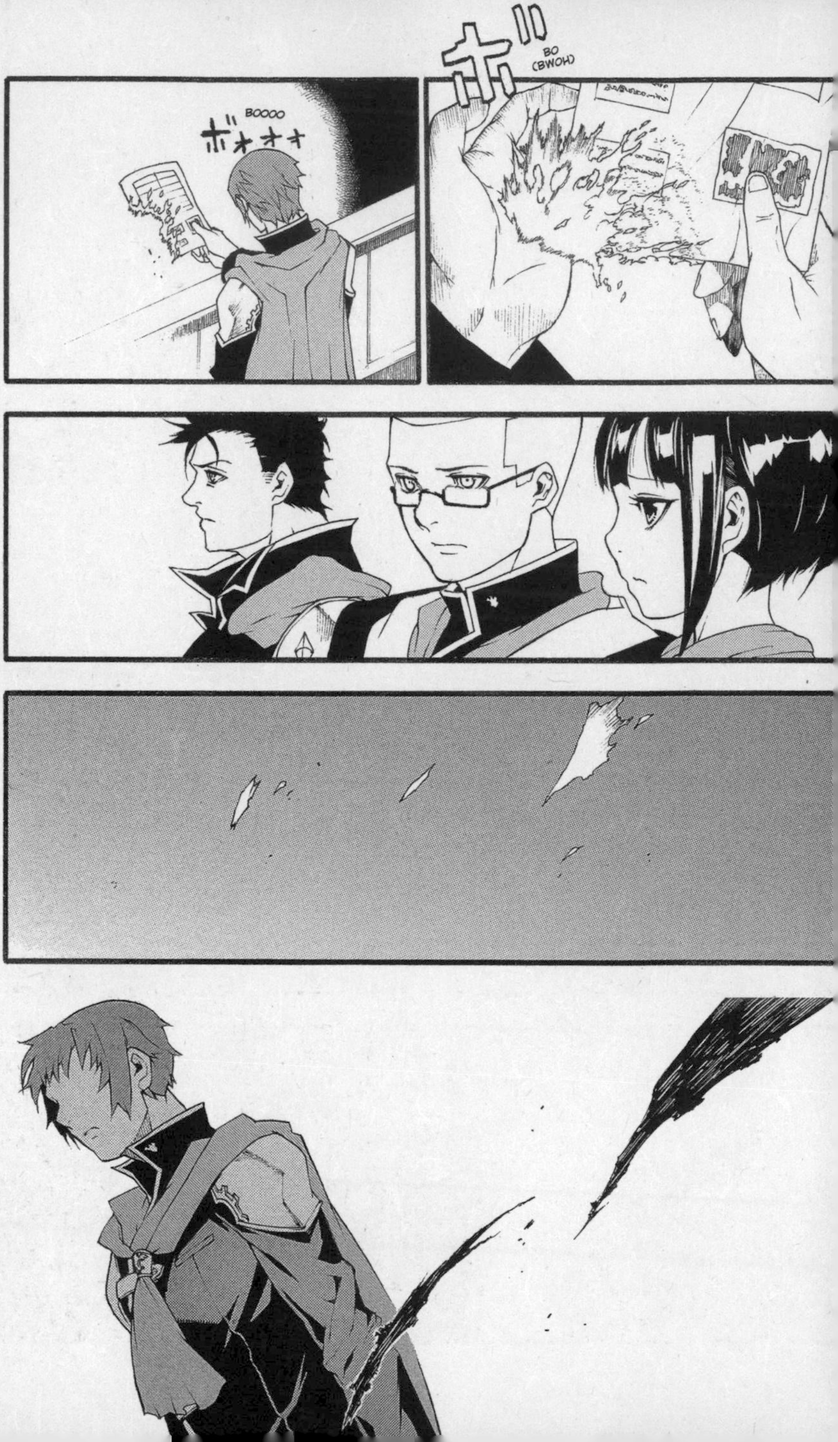ボッ
BO
(BWOH)
ボォオオ
BOOOO

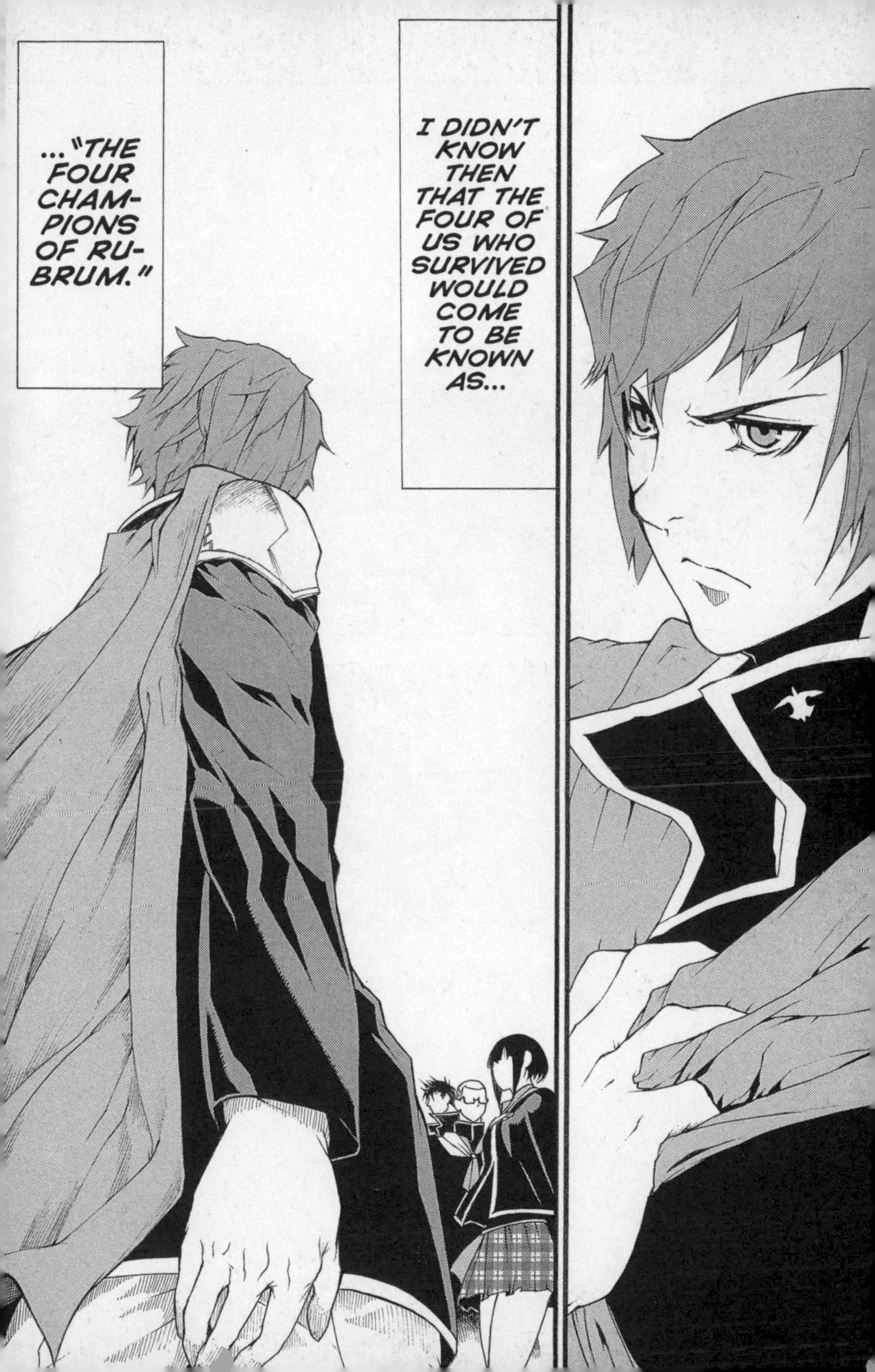
I DIDN'T KNOW THEN THAT THE FOUR OF US WHO SURVIVED WOULD COME TO BE KNOWN AS...
..."THE FOUR CHAMPIONS OF RUBRUM."

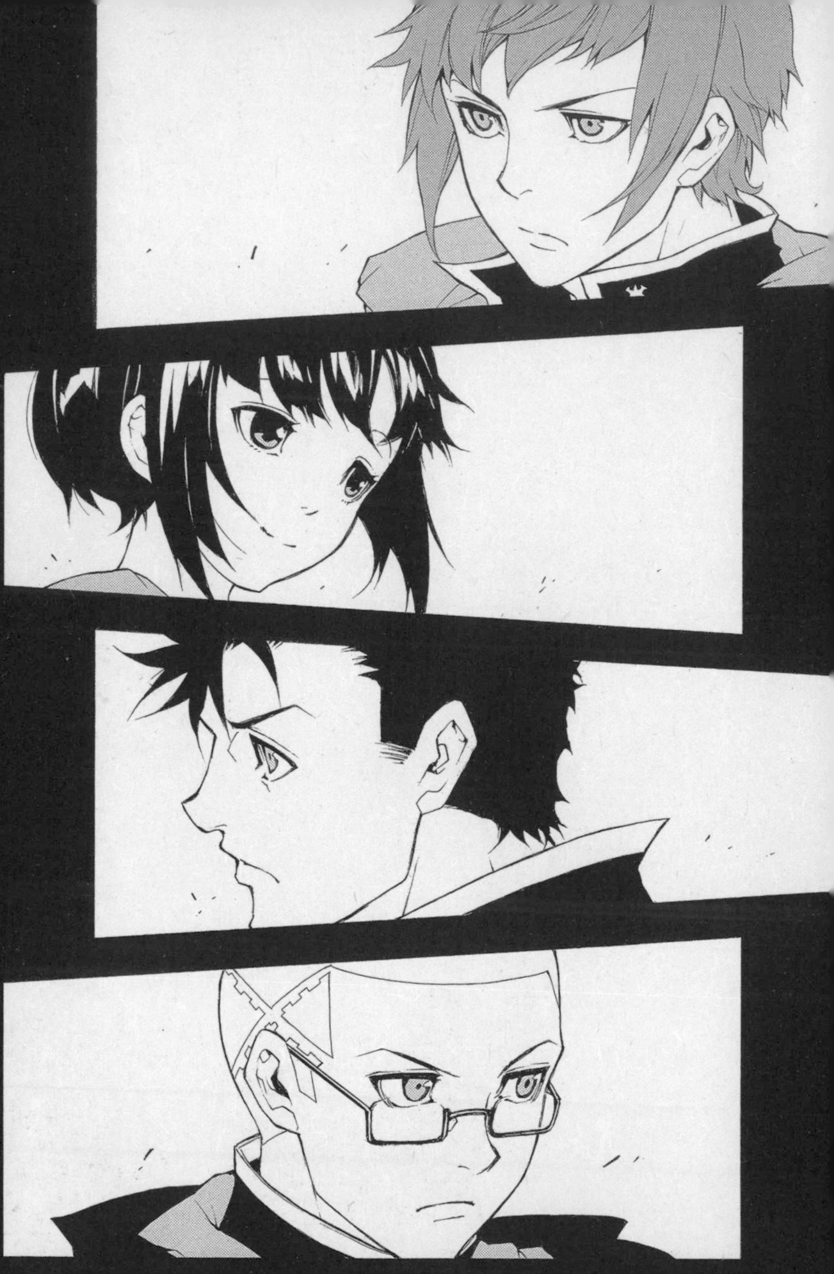

FINAL FANTASY 零式 TYPE-0™

SIDE STORY

The Ice Reaper

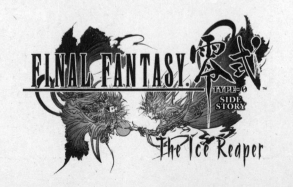

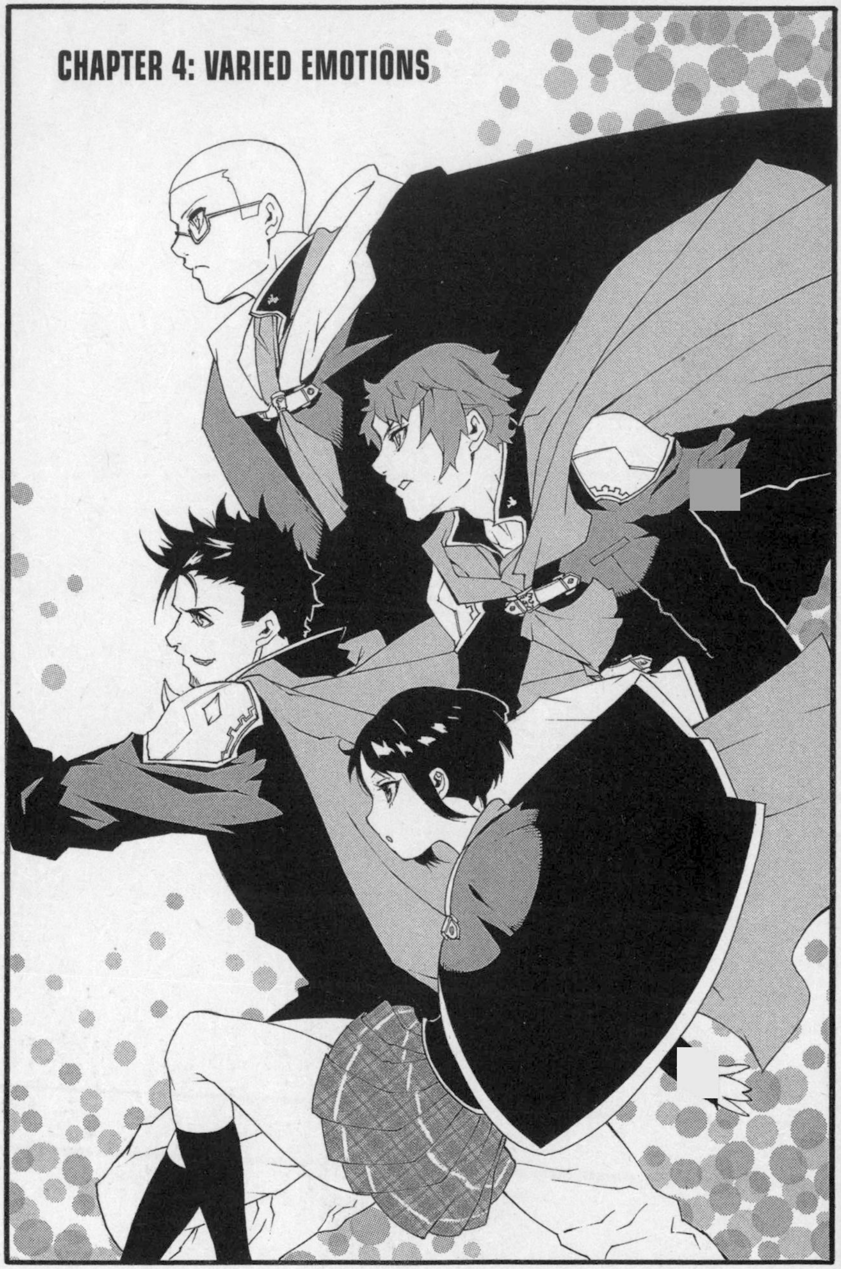
CHAPTER 4: VARIED EMOTIONS

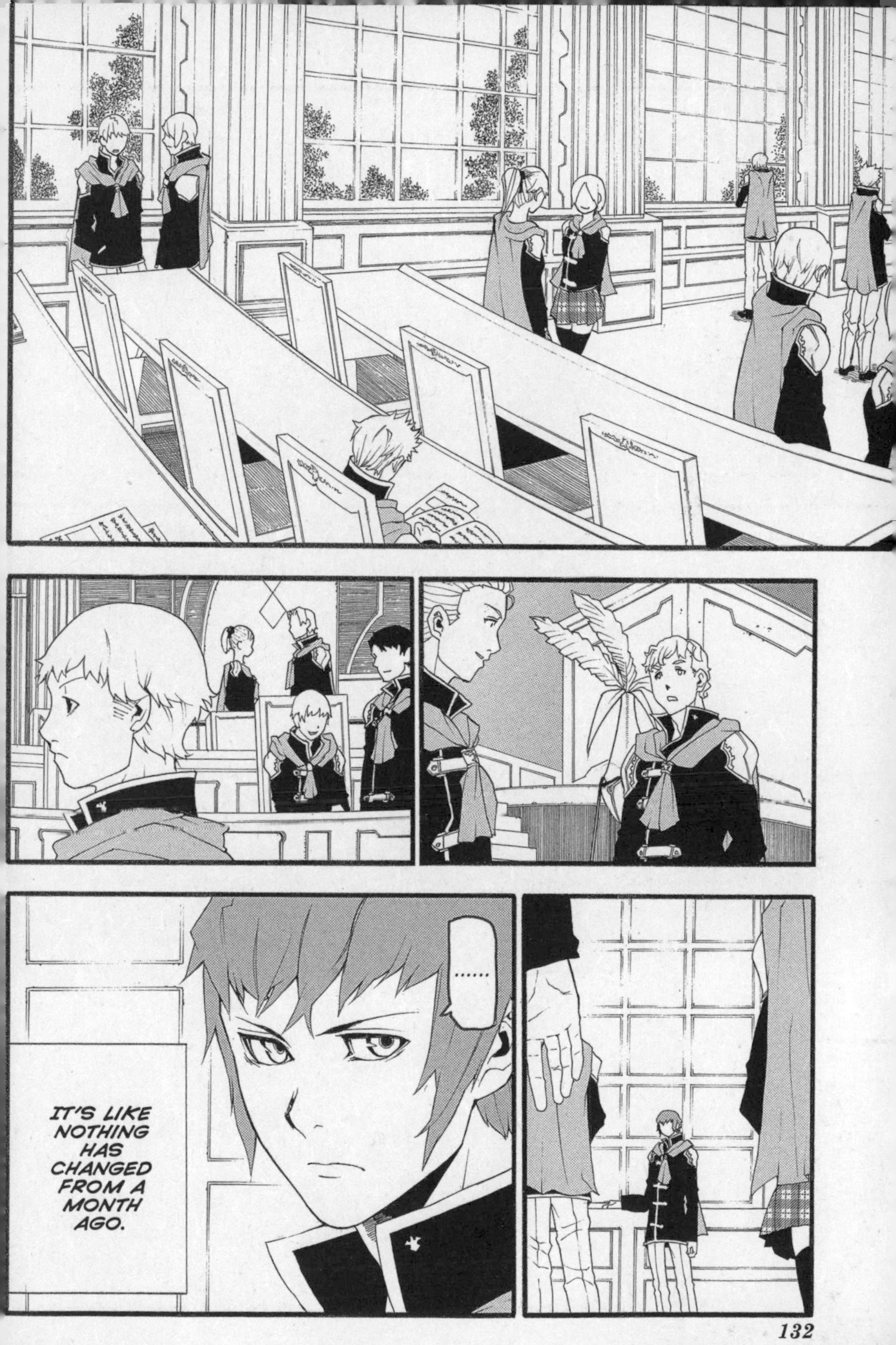
......
IT'S LIKE NOTHING HAS CHANGED FROM A MONTH AGO.

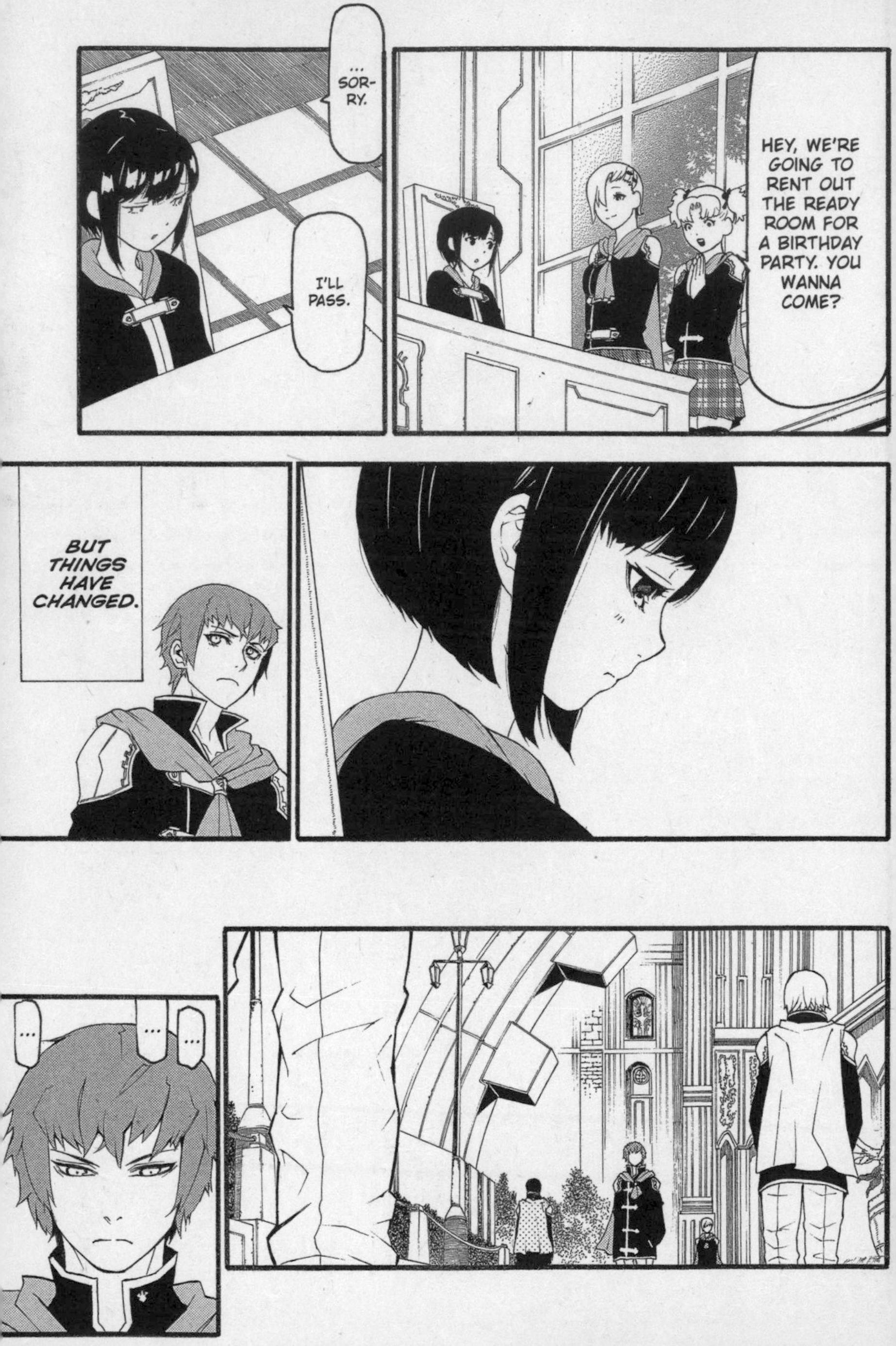
HEY, WE'RE GOING TO RENT OUT THE READY ROOM FOR A BIRTHDAY PARTY. YOU WANNA COME?
... SOR-RY.
I'LL PASS.
BUT THINGS HAVE CHANGED.
...
...
...

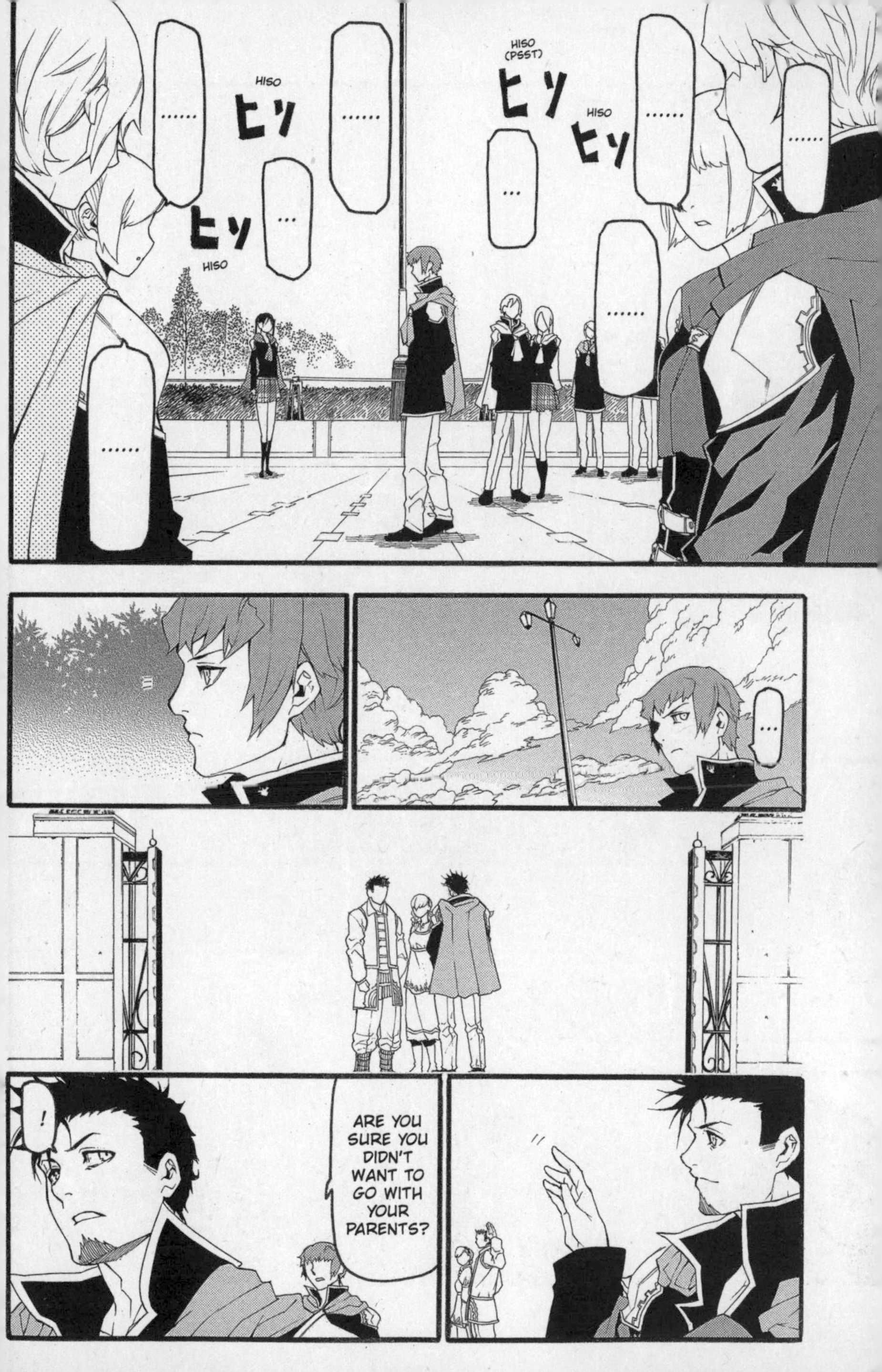

......
......
HISO (PSST)
ヒソ
HISO
ヒソ
...
......
......
HISO
ヒソ
...
......
ヒソ
HISO
......
...
ARE YOU SURE YOU DIDN'T WANT TO GO WITH YOUR PARENTS?
!

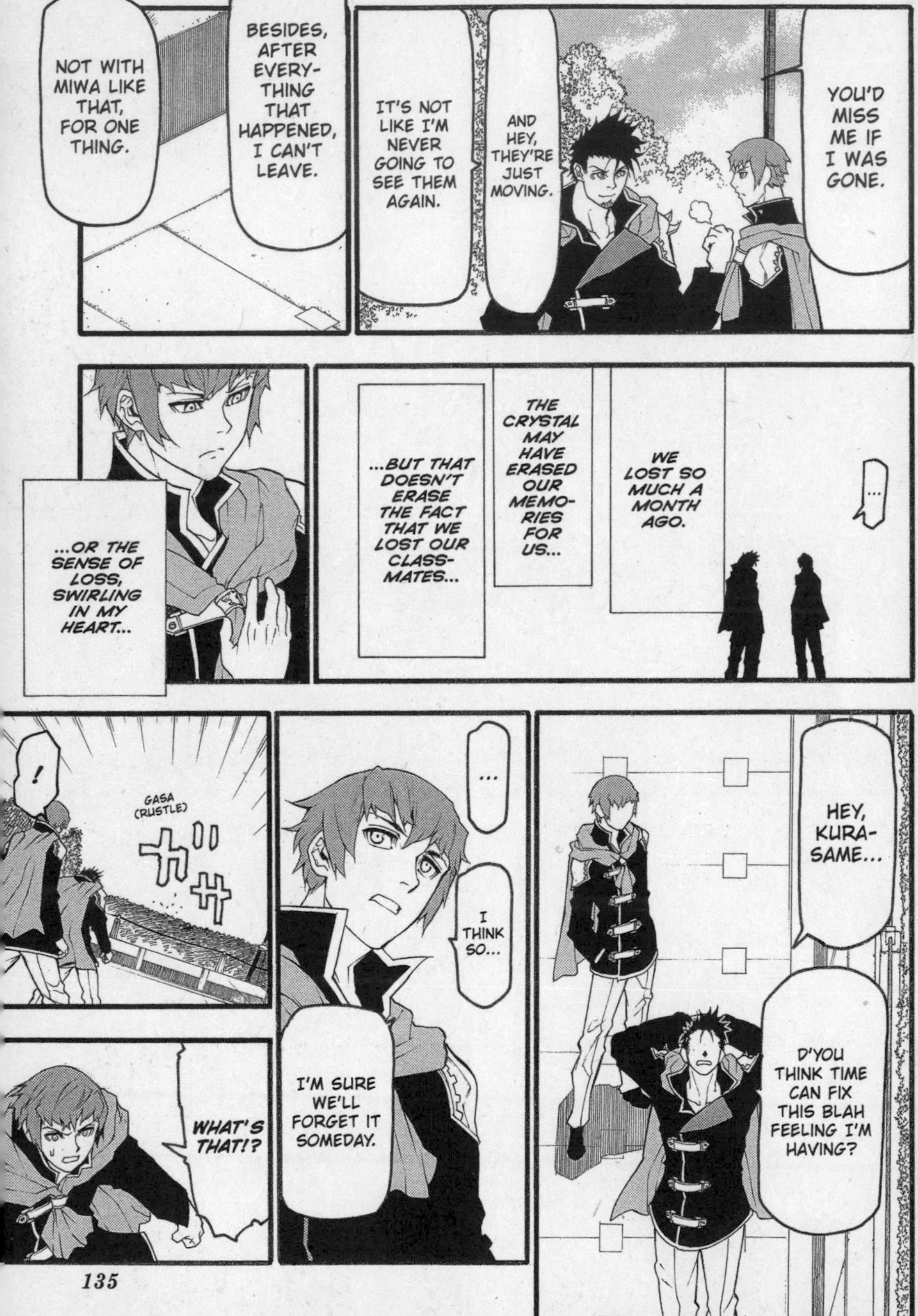
YOU'D MISS ME IF I WAS GONE.
AND HEY, THEY'RE JUST MOVING.
IT'S NOT LIKE I'M NEVER GOING TO SEE THEM AGAIN.
BESIDES, AFTER EVERYTHING THAT HAPPENED, I CAN'T LEAVE.
NOT WITH MIWA LIKE THAT, FOR ONE THING.
...
WE LOST SO MUCH A MONTH AGO.
THE CRYSTAL MAY HAVE ERASED OUR MEMORIES FOR US...
...BUT THAT DOESN'T ERASE THE FACT THAT WE LOST OUR CLASSMATES...
...OR THE SENSE OF LOSS, SWIRLING IN MY HEART...
HEY, KURASAME...
D'YOU THINK TIME CAN FIX THIS BLAH FEELING I'M HAVING?
...
I THINK SO...
I'M SURE WE'LL FORGET IT SOMEDAY.
!
GASA (RUSTLE)
ガサ
WHAT'S THAT!?

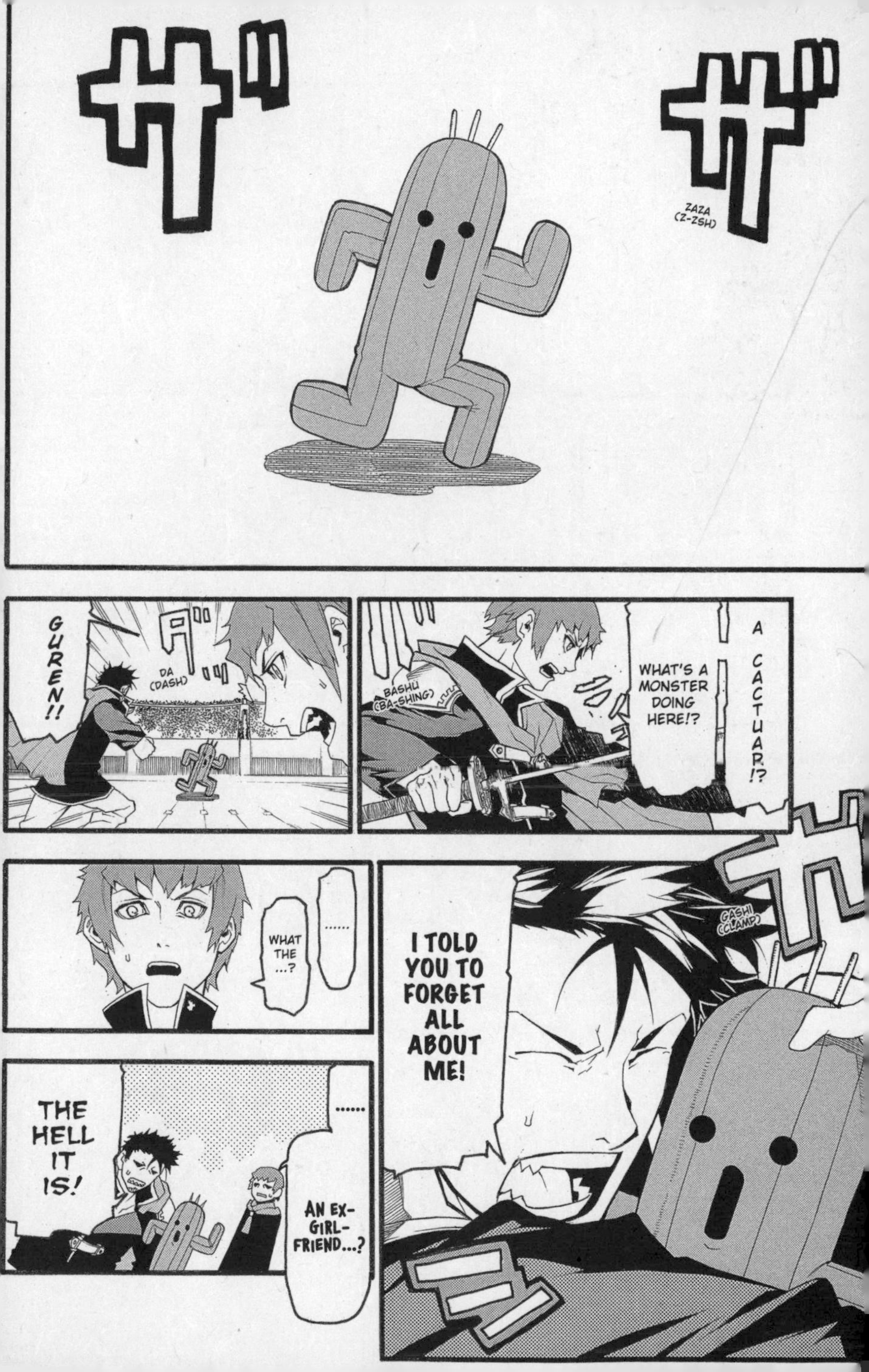
ZAZA (Z-ZSH)
A CACTUAR!?
WHAT'S A MONSTER DOING HERE!?
BASHU (BA-SHING)
GUREN!!
DA (DASH)
GASHI (CLAMP)
I TOLD YOU TO FORGET ALL ABOUT ME!
......
WHAT THE ...?
......
AN EX-GIRL-FRIEND...?
THE HELL IT IS!

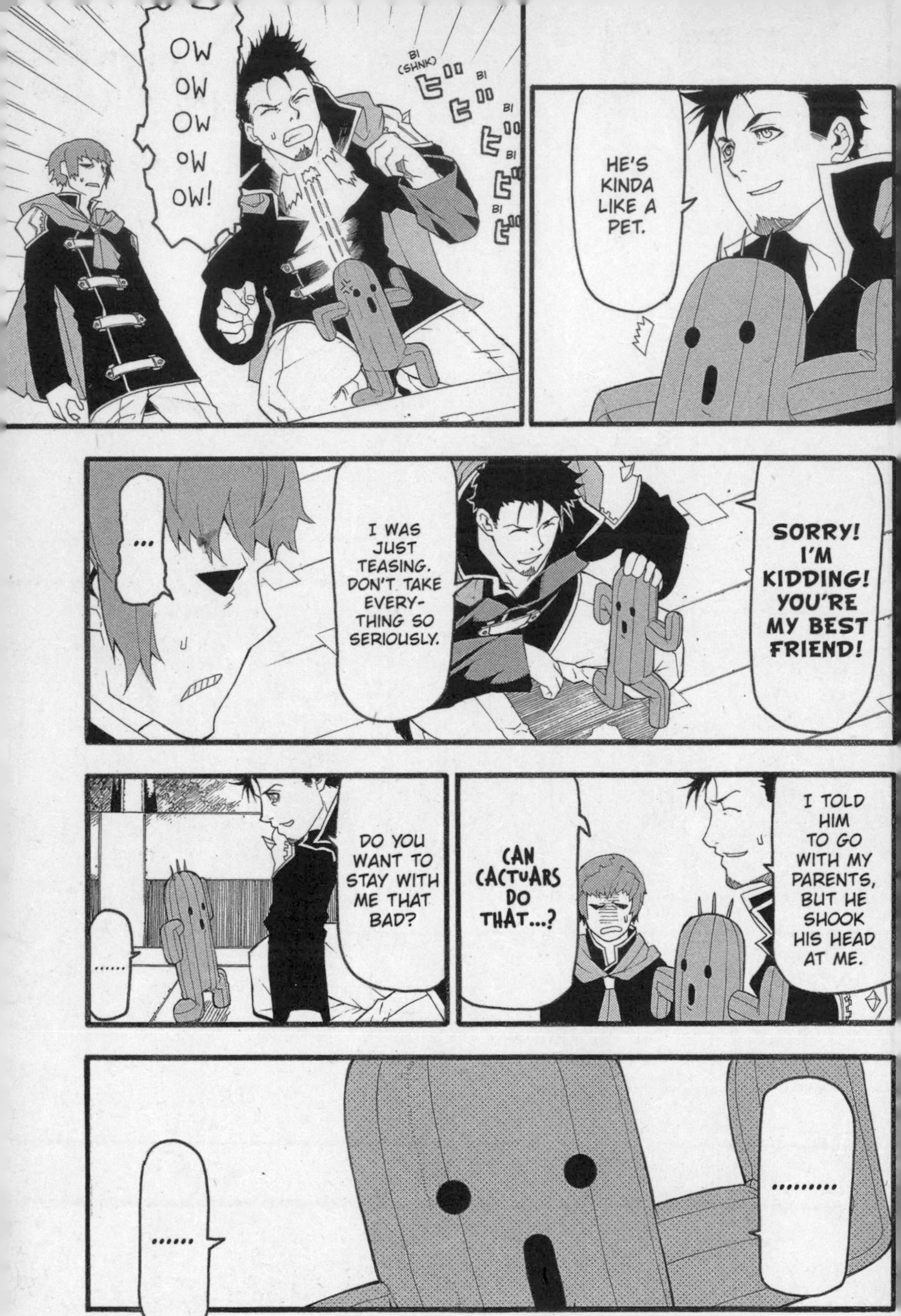
HE'S KINDA LIKE A PET.
OW OW OW OW OW!
BI (SHNK)
BI
BI
BI
BI
SORRY! I'M KIDDING! YOU'RE MY BEST FRIEND!
I WAS JUST TEASING. DON'T TAKE EVERY-THING SO SERIOUSLY.
...
I TOLD HIM TO GO WITH MY PARENTS, BUT HE SHOOK HIS HEAD AT ME.
CAN CACTUARS DO THAT...?
DO YOU WANT TO STAY WITH ME THAT BAD?
......
....
......

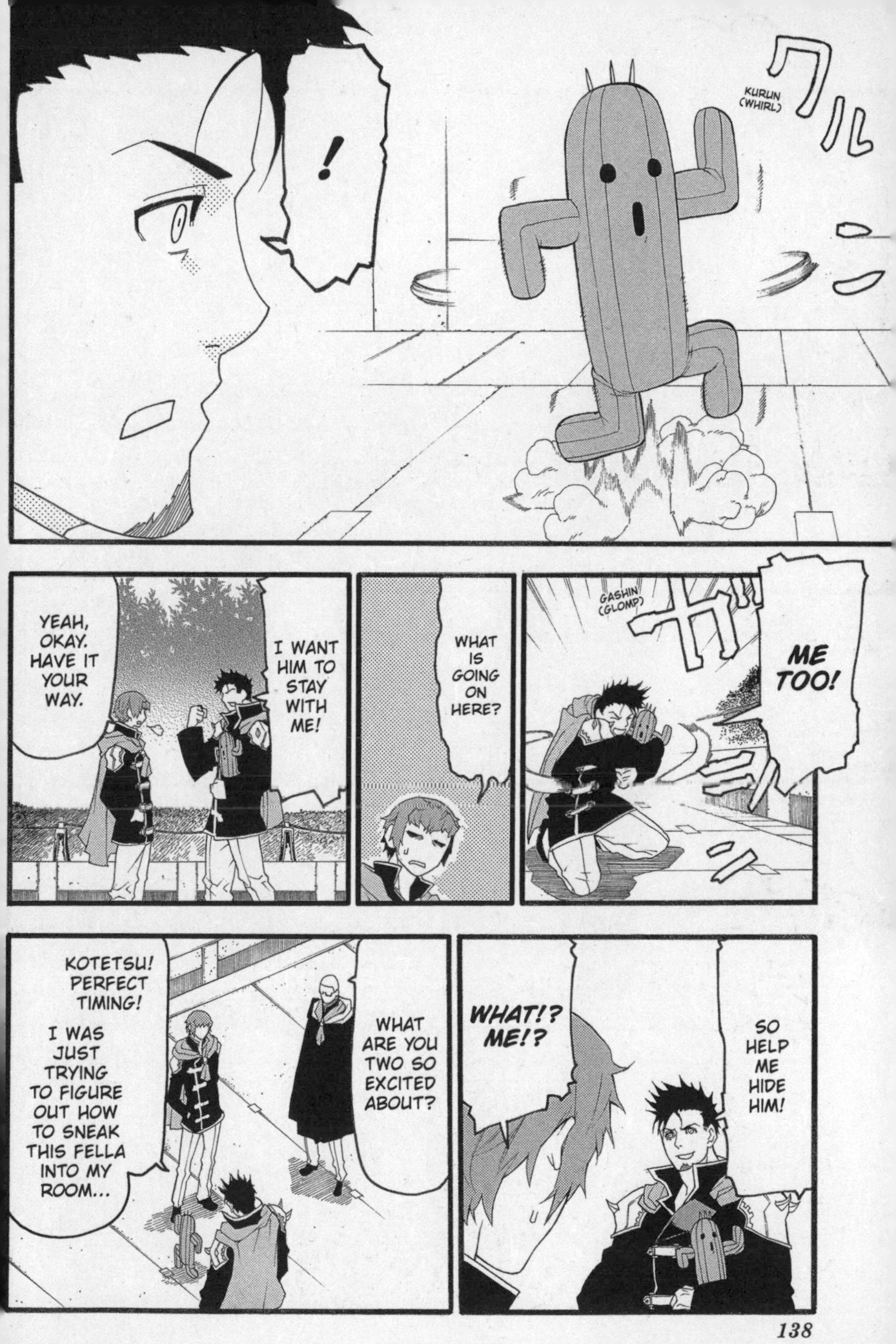
KURUN (WHIRL)
!
GASHIN (GLOMP)
ME TOO!
WHAT IS GOING ON HERE?
I WANT HIM TO STAY WITH ME!
YEAH, OKAY. HAVE IT YOUR WAY.
SO HELP ME HIDE HIM!
WHAT!? ME!?
WHAT ARE YOU TWO SO EXCITED ABOUT?
KOTETSU! PERFECT TIMING!
I WAS JUST TRYING TO FIGURE OUT HOW TO SNEAK THIS FELLA INTO MY ROOM...

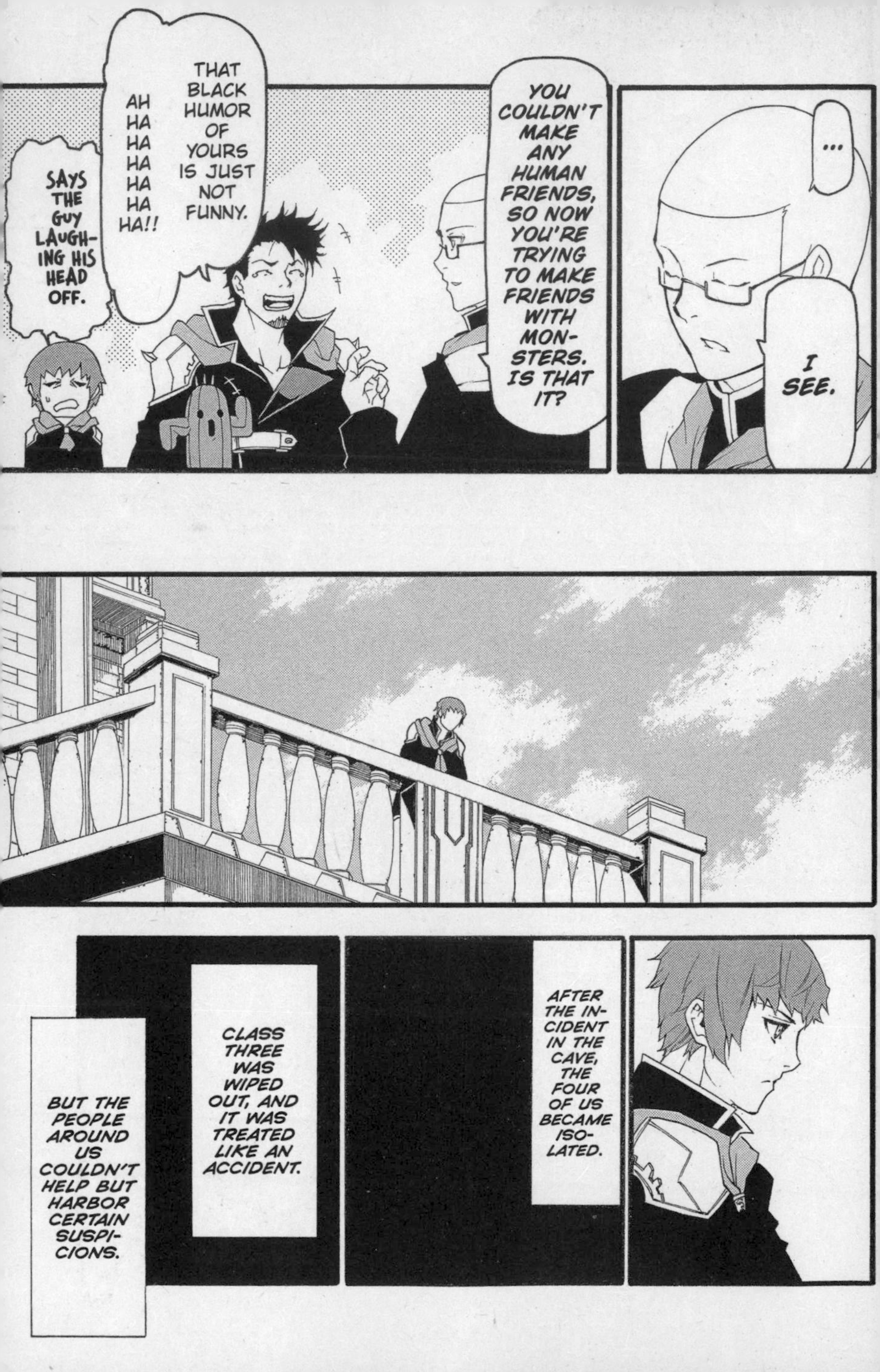
...
I SEE.
YOU COULDN'T MAKE ANY HUMAN FRIENDS, SO NOW YOU'RE TRYING TO MAKE FRIENDS WITH MON-STERS. IS THAT IT?
THAT BLACK HUMOR OF YOURS IS JUST NOT FUNNY.
AH HA HA HA HA HA HA!!
SAYS THE GUY LAUGH-ING HIS HEAD OFF.
AFTER THE IN-CIDENT IN THE CAVE, THE FOUR OF US BECAME ISO-LATED.
CLASS THREE WAS WIPED OUT, AND IT WAS TREATED LIKE AN ACCIDENT.
BUT THE PEOPLE AROUND US COULDN'T HELP BUT HARBOR CERTAIN SUSPI-CIONS.

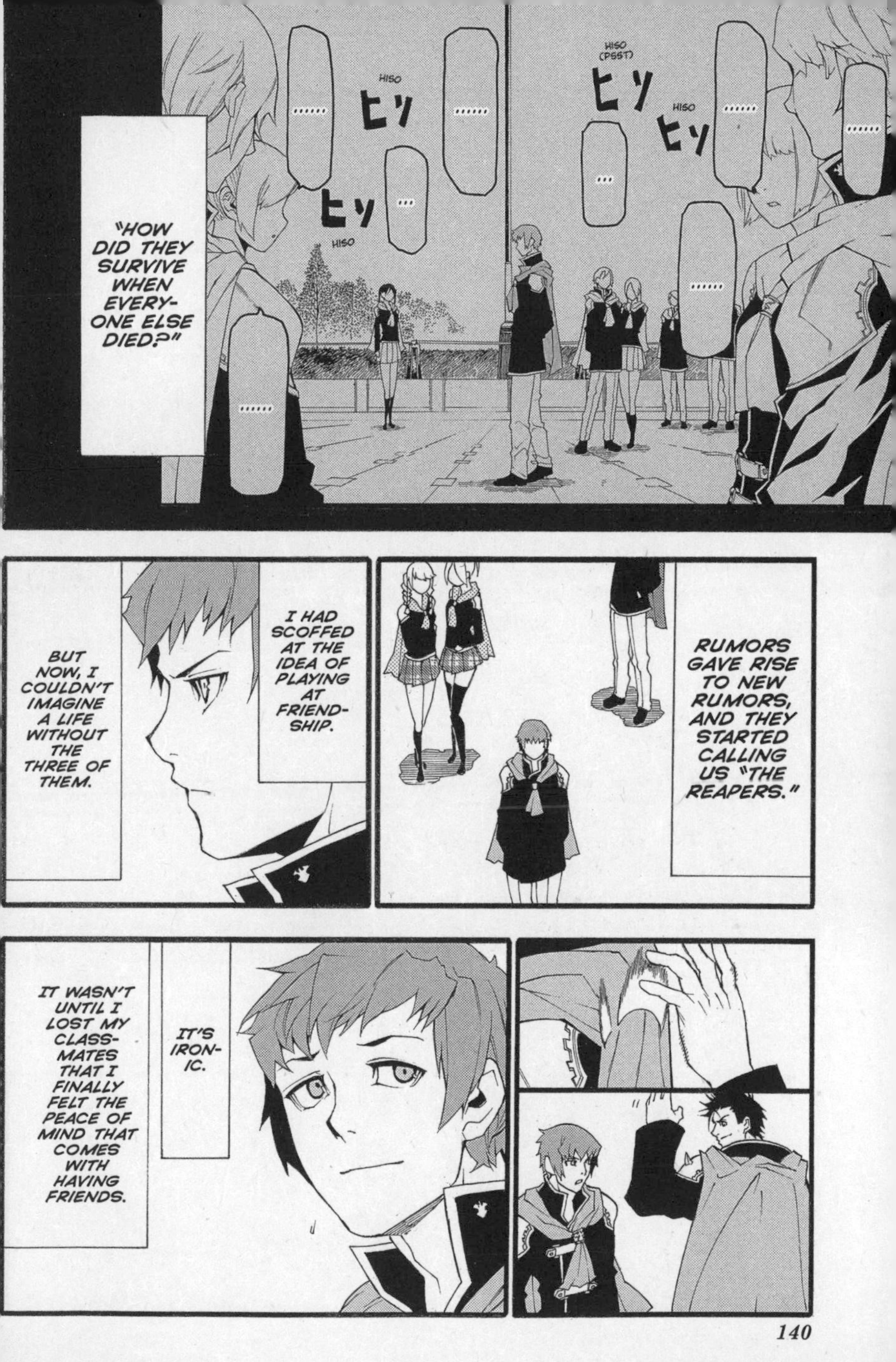

HISO (PSST)
ヒソ
HISO
ヒソ
......
......
...
......
......
HISO
ヒソ
......
...
HISO
ヒソ
"HOW DID THEY SURVIVE WHEN EVERYONE ELSE DIED?"
......
RUMORS GAVE RISE TO NEW RUMORS, AND THEY STARTED CALLING US "THE REAPERS."
I HAD SCOFFED AT THE IDEA OF PLAYING AT FRIENDSHIP.
BUT NOW, I COULDN'T IMAGINE A LIFE WITHOUT THE THREE OF THEM.
IT'S IRONIC.
IT WASN'T UNTIL I LOST MY CLASSMATES THAT I FINALLY FELT THE PEACE OF MIND THAT COMES WITH HAVING FRIENDS.

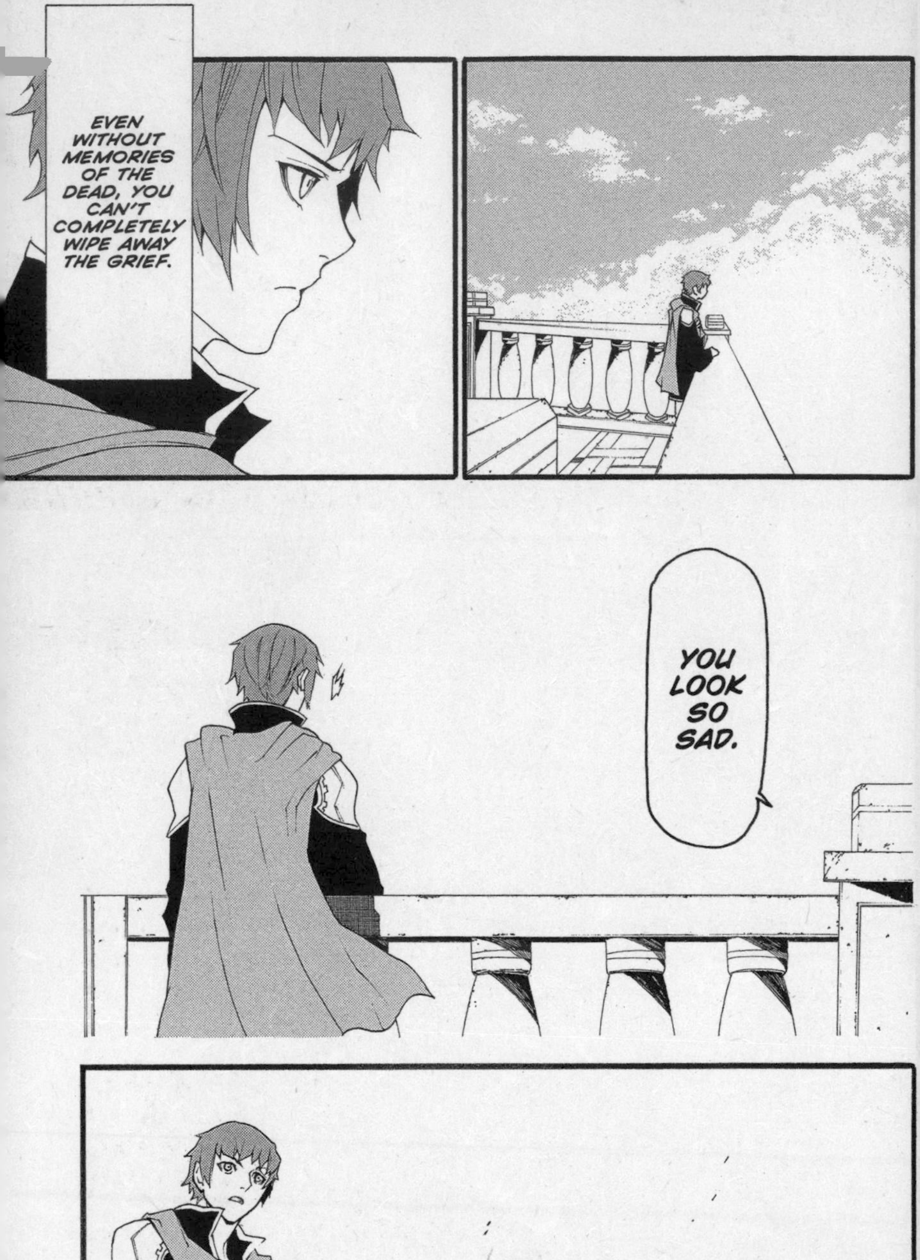
EVEN WITHOUT MEMORIES OF THE DEAD, YOU CAN'T COMPLETELY WIPE AWAY THE GRIEF.
YOU LOOK SO SAD.

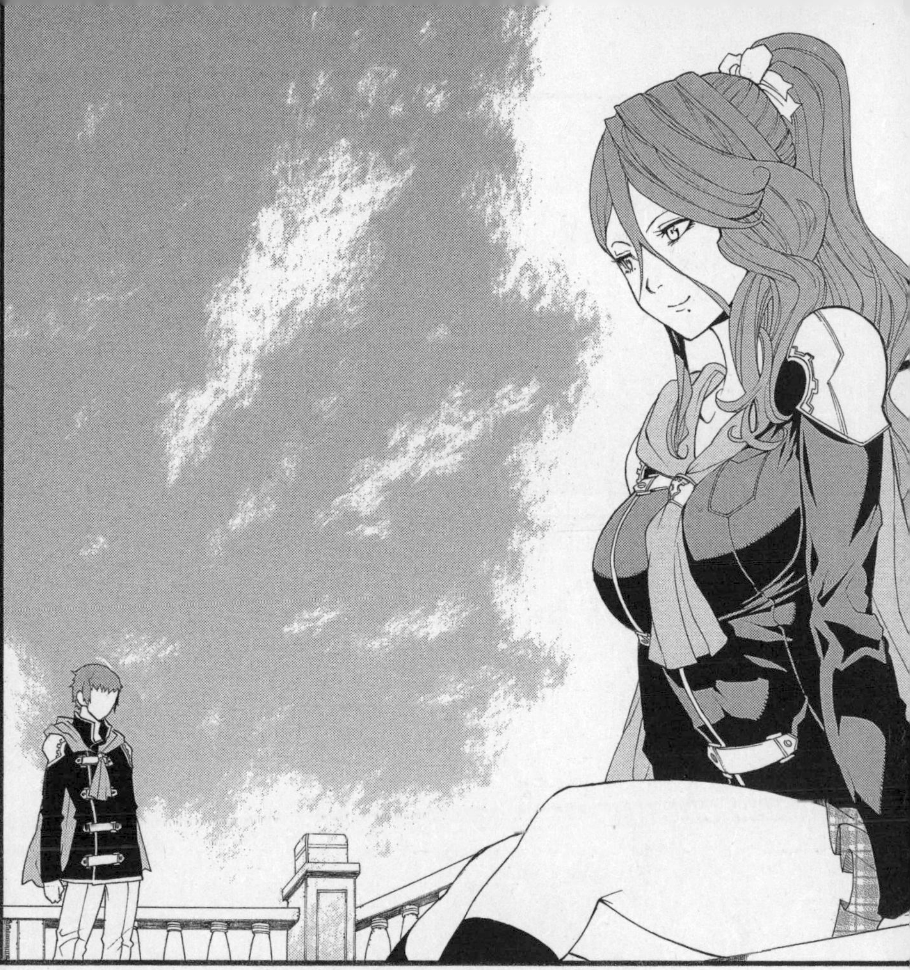

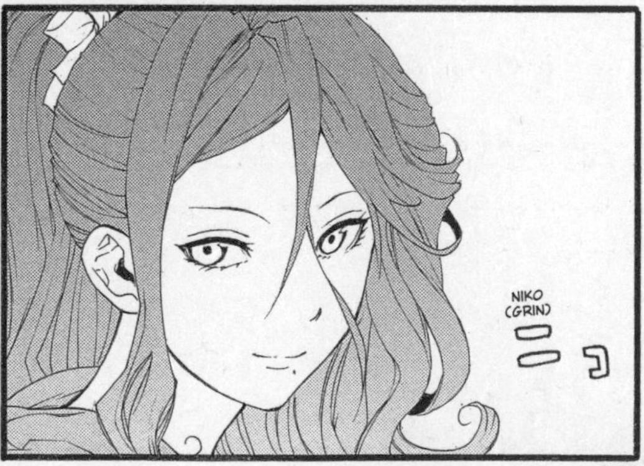
NIKO
(GRIN)

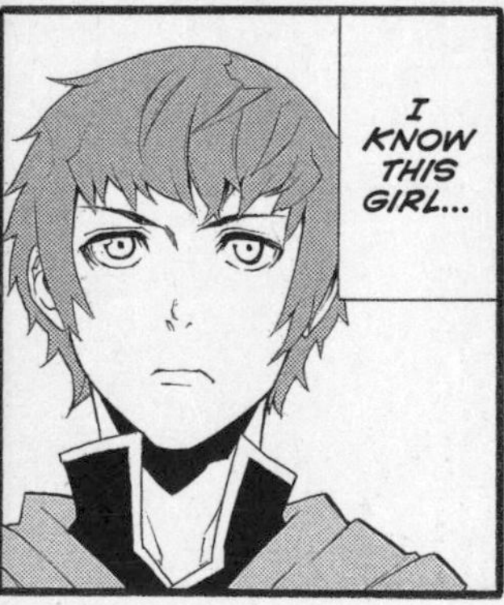
I KNOW THIS GIRL...

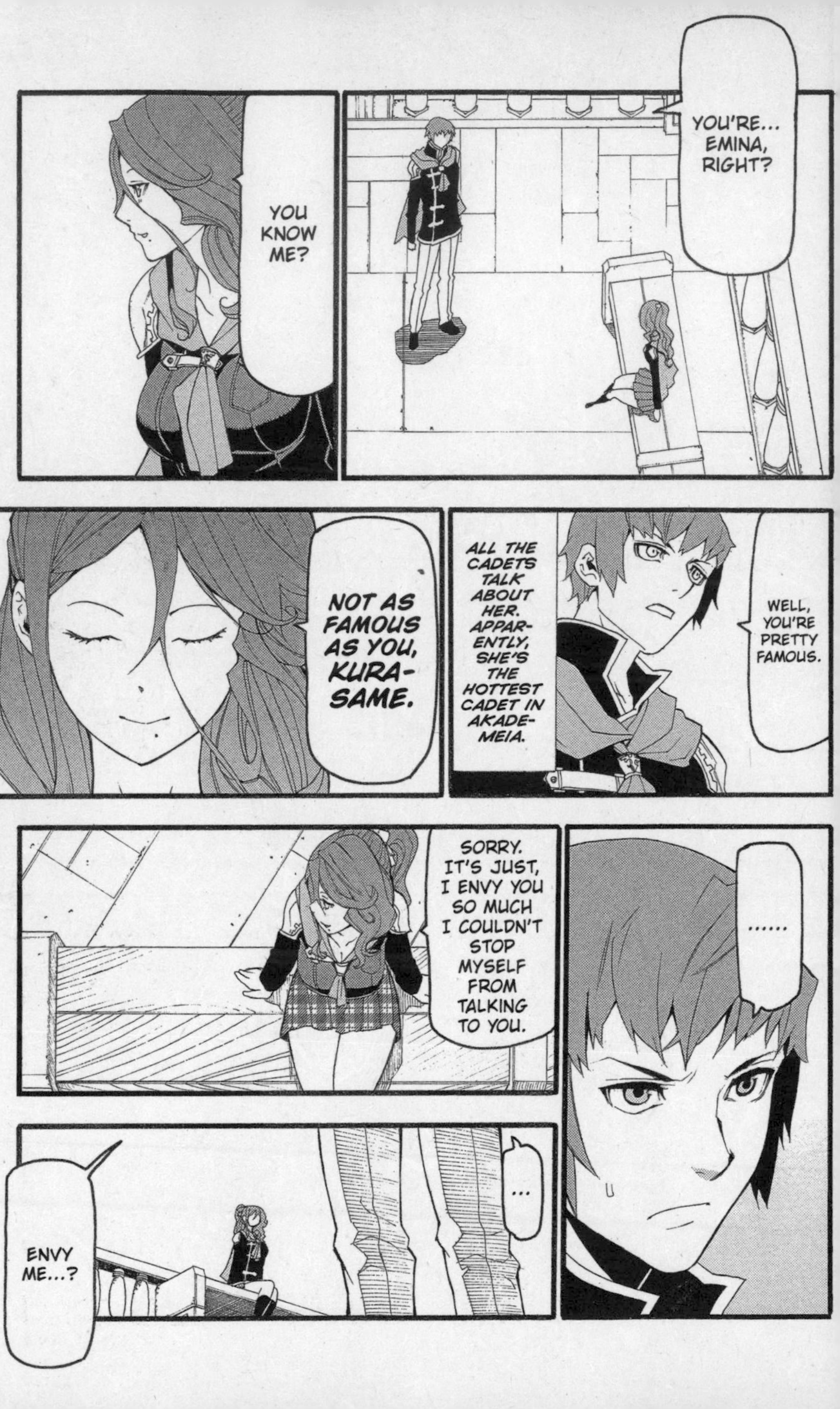
YOU'RE... EMINA, RIGHT?
YOU KNOW ME?
WELL, YOU'RE PRETTY FAMOUS.
ALL THE CADETS TALK ABOUT HER. APPARENTLY, SHE'S THE HOTTEST CADET IN AKADEMEIA.
NOT AS FAMOUS AS YOU, KURASAME.
......
SORRY. IT'S JUST, I ENVY YOU SO MUCH I COULDN'T STOP MYSELF FROM TALKING TO YOU.
...
ENVY ME...?

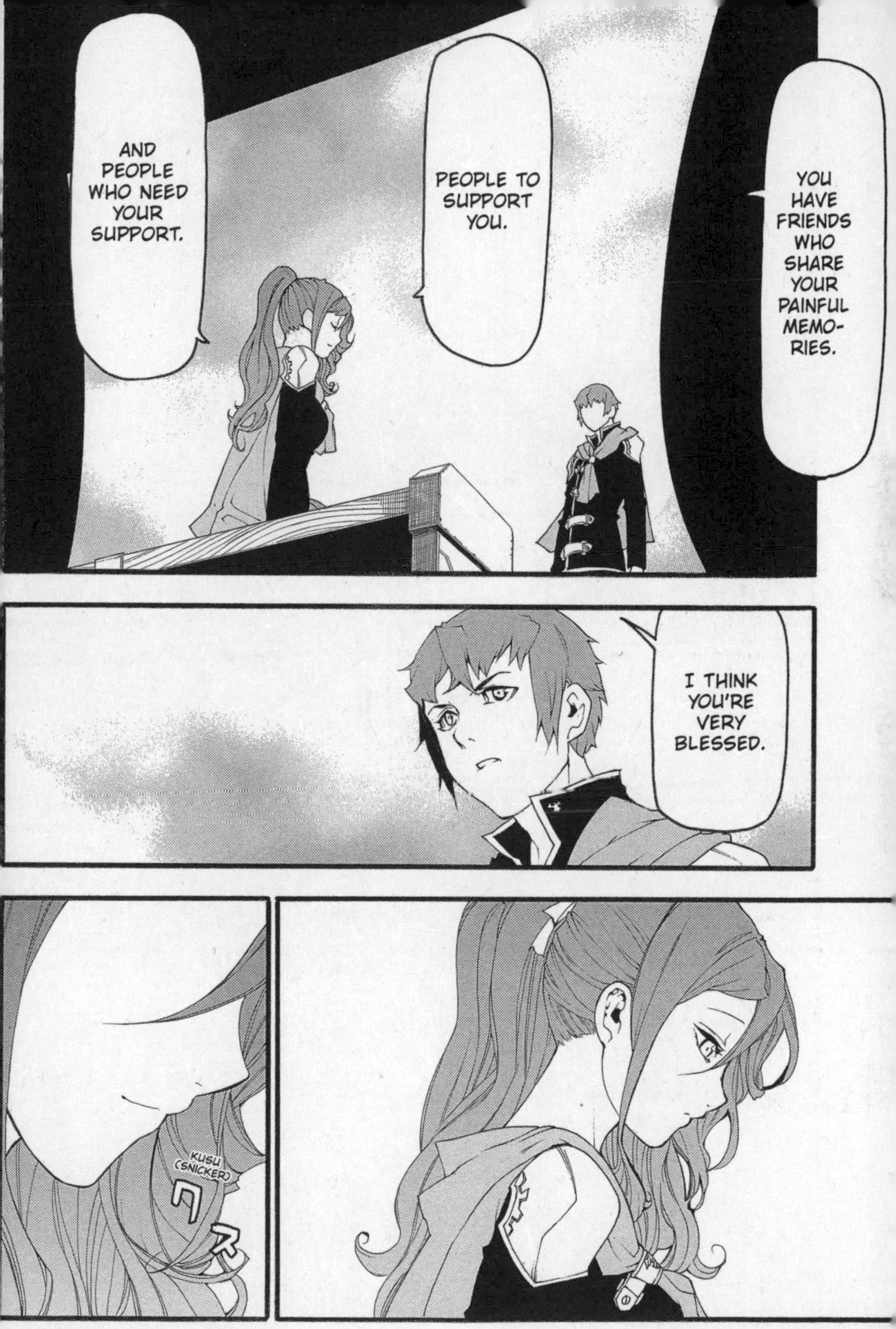
YOU HAVE FRIENDS WHO SHARE YOUR PAINFUL MEMORIES.
PEOPLE TO SUPPORT YOU.
AND PEOPLE WHO NEED YOUR SUPPORT.
I THINK YOU'RE VERY BLESSED.
KUSU (SNICKER)

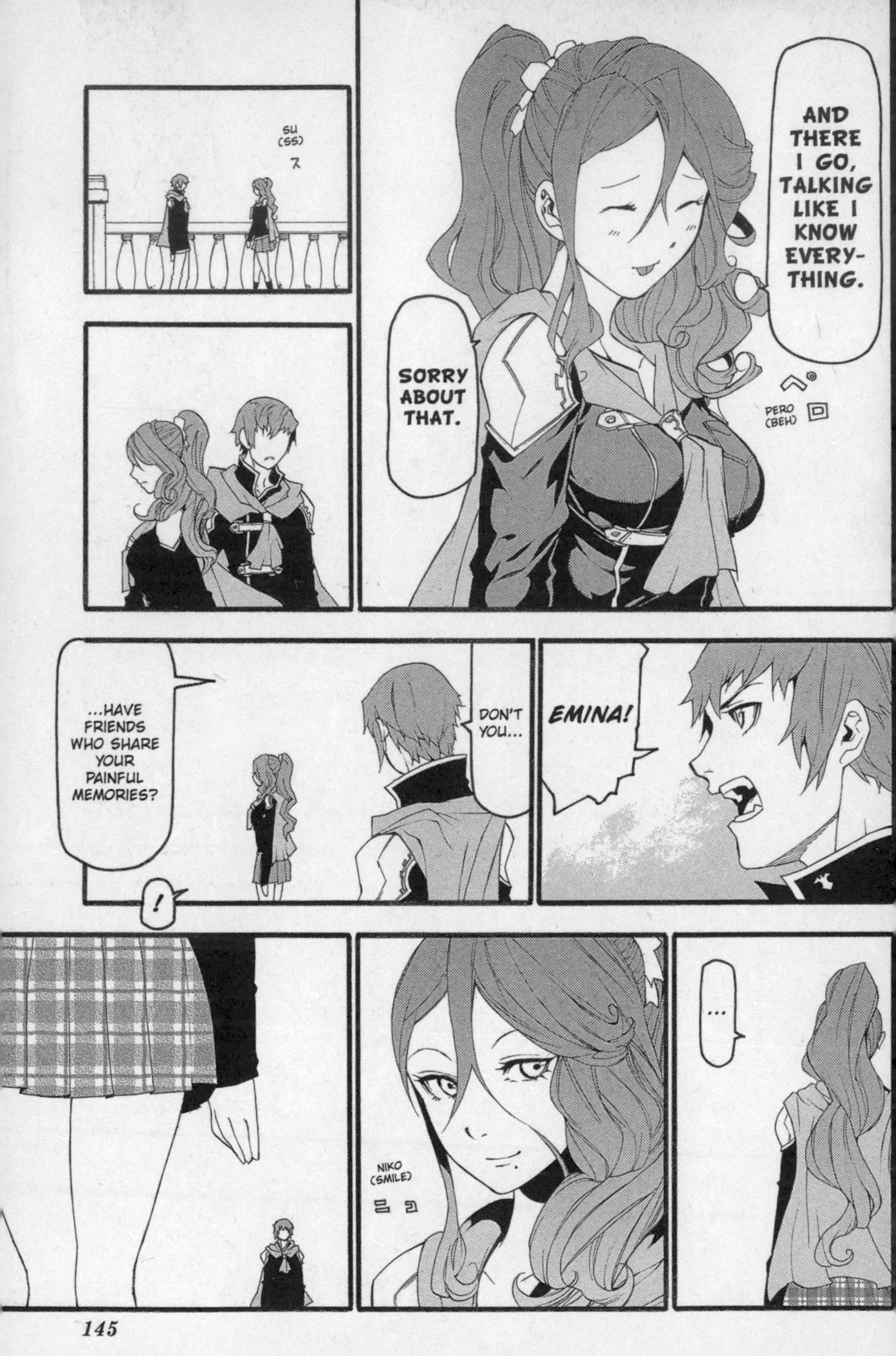
AND THERE I GO, TALKING LIKE I KNOW EVERY-THING.
SORRY ABOUT THAT.
PERO (BEH)
ぺろ
SU (SS)
ス
EMINA!
DON'T YOU...
...HAVE FRIENDS WHO SHARE YOUR PAINFUL MEMORIES?
...
NIKO (SMILE)
ニコ
!

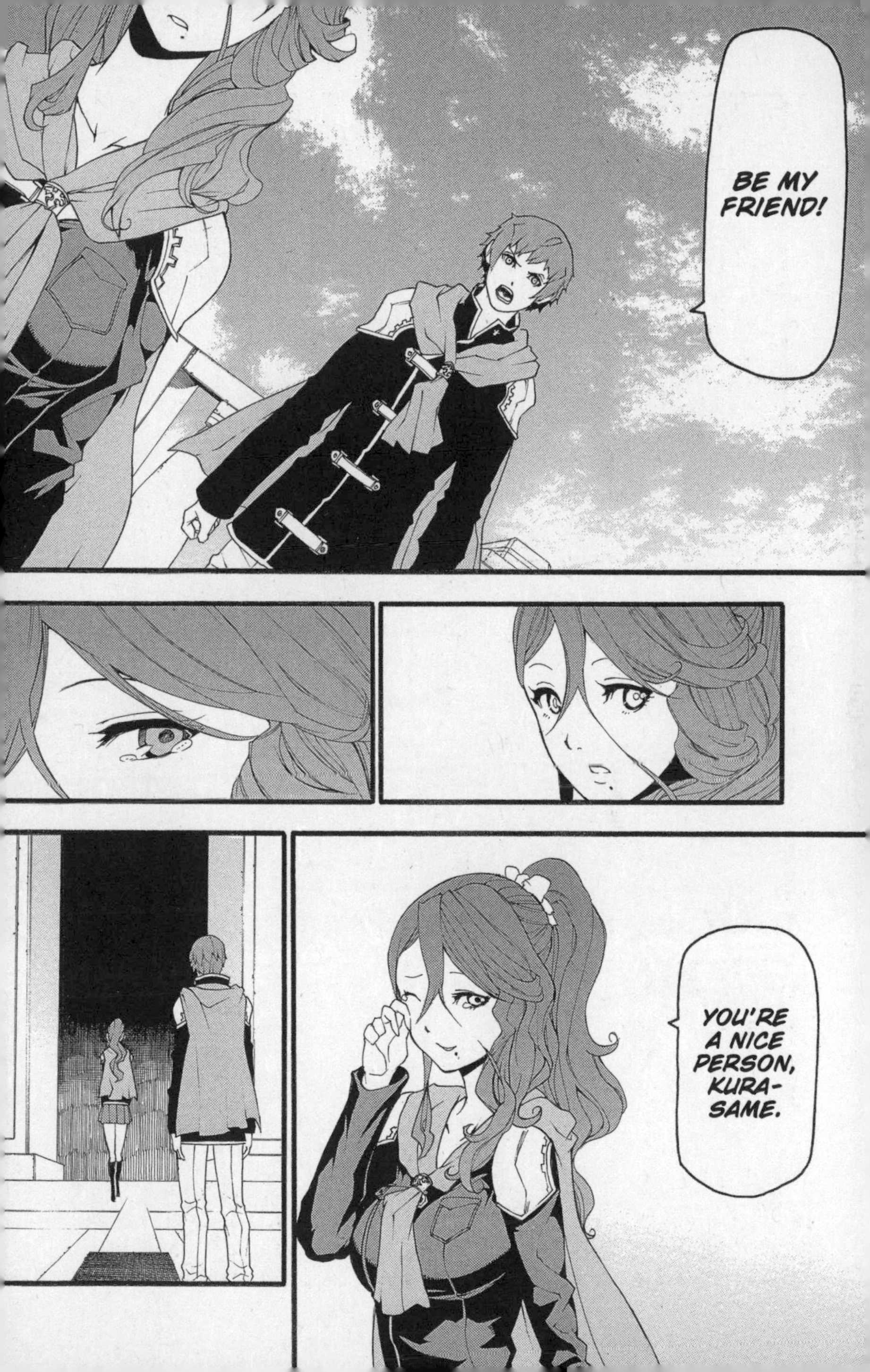
BE MY FRIEND!
YOU'RE A NICE PERSON, KURA-SAME.

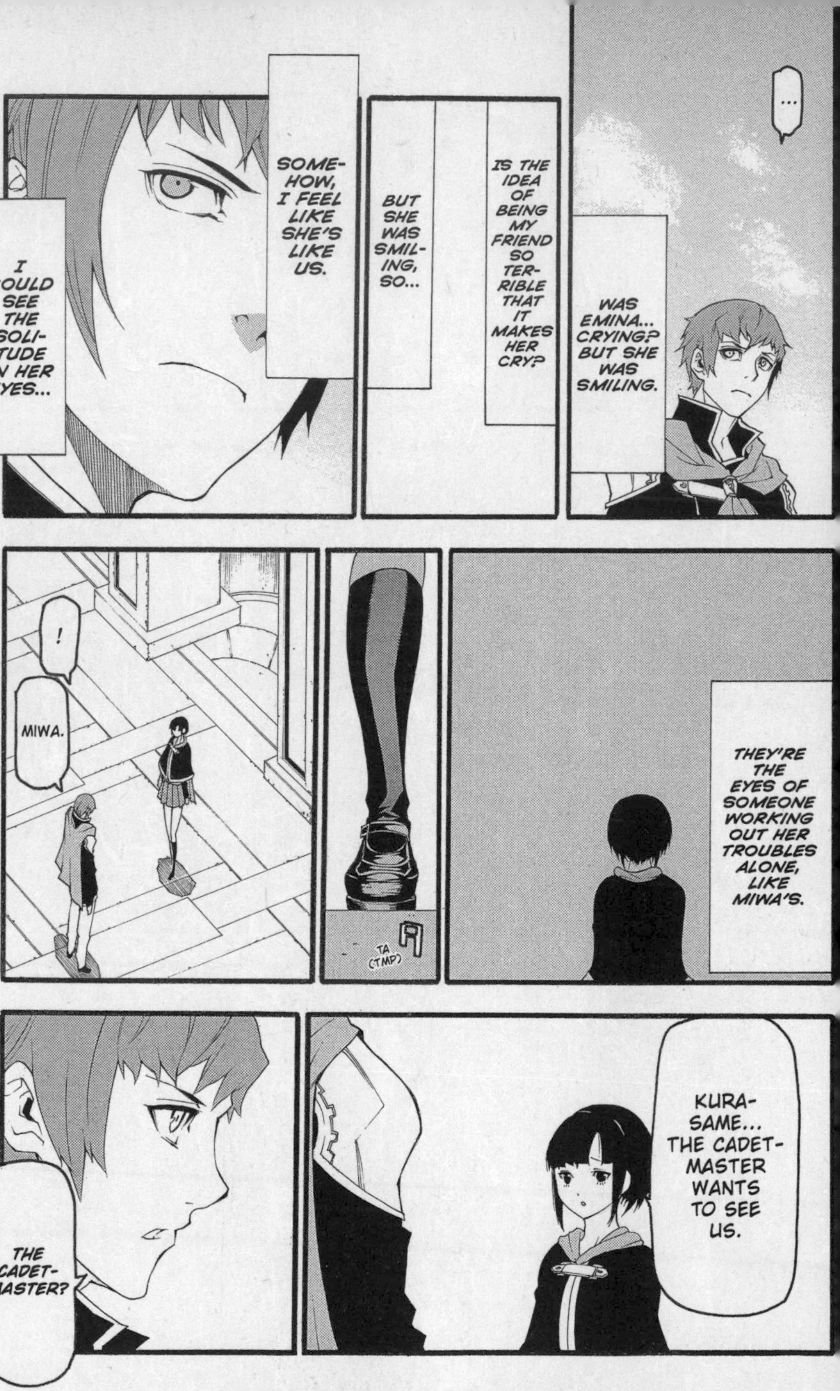
...
WAS EMINA... CRYING? BUT SHE WAS SMILING.
IS THE IDEA OF BEING MY FRIEND SO TERRIBLE THAT IT MAKES HER CRY?
BUT SHE WAS SMILING, SO...
SOMEHOW, I FEEL LIKE SHE'S LIKE US.
I COULD SEE THE SOLITUDE IN HER EYES...
THEY'RE THE EYES OF SOMEONE WORKING OUT HER TROUBLES ALONE, LIKE MIWA'S.
TA (TMP)
!
MIWA.
KURASAME... THE CADET-MASTER WANTS TO SEE US.
THE CADET-MASTER?

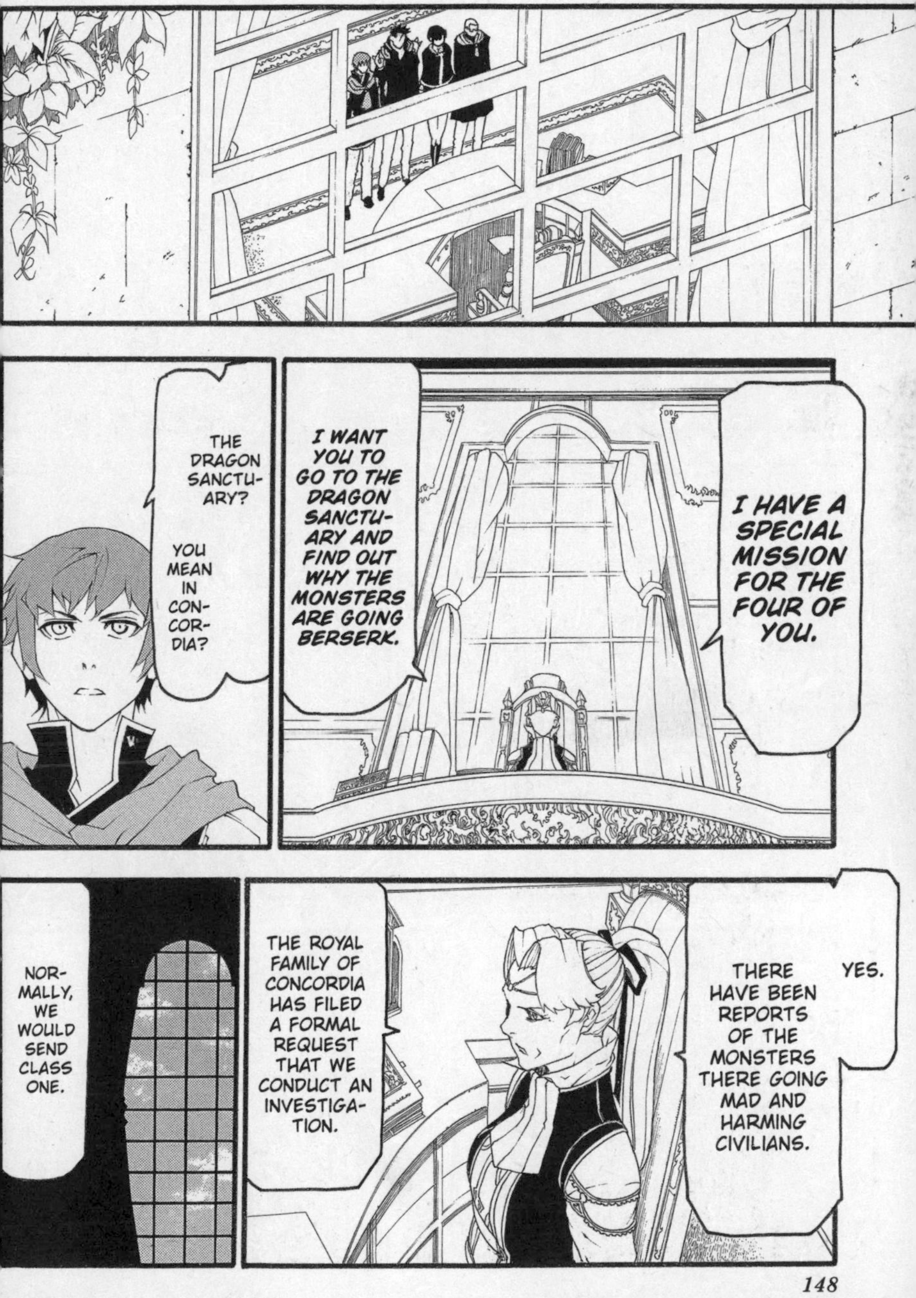
I HAVE A SPECIAL MISSION FOR THE FOUR OF YOU.
I WANT YOU TO GO TO THE DRAGON SANCTUARY AND FIND OUT WHY THE MONSTERS ARE GOING BERSERK.
THE DRAGON SANCTUARY?
YOU MEAN IN CONCORDIA?
YES.
THERE HAVE BEEN REPORTS OF THE MONSTERS THERE GOING MAD AND HARMING CIVILIANS.
THE ROYAL FAMILY OF CONCORDIA HAS FILED A FORMAL REQUEST THAT WE CONDUCT AN INVESTIGATION.
NORMALLY, WE WOULD SEND CLASS ONE.

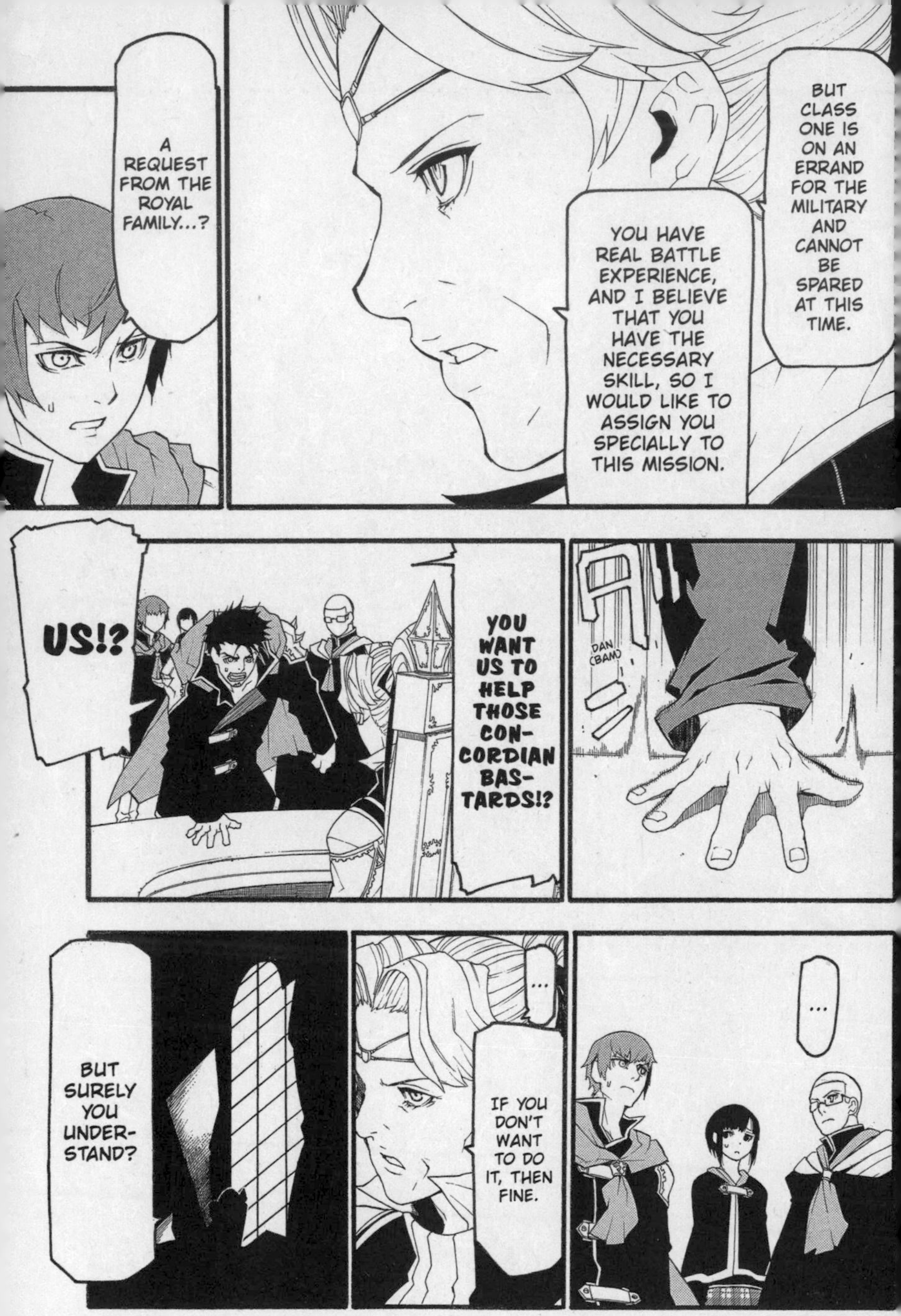
BUT CLASS ONE IS ON AN ERRAND FOR THE MILITARY AND CANNOT BE SPARED AT THIS TIME.
YOU HAVE REAL BATTLE EXPERIENCE, AND I BELIEVE THAT YOU HAVE THE NECESSARY SKILL, SO I WOULD LIKE TO ASSIGN YOU SPECIALLY TO THIS MISSION.
A REQUEST FROM THE ROYAL FAMILY...?
DAN (BAM)
YOU WANT US TO HELP THOSE CON-CORDIAN BAS-TARDS!?
US!?
...
...
IF YOU DON'T WANT TO DO IT, THEN FINE.
BUT SURELY YOU UNDER-STAND?

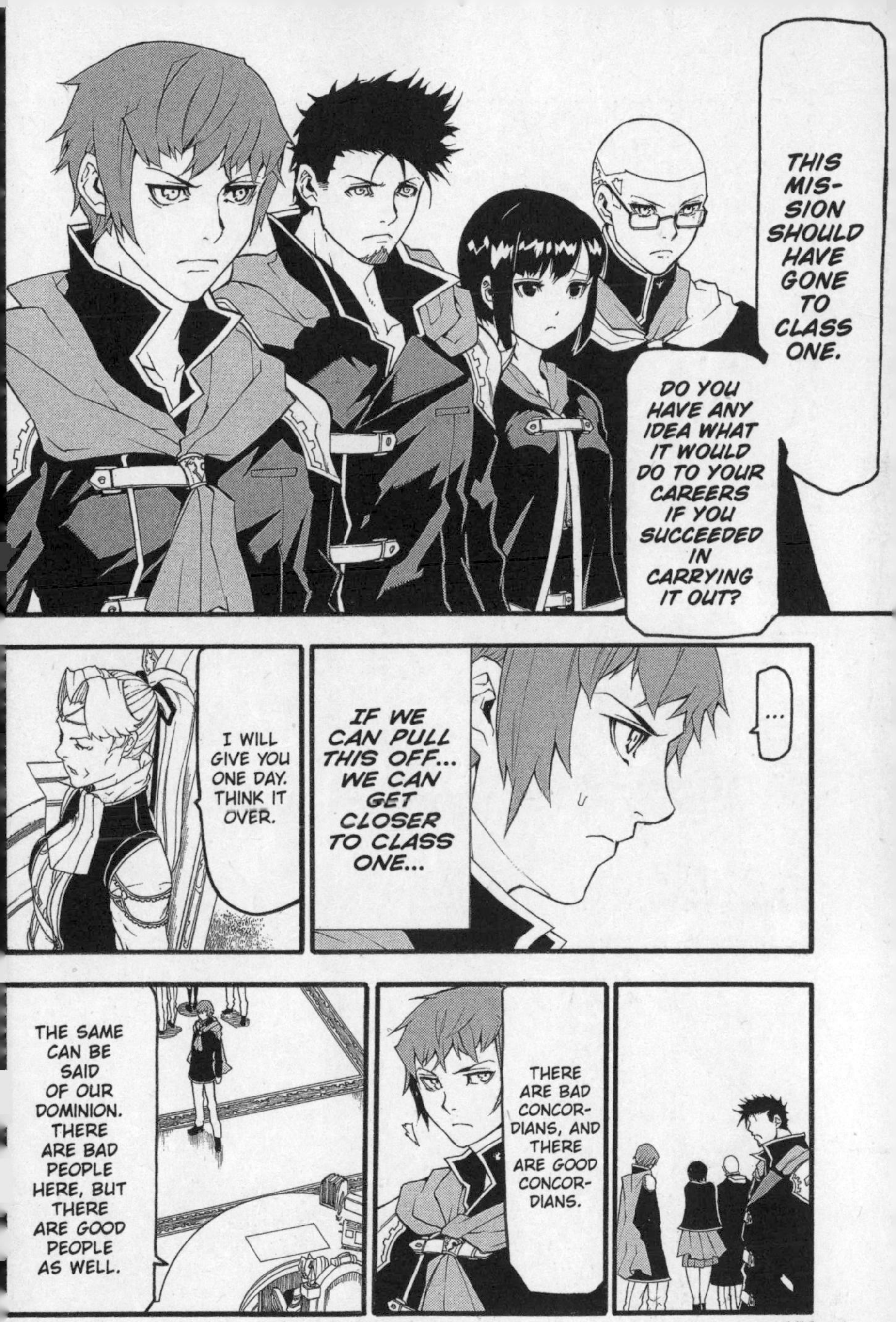
THIS MISSION SHOULD HAVE GONE TO CLASS ONE.
DO YOU HAVE ANY IDEA WHAT IT WOULD DO TO YOUR CAREERS IF YOU SUCCEEDED IN CARRYING IT OUT?
...
IF WE CAN PULL THIS OFF... WE CAN GET CLOSER TO CLASS ONE...
I WILL GIVE YOU ONE DAY. THINK IT OVER.
THERE ARE BAD CONCORDIANS, AND THERE ARE GOOD CONCORDIANS.
THE SAME CAN BE SAID OF OUR DOMINION. THERE ARE BAD PEOPLE HERE, BUT THERE ARE GOOD PEOPLE AS WELL.

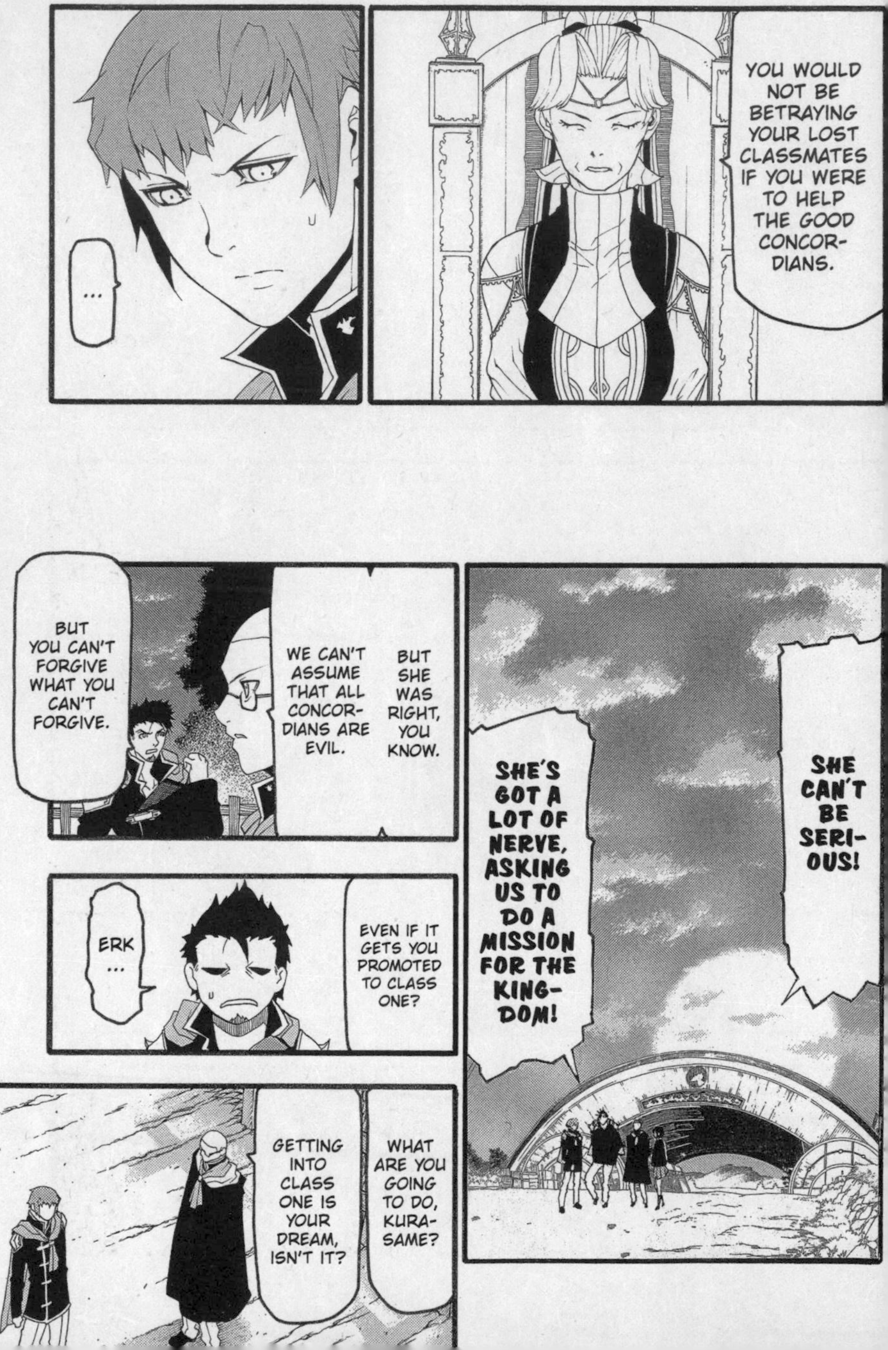
YOU WOULD NOT BE BETRAYING YOUR LOST CLASSMATES IF YOU WERE TO HELP THE GOOD CONCORDIANS.
...
SHE CAN'T BE SERIOUS!
SHE'S GOT A LOT OF NERVE, ASKING US TO DO A MISSION FOR THE KINGDOM!
BUT SHE WAS RIGHT, YOU KNOW.
WE CAN'T ASSUME THAT ALL CONCORDIANS ARE EVIL.
BUT YOU CAN'T FORGIVE WHAT YOU CAN'T FORGIVE.
EVEN IF IT GETS YOU PROMOTED TO CLASS ONE?
ERK ...
WHAT ARE YOU GOING TO DO, KURASAME?
GETTING INTO CLASS ONE IS YOUR DREAM, ISN'T IT?

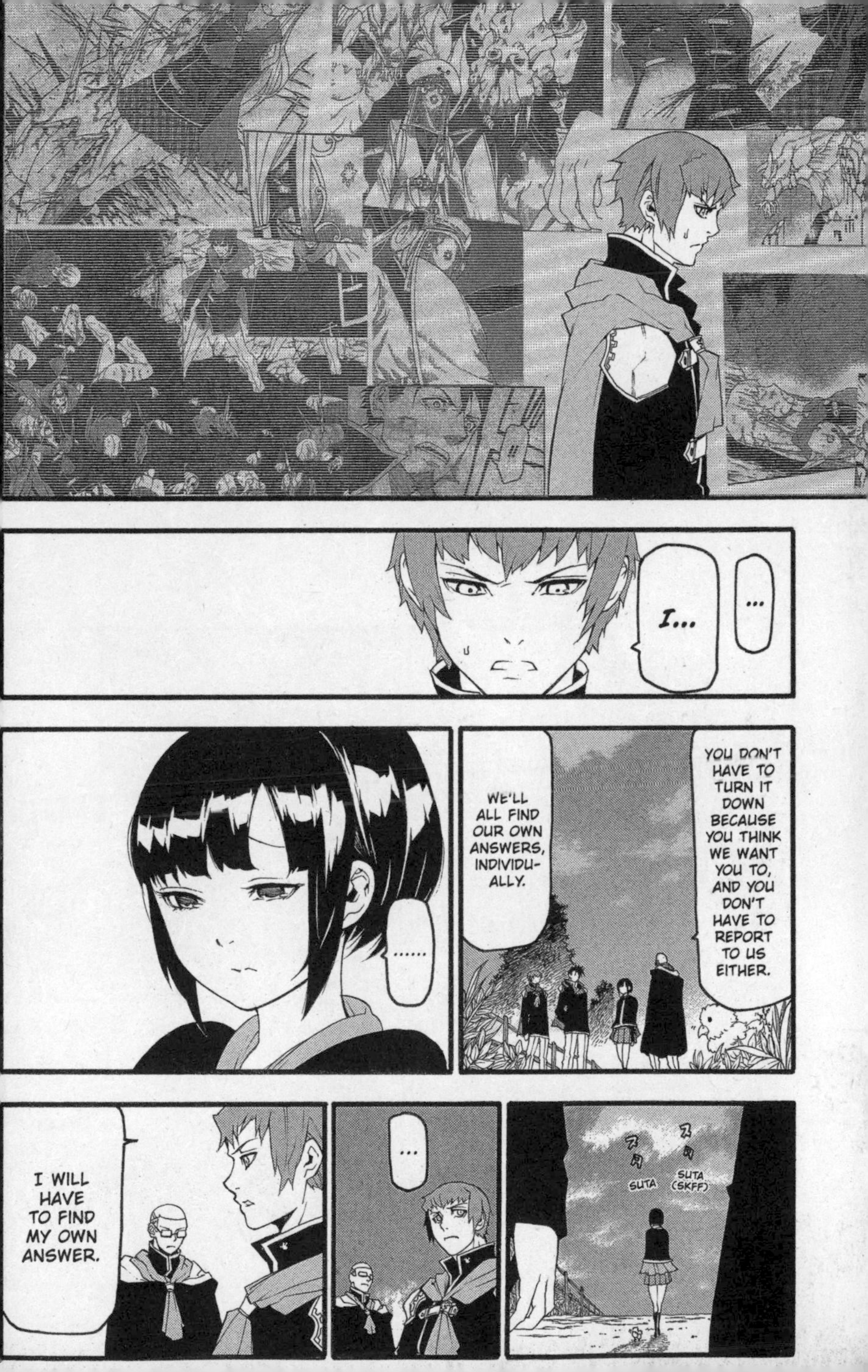
...
I...
YOU DON'T HAVE TO TURN IT DOWN BECAUSE YOU THINK WE WANT YOU TO, AND YOU DON'T HAVE TO REPORT TO US EITHER.
WE'LL ALL FIND OUR OWN ANSWERS, INDIVIDU-ALLY.
......
SUTA (SKFF)
SUTA
...
I WILL HAVE TO FIND MY OWN ANSWER.

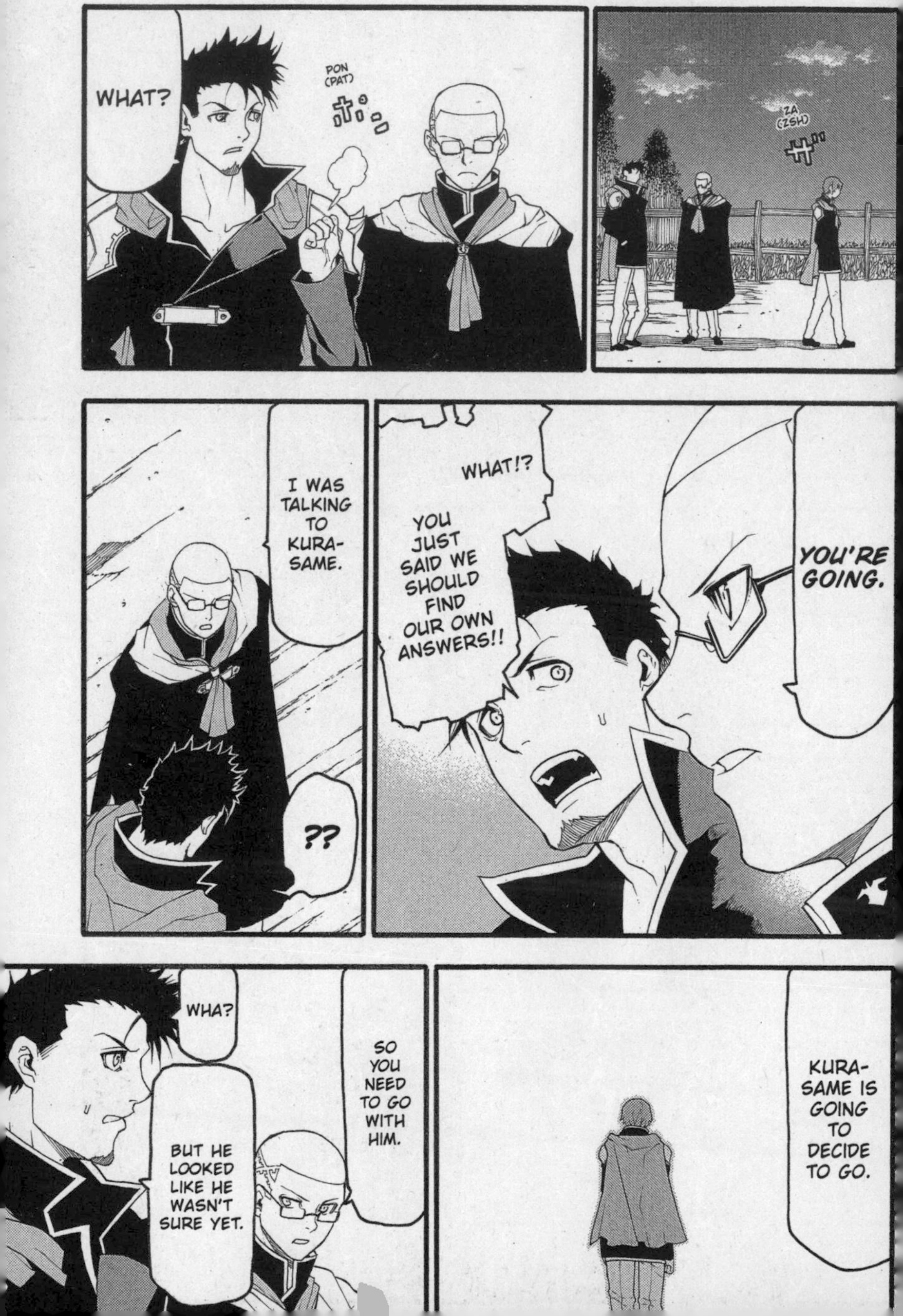
ZA (ZSH)
PON (PAT)
WHAT?
YOU'RE GOING.
WHAT!?
YOU JUST SAID WE SHOULD FIND OUR OWN ANSWERS!!
I WAS TALKING TO KURA-SAME.
??
KURA-SAME IS GOING TO DECIDE TO GO.
SO YOU NEED TO GO WITH HIM.
WHA?
BUT HE LOOKED LIKE HE WASN'T SURE YET.

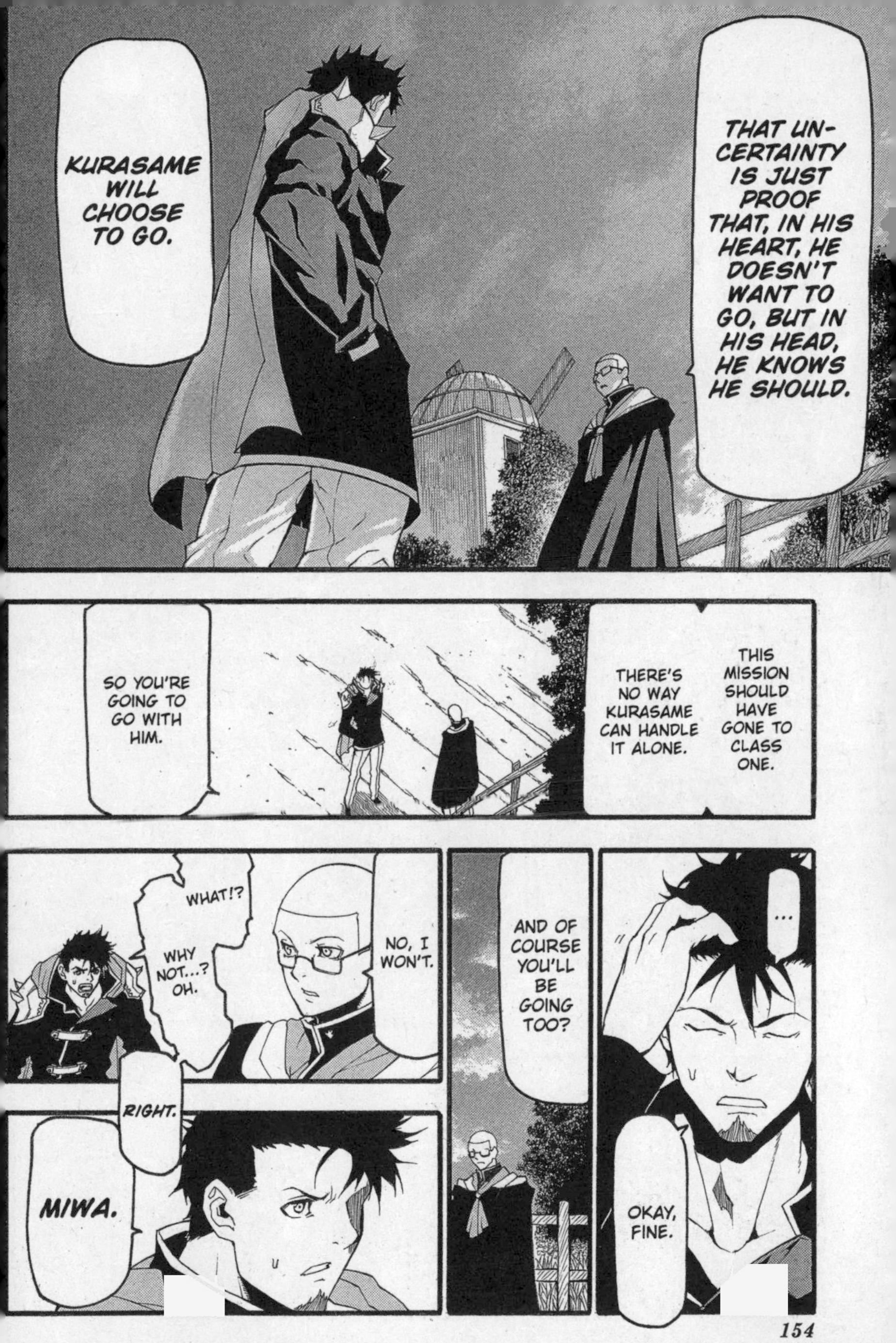
THAT UN-CERTAINTY IS JUST PROOF THAT, IN HIS HEART, HE DOESN'T WANT TO GO, BUT IN HIS HEAD, HE KNOWS HE SHOULD.
KURASAME WILL CHOOSE TO GO.
THIS MISSION SHOULD HAVE GONE TO CLASS ONE.
THERE'S NO WAY KURASAME CAN HANDLE IT ALONE.
SO YOU'RE GOING TO GO WITH HIM.
...
OKAY, FINE.
AND OF COURSE YOU'LL BE GOING TOO?
NO, I WON'T.
WHAT!?
WHY NOT...? OH.
RIGHT.
MIWA.

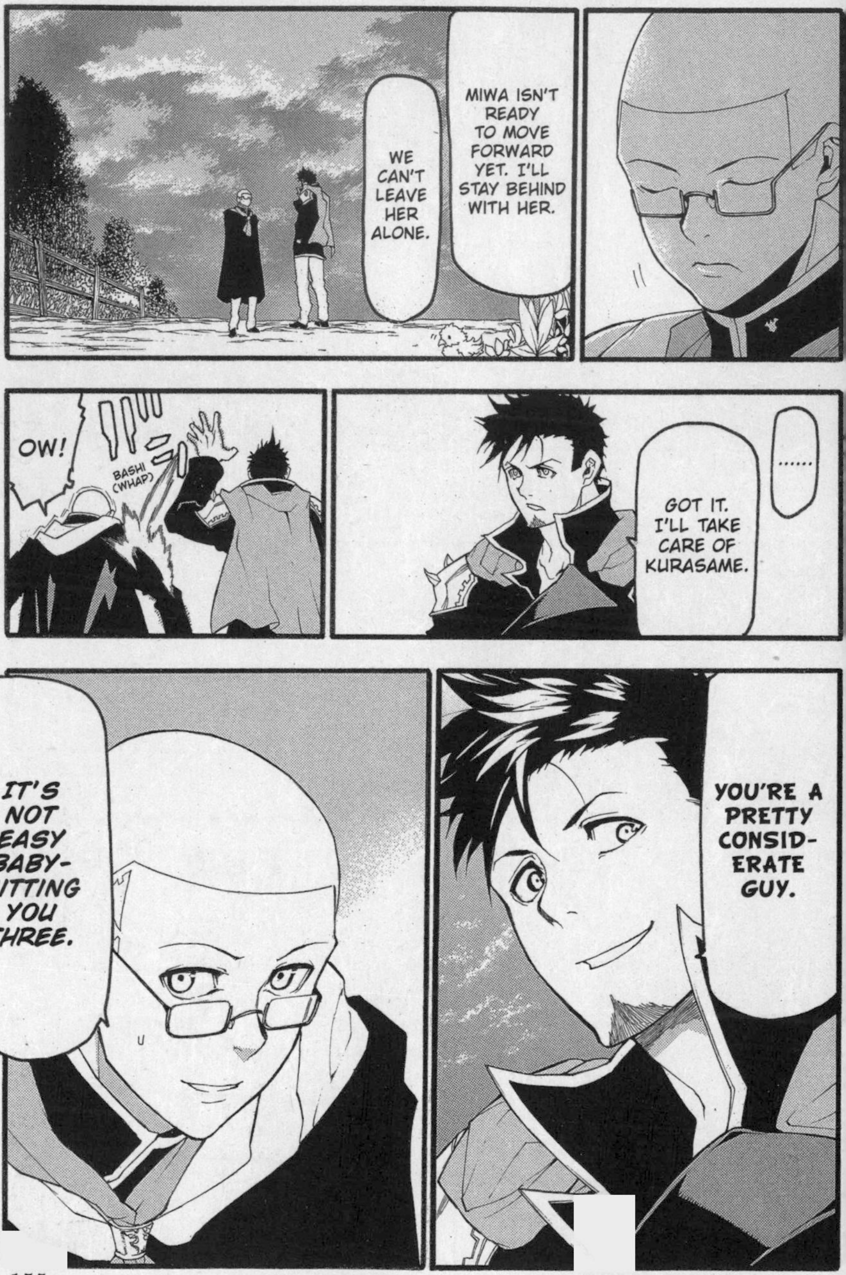
MIWA ISN'T READY TO MOVE FORWARD YET. I'LL STAY BEHIND WITH HER.
WE CAN'T LEAVE HER ALONE.
......
GOT IT. I'LL TAKE CARE OF KURASAME.
BASHI (WHAP)
OW!
YOU'RE A PRETTY CONSID-ERATE GUY.
IT'S NOT EASY BABY-SITTING YOU THREE.

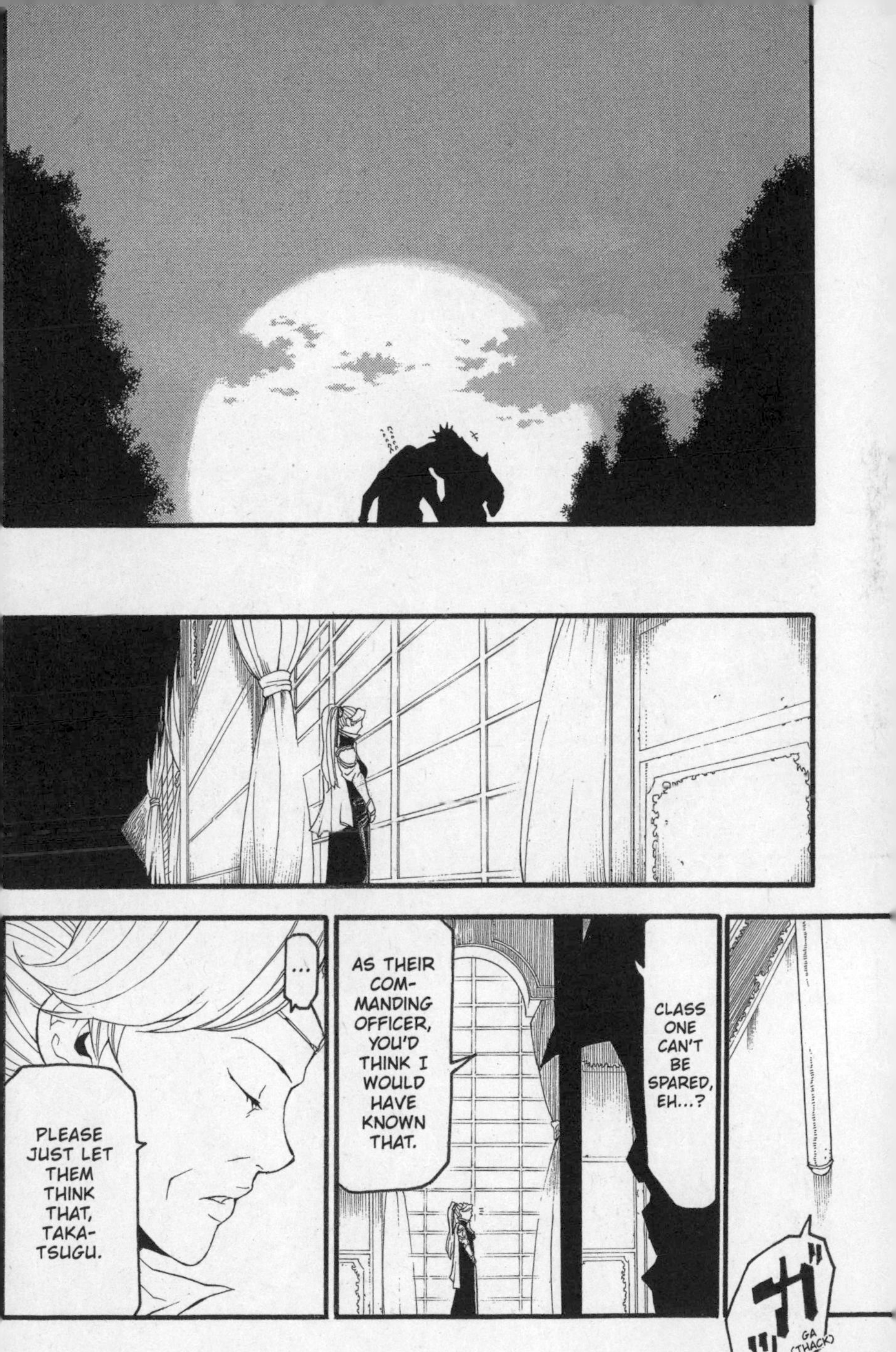
ガッ
GA (THACK)
CLASS ONE CAN'T BE SPARED, EH...?
AS THEIR COM-MANDING OFFICER, YOU'D THINK I WOULD HAVE KNOWN THAT.
...
PLEASE JUST LET THEM THINK THAT, TAKA-TSUGU.

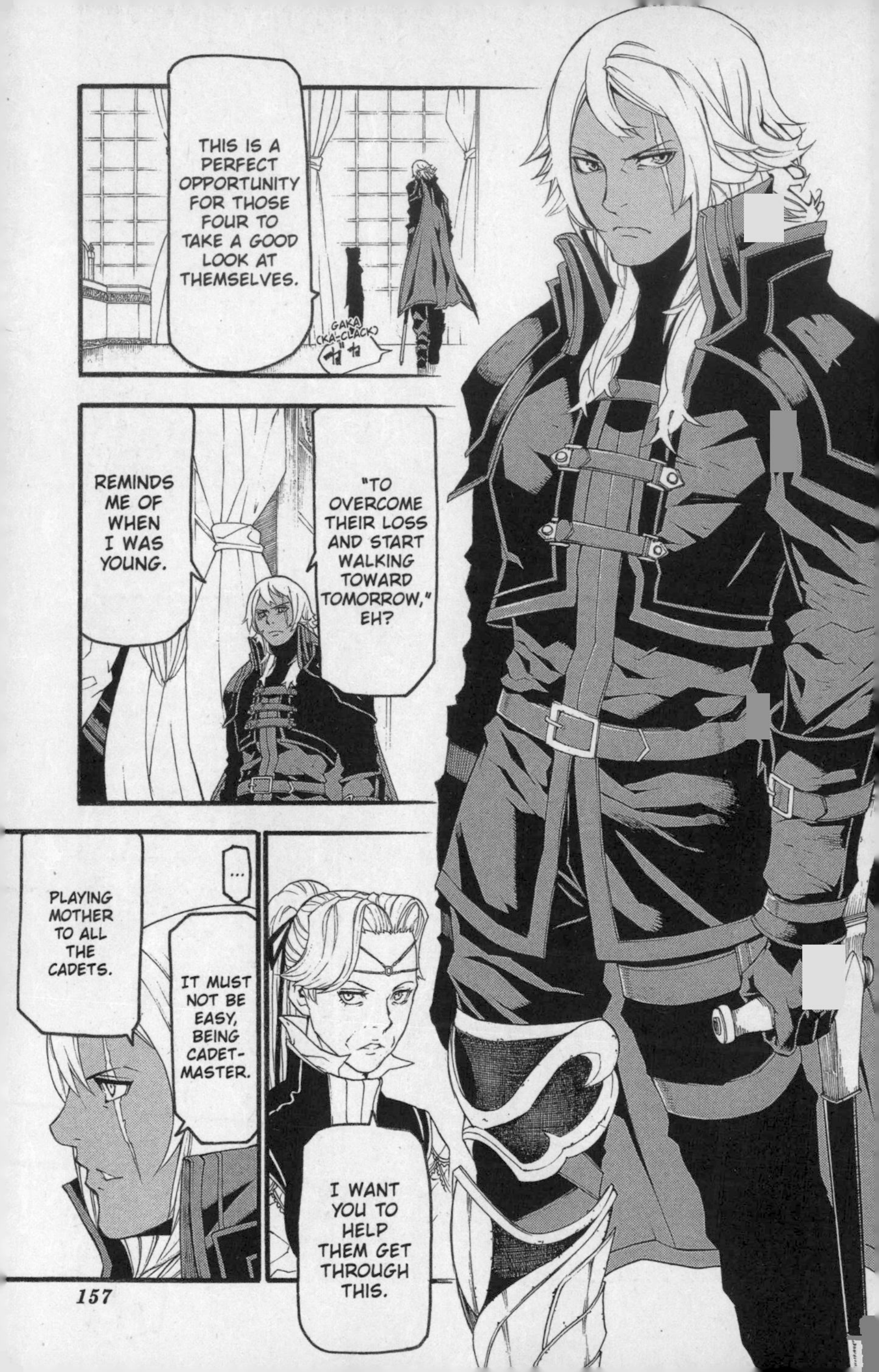
THIS IS A PERFECT OPPORTUNITY FOR THOSE FOUR TO TAKE A GOOD LOOK AT THEMSELVES.
GAKA (KA-CLACK)
"TO OVERCOME THEIR LOSS AND START WALKING TOWARD TOMORROW," EH?
REMINDS ME OF WHEN I WAS YOUNG.
...
PLAYING MOTHER TO ALL THE CADETS.
IT MUST NOT BE EASY, BEING CADET-MASTER.
I WANT YOU TO HELP THEM GET THROUGH THIS.

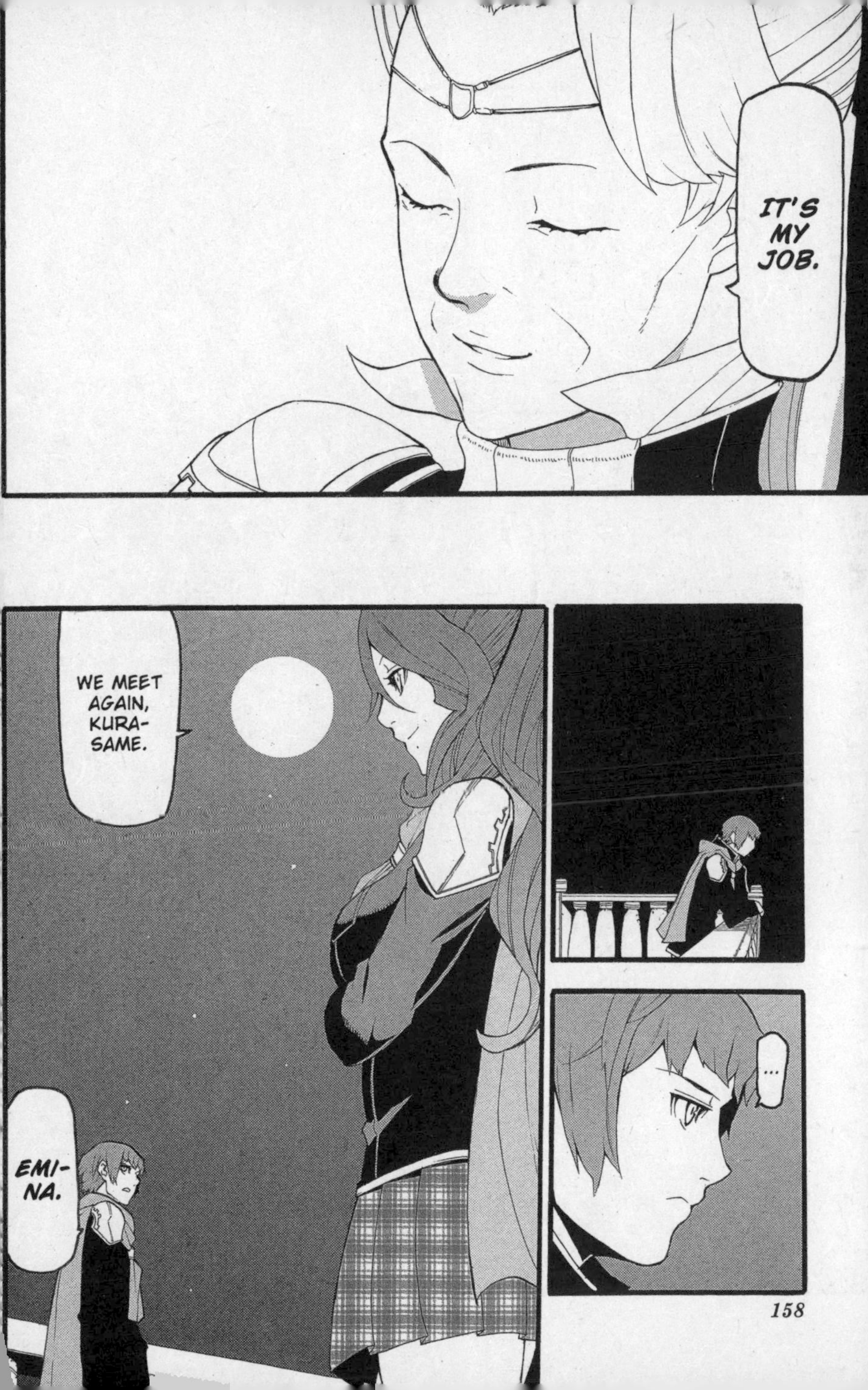
IT'S MY JOB.
...
WE MEET AGAIN, KURA-SAME.
EMI-NA.

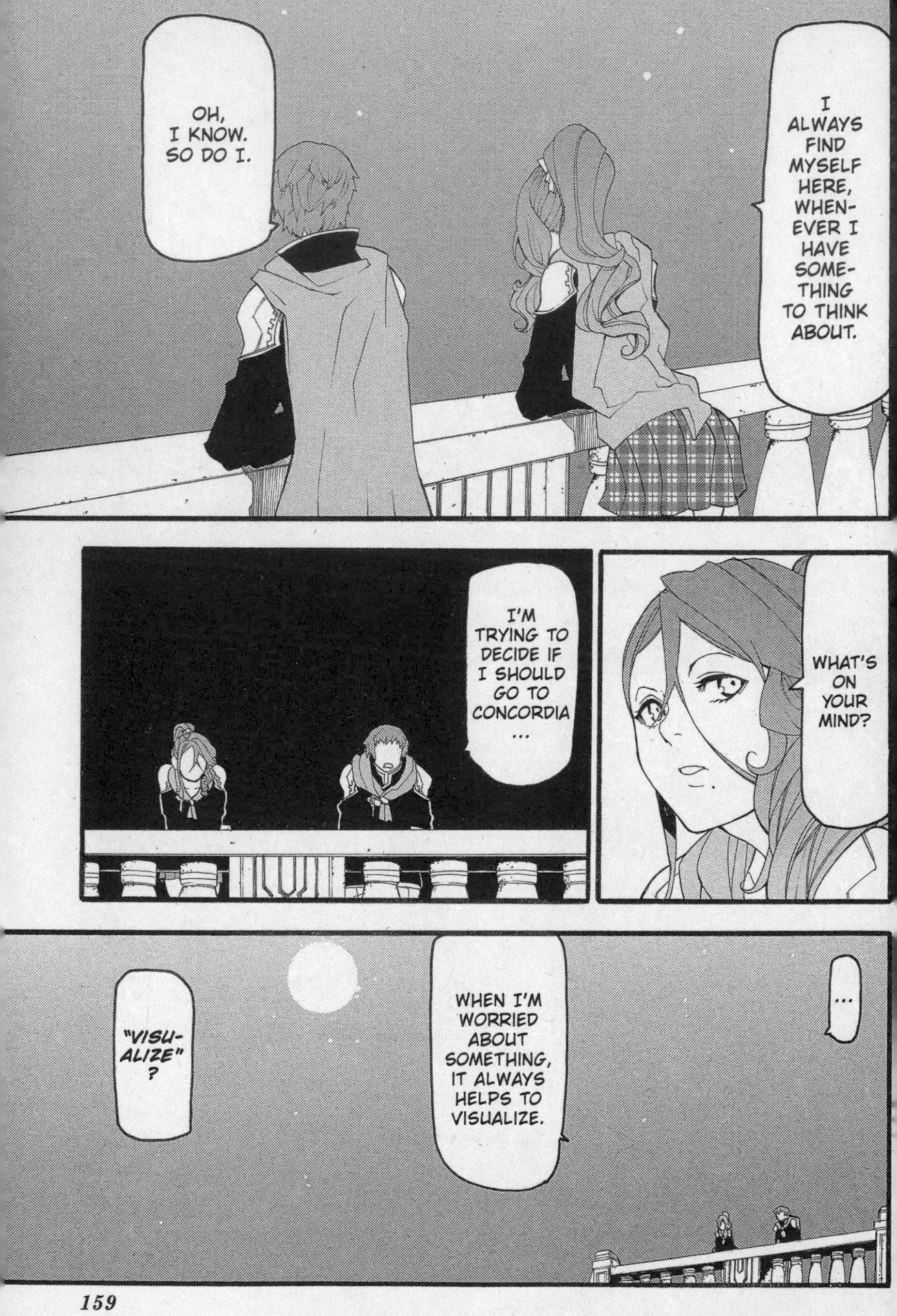
I ALWAYS FIND MYSELF HERE, WHENEVER I HAVE SOMETHING TO THINK ABOUT.
OH, I KNOW. SO DO I.
WHAT'S ON YOUR MIND?
I'M TRYING TO DECIDE IF I SHOULD GO TO CONCORDIA...
...
WHEN I'M WORRIED ABOUT SOMETHING, IT ALWAYS HELPS TO VISUALIZE.
"VISUALIZE"?

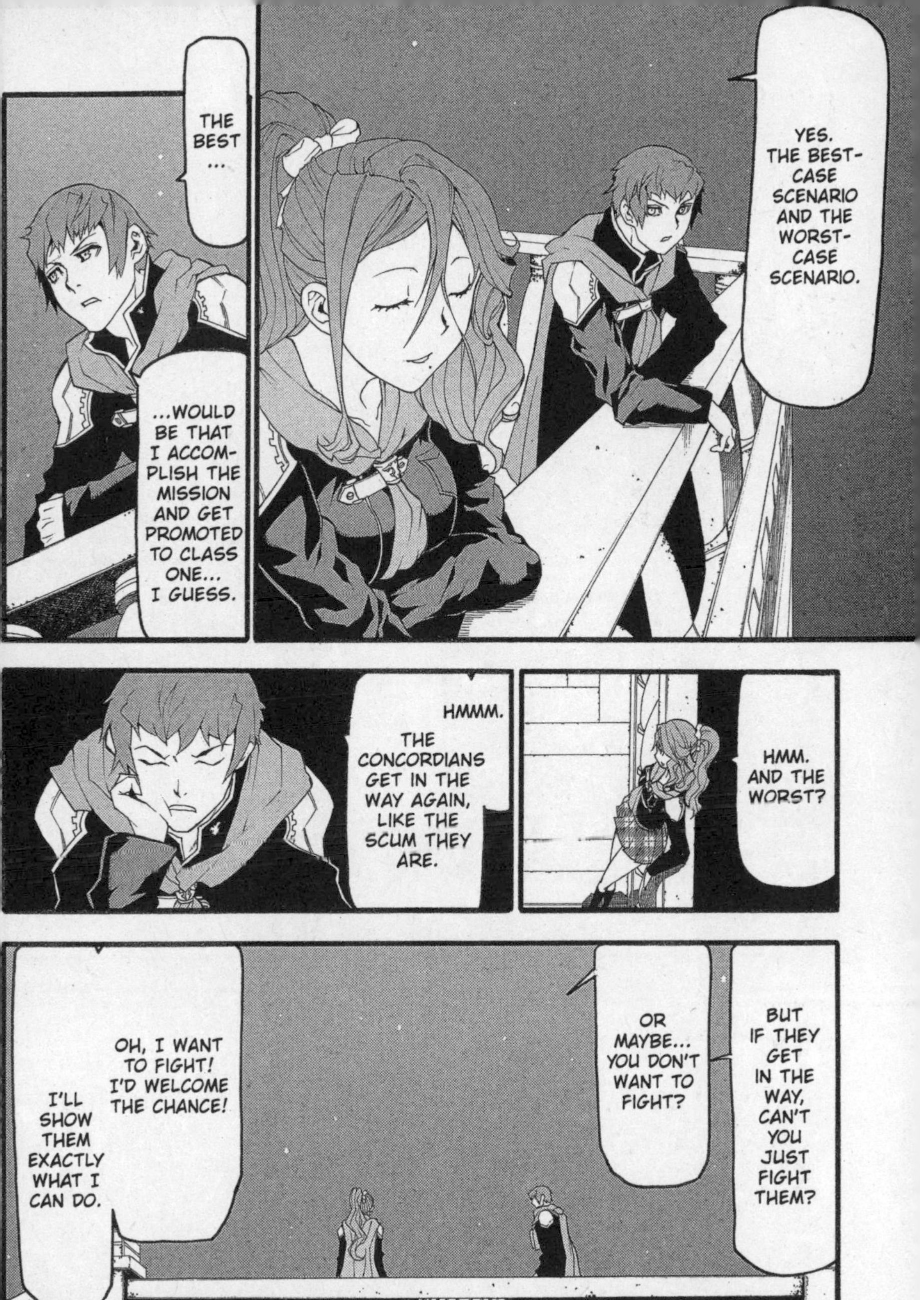
YES. THE BEST-CASE SCENARIO AND THE WORST-CASE SCENARIO.
THE BEST...
...WOULD BE THAT I ACCOMPLISH THE MISSION AND GET PROMOTED TO CLASS ONE... I GUESS.
HMM. AND THE WORST?
HMMM.
THE CONCORDIANS GET IN THE WAY AGAIN, LIKE THE SCUM THEY ARE.
BUT IF THEY GET IN THE WAY, CAN'T YOU JUST FIGHT THEM?
OR MAYBE... YOU DON'T WANT TO FIGHT?
OH, I WANT TO FIGHT! I'D WELCOME THE CHANCE!
I'LL SHOW THEM EXACTLY WHAT I CAN DO.

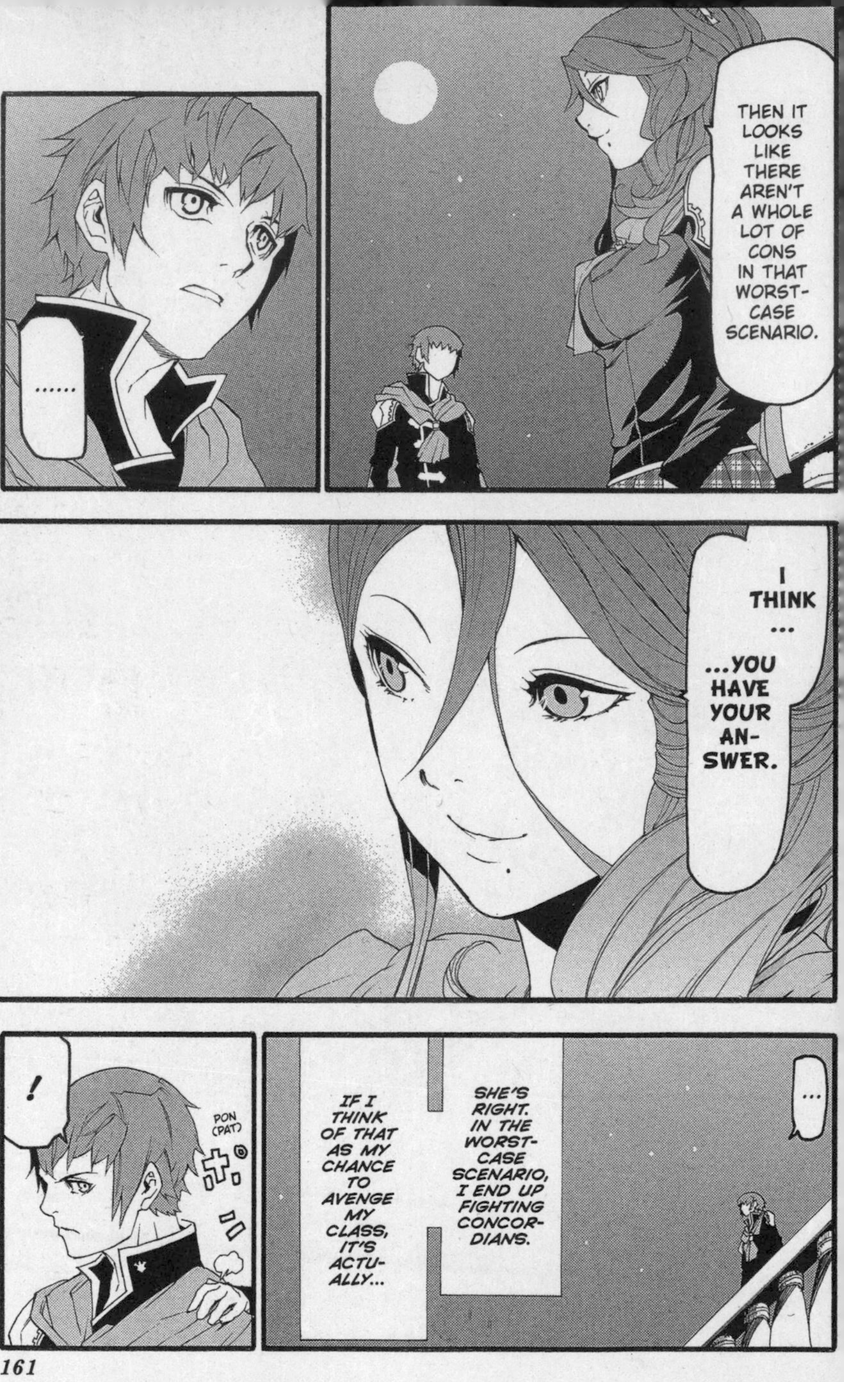
THEN IT LOOKS LIKE THERE AREN'T A WHOLE LOT OF CONS IN THAT WORST-CASE SCENARIO.
......
I THINK ...
...YOU HAVE YOUR AN-SWER.
...
SHE'S RIGHT. IN THE WORST-CASE SCENARIO, I END UP FIGHTING CONCOR-DIANS.
IF I THINK OF THAT AS MY CHANCE TO AVENGE MY CLASS, IT'S ACTU-ALLY...
!
PON (PAT)

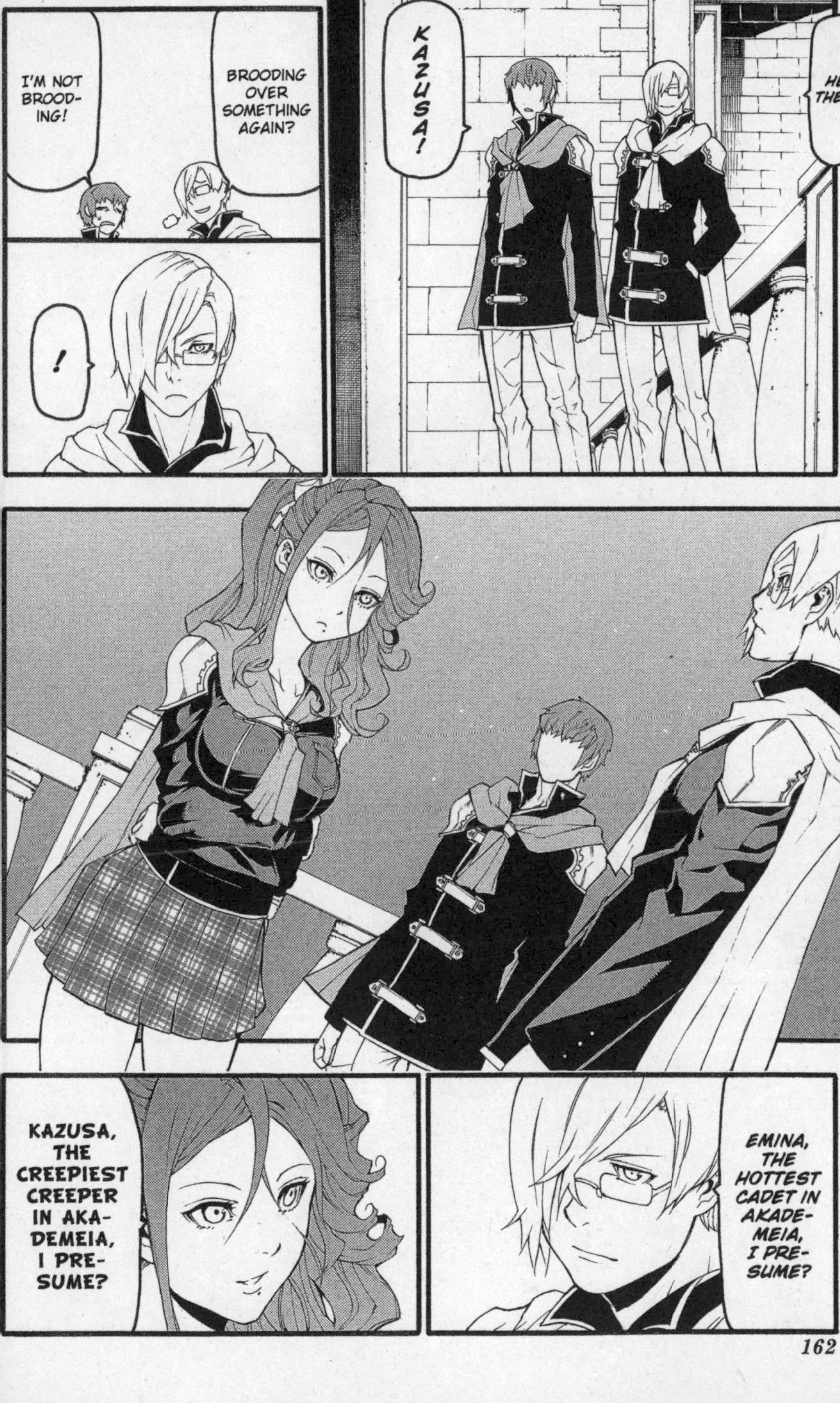
HEY, THERE.
KAZUSA!
BROODING OVER SOMETHING AGAIN?
I'M NOT BROOD-ING!
!
EMINA, THE HOTTEST CADET IN AKADE-MEIA, I PRE-SUME?
KAZUSA, THE CREEPIEST CREEPER IN AKA-DEMEIA, I PRE-SUME?

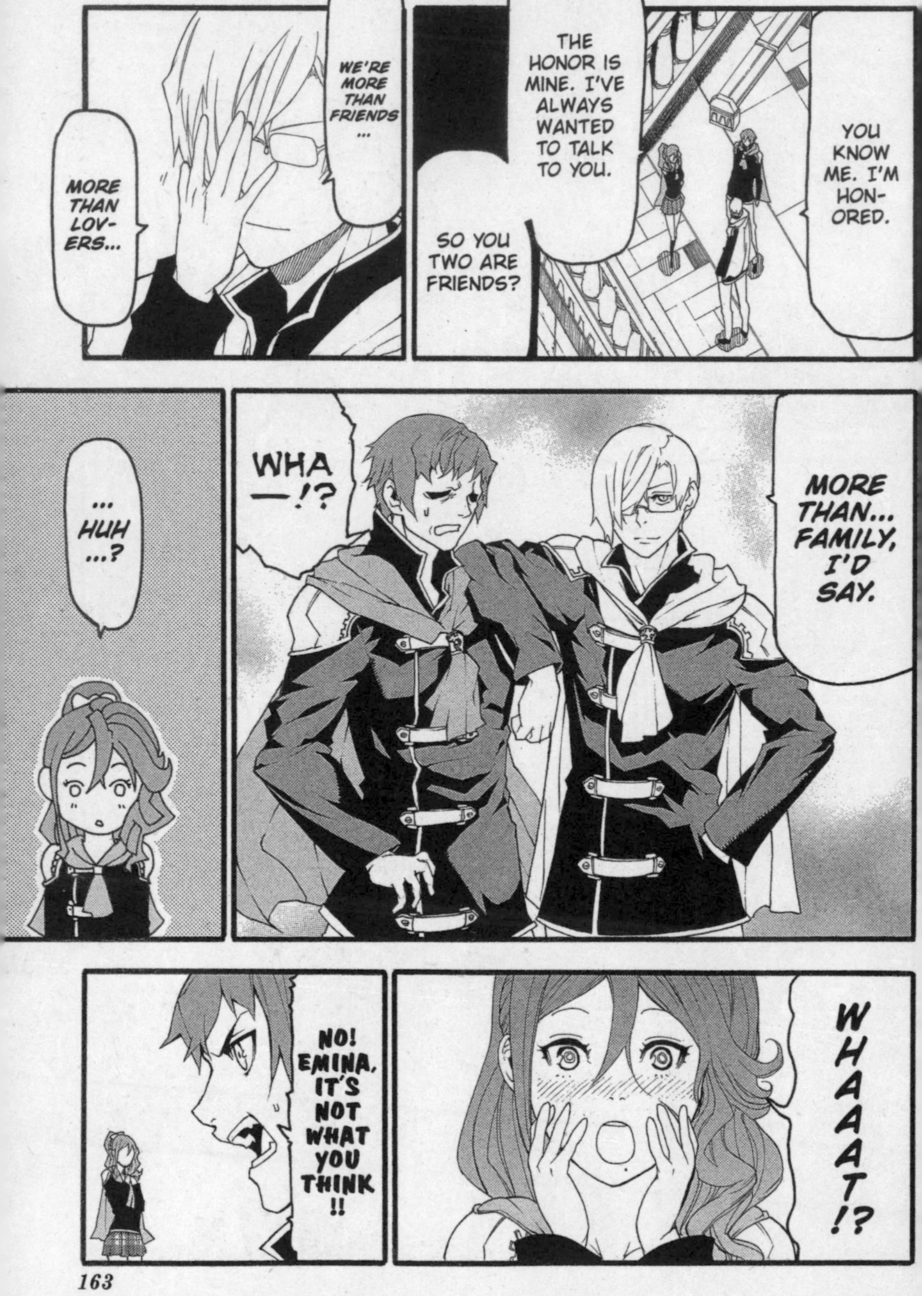
YOU KNOW ME. I'M HONORED.
THE HONOR IS MINE. I'VE ALWAYS WANTED TO TALK TO YOU.
SO YOU TWO ARE FRIENDS?
WE'RE MORE THAN FRIENDS...
MORE THAN LOVERS...
MORE THAN... FAMILY, I'D SAY.
WHA—!?
...HUH...?
WHAAAAT!?
NO! EMINA, IT'S NOT WHAT YOU THINK!!

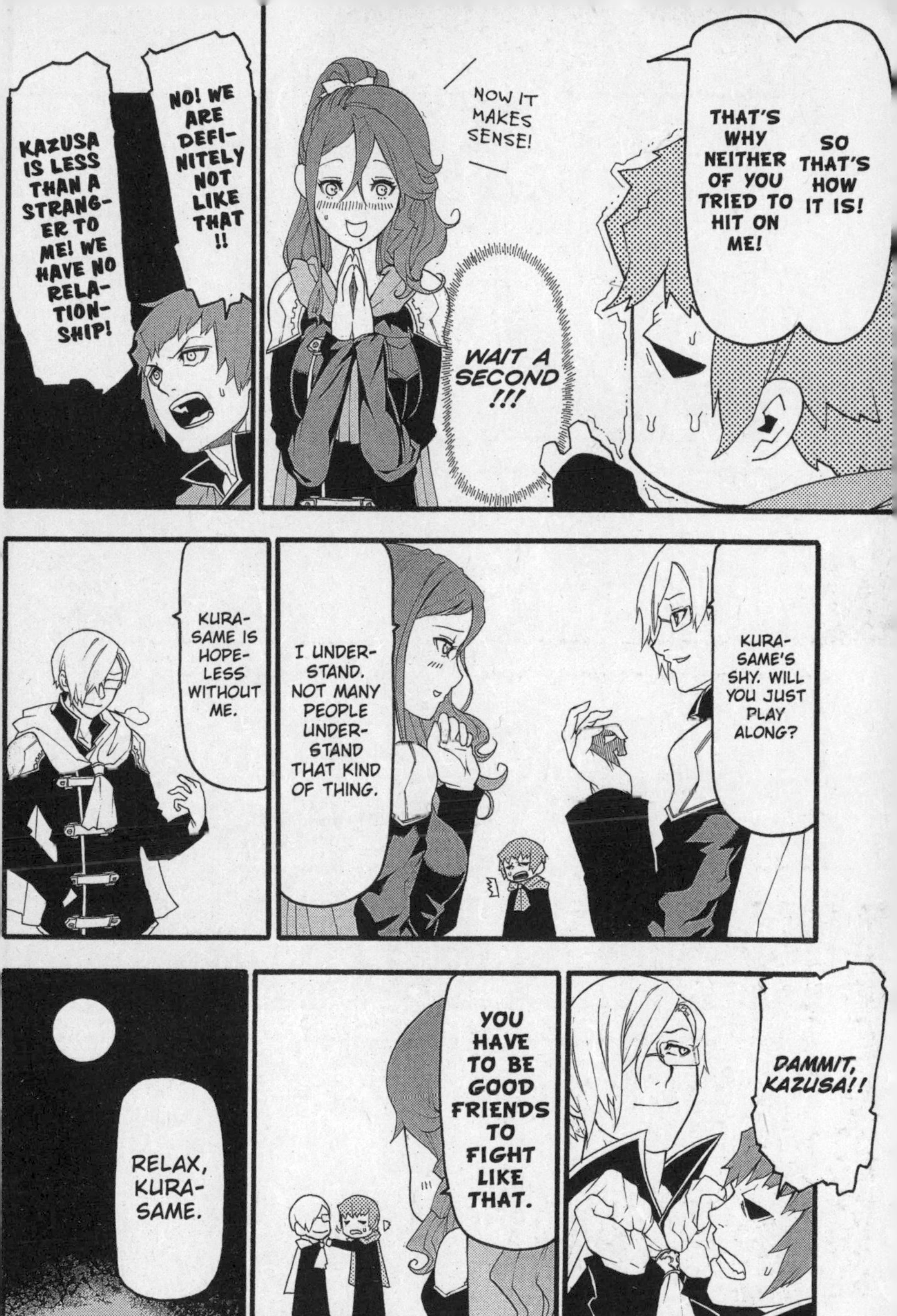
SO THAT'S HOW IT IS!
THAT'S WHY NEITHER OF YOU TRIED TO HIT ON ME!
NOW IT MAKES SENSE!
WAIT A SECOND!!!
NO! WE ARE DEFINITELY NOT LIKE THAT!!
KAZUSA IS LESS THAN A STRANGER TO ME! WE HAVE NO RELATIONSHIP!
KURASAME'S SHY. WILL YOU JUST PLAY ALONG?
I UNDERSTAND. NOT MANY PEOPLE UNDERSTAND THAT KIND OF THING.
KURASAME IS HOPELESS WITHOUT ME.
DAMMIT, KAZUSA!!
YOU HAVE TO BE GOOD FRIENDS TO FIGHT LIKE THAT.
RELAX, KURASAME.

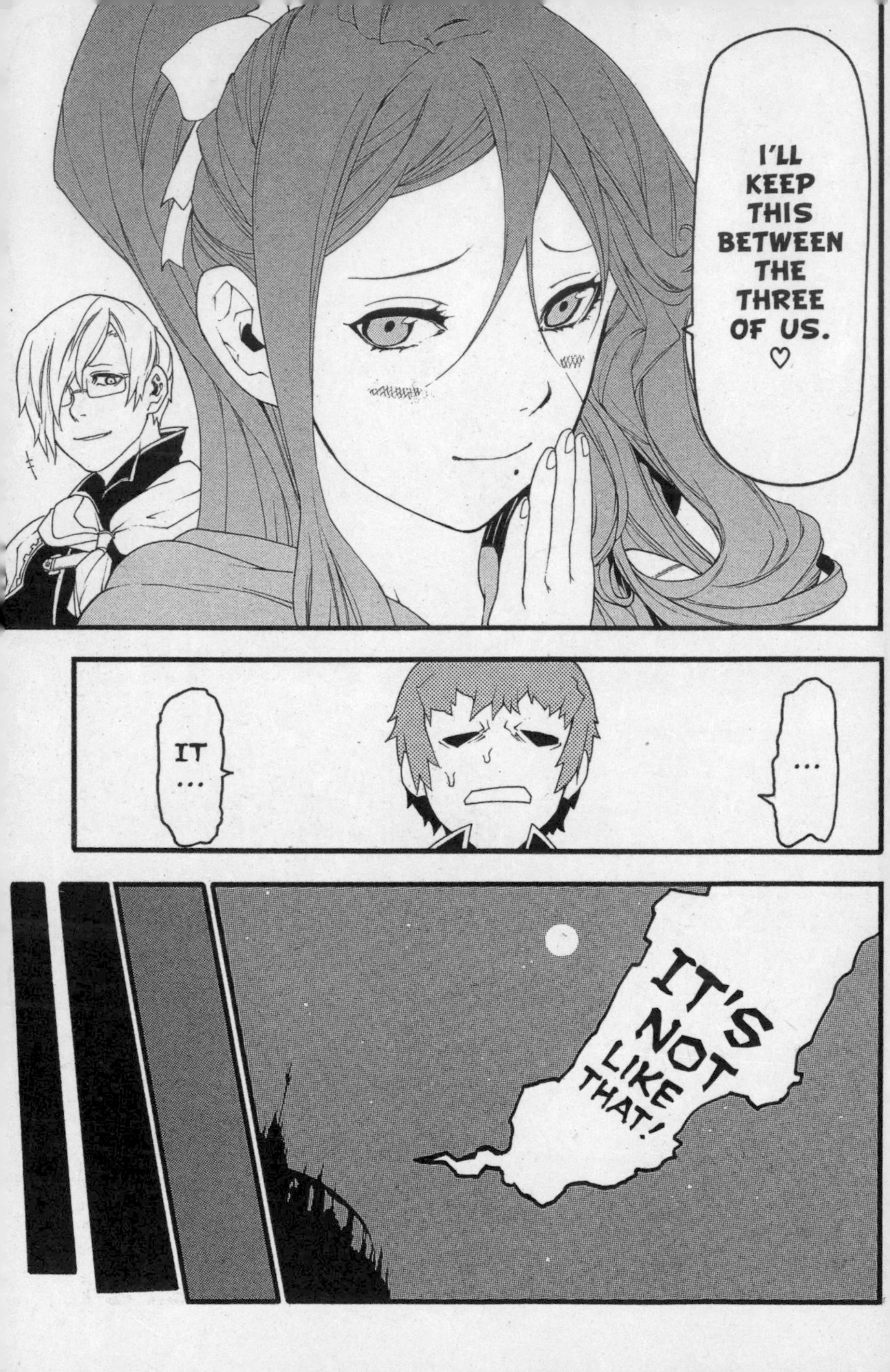

I'LL KEEP THIS BETWEEN THE THREE OF US. ♡
...
IT ...
IT'S NOT LIKE THAT!

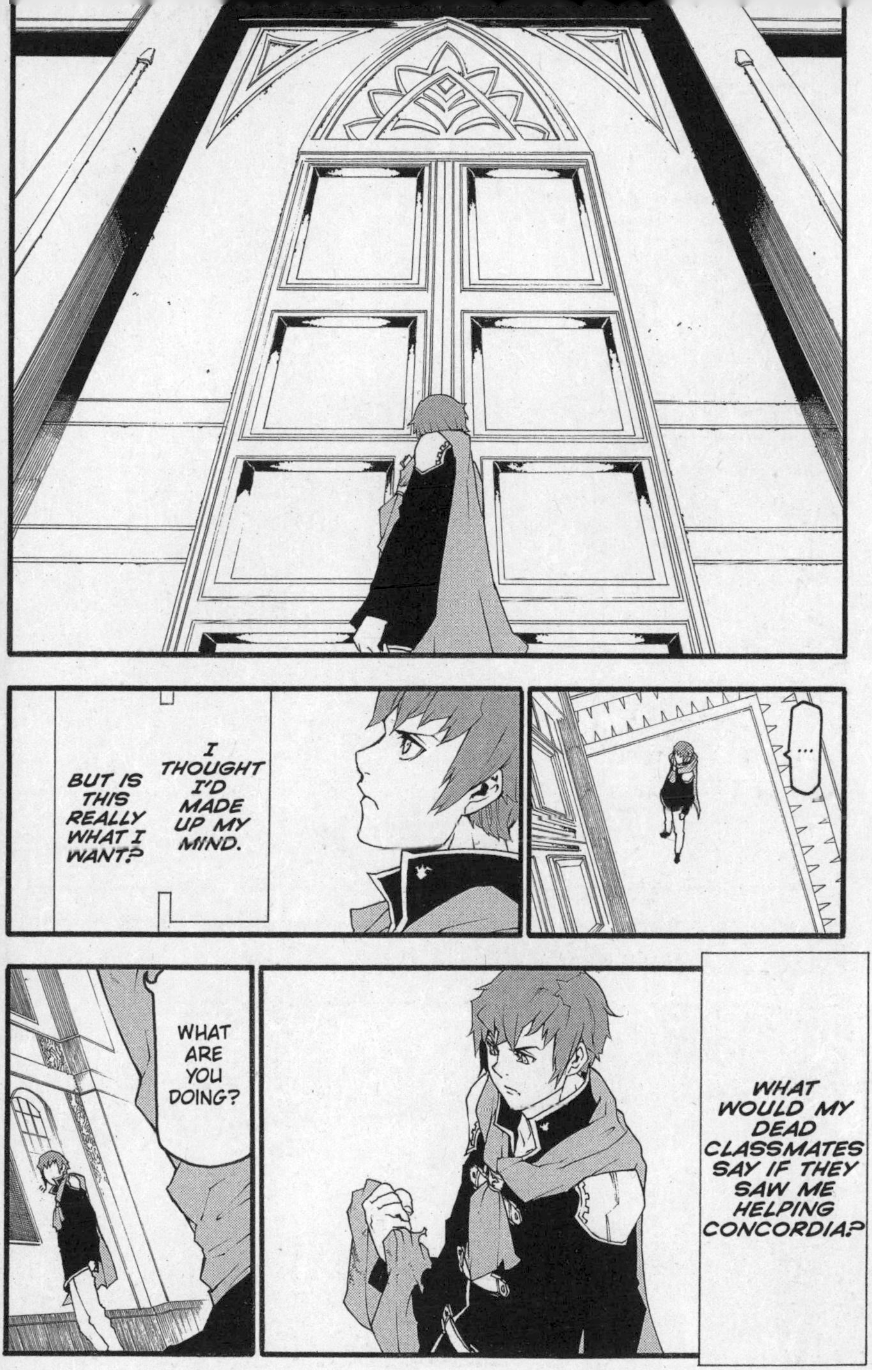
...
I THOUGHT I'D MADE UP MY MIND.
BUT IS THIS REALLY WHAT I WANT?
WHAT WOULD MY DEAD CLASSMATES SAY IF THEY SAW ME HELPING CONCORDIA?
WHAT ARE YOU DOING?

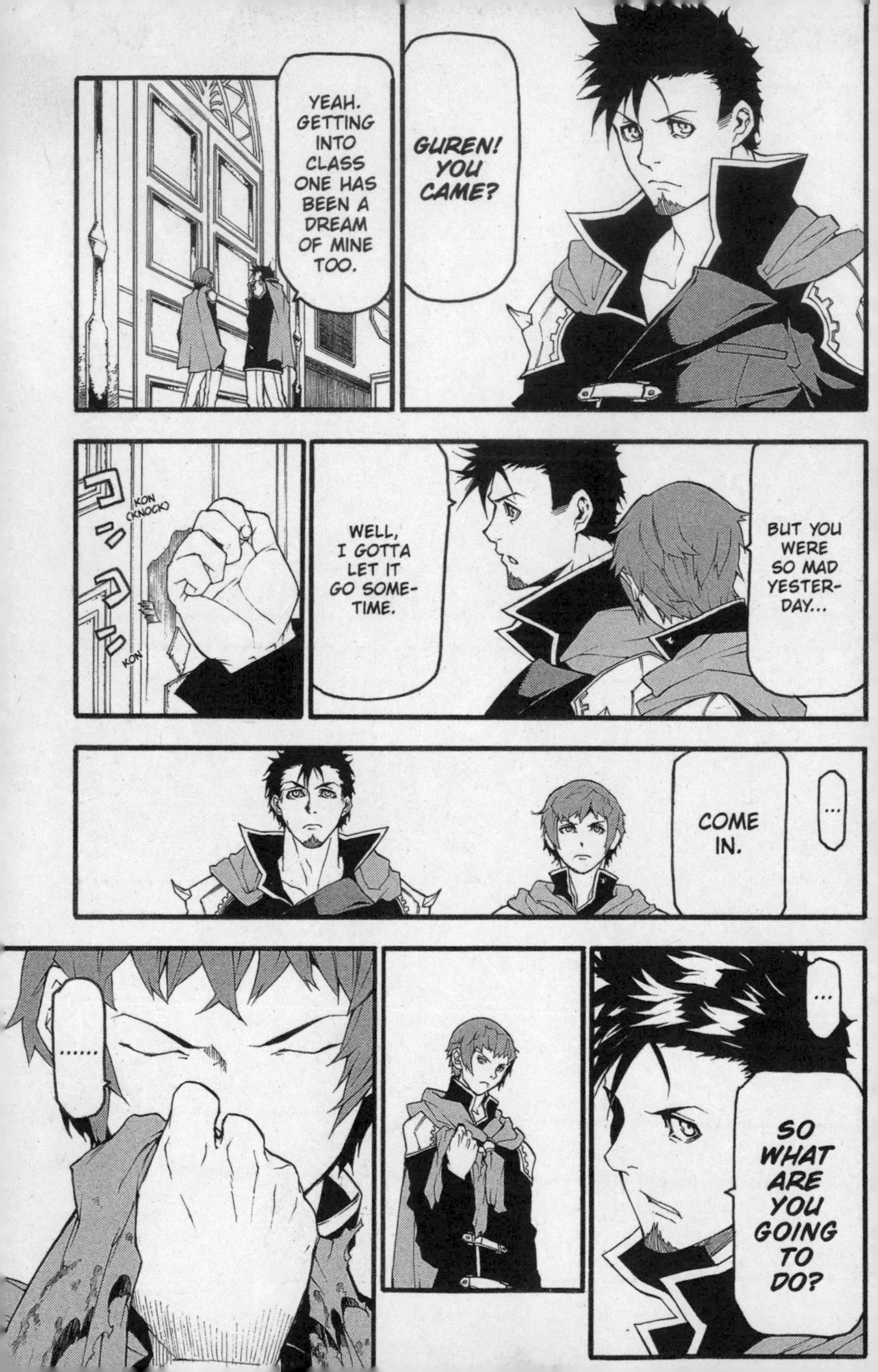
GUREN! YOU CAME?
YEAH. GETTING INTO CLASS ONE HAS BEEN A DREAM OF MINE TOO.
BUT YOU WERE SO MAD YESTER-DAY...
WELL, I GOTTA LET IT GO SOME-TIME.
KON (KNOCK)
KON
...
COME IN.
...
SO WHAT ARE YOU GOING TO DO?
......

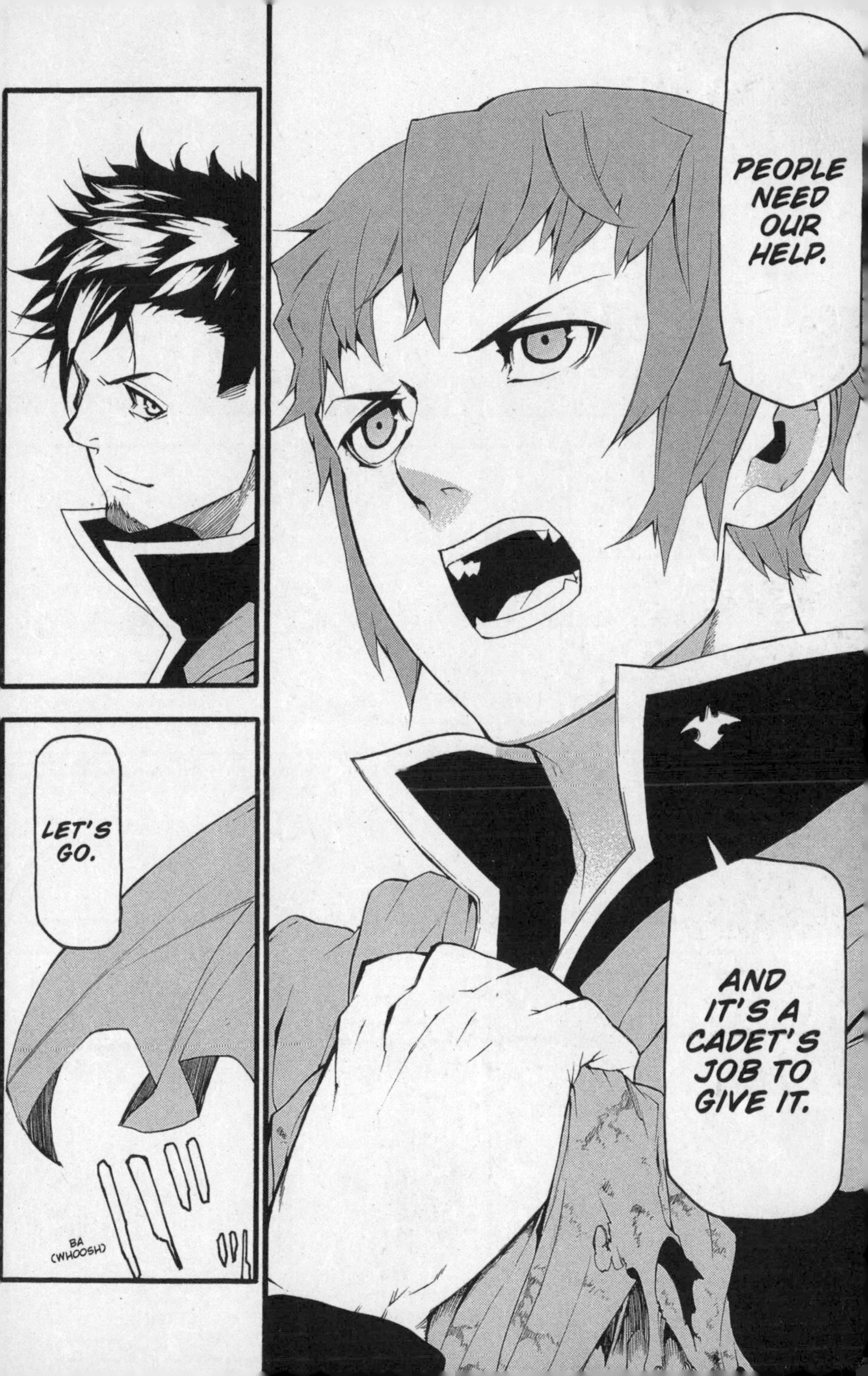
PEOPLE NEED OUR HELP.
AND IT'S A CADET'S JOB TO GIVE IT.
LET'S GO.
BA (WHOOSH)

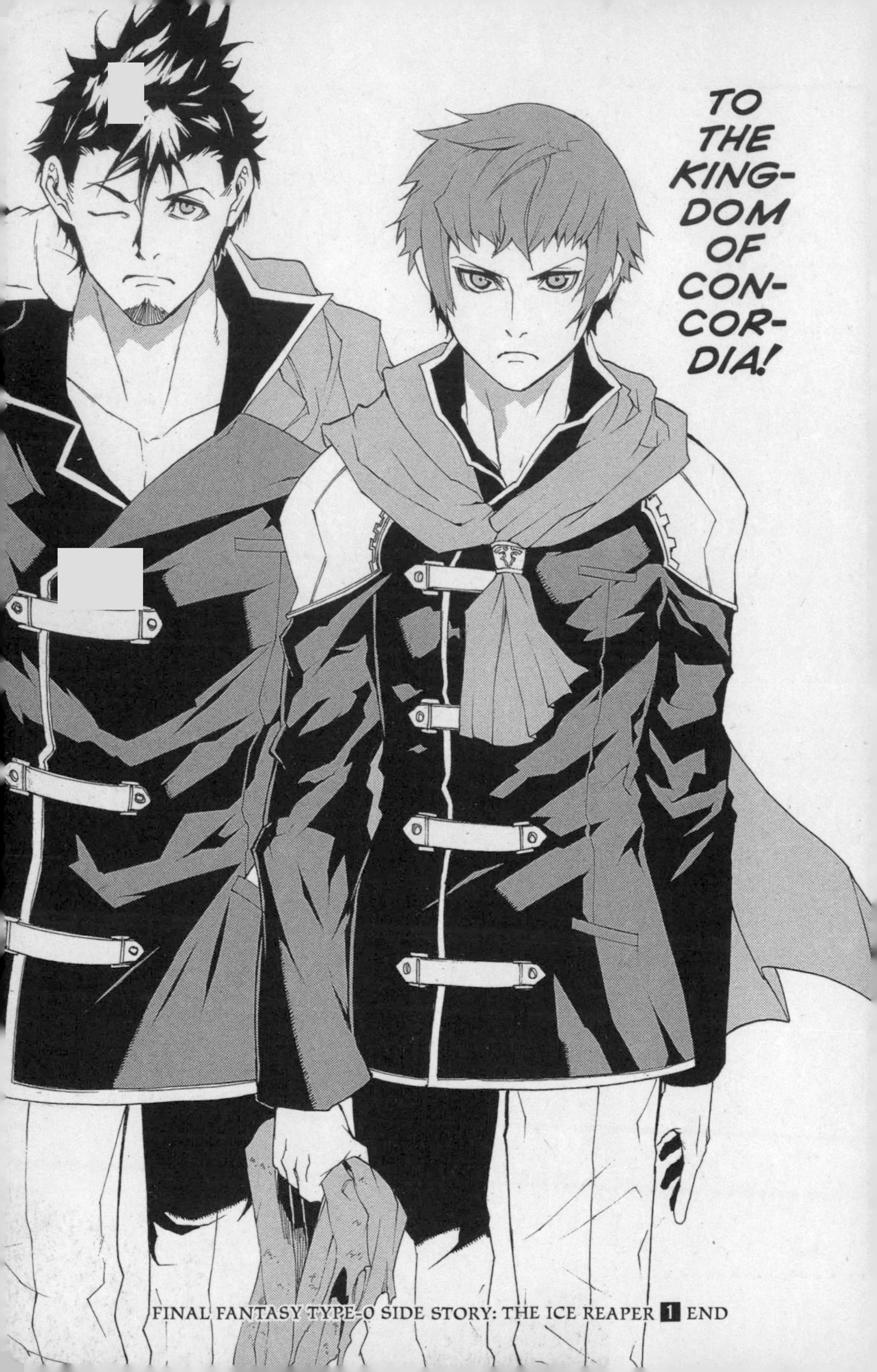
TO THE KINGDOM OF CONCORDIA!
FINAL FANTASY TYPE-0 SIDE STORY: THE ICE REAPER 1 END

Read on for a special preview of

FINAL FANTASY 零式 TYPE-0 SIDE STORY™

The Ice Reaper

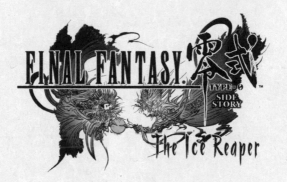

Volume 2!

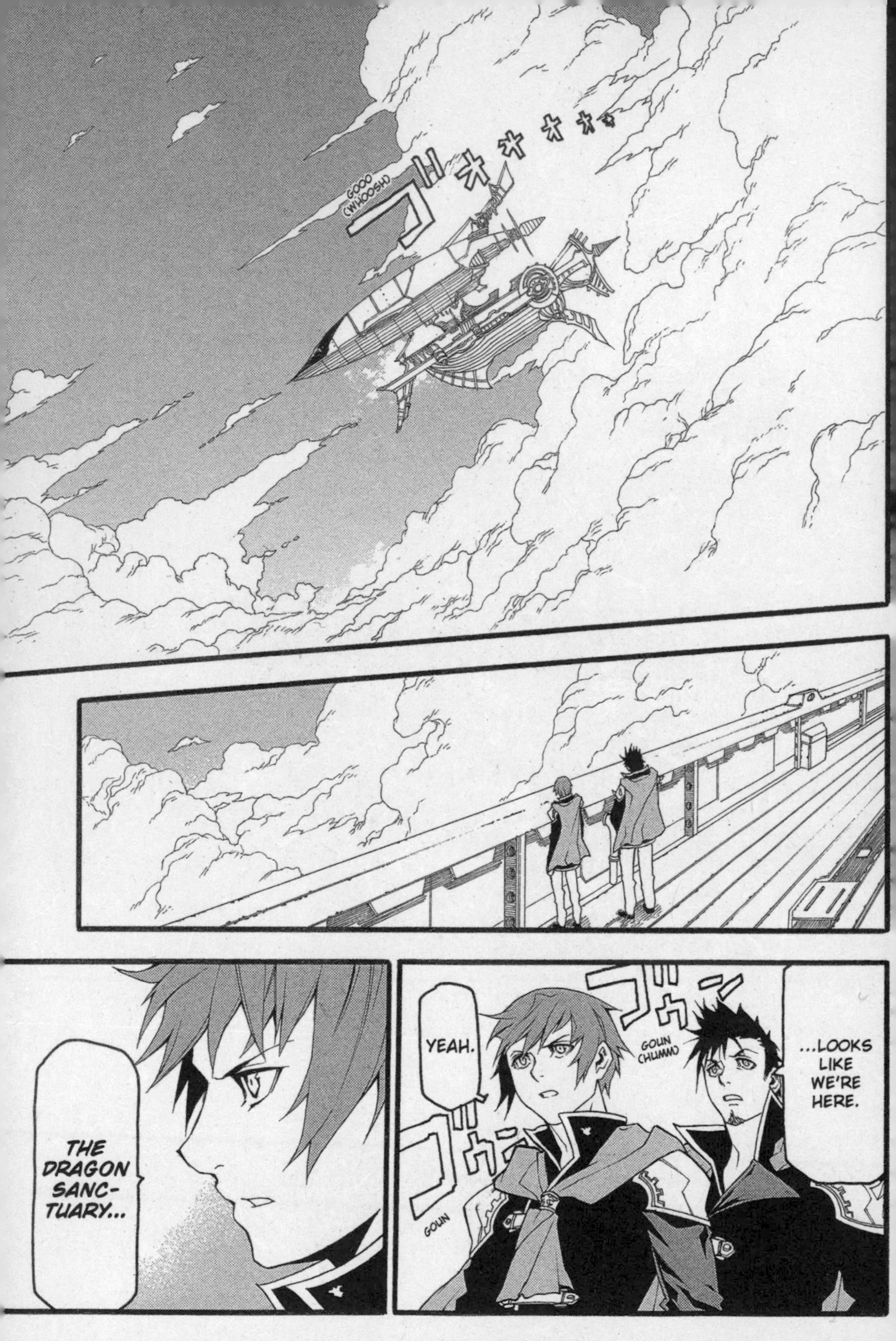
GOOO (WHOOSH)
...LOOKS LIKE WE'RE HERE.
GOUN (HUMMM)
YEAH.
GOUN
THE DRAGON SANCTUARY...

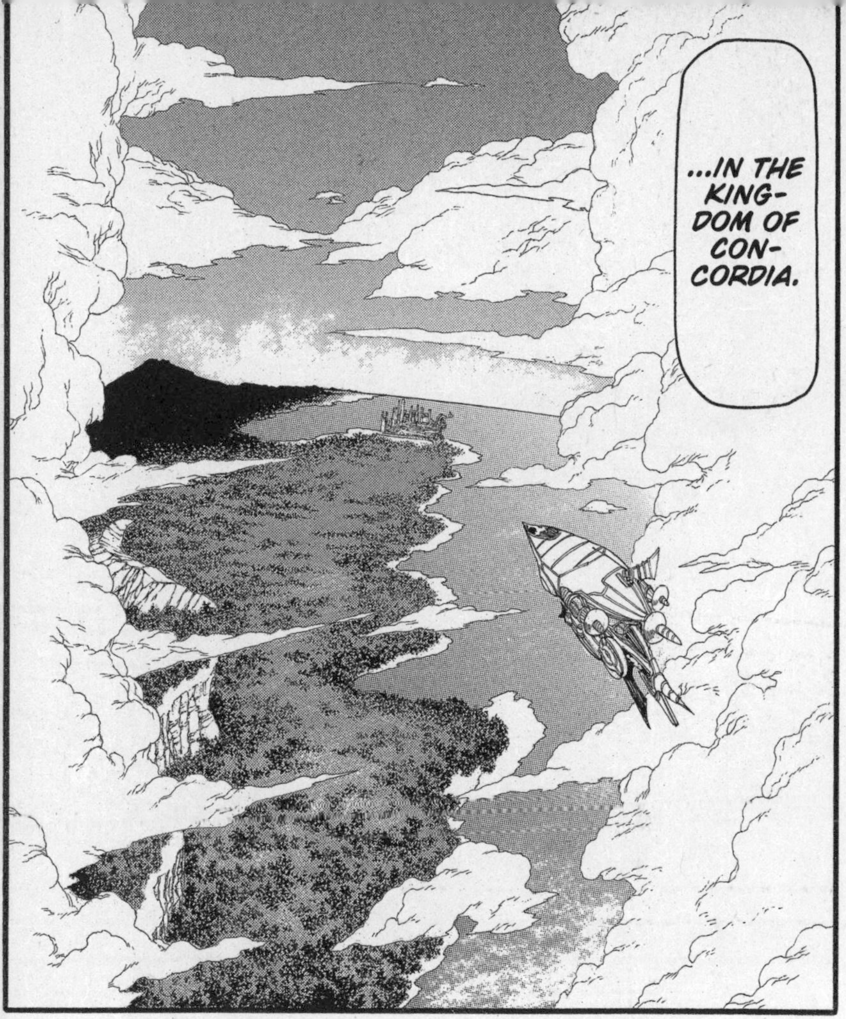
...IN THE KING-DOM OF CON-CORDIA.

CHAPTER 5: CHANCE ENCOUNTERS

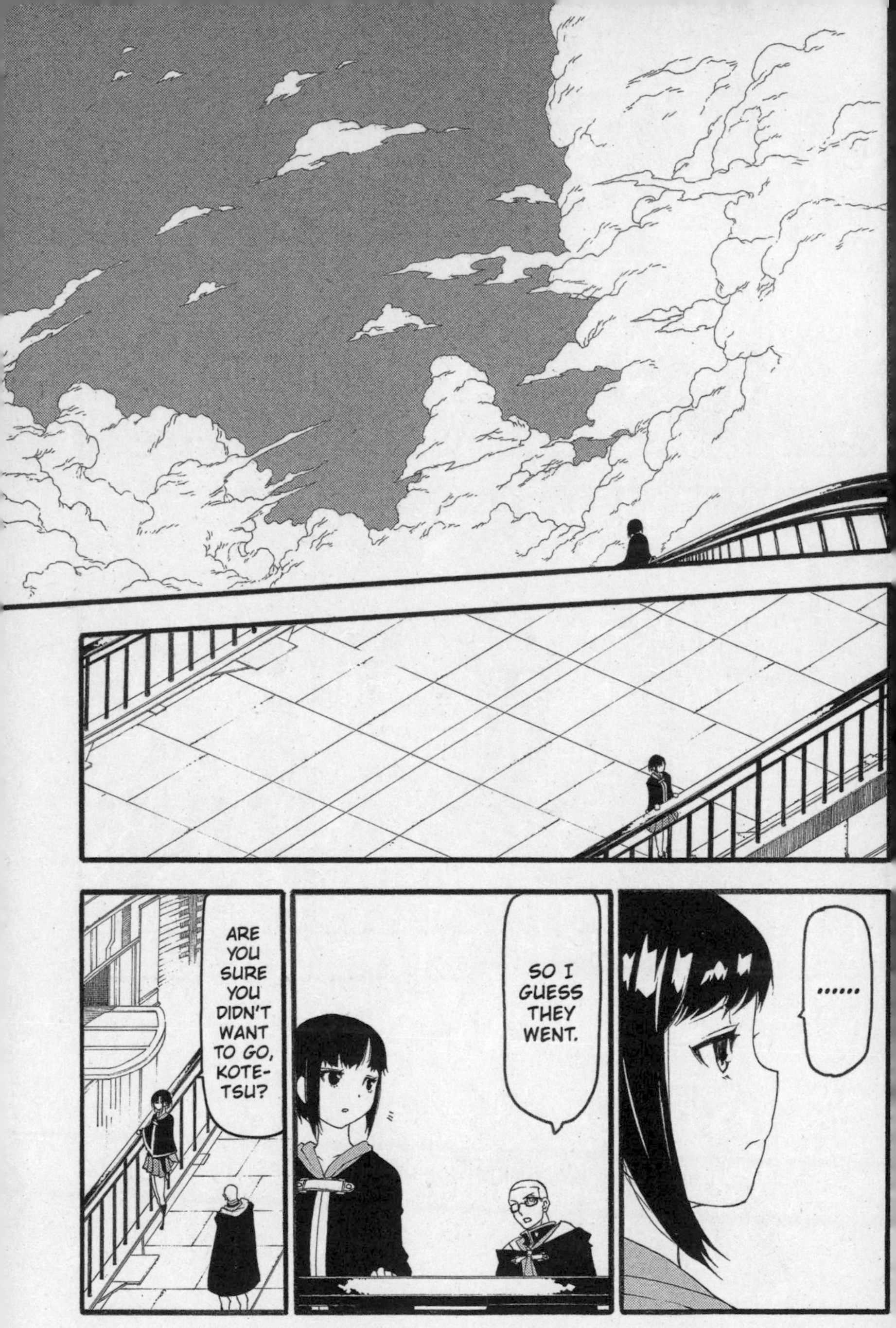
......
SO I GUESS THEY WENT.
ARE YOU SURE YOU DIDN'T WANT TO GO, KOTE-TSU?

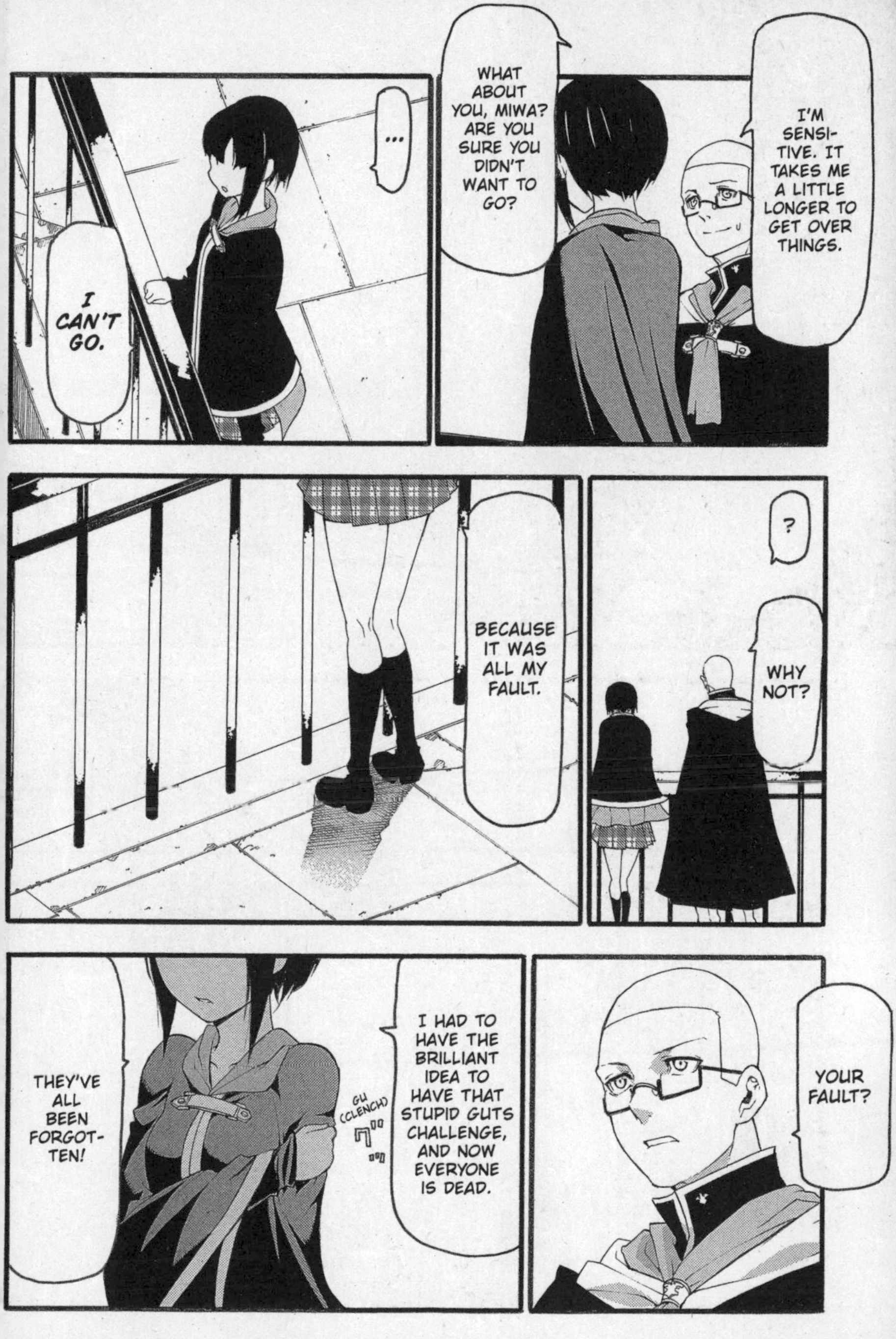
I'M SENSITIVE. IT TAKES ME A LITTLE LONGER TO GET OVER THINGS.
WHAT ABOUT YOU, MIWA? ARE YOU SURE YOU DIDN'T WANT TO GO?
...
I CAN'T GO.
?
WHY NOT?
BECAUSE IT WAS ALL MY FAULT.
YOUR FAULT?
I HAD TO HAVE THE BRILLIANT IDEA TO HAVE THAT STUPID GUTS CHALLENGE, AND NOW EVERYONE IS DEAD.
GU (CLENCH)
THEY'VE ALL BEEN FORGOTTEN!

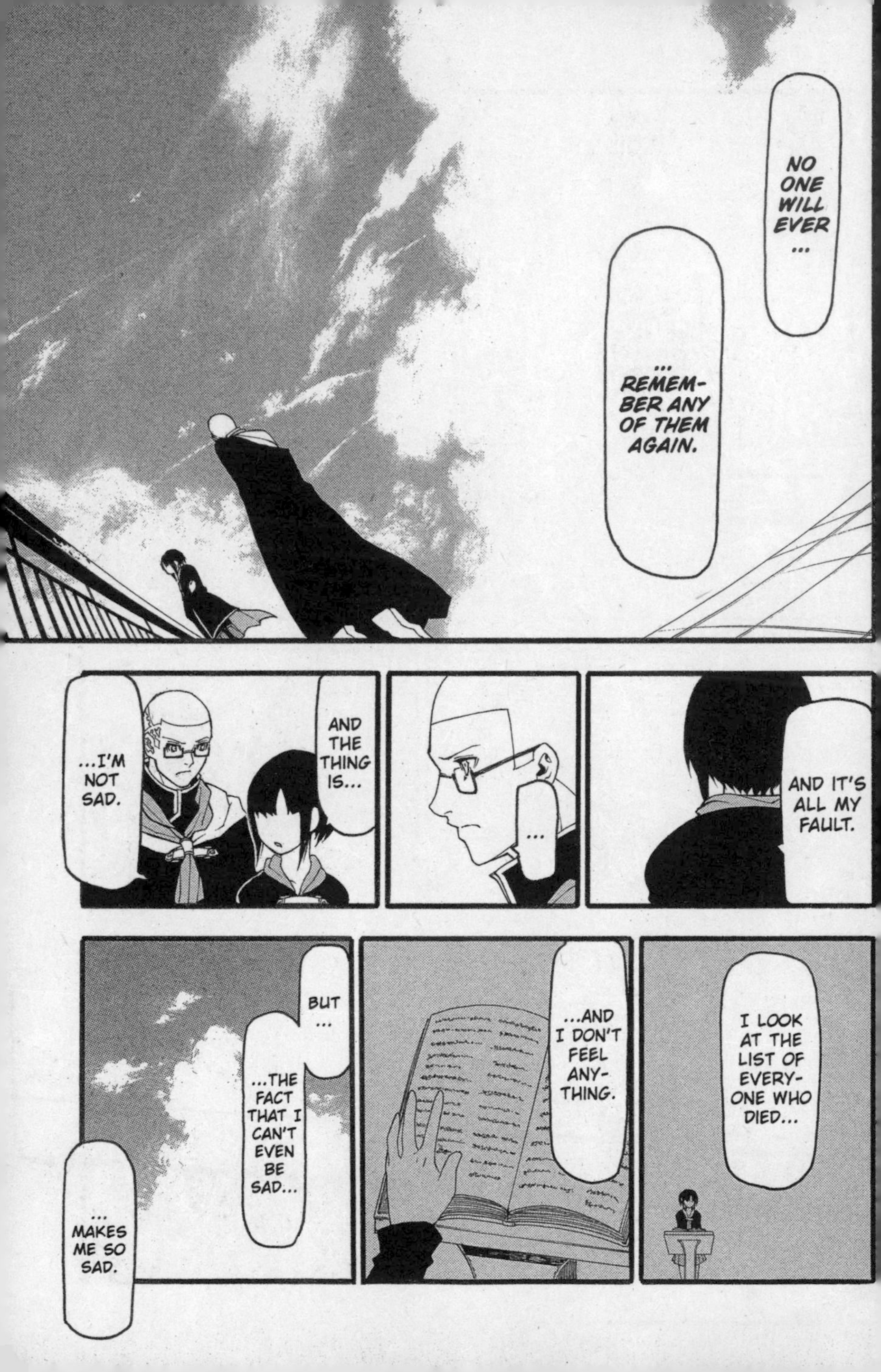
NO ONE WILL EVER ...
... REMEMBER ANY OF THEM AGAIN.
AND IT'S ALL MY FAULT.
...
AND THE THING IS...
...I'M NOT SAD.
I LOOK AT THE LIST OF EVERYONE WHO DIED...
...AND I DON'T FEEL ANYTHING.
BUT ...
...THE FACT THAT I CAN'T EVEN BE SAD...
... MAKES ME SO SAD.

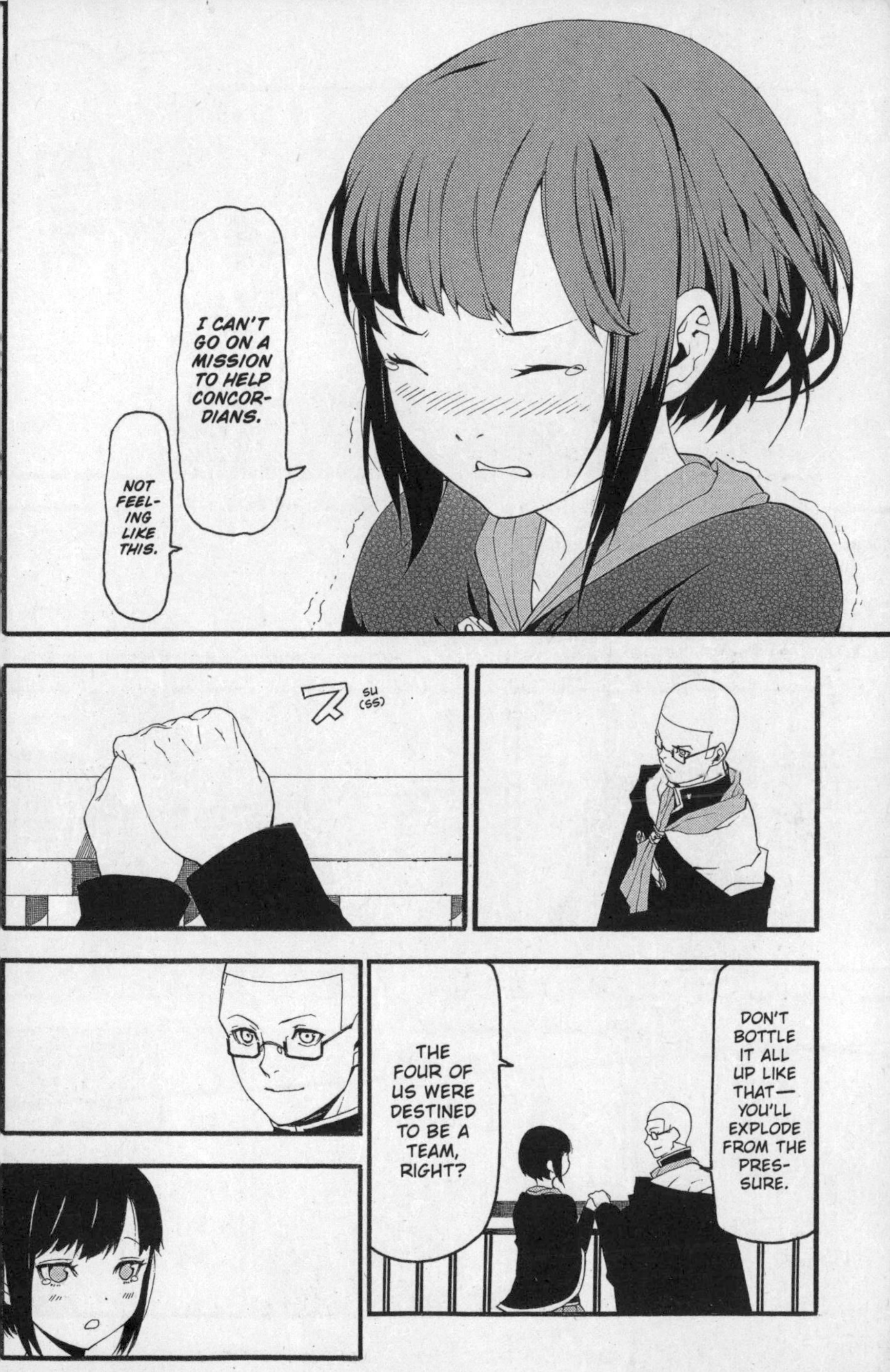
I CAN'T GO ON A MISSION TO HELP CONCOR-DIANS.
NOT FEEL-ING LIKE THIS.
ス
SU (SS)
DON'T BOTTLE IT ALL UP LIKE THAT— YOU'LL EXPLODE FROM THE PRES-SURE.
THE FOUR OF US WERE DESTINED TO BE A TEAM, RIGHT?

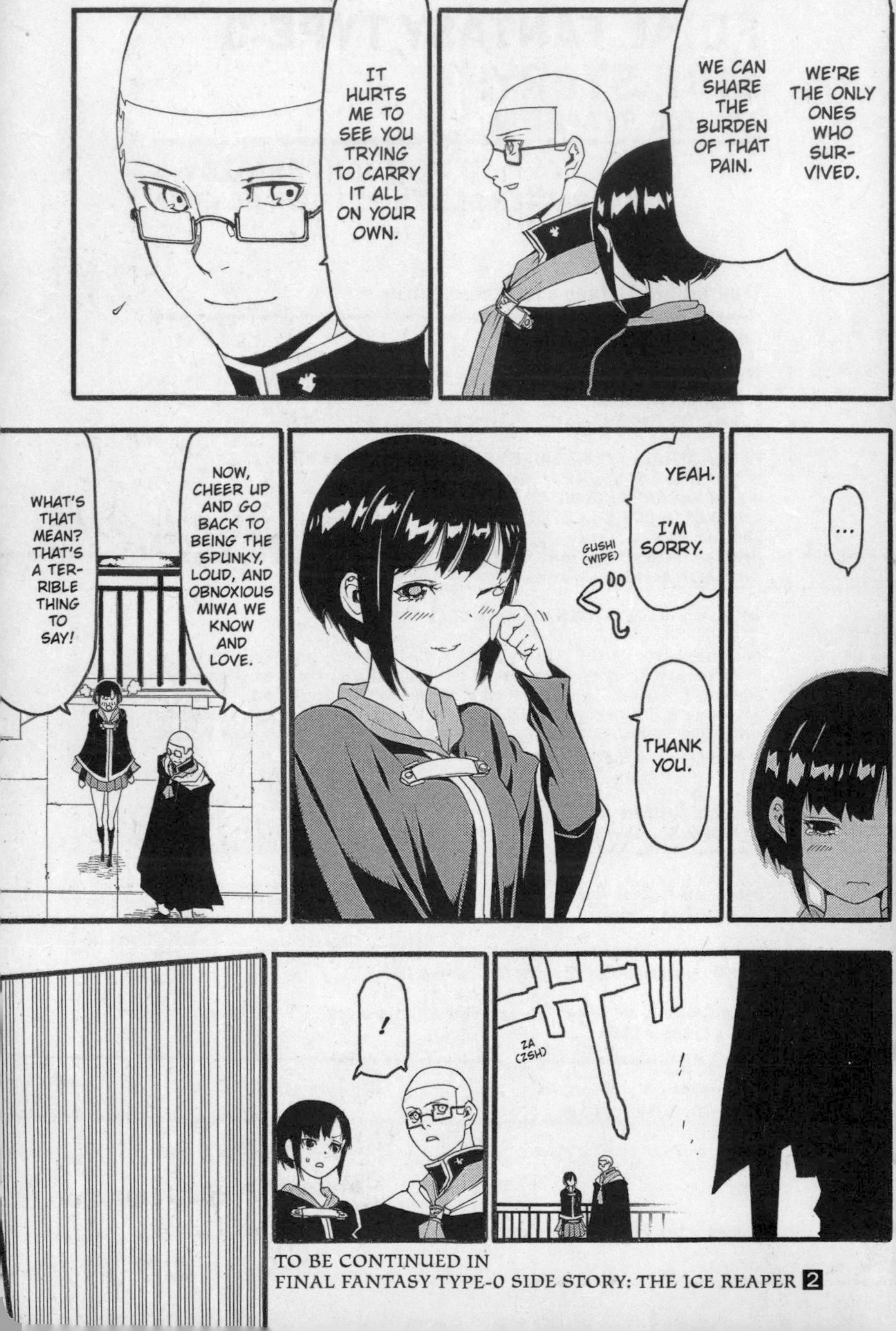
WE'RE THE ONLY ONES WHO SURVIVED.
WE CAN SHARE THE BURDEN OF THAT PAIN.
IT HURTS ME TO SEE YOU TRYING TO CARRY IT ALL ON YOUR OWN.
...
YEAH.
I'M SORRY.
GUSHI (WIPE)
THANK YOU.
NOW, CHEER UP AND GO BACK TO BEING THE SPUNKY, LOUD, AND OBNOXIOUS MIWA WE KNOW AND LOVE.
WHAT'S THAT MEAN? THAT'S A TERRIBLE THING TO SAY!
ZA (ZSH)
!
!

TO BE CONTINUED IN
FINAL FANTASY TYPE-0 SIDE STORY: THE ICE REAPER 2

FINAL FANTA[SY]
SIDE STORY:
THE ICE REAPER ❶

TAKATOSHI SHIOZAWA
CHARACTER DESIGN: TETSUYA NOMURA

Translation: Alethea and Athena Nibley

Lettering: Lys Blakeslee

FINAL FANTASY TYPE-0 GAIDEN HYOKEN NO SHINIGAMI Vol. 1
© 2012 Takatoshi Shiozawa / SQUARE ENIX CO., LTD.
© 2011 SQUARE ENIX CO., LTD. All rights reserved.
CHARACTER DESIGN: TETSUYA NOMURA
First published in Japan in 2012 by SQUARE ENIX CO., LTD. English translation rights arranged with SQUARE ENIX CO., LTD. and Hachette Book Group through Tuttle-Mori Agency, Inc., Tokyo.

Translation © 2015 by SQUARE ENIX CO., LTD.

Yen Press
Hachette Book Group
1290 Avenue of the Americas
New York, NY 10104

www.HachetteBookGroup.com
www.YenPress.com

Yen Press is an imprint of Hachette Book Group, Inc. The Yen Press name and logo are trademarks of Hachette Book Group, Inc.

The publisher is not responsible for websites (or their content) that are not owned by the publisher.

First Yen Press Edition: July 2015

ISBN: 978-0-316-30540-2

10 9 8 7 6 5 4 3 2 1

BVG

Printed in the United States of America